Perspectives on Anxiety, Panic, and Fear

Volume 43 of
the Nebraska Symposium
on Motivation

University of Nebraska Press
Lincoln and London 1996

Volume 43 of the Nebraska Symposium on Motivation

Perspectives on Anxiety, Panic, and Fear

Richard A. Dienstbier
Debra A. Hope

Series Editor
Volume Editor

Presenters
Carroll E. Izard

Unidel Professor of Psychology at the University of Delaware

Eric A. Youngstrom

University of Delaware

Jeffrey A. Gray

Professor of Psychology at the Institute of Psychiatry, University of London

Neil McNaughton

Associate Professor at the University of Otago and Director of the Neuroscience Research Centre

Susan Mineka

Professor of Psychology at Northwestern University

Richard Zinbarg   *Assistant Professor at the University of Oregon*

Richard J. McNally   *Professor at Harvard University*

David H. Barlow   *Distinguished Professor of Psychology at the University of Albany, State University of New York, and Director of the Phobia and Anxiety Disorders Clinic*

Bruce F. Chorpita   *University at Albany, State University of New York*

Julia Turovsky   *University at Albany, State University of New York*

Perspectives on Anxiety, Panic, and Fear is Volume 43 in the series
CURRENT THEORY AND RESEARCH
IN MOTIVATION

The passage quoted on pages 73–77 is from
*The neuropsychology of anxiety: An enquiry into the
functions of the septo-hippocampal system*, by J. A. Gray,
1982, Oxford: Oxford University Press. Reprinted by
permission of Oxford University Press.

"The Library of Congress has cataloged
this serial publication as follows:"
Nebraska Symposium on Motivation.
Nebraska Symposium on Motivation.
[Papers] v. [1]–1953–
Lincoln, University of Nebraska Press.
v. illus., diagrs. 22cm. annual.
Vol. 1 issued by the symposium under
its earlier name: Current Theory and
Research in Motivation.
Symposia sponsored by the Dept. of
Psychology of the University of Nebraska.
1. Motivation (Psychology)
BF683.N4   159.4082   53-11655
Library of Congress

Preface

The volume editor for this 43d volume of the Nebraska Symposium is Professor Debra A. Hope, who coordinated the symposium that led to this volume with enthusiasm and total dedication. She planned this volume, selected and invited the contributors, and co-ordinated all aspects of the editing. My thanks to our contributors for excellent presentations and for the timely production of similarly excellent chapters.

With this volume, we have continued to employ procedures that were designed to facilitate attendance at the symposium by scholars other than our main presenters. Specifically, to allow other scholars the possibility of traveling to the symposium as participants, we invited posters on topics relevant to the main theme of each volume. Since this is a tradition we intend to continue, we urge you, our readers, to consider such poster submissions when you receive future symposium announcements.

This symposium series is supported largely by funds donated in the memory of Professor Harry K. Wolfe to the University of Nebraska Foundation by the late Professor Cora L. Friedline. This symposium volume, like those of the recent past, is dedicated to the memory of Professor Wolfe, who brought psychology to the University of Nebraska. After studying with Professor Wilhelm Wundt,

Professor Wolfe returned to this, his native state, to establish the first undergraduate laboratory of psychology in the nation. As a student at Nebraska, Professor Friedline studied psychology under Professor Wolfe.

We are grateful to the late Professor Friedline for this bequest and to the University of Nebraska Foundation for continued financial support for the series.

RICHARD A. DIENSTBIER
Series Editor

Contents

Introduction

Debra A. Hope
University of Nebraska–Lincoln

In recent years the Nebraska Symposium on Motivation has returned explicitly to the theme of motivation. The 43d volume is no exception. In the spring of 1995, leading researchers and theorists came together in Lincoln, Nebraska, to offer their perspectives on anxiety, panic, and fear. Clearly, the theme of this year's symposium is closely tied to motivation.

The last 15 years have seen an explosion of research on anxiety-related topics, particularly within clinical psychology. Two themes from this research are evident in this year's symposium. First, it is increasingly clear that it is appropriate to consider anxiety, panic, and fear as separate but related constructs, as reflected in the volume title. Izard and Youngstrom, Gray and McNaughton, and Barlow, Chorpita, and Turovsky build a strong case that fear is a basic emotion that humans share with many animal species. Fear appears to have specific neural-chemical pathways and can be isolated from other emotions, such as sadness or interest, on various psychological measures. Barlow and his colleagues argue that panic is an inappropriate activation of the fear response in the absence of danger, literally a "false alarm." Using Gray and McNaughton's terminology, panic represents the activation of the neuropsychological fight/flight system, but anxiety is associated with a separate neuropsychological circuit known as the behavioral inhibition system. Finally, several of the authors suggest that anxiety represents a combination of emotions of which fear is but one. Izard and Youngstrom report that anxiety is often composed of interest, excitement, guilt, and shyness, in addition to fear. Barlow and his colleagues, who prefer the term "anxious apprehension," emphasize the future orientation inherent in anxiety. This recognition of the distinction among the three constructs represents more than technical nomenclature. It has important implications for understanding normal and abnormal manifestations of anxiety, panic, and fear as well as for the development of pharmacological and psychosocial interventions.

The second major theme in anxiety-related research that is also evident in the symposium is the multidimensional nature of anxiety, panic, and fear. By exploring the emotional, neuropsychological, conditioning, and cognitive aspects of anxiety-related phenomena, the first four chapters provide the building blocks for Barlow's comprehensive theory, which is presented in the fifth chapter. As the reader will see, however, each chapter also draws on the work of the other authors—an indication of the extent to which the authors recognize the interrelatedness of their perspectives.

Izard and Youngstrom open the volume with a review of Differential Emotions Theory as applied to the symposium topic. At a time when cognitive theories and therapies have been highly influential, Izard and Youngstrom remind us of the importance of emotion and argue cogently for the primacy of emotion over cognition under some circumstances. They also offer intriguing insights into how culture and gender may influence the expression of fear-related emotions.

In the second chapter, Gray and McNaughton update Gray's theory as presented in his 1982 book on the neuropsychology of anxiety. Gray's original theory is summarized early in the chapter, followed by an update and revision based on more recent research. Readers familiar with Gray's work will recognize the septo-hippocampal system, known as the Behavioral Inhibition System, that appears to form the neuropsychological substrate of anxiety. Acknowledging the increased importance of the phenomena of panic in the last 10 years, Gray and McNaughton outline the role of the central gray, medial hypothalamus, and amygdala in the fight/flight system.

In what for many readers may be the most surprising chapter in the volume, Mineka and Zinbarg update us on what modern conditioning theory contributes to our understanding of anxiety, fear, and panic. Traditional learning explanations of anxiety-related phenomena have been discounted in favor of more cognitive models in recent years. Mineka and Zinbarg argue strongly that this discounting fails to recognize advances in learning theory that offer parsimonious, testable hypotheses about the etiology and treatment of anxiety disorders. Outdated "Stress-in-Total-Isolation Anxiety Models" (SITIA) are compared with "Stress-in-Dynamic-Context Anxiety Models" (SIDCA) using concepts such as preparedness, temperament, and compound and contextual cues in order to address the shortcomings of SITIA models.

The application of experimental cognitive psychology paradigms to anxiety, panic, and fear has yielded substantial information about the information-processing aspects of anxiety-related disorders that were previously unavailable with self-report measures. McNally offers an excellent overview of this burgeoning body of research while placing it in the context of important experimental cognitive theories about the nature of the human information-processing system. Information-processing research has sometimes been accused of relying on alluring, computer-driven, experimental paradigms in the absence of cogent theory or even an understanding of what processes are tapped by the paradigms. Thus McNally's discussion of this research within an established theoretical framework is a particularly significant contribution.

The volume concludes with an updated and condensed version of Barlow's 1988 theory of emotional disorders. Barlow, Chorpita, and Turovsky draw from work on emotion, neurophysiology, attributions, learning, ethology, attention, and child development to describe how the inappropriate activation of fear (e.g., a panic attack) can trigger a cascade of events that eventually becomes a clinical anxiety disorder. Within the model, Barlow and colleagues outline how internal or environmental cues can initiate a feedback loop of negative affect, attentional shifts, increased arousal, and possible behavioral disruption and/or avoidance. Barlow and colleagues extend the model to include other disorders of emotion such as anger, depression, and mania which are thought to represent inappropriate activation of other basic emotions—anger, sadness, and excitement, respectively.

During the Symposium Discussion and Integration Session, Dianne Chambless, the discussant, highlighted several themes that appear across the various papers and warrant further research. First, as mentioned by all of the authors, an individual's perception of the controllability of internal and external events appears to be central to our understanding of anxiety-related phenomena. Second, the notion of "unconscious" has resurfaced as a legitimate topic of research, although, as McNally pointed out, contemporary discussions of "processing without awareness" differ substantially from the psychoanalytic notion of an unconscious laden with symbolic content. Third, the role of the human information-processing system in anxiety, panic, and fear was acknowledged by all of the authors as well. Although this may simply reflect the current dominance of cognitive models, it seems likely that any comprehensive understanding of anxiety, panic, and fear must consider how the processing of external and internal stimuli affects neuropsychological events, emotions, and behavior.

It seems clear that anxiety, panic, and fear are complex phenomena that require a multidimensional approach ranging from neuroanatomy to conditioning. Like the proverbial blind person grasping the tail of the elephant, we will have difficulty understanding the true nature of these phenomena if we limit ourselves to a single perspective. I hope this volume encourages students, researchers, and clinicians to broaden their understanding of anxiety, panic, and fear.

Acknowledgments

I want to thank the people who were helpful in making this year's symposium a reality. First, I am grateful to the volume contributors for preparing excellent presentations and strong, scholarly manuscripts for publication here. Dianne Chambless was an outstanding discussant, making numerous insightful and stimulating points. Although she elected not to contribute a chapter to the volume, her involvement is apparent in nearly all of the other chapters. I appreciate the invaluable assistance of Claudia Price-Decker, Rebecca Barnes, and their staff in organizing this symposium. They took care of a myriad of organizational details so that everything went smoothly. Without the enthusiasm and support of the graduate and undergraduate students on my research team, this symposium would never have occurred. I also want to thank my colleagues in the Department of Psychology for the opportunity to chair this prestigious event and for their ongoing support. In particular, I appreciate the guidance of Richard Dienstbier, the series editor, who always found the time to answer my questions. Finally, I would like to dedicate my work on this 43d Nebraska Symposium to my mother, Lorraine Izetta Nelson Hope (1920–1994). She taught me what is important in life.

The Activation and Regulation of Fear and Anxiety

Carrol E. Izard and
Eric A. Youngstrom
University of Delaware

We believe that in the years ahead significant advances in our knowledge of the activation and regulation of fear and anxiety will be largely a function of our interest and competence in dealing with individuals as complex systems. More accurately, individuals are complex *supersystems*, consisting of numerous interacting modular systems. The emotions, perception, cognition, and action are processes or products of these complex systems.

We believe that increasing our knowledge of the modular and systemic nature of the emotions and the conditions in which they operate as relatively independent systems and the conditions for their optimal interaction with the cognitive and action systems will improve our understanding of the development of normal and abnormal personality and behavior. For example, research on the separable operations of the emotions and cognitive systems should increase our knowledge of the dissociative phenomena that characterize posttraumatic stress disorders and other fear-related psychological syndromes. There is now solid neuroanatomical evidence (Zola-Morgan, Squire, Alvarez-Royo, & Clower, 1991) to support

This work was supported by NSF grant SBR-9108925 and the William T. Grant Foundation Award 93-1548-93. We are especially grateful to Celeste Hughes, staff assistant, for her help in preparing the manuscript and figures.

the long-held clinical hunch that fear-related behaviors can be functionally separated from the fear-relevant memories.

We need to know more about how connections among systems are developed and maintained so we can engineer better techniques for helping troubled people eliminate poor connections in favor of better ones. Making such adjustments in intersystem connections may be most difficult when they involve the fear system. This is so because of the powerful effects of intense fear on our thoughts and actions.

A great challenge for psychology that can engage us well into the 21st century is explaining normal and abnormal developmental changes in the context of a level of stability (cf. M. D. Lewis, 1995). Increasing our knowledge of the overall emotions system and each discrete emotion system at the neural, expressive, and phenomenal levels may be the key to progress in this domain. Emotions certainly have chracteristics that are stable over the life span as attested by the robust relations between emotion feeling states and dimensions of personality (Izard, Libero, Putnam, & Haynes, 1993; Watson & Clark, 1992). At the same time, emotions are well-known in folk psychology and science as causes of both subtle and dramatic change. Proneness to fear or trait anxiety can be a stable characteristic of the individual, but a situationally induced experience of intense fear (or a major increase in ongoing fear) produces profound physiological and psychological changes.

A Systems View of Emotions

In differential emotions theory (DET) we have described the emotions as a system and each discrete emotion as a component modular system (Izard, 1971, 1977, 1991). As suggested by the foregoing ideas adapted from complex systems research, we propose that the significant changes in the development and functioning of personality and social relationships are mediated by the processes of forming, maintaining, and modifying connections among systems. We envision connections at both the conceptual and neural levels, the former depending on the later. Connections with and through the emotions system are pivotal in normal and abnormal development. For example, as Tomkins (1962) observed, reason without emotion is impotent, and as Damasio (1994) argued, rationality itself, at least in terms of social communication, is achieved *only through input of appropriate emotion*. The language of these observations is consistent with the proposition that personality consists of interacting modular systems.

We believe that the arguments for the modularity of brain and mind generalize to the emotions. Neuroscientists conceive of the brain as consisting of numerous functionally distinct areas of interconnected neurons or modules (LeDoux, 1987; Zola-Morgan et al., 1991). A module or set of modules constitutes a neural network or system, and there are neural systems within larger systems. Scientists of different disciplines have contributed to the case for a similar modularity of mind (Fodor, 1983; Schneider, Casey, & Noll, 1994).

The basic idea of modularity, as Gould (1993) put it, is that the apparent *wholeness* of any life form is *decomposable* into relatively independent and dissociable modules. He illustrated the point by reference to the mind of a well-known musician, noting that one can have an extraordinary musical talent module in the context of many average or even below average modules of mind. As Gould and many others have observed, such was the case of Wolfgang Mozart. The musical module that made Mozart an impressive composer and performer by age four and an international celebrity by age eight was housed among many ordinary modules of mind.

The emotions are part of the brain and mind and share their modularity. In the case of affect, modularity means separate and distinct emotions, and thus the modules of the emotions system include joy and sadness and anger and fear. Fear, like any other emotion, is best understood as a functional part of a larger emotions system. From his evolutionary perspective, Gould (1993) made a telling argument for the modularity or discreteness of the emotions. He maintained that if the array of human emotions were locked together in a single glob in "our unique consciousness, then a historical origin from simpler systems becomes impossible" (but cf. Dawkins, 1986).

The concept of modular, discrete, and dissociable emotions systems is incongruent with theories of emotions, psychopathology, and psychotherapy that view emotion and cognition as *integral* and *inseparable*. To paraphrase Gould (1993), *integral wholeness* may

Components I and II can operate through cortical or
subcortical pathways. Neurohormonal processes (I) can lead
to an emotion state (III) without observable expression.

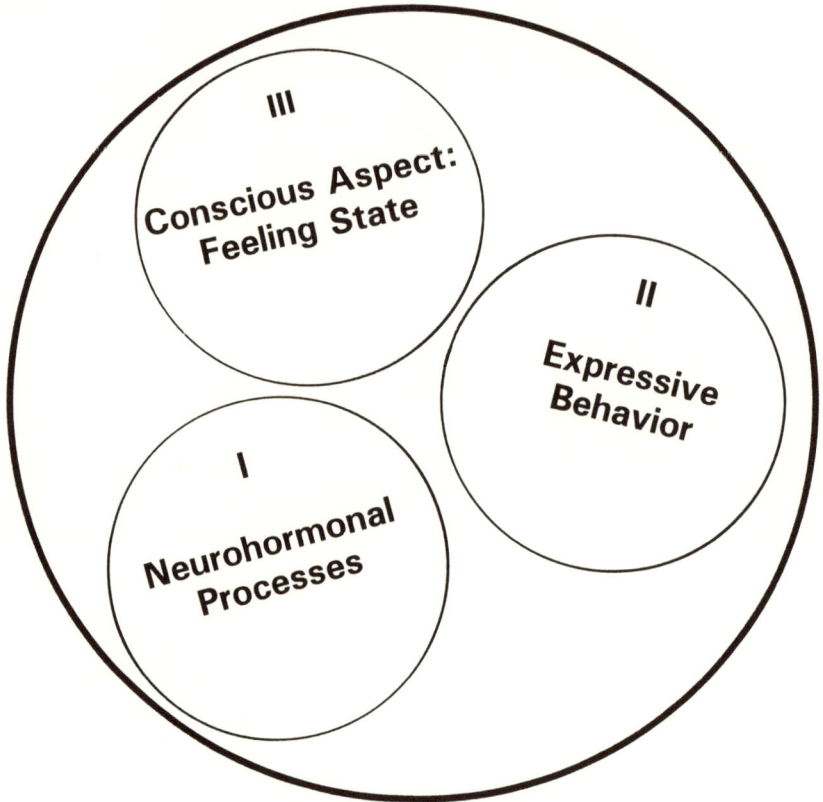

Figure 1. Components of an emotion system (e.g., fear system).

sound warm, fuzzy, and romantic, but dissociability is the way it is
in nature.

The concept of independent and dissociable functional units or
modules is essential to our understanding of complex living systems
and their actions. How else than with the principle of dissociable
systems can we explain an outburst of wanton violence in a previously tranquil personality, the failure of cognitive psychotherapy

with phobic patients, the failure of animals with dysfunctional visual cortex to extinguish a fear response conditioned to visual stimuli (LeDoux, Iwata, Cicchetti, & Reis, 1988), the differential capacity for memory of emotional and nonemotional material (Cahill, Prins, Weber, & McGaugh, 1994), and the disconnection of emotion and memory in various dissociative disorders? In summary, how, without a concept of dissociable emotions and cognitive systems, can we explain the insufficiency of reason in managing emotions?

A SINGLE EMOTION AS A SYSTEM

An advantage in considering a particular discrete emotion within the framework of a systems approach is that such a perspective requires attention to all components or aspects of the emotion. Considering neurochemical processes, neuromotor activity, or feeling as emotion is like considering the trunk of the elephant as the whole animal. Each discrete emotion, like fear, consists of three interacting components—neural evaluative, sensorimotor/neuromuscular, and somatosensory/feeling. Neural processes that determine the affective significance of events are followed by somatosensory and motor activity and a distinct quality of consciousness or feeling state. The continuous flow of emotion experience in daily life is dependent on the interaction of these three components or processes, but each component has distinct functions.

THE NEURAL SUBSTRATES AND THEIR FUNCTIONS

Current evidence indicates that the first component of emotion, the neural aspect, involves brain-stem central gray, thalamus, amygdala, hypothalamus, locus coeruleus, habenula, perirhinal cortex, and neocortex, particularly prefrontal cortex. The amygdala is considered to be the sensory gateway to the emotions (Davis, 1992; LeDoux, 1987). Efferent fibers from the amygdala project to the basal forebrain and several deep subcortical structures (Aggleton & Mishkin, 1986). The great complexity and extent of the emotion circuitry and its roots in phylogenetically old structures are consistent with the notions that emotions are a fundamental part of our evolutionary heritage and have inherently adaptive functions.

There is consensus among neuroscientists that a principal function of the amygdala is to evaluate stimuli for their emotional significance. It is capable of detecting the gross physical characteristics of a stimulus and processing the sensory information very rapidly. In some situations, the amygdala can process stimulus information and activate emotion responses without involving the neocortex and the cognitive functions subserved by it. (See Davis, 1992, for a review of the role of the amygdala in fear and anxiety.)

Fear conditioning and other research with nonhuman animals indicate that the hypothalamus controls emotion responses involving activity of the autonomic nervous system such as heart rate and blood pressure, as well as some observable expressive behavior (see LeDoux, 1987, for a review). LeDoux et al. (1988) found that brainstem central gray controls some fear-elicited motor reponses such as freezing.

THE NEUROMUSCULAR AND SENSORY FEEDBACK COMPONENT AND ITS FUNCTIONS

The neuromuscular aspect, the second component of emotion, refers to central efferent commands and striated muscle activity generated by the neural evaluative processes. These include observable patterned movements of face and body that signal feeling or behavioral intentions. There are several facets of the neuromuscular component:

> *Neuromuscular Activity*
> *Expressive Behavior*
> 1. Central nervous system;
> 2. full facial expressions;
> 3. components of expressions;
> 4. posture;
> 5. vocal expressions;
> 6. head/eye movement;
> 7. muscle action potentials.

We shall focus on facial expression.

General functions of emotion expressions. Because patterns of facial movement have been the subject of much research and considerable debate, a few caveats regarding their role in emotion are in order. Although everyone agrees that patterns of facial movement have signal value, there is disagreement on the nature of the message (Fridlund, 1994). In a recent review, Izard (in press) concluded that facial expression may signal feelings, social motives, or behavioral intentions, or any combination of these three, or they may represent attempts to disguise or mask inner states. Nevertheless, there must have been a link between expression on the one hand and behavioral intentions on the other for facial expression to have evolved into such an integral part of primate social life. So, too, there must be a veridical link between expression and feeling in ontogeny, for otherwise there would be no basis for explaining emotion communication and the emotional bond between the preverbal infant and its mother.

However, *observable* expression is a dissociable component of emotion. Social learning can make the link between expression and feeling a very flexible one. Thus one can learn to smile while feeling fear. Gaining control over facial expressions during early childhood not only increases their utility as a social tool, it makes expression a mechanism for the regulation of feeling (see Izard, 1990, for a review). As discussed later, this has many implications for therapeutic interventions.

Emotion expressions have both intraindividual and social functions. The principal intrapsychic function of expressive behavior is emotion-feeling activation and regulation, to be discussed in a later section. There is exciting research to be done on the mechanisms of expressive behavior's connections to emotion feelings and other emotion responses and the potential of using voluntary muscle activity as a means of controlling emotion.

Facial expressions have sevral interpersonal or communicative functions, and these are best understood in the context of social interactions and relationships. Previous papers have described these functions for the general case of emotion expression (e.g., Izard, 1989). Here, we shall define the social-communicative functions of expressive behavior for the specific emotion of fear.

Specific functions of fear expressions. The principal function of a fear expression is to signal conspecifics of imminent danger. It signals the motivation and intent to engage in protective behavior.

Ethologists have argued that this feature of an expression or display was necessary for natural selection or other evolutionary processes to lock the behavior pattern into the genome (Andrew, 1963).

An effective signal of danger or threat need not be a full-face configuration of facial movements. Such a configuration rarely occurs in adult interactions. This may be due in part to innate tendencies because of the adaptive advantage of making the fear signal less obvious to the threatening agent. Of course, in a case like fear of snakes, it might not matter whether the threatening agent sees a full display of fear signals.

In addition to the function of a fear pattern in signaling feelings or intentions is the related function of motivating or influencing the behavior of observing conspecifics. There are several possible scenarios here. A fear pattern may signal submission and motivate leniency in a dominant or threatening individual, whereas it might facilitate a vicarious fear feeling and self-protective behavior in infants or children. The work of Mineka and her colleagues (Mineka, Davidson, Cook, & Keir, 1984) suggests that expressive behavior in a wild-reared monkey mother may be an important factor in the observational learning of fear by her laboratory-reared offspring. That research also showed that mothers were somewhat more effective models than other adults in teaching fear to juveniles.

The effectiveness of human mothers' fear expressions in controlling the behavior of their infants is well illustrated by the work of Campos, Emde, and their colleagues (Sorce, Emde, Campos, & Klinnert, 1985). They studied social referencing in infants who had acquired the ability for self-locomotion. Social referencing is operationally defined as looking at the face of another in an ambiguous situation. The stimulus, a visual cliff modified to show an apparent drop-off of about 12 inches, provided a situation of uncertainty and possible danger to the infants. The mother stood by the deep side of the visual cliff (which shows the apparent drop-off), while the infant was placed on the shallow side. When mothers smiled, 74% of their infants crossed over to the deep side, but when mothers expressed fear, none of the infants crossed.

When the experimenters used the typical visual cliff with an apparent 42-inch drop-off, infants would not cross to a smiling mother. The cliff-induced fear feeling provided the information that organized and motivated the infant's avoidance behavior. We infer that the infant's own appraisal of danger and the accompanying fear and anticipation of fear was a stronger motivation than that mediated by the mother's happy expression.

THE EXPERIENTIAL/FEELING COMPONENT AND ITS FUNCTIONS

Several facets of the third, experiential or conscious, component of emotion are shown here:

Emotion Experience
1. Motivation;
2. action readiness;
3. action tendency;
4. biasing of perception;
5. cues for cognition and action;
6. feeling state.

The core of the emotion component that achieves consciousness is a *feeling* or *motivational state*. Emotion feeling is defined in part by the information it provides to the cognitive system (Izard, 1971; cf. Ortony, Clore, & Collins, 1988). Emotion feelings are fundamentally cue-producing phenomena. Some of the information is particularly relevant to cognitive processes. It is the information in an emotion feeling that biases perceptual activity and creates selective perception.

General functions of emotion feelings. Because we emphasize the modularity and separate functions of the emotions and cognitive systems, we think it important to distinguish these two types of systems. Their most important distinguishing feature is their relation to the dynamics or causal processes in behavior. Cognition without emotion, if there were such a thing, does not drive further thought or instigate any action. The apparent pull or push of a novel idea or goal-concept comes from the affect associated with it. The greater the pull of the abstraction in memory or anticipation, the higher the level of associated emotion, for example, interest-excitement. In contrast to "pure" cognition as representation of object or idea, emotion *is* motivation. There will be more discussion of the role of cognition in affective phenomenon and emotion-cognition relations when we discuss the concept of patterning in the section on anxiety.

Therefore, emotion is causal in the most fundamental sense. It is primal in any causal chain or sequence. Emotion is prime cause not only because of its inherent motivational power but because it comes first and influences the perception, cognition, and action that follows.

In the early days of the emotion research revival, we showed that induced joy and anger feelings had significantly different effects on the resolution of binocular rivalry, a fundamental perceptual process. When facial expressions of anger and joy or interpersonal scenes of friendly or hostile encounters were presented simultaneously, the induction of anger feelings led to the perception of a greater number of anger expressions and hostile interpersonal scenes (Izard, Wehmer, Livsey, & Jennings, 1965). Now there are many other experimental illustrations of the effects of emotions on basic perceptual processes, some of which can be found in a recent collection of paper titled *The Heart's Eye* (Niedenthal & Kitayama, 1994).

In one series of studies, for example, experimenters induced joy or sadness by having subjects listen to selections of classical music that had been prerated as potent elicitors of these specific emotions (Niedenthal, Setterlund, & Jones, 1994). In Experiment 1, subjects had to make a lexical decision as to whether stimulus words had a happy or sad connotation. Happy subjects made faster decisions about words that were congruent with their emotion feelings. Experiment 2 provided a clear replication of these findings. In Experiment 3, the subjects made rapid gender discriminations among photographs of happy and sad facial expressions of males and females. The experimenters predicted that congruence between subjects' emotion feelings and stimulus facial expressions would facilitate judgments "because the feelings of the perceiver should activate representations of faces that express similar emotion, and a holistic perception of the face is required for the gender judgment" (Niedenthal et al., 1994, p. 103). As predicted, happy and sad subjects made faster gender discriminations of faces with happy and sad expressions, respectively.

A number of nicely controlled experiments on preconscious and automatic perception indicate that the evaluative processes that lead to emotion are continually operating (see Izard, 1977). For example, it has been shown that subjects can detect the affective valence of a rapidly presented word before they have processed sufficient information to define it (see Johnson & Weisz, 1994; Pratto, 1994).

The first author has also long been a proponent of the idea that emotion feelings are primal in organizing and motivating cognition and action and in giving meaning and significance to life events (Izard, 1971). Very similar thoughts were expressed recently by the neurologist Antonio Damasio (1994).

> I see feelings as having a truly privileged status. They are represented at many neural levels, including the neocortical, where they are the neuroanatomical and neurophysiological equals of whatever is appreciated by other sensory channels. But because of their inextricable ties to the body, they come first in development and retain a primacy that subtly pervades our mental life. Because the brain is the body's captive audience, feelings are winners among equals. And since what comes first constitutes a frame of reference for what comes after, feelings have a say on how the rest of the brain and cognition go about their business. Their influence is immense. (pp. 159–160)

A voice from yet another scientific discipline, cognitive artificial intelligence/computer science, has recently sounded a clarion call for attention to emotion feelings. We refer to David Gelernter and his book *The Muse in the Machine* (1994). He claims that intelligent thinking is impossible without the body and without emotion. Referring to his so-called spectrum model of mind, he said, "The spectrum idea puts emotion at the center of the cognitive universe. It makes emotion the glue of thought; it makes emotion the force that engenders creativity" (p. 149).

If the message from these scientists is even partly right, then there is a great need for scientists and clinicians to focus more attention on feelings. If Tomkins (1963) was correct in saying that fear is the most toxic of all the negative emotions, and we believe he was correct, then scientific attention should be directed toward the theme of this symposium—fear, anxiety, and panic.

Specific functions of fear feelings. In evolutionary perspective, the first function of fear feelings is to motivate self-protective behavior,

behavior that leads to the attenuation of the threat or danger. It also focuses appraisal processes that can help guide action (see Mineka & Zinbarg, this volume). Because of the potency of fear feeling, the motivation to escape or to reduce threat dominates all functional systems. Any emotion feeling tends to bias perception. Intense fear feeling exercises such tight control over information processing that it tends to eliminate all parts of the perceptual field that hold no promise of an escape route (cf. Easterbrook, 1959). Evidence indicates that fear has profound effects on cognition in general (see Mineka & Zinbarg, this volume). It reduces working memory (Hope, Heimberg, & Klein, 1990), increases superficial processing (Baron, Inman, Kao, & Logan, 1992), generates cognitive bias (McNally, this volume), and tends to put indelible traces in memory (LeDoux, Romanski, & Xagoraris, 1989). Furthermore, a strong fear stimulus offers us no alternatives. The information in the stimulus is peremptory. Compulsory processing proceeds automatically, and all channels not involved with the fear stimulus are shut down.

So how do we reconcile the seemingly degrading effects of fear feelings on perception, cognition, and action with the notion that all emotions, their expression and feeling components, have an inherently adaptive function? The infant's response to the mother's signals regarding the visual cliff demonstrates an adaptive function of the fear expression. If we assume that the infant experiences a vicarious fear feeling, then it is reasonable that fear feeling is the proximal cause of the infant's choosing a safe maneuver. This assumption seems consistent with the infant's refusal to cross a deeper apparent drop-off, despite a smile on the mother's face.

When fear is mediated by cognitive processes, an effective response is predicated on a reasonably objective and realistic account of the threatening situation. Several factors will determine whether the appraisal is appropriate and whether the fear feeling will perform its inherently adaptive function. These include trait emotionality, in particular fear proneness or trait anxiety, the strength of adaptive connections among the emotions, cognitive, and action systems, and the effectiveness of one's skills and competencies for coping with threat. The fear thresholds set by genes, experience, and developmental processes will determine the likelihood that some level of fear feeling exists in consciousness. As already indicated, emotion and cognition interact as they operate in feedback-feedforward loops. There are nonlinear sequences of emotion-per-ception-cognition interactions in fear-eliciting situations. Thus on-going emotion influences ongoing cognitive activity, and the prod-ucts of appraisal processes have a feedback effect on whatever emotion exists in consciousness. Ongoing fear or trait anxiety will amplify newly activated feelings of fear.

Hence for fear feeling to perform its adaptive functions, the ap-praisal systems must operate in conjunction with a fear system that is at least moderately well regulated. When trait fear or trait anxiety are low, the appraisal system can assess potential danger with a rea-sonable degree of accuracy and activate fear when the danger is real and imminent (see McNally, this volume). Put another way, this is a reminder that fear feeling in response to danger is normal and adap-tive in the sense that the fear feeling motivates behavior to reduce the threat.

When high emotion arousal or inadequate knowledge causes the cognitive appraisal system to miscalculate, and the readout says "danger" when there is none, the individual's subsequent thought and actions cannot be adaptive in the long run. If the behavior suc-ceeds in reducing the misperceived threat but does nothing to adjust the appraisal system, the apparently adaptive but needless escape-oriented behavior will be rewarded and perpetuated at great cost to the individual's biological and psychological systems. Escape-ori-ented thought and actions motivated by fear feeling are truly adap-tive only in truly dangerous situations.

Another requirement for fear feeling having an adaptive effect is appropriate connections or communication lines among the emo-tions, cognition, and action systems. We are referring to the inter-system connections that we conceive as the main agenda in emo-tional and personality development (Ackerman, Abe, & Izard, in press; Izard, 1994a). Such connections link the motivational power of emotions to appropriate thought and action in an endless variety of emotion-eliciting situations. An example is the child's learning the appropriate cognitive and motor activities in response to the mother's fear expression in a particular situation. It is these inter-system connections that enable one to learn techniques for coping with threat. This leads to yet another factor that helps determine whether a fear feeling will fulfill its inherently adaptive function.

This factor is the status of relevant skills or abilities that enable person-environment transactions that decrease the appraised threat. To take an extreme example, if you learn that your boat is sinking in deep water far from shore, and you cannot swim, the adaptiveness of fear feeling will be severely constrained. This indicates that we need cognitive and motor skills for coping with a wide range of potentially threatening situations.

Such a set of competencies, which emerge as a function of genes and environment and developmental processes, cannot be so comprehensive that they take care of all contingencies. It is necessary that the individual develop general-purpose mechanisms for regulating emotions and that these mechanisms work even while the individual is experiencing fear in the fear-eliciting situation. If fear feeling can be regulated and kept at lower levels of intensity, it will not preclude the cognitive evaluation of behavioral alternatives and the learning of new coping skills within the threatening situation.

There are probably other criteria or conditions for effective use of the inherent adaptive function of fear feeling. Rather than trying to delineate all of them, we shall conclude our consideration of this issue with two points. First, fear feeling does indeed have an inherently adaptive function. This seems readily acceptable if we adopt an evolutionary or developmental perspective. Second, the adaptiveness of fear feeling is not automatic or guaranteed in all situations. The individual has to be prepared to capitalize on it.

In summary, each discrete emotion consists of three components—neural, expressive, and experiential. The components normally interact harmoniously in the processes of emotion activation and regulation. The neurobiological substrates set emotion activation thresholds and evaluate the emotional significance of stimuli. The expressive component is a key factor in social communication and social relationships, but it also plays a role in emotion activation and regulation. Whereas the expressive component of emotion is important in motivating the behavior of observers, the third component—emotion experience or feeling state—is primary in motivating one's own thought and action.

Four Systems for Emotion Activation and Regulation

The cognitive and noncognitive approaches to explaining emotion activation and regulation can be integrated in a multisystem model.

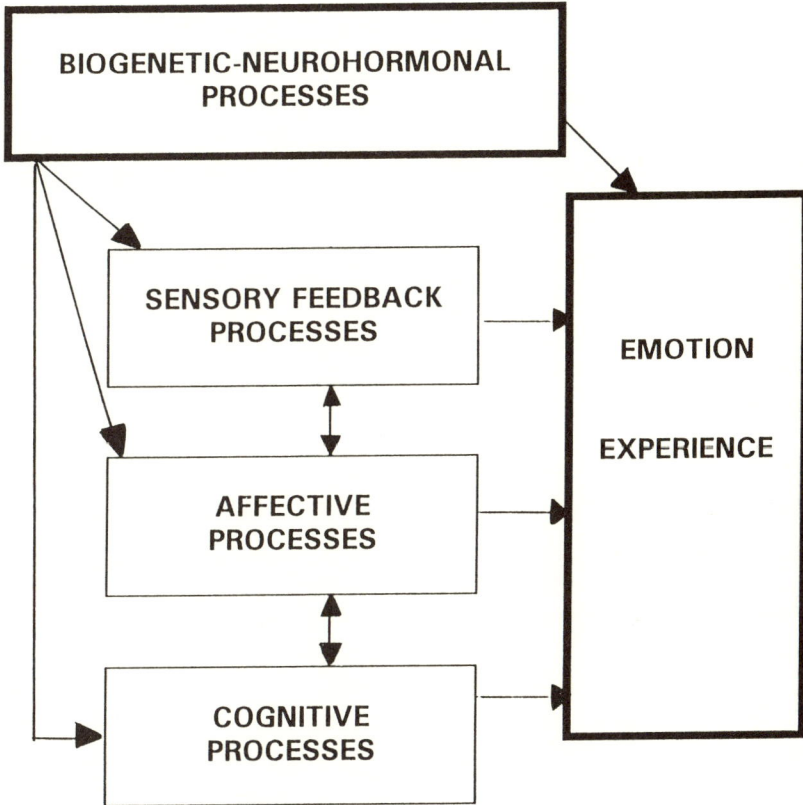

Figure 2. A multisystem model of emotion activation and regulation.

We have proposed four types of systems: biogenetic-neurohormonal, somatosensory, affective, and cognitive. The first three *can* and *do* operate independently of cognition.

In the framework of DET emotion activation and regulation, biogenetic-neurohormonal processes and "spontaneous" or automatic neural evaluative processes are responsible for a substantial part of trait emotionality or the emotion component of traits of personality. Personality traits add to the biogenetic-neurohormonal processes yet another layer of focusing mechanisms and filters that act on all emotion-eliciting information, whether simple sensory data from pain or high-level cognition. Thus a person who is high on fear proneness or trait anxiety will more readily respond to threat with significant increases in feelings of fear and anxiety.

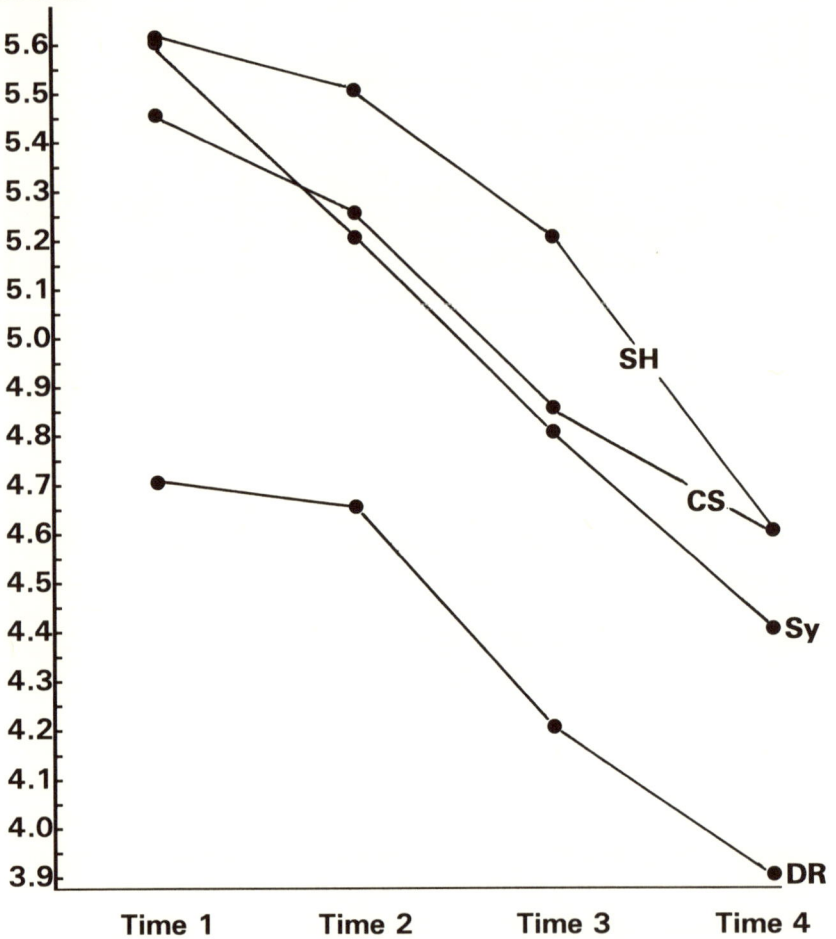

(*SH* = Shame; *CS* = Contempt; *Sy* = Shyness;
DR = Disgust)

NOTE: Time 4 means are for state DES scores aggregated over 3 occasions: 13, 18, and 24 months after childbirth.

Figure 3. Mothers' Differential Emotion Scale (DES) means that changed significantly during the period 2.5–6 months after childbirth. From "Stability of Emotion Experiences and Their Relations to Traits of Personality," by C. E. Izard, D. Z. Libero, P. Putnam, and O. M. Haynes, 1993, *Journal of Personality and Social Psychology, 64,* p. 854. Copyright by the American Psychological Association. Adapted with permission.

BIOGENETIC-NEUROHORMONAL PROCESSES

For each discrete emotion, biogenetic-neurohormonal processes set the range for the threshold of activation and actually generate and regulate emotion by controlling changes in levels of hormones and neurotransmitters that control neural activity. Some data consistent with this notion were provided by a longitudinal study of mothers' emotion feelings during the first six months following childbirth (Izard et al., 1993). As shown in Figure 3, the frequency with which mothers experienced certain depression-related emotions declined steadily over the first half-year after giving birth. These negative emotions are among those that are elevated or experienced more frequently in depression, and clinical investigations have indicated that one of the factors in postpartum depression is change in levels and balance of hormones (Izard et al., 1993).

Evidence from neuroendocrinology suggests that neural processes, such as those related to the opioid peptides, might set the thresholds for positive emotions and affiliative social behavior (Panksepp, Herman, Conner, Bishop, & Scott, 1978). More recent neurohormonal research indicates that oxytocin, a 9-amino-acid peptide, could also be a molecular basis for regulating positive emotion thresholds and the development of social bonds (Insel, 1993) and Extraversion.

As with the positive emotions and the affiliative social behavior of Extraversion, some studies suggest a neurohormonal basis for low thresholds for fear, other negative emotions, and Neuroticism. Reduced oxytocin in the cerebrospinal fluid of anorexics may help account for their fears of adverse changes in body image (Altemus & Gold, 1993), and increased testosterone levels may increase certain types of aggression in a variety of species, including nonhuman and human primates (Siegel & Demetrikopoulos, 1993). Such findings from neurohormonal research seem consistent with the notion that the biogenetic-neurohormonal systems are determinants of "spontaneous" neural processes of emotion activation and regulation.

The biogenetic-neurohormonal emotion activating and regulating systems are the most impervious of such systems to exogenous influences and the effects of other emotion activating and regulating systems for several reasons. First, these biological substrates of emotions are components of, or have neural connections to, larger

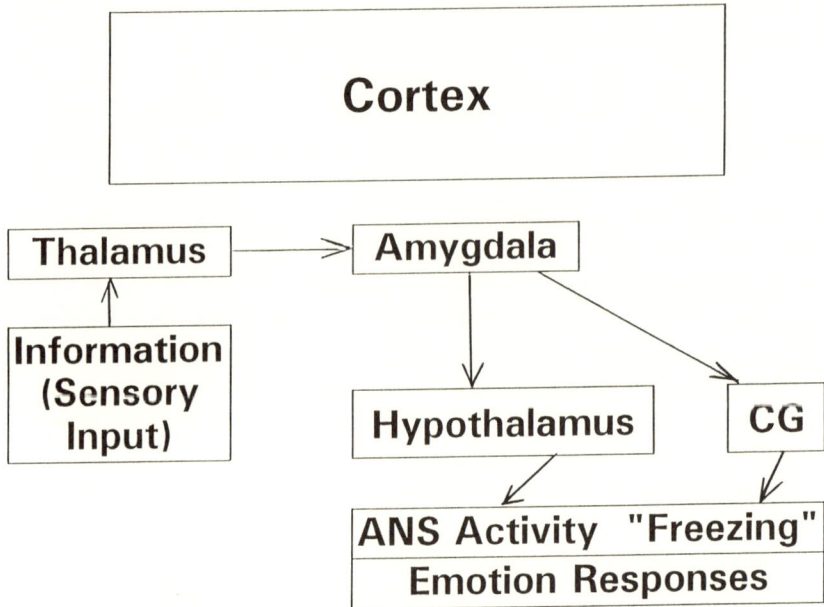

Figure 4. Emotion without neocortex. From *Handbook of Physiology: Vol. 5. Higher Functions of the Brain* (p. 437), J. Plum, Ed., 1987, Bethesda MD: American Physiological Society. Copyright by the American Physiological Association. Adapted with permission.

systems that serve critical functions in survival and adaptation. In the first of the foregoing examples, the neural substrates of postpartum emotion or mood changes are part of the neural substrates of the reproductive system. And the positive mood source, oxytocin, which emerged with mammals may be crucial to mother-infant attachment and primate social life (Insel, 1993). Second, because biogenetic-neurohormonal processes operate silently, they are less likely to become part of focal awareness and get attention as causal factors in emotions. Third, because they operate silently and automatically, they are less amenable to voluntary control. Despite the relative intractability and insulation of these biogenetic-neurohormonal processes, they constrain and influence all the other emotion activating and regulating systems. All incoming sensory data or information is focused and filtered by these processes.

The neurophysiological basis for emotion without cognition. Data relating to the neural basis of noncognitive emotion activating processes come from a series of carefully controlled experiments on animal behavior. LeDoux and his colleagues (LeDoux, 1987; LeDoux et al., 1988) showed that the conditioning of fear reactions to acoustic stimuli could be mediated by a thalamoamygdala pathway that does not involve the neocortex (see Figure 4). Similarly, animals without visual cortex were still able to acquire conditioned fear responses to a flashing light. Because the thalamoamygdala circuit bypasses the neocortex, higher-order cognitive processes cannot account for conditioned emotion responses mediated subcortically.

Having demonstrated that fear expression and behavior can be activated by acoustic or visual stimuli in the absence of auditory or visual cortex, LeDoux (1989) concluded that his data supported the hypothesis that separate systems process emotional and nonemotional information (cf. Izard, 1984; Zajonc, 1984). This conclusion is also consistent with the position of several investigators in developmental and social psychology that the emotions constitute a separate system (Cicchetti, 1990; Izard, 1984; Zajonc, 1980).

Le Doux's research also showed that in animals with cortical lesions, subcortically mediated emotion responses tend to be locked in memory and highly resistant to extinction (LeDoux et al., 1989). The conditioned stimulus (CS) was readministered to lesioned and sham (control) animals in five test sessions over a 30-day period. The sham-operated animals showed gradual and ultimately complete extinction of fear behavior. In contrast, the animals without visual cortex failed to extinguish the fear responses. Apparently, emotion-related memories that are mediated subcortically continue for an indefinite period.

NEUROMUSCULAR AND SENSORY FEEDBACK PROCESSES IN FEAR ACTIVATION AND REGULATION

Since Darwin and James, emotions theory has contained the idea that there is a close connection between emotion feeling states and muscle activity. The muscle activity that has drawn the most attention in recent research on emotions is that involved in facial expressions. Facial expression has been considered to be a factor or contributor to the activation and regulation of emotion feeling.

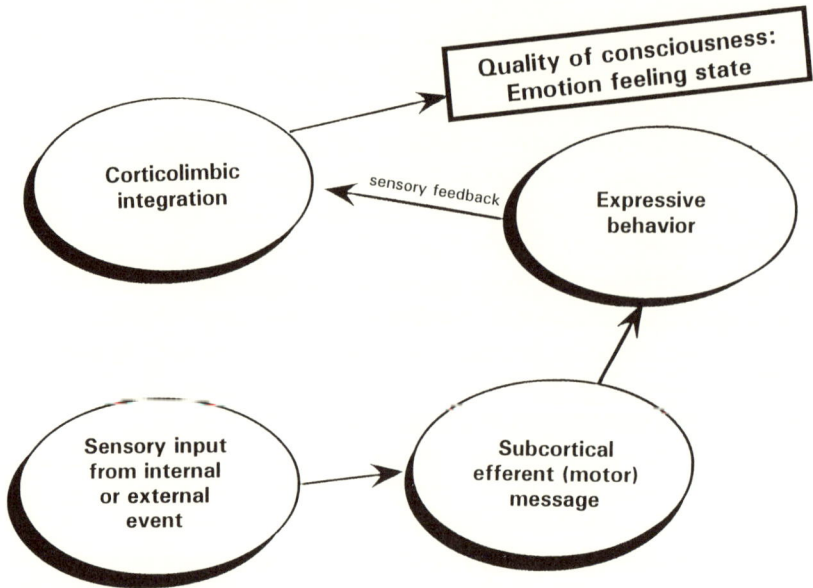

Figure 5. The feedback hypothesis of emotion activation.

Facial muscle activity (expression) and sensory feedback in emotion activation. Figure 5 depicts the hypothesized sequence of events when sensory feedback processes activate and regulate fear feelings. In the first controlled experiment on the effects of feedback from facial expression on emotion experience, Laird (1974) instructed subjects to pull the corners of their mouths back and up or to pull the corners of their brows downward. The facial movements simulating a smile made subjects happier and caused them to rate cartoons more positively. Contrariwise, the movements of the anger frown had the opposite effect.

Since Laird's original study, psychologists have published about 30 experiments that tested the facial feedback hypothesis. The published accounts support the hypothesis, with varying degrees of strength.

Skeptics have argued that methodological flaws (such as experimental demand and subjects' expectations) vitiate the expression effect on emotion feeling states. The criticisms notwithstanding, the weight of published evidence indicates that expressive behavior can activate emotion feelings and that in some cases the feelings are elicited without causal cognitive antecedents. Three explanatory mechanisms have been proposed—self-perception of the expressive behavior (Laird, 1974); changes in cerebral blood temperature and brain neurochemistry resulting from the effects of facial muscle actions on blood flow to the cavernous sinus (Zajonc, Murphy, & Inglehart, 1989); and sensory feedback from expressive behavior (Gellhorn, 1964; Izard, 1977; Tomkins, 1962).

Sensory feedback processes in emotion regulation. The evidence supporting the hypothesis that facial expressions contribute to the activation of emotion feelings also supports a corollary of that hypothesis: emotion-expressive behavior is a somatosensory mechanism for the regulation of emotion experiences. As in the case of the emotion activation hypothesis, the emotion regulation corollary can also be traced to Darwin (1872/1965) and James 1890/1950). As already noted, Darwin believed that there was a direct relation between voluntarily produced expressive behavior and the subjective experience of emotion. Similarly, James wrote, "Refuse to express a passion and it dies . . . and if you wish to experience an emotion . . . go through the outward movements" (p. 463).

Compared to the evidence for the role of experimenter-manipulated emotion expression in emotion activation, the evidence for the effect of intentional, motivated, and subject-controlled expressive behavior on altering ongoing emotion experiences is substantially stronger. The effect size for ten studies of experimenter-manipulated expression was .275, whereas that for six studies of subject-controlled expression was .457 (Izard, 1990). The data indicate that individuals who can effectively regulate expressive behavior can exercise considerable control over their emotion experiences. This technique of emotion regulation, which integrates cognitive and motor processes, is illustrated in an early study of imagery-induced emotions.

In that study, the subjects were a group of a professional Russian actors, trained in the Stanislavski method, and a group of staff members at the Institute of Higher Nervous Activity in Moscow. Because there were no significant differences between groups, we will focus on the overall results. The subjects were instructed to imagine and relive each of four different emotion scenes under each of three different conditions. The four emotions were joy, sadness, anger, and fear. For each emotion, an electrode was placed over a

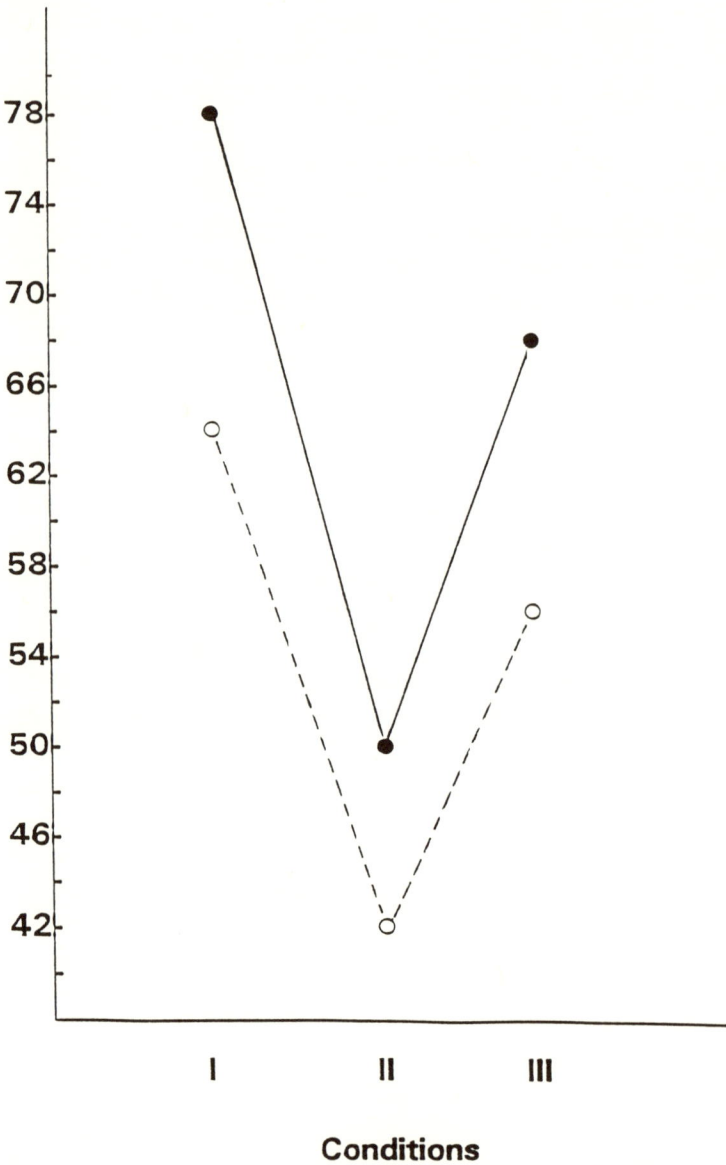

Figure 6. Average EMG of mimical muscles (in range units) for first, second, and third conditions (Condition 1—imagining the emotion scene, feeling the emotion, and expressing it freely; Condition 2—imagining the emotion-eliciting scene, feeling the emotion, but inhibiting the expression; Condition 3—expressing the emotion but inhibiting the feeling). Solid line represents responses of actors, dashed line others.

Heart Rate

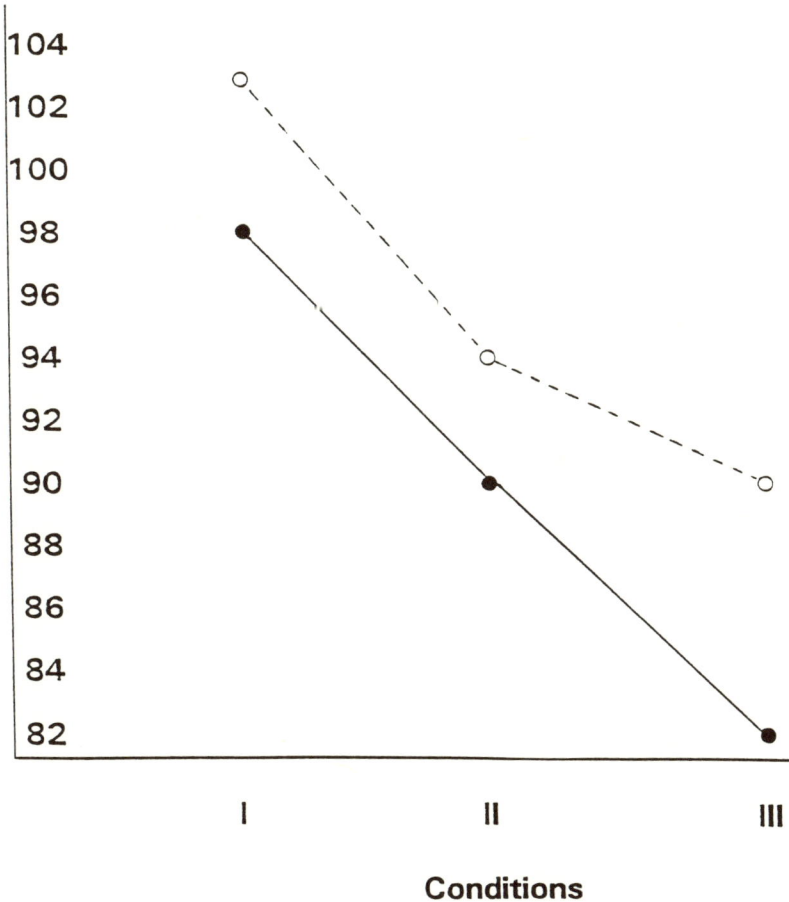

Figure 7. Average heart rate throughout first, second, and third conditions (Condition 1—imagining the emotion scene, feeling the emotion, and expressing it freely; Condition 2—imagining the emotion-eliciting scene, feeling the emotion, but inhibiting the expression; Condition 3—expressing the emotion but inhibiting the feeling). Solid line represents responses of actors, dashed line others. Figures 6 and 7 from "Comparative Analysis of Mimical and Autonomic Components of Man's Emotional State," by M. N. Rusalova, C. E. Izard, and P. V. Simonov, 1975, *Aviation, Space, and Environmental Medicine, 46,* pp. 1132–1134. Copyright by the Aerospace Medical Association. Reprinted with permission.

key facial muscle involved in its expression, and muscle activity was recorded electromyographically (EMG). In Condition 1, subjects were told to imagine the particular emotion scene as vividly as possible, feel the emotion, and express it freely. In Condition 2, they were told to imagine the emotion-eliciting scene, feel the emotion, but inhibit the expression. In Condition 3, subjects were asked to express the emotion but inhibit the feeling.

We obtained an electrocardiograph so we could use heart rate as an index of emotion activation. Because subjects were seated throughout the experiment and instructed to minimize bodily movement to avoid displacing the hard-wired electrodes, we assumed that significant changes in heart rate would be a function of emotion rather than movement or other artifact.

Facial EMG revealed increased muscle activity in the muscles predicted to be involved in the emotion-specific expressions. As can be seen in Figure 6, EMG scores averaged across emotions also provided a manipulation on the effectiveness of the instructions. As expected, Condition 1 showed the most facial (EMG) activity, Condition 3 the next most, and Condition 2 the least.

As shown in Figure 7, cardiac activity averaged across emotions also followed the predicted pattern. Heart rate was highest in Condition 1, in which the emotion was felt and freely expressed. Heart rate was next highest when the subjects felt the emotion but inhibited the expression, and heart rate was lowest when subjects were instructed to make the expression without feeling the emotion.

The substantial effect size for self-controlled expression has direct implications for the socialization of emotions (Izard, 1990). The evidence suggests that infants or children who consciously imitate expressive behavior of parents with psychological disorders may be placing themselves at risk for similar mental health problems.

Sensory feedback and emotion dynamics in the regulation of fear. The robust effect of subject-controlled expression on physiological systems and verbal report of emotion feelings also has implications for psychotherapy and the self-management of the feelings of fear, a conclusion that seems consistent with Barlow's (1988) analysis of anxiety disorders and their treatment. The data on sensory feedback suggest that subtle expressions of anger can be used to inhibit feelings of fear. The motivational thrusts of feelings of anger and feelings of fear are incompatible, and expression-activated anger feelings would necessarily attenuate or deactivate fear feelings.

The possible functions of expressive behavior in generating and regulating emotion feelings, as when anger expression alleviates feelings of fear, help illustrate the value of a systems perspective. This illustration points to the effects of two interacting components within an emotion system and the dynamic relations between two antagonistic emotion systems.

Several techniques could facilitate the use of expressive behavior in alleviating fear feelings. First, patients could be trained to become more aware of fear-related neuromuscular activity in the face and body. Second, they could then be taught to combine the monitoring of somesthetic signals of fear with well-known muscle relaxation techniques. Third, patients could be trained to encode low-intensity facial, postural, and instrumental action patterns that are antagonistic to fear. Assuming the validity of the facial feedback data, either joy or anger expressive patterns would activate emotion feelings antagonistic to fear. Although the sympathetic nervous system can prepare an animal for fight *or* flight, once the choice is implemented there are remarkable differences in the two kinds of behavior and probably their neurophysiology. Self-report data on fear-eliciting situations show a remarkable absence of anger and joy (Bartlett & Izard, 1972).

Our position on the qualified adaptiveness of fear feeling was supported in a study of the effects of exposure therapy on posttraumatic stress disorder (PTSD) patients. The amount of improvement was positively related to the amount of facial expression of fear during the first reliving of the traumatic event (Foa, Riggs, Massie, & Yarczower, 1995). We assume that more facial expressions of fear were indicative of a more realistic reliving of the trauma, more fear feeling during the therapy session, and hence more opportunity for making lasting connections between fear feelings and appropriate cognitions and actions.

AFFECTIVE PROCESSES IN FEAR ACTIVATION AND REGULATION

Tomkins (1963) speculated that intense sadness extended over time would activate anger. Clinical opinion and empirical data support

Tomkins's idea that one emotion can cause another (Finman & Berkowitz, 1989). Thus a situation that elicits joy typically elicits interest, and interesting situations and endeavors lead to joy. Sadness, which is generally recognized as the dominant emotion in depression, is almost always reported to co-occur with anger in depressive clients.

There is even stronger support for the notion that the affective processes in pain elicit emotions (Izard, Hembree, & Huebner, 1987). Data suggest a causal relation between pain and anger. There is also evidence that sensory information in tastes and odors can lead to emotion without cognitive mediation (for a review, see Izard, 1993).

COGNITIVE PROCESSES IN EMOTION ACTIVATION

Cognition is considered by some theorists to be the necessary antecedent of emotion (e.g., Lazarus, 1991) and by several others to be the most frequent and important determinant. This is close to popular belief or the commonsense view. Insofar as people reflect on the causes of their emotions, they probably attribute their feelings to their view of things and to their beliefs and desires. There can be no doubt that cognitive-evaluative processes are distal causes of emotion.

Feeling-cognition interaction in fear activation and regulation. In the following analysis of fear acquisition and regulation, the first author is much indebted to an insightful and integrative review done by Paul Harris for a book chapter we coauthored (Izard & Harris, 1995). We agree with, and borrow from, Harris's analysis of the shortcomings of the conditioning approach. We differ a bit from him in placing more emphasis on the roles of biogenetic-neurohormonal processes and the emotion systems in fear acquisition and regulation.

One of the first problems confronting the conditioning paradigm for explaining the acquisition of fear is the difficulty in linking the emotion to a specific causal stimulus or even to a coherent set of causal stimuli. For example, there is no common physical parameter for the stimuli that Bowlby (1973) and others consider natural clues to danger and hence fear elicitors—strangers, large animals, heights, sudden change in intensity of stimulation, being left alone.

The conditioning paradigm assumes that fear is activated by a number of discrete unconditioned stimuli. New fears (or more precisely new fear elicitors) are learned through the association of previously neutral stimuli with the unconditioned stimulus. There have been numerous demonstrations of the effectiveness of the conditioning procedure for establishing fear in animals. We need only point to the work of Gray and Mineka and their colleagues (Gray, 1982; Mineka, 1988; Mineka et al., 1984). Gray has taught us much about fear conditioning and its neural substrates, and Mineka has gone beyond the traditional procedures and shown that fears can be learned by observation of expressive behavior and that the learning process is influenced by the status of the model and by individual differences in the observer. We laud rather than question these findings.

Our questions, which are of two sorts, are about broader issues. Does conditioning explain very many of the fears and anxieties seen by clinicians? Can conditioning explain the other emotions involved in the affective symptomatology of anxiety? Later we shall summarize arguments and evidence that, at least at the phenomenological level, anxiety includes emotions other than fear. Furthermore, clinical investigators frequently report that even though fear may be dominant in conditions such as posttraumatic stress disorder, anger and guilt also play a role. So there are more questions: Can conditioning explain the presence of the other emotions in the anxiety pattern? Can conditioning explain the way the pattern or set of emotions in anxieties and phobias interact to influence the perception, cognition, and actions of the patient?

Some versions of the conditioning paradigm for explaining the acquisition of fears ignore aspects of the emotions system and the appraisal system. They do not take into account the influence of trait emotionality on the initial fear experience and the processes of generalization. Furthermore, even though conditioning and generalization may explain the acquisition of some new fears or fear elicitors, the appraisal system, as influenced by personality and the emotions system, will assess the potential danger of the array of neutral stimuli that become associated with the fear experience. Thus trait emotionality and the emotions system increase the selectivity of generalization processes.

In summary, both trait emotionality and the appraisal system contribute to the processes involved in fear acquisition. This helps explain the diversity and idiosyncrasy of fears stemming from a single traumatic event. Harris demonstrated the role of cognition and the appraisal system in an analysis of a study of adolescent survivors of the sinking of a cruise ship (Yule, Udwin, & Murdoch, 1990). A tanker collided with the cruise ship and caused it to take water rapidly and list as it sank. Night fell by the time of the rescue. The children, some of whom could not swim, were forced to negotiate the tilted decks and jump onto tugboats alongside the cruiser or into the water. The disaster took the lives of one seaman, one teacher, and one schoolgirl.

Five months after the disaster, the children were questioned about their fears. Only some of their fears—deep water, swimming, traveling by boat—seemed to confirm the standard conditioning model. The conditioning model's principle of generalization offers, at best, an incomplete explanation of the array of reported fears. The children's fears did not include some stimuli judged to be closely related to the traumatic experience: loud sirens, dark places, being in a crowd. But their fears did include several stimuli judged to be *unrelated* to the incident: traveling by train, going to school, talking to the class.

Harris offered an alternative explanation based on the cognitive processes of flashbacks and intrusive thoughts about the disaster. The power of memory and mental rehearsal to elicit emotion has been recognized by psychologists since William James (1890/1950). Thus anything that triggers a flashback memory of a trauma-induced fear might become a newly feared stimulus. For example, going to school entailed seeing classmates and teachers whose images could cue a flashback of the tragedy. We think this analysis is essentially correct and would only emphasize that the triggering of the flashback and its effects are modulated by trait emotionality and ongoing emotion.

For example, flashback memories of fearful incidents are more likely to occur in situations that are at least mildly threatening and when the individual is already experiencing apprehension or mild

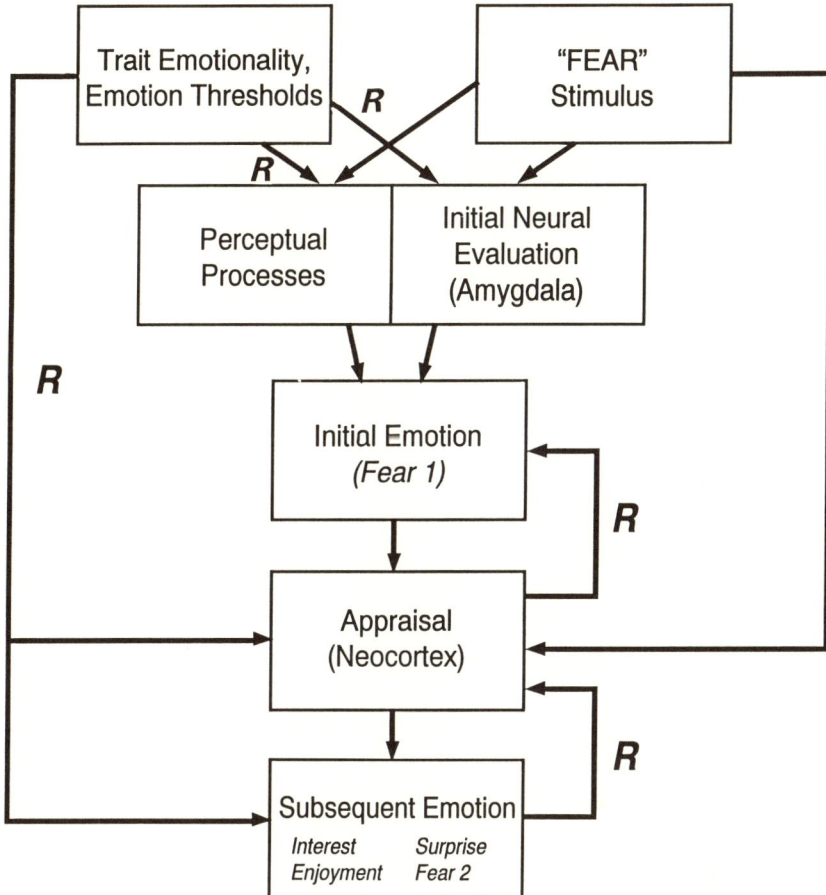

Figure 8. Nonlinear processes in fear activation and regulation.

fear (Bower, 1981). Either trait anxiety or a situational anxiety could increase the likelihood of flashbacks and the fear experience. In this case, mild fear contributed to the activation of intense and potentially uncontrollable fear. The likelihood that such intense fear will be created frequently and result in psychopathology is a function, in part, of trait emotionality (specifically, fear proneness) and other facets of personality.

Just as the emotions system and personality interact with and influence appraisal processes in emotion activation, so do emotions and traits influence the role of cognitive and behavioral techniques in emotion regulation. The nonlinear interactions of emotion and cognition in fear acquisition/activation and regulation are depicted in Figure 8.

Thus just as emotions are conceived as part of a problem, so should they be seen as part of the solution. As Harris noted (Izard & Harris, 1995), Jersild (1947) anticipated Bandura (1977) and others by 30 years when he observed that a child could be helped in overcoming a fear by active and successful participation in an appropriate fear-eliciting experience.

It is through successful coping while actually experiencing real fear, as Jersild noted, that children are able to change their self-concept regarding their ability to cope in fearful situations. This is a fundamental developmental process that has an enduring quality. Practicing or rehearsing successful coping behavior while experiencing a safe level of fear (or other relevant emotion) also seems to be an essential element of any effective psychotherapy or intervention.

The value of coping and learning while experiencing fear can be explained by the research we have already reviewed on the relative independence of the emotions system and the memory system for emotion-related information and by the influence of emotion arousal on memory. Given the capacity of the emotions and cognitive systems to operate independently, it is no wonder that *inefficacy* characterizes simple cognitive instructions or any therapeutic techniques that do not involve coping in the face of the troublesome emotion and emotion-eliciting conditions.

Fear, Personality, and Psychopathology

We believe that a complete explanation of emotion activation and regulation is not available either in cognitive theories of emotion activation or the roughly equivalent commonsense view. Noncognitive processes affect these phenomena. For example, biogenetically controlled flow and balance of hormones and neurotransmitters, "spontaneous" neural activity, also mediate genetic contributions to personality traits. Personality traits consist in part of emotions that are always in consciousness or readily available to it.

A recent advance in the field of emotions comes from the study of their role in personality and psychopathology. Emotions are only one of the several subsystems of personality, but they are considered the principal motivational system.

In the study of emotion-personality relations, most researchers focus on the experiential component of emotion. The facets of emotion experience include feeling/motivational state. Some of these terms also describe functions of feelings and provide clues as to how emotion feelings can influence other systems.

FEAR-PERSONALITY/PSYCHOPATHOLOGY RELATIONS

Several features of the fear feeling mediate the influence of this powerful emotion on personality and psychopathology. We view the descriptions of these features as principles for understanding fear-behavior relations.

- Fear feeling, like the feeling states of each of the basic emotions, has unique motivational properties. We have already described how this characteristic fear feeling creates highly selective perception and tightly organizes thought and action in a particular way in a manner consistent with the intensity of the feeling.
- Proneness to fear is stable over time and across developmental stages (Kagan, 1994; Scarr-Salapatek, 1976). The fear feeling is essentially the same at any age. It is the connected cognition and actions that change with development. The fear feeling serves its adaptive, protective function for the infant on the visual cliff and for the adult driving on a busy ice-covered bridge or walking after dark in a high-crime urban area.
- Each individual has a characteristic fear activation threshold. Thresholds are a function of the reciprocal influences of genetic and environmental factors in development. Positive emotionality has been found to be influenced relatively more by environment or surrounding social climate than negative emotionality (Watson, Clark, & Tellegen, 1988), suggesting that there is a larger genetic component in fear and other negative emotions. Individual differences in fear thresholds and the stability of the fear feeling over time help explain how a biogenetic

Table 1

Correlations: Emotions and Neuroticism, Emotions and Extraversion

DES Emotion Experience	EPQ Neuroticism	EPQ Extraversion
Interest	-.27	.35*
Enjoyment	-.32*	.36*
Surprise	-.04	.21
Sadness	.44**	-.16
Anger	.32*	-.07
Disgust	.34*	.00
Contempt	.46**	.00
Fear	.40**	.02
Shyness	.46**	-.11
Shame	.41**	-.33*
Guilt	.41**	.04
Self-Hostility	.46**	-.07

*$p < .01$, two-tailed. **$p < .001$, two-tailed.

proneness, combined with a chronically threatening environment, can result in long-term phobias and anxiety disorders.
- Fear tends to form stable links to certain other emotions, and
  this leads to characteristic patterns of emotions in various anxiety disorders. We shall return to this point in a later section on
  patterns of emotion feelings in anxiety.
- Fear tends to become linked to particular types of thoughts and
  memories to form particular types of affective cognitive structures or schemas. These are the schemas of anxieties and phobias. Whereas interest and enjoyment link to children's play
  and the creative endeavors of adults, anger to plans or fantasies
  of revenge, guilt to ruminations about efforts at reconciliation,
  shame to dreams of self-efficacy, fear feelings connect to images
  of threat or danger and real or imagined efforts to achieve feelings of safety and security.

We have already discussed the durability of memories associated with feelings of fear. The tenacious grip of a phobia is undoubtedly explained in large measure by the very characteristic of the fear
feeling that makes it adaptive in appropriately appraised situations.
The fear feeling is a compelling signal to change mental and motor
processes in the direction of safety, and sometimes these changes
move us toward our most basic instinctlike patterns of protective behavior. Such patterns are not always adaptive in contemporary life

situations, particularly when the appraisal system is malfunctioning and the level of threat is misperceived. Emotion feelings often arrive in consciousness with excess baggage: faulty appraisals, misattributions, compulsive schema, intrusive thoughts.

Emotion-cognition sequences and their connections to actions are the building blocks of our behavioral repertoire and personality traits. The interfacing of the emotions system, the cognitive system, and the action system is the source of both adaptive and maladaptive characteristics. Studies of the relations among measures of emotion experience and personality traits provide support for this proposition and the five premises of emotion-behavior relations. Table 1 shows that, as expected, the positive emotion feelings of interest and enjoyment correlate positively and the negative emotion feelings of shyness negatively with Eysenck's (1956) Extraversion. The negative emotion feelings, including fear, are strongly associated with Eysenck's Neuroticism (Izard et al., 1993). Similar findings have been reported by other investigators using a five-factor model of personality (Watson & Clark, 1992). Studies with both models of personality found that fear was a prominent correlate of Neuroticism. Indeed, this research suggests that Eysenck was correct in his basic definition of the personality dimension of Neuroticism as negative emotionality.

From the perspective of DET, one could argue that low thresholds for social interest and enjoyment are the basic determinants of the personality dimension of Extraversion. One could argue that low thresholds for fear and other negative emotions are basic determinants of the Neuroticism dimension of personality.

Fear Activation and Regulation: Concluding Remarks

Data from diverse sources, including neuroscience and developmental and clincial psychology, also support the hypothesis of a functionally distinct emotions system that consists of the fear system and other functionally distinct discrete emotion systems. The fear system, like other discrete emotion systems, has three dissociable components (neural, expressive, and experiential), and this dissociability, together with the dissociability of emotion and cognition, helps explain some of the phenomena in various fear-related disorders. An example is the dissociation that may occur with PTSD, which is often characterized by a splitting of the emotion and cognition associated with the context of the trauma. Because of this, patients with PTSD may experience strong emotions that they are unable to articulate verbally.

The possible role of biogenetic-neurohormonal processes in personality and psychopathology is another reminder of the need for attention to a multisystem model for the activation and regulation of fear and other emotions. In particular, the evidence from neuroscience enables us to underscore a central theme of the multisystem model. Findings from both neurohormonal and neuroanatomical research suggest that there really are noncognitive emotion activating and regulating processes.

Contributions from neuroscience also suggest that trait emotionality, fear proneness, and dimensions of personality may be determined in part by biogenetic or neurohormonal processes. These silent and automatic processes, together with the peremptory effects of fear on perception, cognition, and action, help explain a theme common to all the papers in this symposium: fear-related disorders lead to a sense of uncontrollability. Of all the emotions, fear poses the most powerful threat to one's sense of self-efficacy and self-control.

The interfacing and integration of certain aspects of neuroscience, cognitive science, and emotions theory present a great challenge for the future. We need much better communication and more sharing of concerns across these disciplines. For example, the neuroscientists who are providing evidence for fear activation or fear conditioning without cortically mediated cognition do not give much attention to the issue of levels or types of cognition that could occur in, or be associated with, fear circuits that do not involve the neocortex (J. B. Rosen, personal communication, 1 February 1995). The development of cross-disciplinary concerns of this sort promises to increase our knowledge and control of fear, anxiety, panic, and other problems in normal and abnormal development.

Anxiety as a Pattern of Emotions

Fear is a unifying emotion thread running through the subjective experience of persons suffering from anxiety and its related disorders.

The focus of the fear can vary widely, from the relatively circumscribed targets of animal phobias, to the more pervasive patterns of elicitors experienced in Generalized Anxiety Disorder. The invariant element is the individual awareness of psychological distress, and an emotions perspective does service in focusing attention on what, for the sufferer, may be the most prominent feature of the pathology.

DET hypothesizes that the affective symptomatology of anxiety consists of a pattern of basic emotion feelings. The anxiety pattern always involves the emotion of fear, and all that was discussed previously with regard to the functions and motivational properties of fear feelings is pertinent to a consideration of anxiety. However, the emotion phenomenology of anxiety includes other emotions in addition to fear. These other emotions are hypothesized to have an interactive effect (and not a simple, cumulative one) with the feelings of fear. This nonadditive interaction between fear and other emotions in the anxiety profile has consequences for the regulation and expression of emotion feelings, the diagnosis and treatment of anxiety disorders, and the unique experience of the individual.

Although fear may represent a common element in anxiety's permutations, it is inappropriate to equate anxiety with fear. DET has pointed out that subjective states of fear and anxiety do not have completely overlapping sets of antecedents, nor do they motivate identical behavioral responses (Izard, 1991). Fear has a profoundly noxious quality that compels efforts to change the situation that elicited the emotion. Anxiety, on the other hand, involves a cluster or pattern of emotions that may motivate both approach and avoidance (Buechler & Izard, 1980; Izard, 1991).

Thus it is unlikely that fear is the only emotion operating in anxiety. Evidence suggests that a single emotion system rarely operates in isolation for long periods of time, with the exception of the positive emotion of interest. Instead, emotion-eliciting stimuli often trigger multiple emotion systems (Izard, 1972, 1993; cf. Lewis, 1985). Whether the discrete emotions involved in anxiety operate in a parallel profile or in a series of oscillations is less important than the fact that emotions tend to co-occur in temporal proximity. When several emotions activate, their unique motivational properties interact to produce outcomes qualitatively different from a simple addition of feelings.

THE CONCEPT OF PATTERNING

A pattern of emotions is defined as an interactive set of basic emotions in which the key emotion is experienced with more frequency and intensity than the others. Emotion systems that increase the likelihood of each other's activation, or that become associated with each other through acculturation or the idiosyncrasies of personal history, can be thought of as forming a pattern. The emotion systems in the pattern are causally linked so that the activation of one of them (especially the key emotion) increases the probability that the others in the set will also activate (Blumberg & Izard, 1986; Izard & Ackerman, in press).

Although empirical inquiry into this area is only beginning, the four types of emotion-activating systems discussed earlier suggest mechanisms by which emotion activation could spread to include the various emotions in an anxiety profile. Not only could the cognitive or neurophysiological pathways recruit more than one discrete emotion in response to a given stimulus, but one emotion can activate other emotions in a predictable way (e.g., sadness eliciting anger, Izard, 1993; Tomkins, 1963).

We have confirmed that emotions tend to activate in clusters or patterns through a series of empirical studies using a form of the Differential Emotions Scale (DES) and a Dimensions Rating Scale (DRS) (Bartlett & Izard, 1972). DRS scores for samples of college students appeared to indicate that imagery-induced, fear-eliciting situations increased self-reported levels of tension and impulsiveness and decreased levels of self-assurance and pleasantness. Observed levels of tension were on average higher in the fear situation than for any other emotion, and impulsiveness levels were lower than exhibited in the anger situation but similar to those seen with sadness (and greater than those associated with any other negative emotion situations; Izard, 1991). Examination of DES scores from the same situations designed to elicit fear demonstrated the greatest elevation on the fear subscale of the DES. However, the responses to the same situation also displayed elevations on other basic emotions. The progression of subscale scores in imagery-induced fear ranged from greatest levels of fear, followed by significantly lower scores for guilt and shyness (not significantly different from each other), then sadness, through to a lower end marked by anger, surprise, and interest (not reliably different from each other), and finally joy (Bartlett & Izard, 1972).

A DISTINCT PATTERN OF EMOTIONS IN ANXIETY

What implication does emotion patterning have for an understanding of anxiety? Empirical research employing Differential Emotions Theory has demonstrated that fear is the dominant emotion in the emotional profiles of anxiety sufferers and also that there typically are differences between the profile of emotions reported in anxiety, depression, and fear. Furthermore, there is evidence of some consistency across individuals in the emotions that are reported within each diagnostic group or situation. Both the similarities and differences in profiles of emotion will prove of theoretical and clinical interest.

Although the combination of emotions constituting anxiety is changeable with relation to time, persons, and situations, as well as the intensity and frequency of subjective perception, a series of studies demonstrated considerable commonalities pointing toward the coherence of anxiety profiles. Evidence supporting the concept of anxiety as a pattern of emotions includes the following:

- As people grow more anxious, they generally report increased levels of fear and interest or excitement (which probably need to be construed as vigilance in this context). Other emotions, such as guilt and shyness, may also occur in conjunction with fear in response to anxiety-provoking stimuli or in the baseline levels of emotion feelings described by persons suffering from anxiety (Blumberg & Izard, 1986; Izard, 1972; Lelwica, 1988). Fear has consistently been the dominant emotion feeling in the profiles across the studies.
- Factor analytic studies have shown that terms used to describe anxiety, as well as items from clinical anxiety scales that assess more somatic aspects of anxiety-related dysfunction, consistently correlate most highly with fear and share the next largest amount of variance with a combined sadness/guilt factor. These patterns of relations remain even when items with emotion content are deleted from the anxiety scale. Given the good psychometric properties of the anxiety instrument used (the State/

Trait Anxiety Inventory; Spielberger, Gorsuch, & Lushene, 1970), including its well-established content and convergent validity with other measures of anxiety, this result is interpreted as showing that anxiety involves a set of emotions beyond pure fear (Izard, 1972, 1991; but cf. Spielberger, 1985).

• As eliciting conditions change, the activation of emotion feelings shifts in complicated ways. When people imagine themselves in an anger-eliciting situation, as opposed to a fearful one, more than simply their perceived levels of fear and anger change. Analyses of variance consistently have shown extremely reliable interaction effects between scores on emotion subscales and the eliciting condition (e.g., Izard, 1972). These interaction effects indicate that emotion profiles, and not only levels of a single emotion, are significantly different across varying emotion-eliciting situations.

Corroborating evidence for the validity of the emotion patterns associated with anxiety and depression can also be found in the cognitive literature. Beck's cognitive theory of emotion, while emphasizing the primacy of cognition at the expense of emotion feelings, makes predictions congruent with DET. Cognitions of harm and danger are anticipated to associate with anxiety, whereas thoughts of loss and depression are expected to co-occur with depression (construed by Beck as an emotion feeling; Beck, 1976). These expectations have been confirmed in results reported by Clark (1986) and Wickless and Kirsch (1988), among others. Their findings consistently indicate that the emotions and cognitions not only correlate highly with each other in the expected patterns but that they also display divergent validity. In other words, cognitions of harm and danger were most associated with anxiety, while thoughts of loss and failure related more strongly with reports of depression.

A differential emotions perspective on the phenomenology of anxiety or depression can find support through the reinterpretation of these results along an emotion-theory scaffolding. The correlational nature of these investigations leaves open the question of whether emotion is cause or consequence. DET may offer a more powerful heuristic than a traditional cognitive/behavioral perspective because it acknowledges a reciprocal causal relation between emotion and cognition.

A differential emotions perspective illuminates some of the

findings described by cognition researchers who cannot as readily assimilate the data into a traditional cognitive model. For example, Clark (1986) reported that the degree of disapproval or unacceptability expressed about a given thought also showed a reliable positive relation to the individual's report of depression. This is perhaps surprising from a cognitive vantage but consistent with the view that the discrete emotions of guilt and/or shame are in the profile for depression. The greater the activation of the emotions of guilt and shame, the larger their contribution to the depression experienced subjectively.

In a similar vein, Wickless and Kirsch's (1988) data suggest that dysphoric emotions generally do not occur independently of each other, but that co-occurring emotions typically are patterned in such a way that the dominant emotion feeling shows the strongest relation with the thoughts predicted by Beck's cognitive model. For example, although some reports of anger and sadness accompanied thoughts of threat, the average report across respondents and judges was greatest for feelings of anxiety in situations that produced thoughts of threat. All three categories of cognition examined in this study produce a similar pattern, in which reports of the theoretically anticipated emotion occurred significantly more frequently than reports of the other negative emotions. Their results also underscore the specificity of the anxiety system: anxiety was uniquely predicted only by thoughts of threat in regression analysis, and the inclusion of other cognitions made no substantive improvement in the performance of the model after controlling for cognitions of threat.

Most interesting from a differential emotions perspective, though, is the evidence about patterning of emotions within Wickless and Kirsch's sample. When thoughts of loss were statistically controlled (i.e., partialed out of the dependent variable in a regression analysis), then a negative relation appeared between thoughts of threat and sadness. Apparently, the perception of threat elicits anxiety (fear) and inhibits or attenuates sadness in troublesome situations.

LAWFUL DIFFERENCES IN ANXIETY PATTERNS OF EMOTION

Having marshaled the available indicators that certain emotions will tend to activate in related ways in anxiety-inducing situations, we must also consider the ways in which emotion responses to the same stimuli can be decidedly different. Whereas basic emotions appear to be human universals (Izard, 1971, 1991, and e.g., Ekman, Sorenson, & Friesen, 1969, Scherer & Wallbott, 1994, for similar conclusions), there appear to be noticeable differences in how these emotions are elicited, regulated, symbolically represented, and socially shared (Scherer & Wallbott, 1994). These variations have been observed at the levels of both cultural and individual differences. Psychology has traditionally focused on the individual as the unit of analysis, and the trend is toward heightened multicultural sensitivity. From either of these vantages it is imperative to search for differences in the way that anxiety manifests in patterns of emotion. There is reason to believe that there might be differences in anxiety patterns across gender, age, and culture.

Generic support for the possibility of variations on the anxiety theme came from an empirical test of Cattell's hypothesis (as cited in Izard, 1972) that anxiety represents a "higher order factor" (onto which more discrete emotions and cognitions load); the study factor analyzed four sets of DES data and searched for second-order solutions. In none of the four analyses was there a single second-order factor that showed a strong relation with all of the emotions found to occur in anxiety patterns. In all of the studies, however, there appeared a second-order factor that contained substantial loadings for both fear and at least two of the other emotions commonly co-occurring with fear in anxiety profiles (e.g., interest, sadness, guilt, and shyness, as well as the less frequent surprise, anger, and disgust). These findings are interpreted as revoking both the concept of anxiety as a single overarching factor and also the view that anxiety is a unitary construct. At the same time, these patterns of shared variance support the DET positions that anxiety is a variable pattern of emotions and that fear is the key emotion within the normative anxiety profile.

The suite of studies reported earlier also highlighted some interesting differences across subjective reports of anxiety. The results are telling from interviews conducted with African American college students at two different campuses after a confrontation between students and police ended in the death of two students and the injury of several others. This tragic event allowed for comparisons of emotion patterns across situational differences as well as within individuals' reports of different anxiety-eliciting conditions. The average report of the students from the campus with the recent fatalities (and the continuing atmosphere of tension and hostility) showed significantly higher levels of fear, sadness, guilt, and surprise than did the profile of their counterparts (Izard, 1972).

Although this situation obviously did not have any experimental control, it is important that the two campuses did not show the same differences in emotion responses to imaginal elicitors more removed from the present situation. If potentially confounding variables, such as regional variability or time of year, were responsible for the observed differences in the measure of emotions, then similar patterns should have been observed across the other, imaginal conditions. Since this was not the case, it is credible that the elevated scores on certain negative emotions represented a general response by those students to the threat to their safety and well-being.

The same study also hinted that developmental factors may play a role in the determination of patterns of emotion. African American respondents showed reliable differences in DES subscales when asked to remember their first encounter with racism as opposed to imagining themselves currently involved in a racist exchange. The pattern of emotions followed the hypothesized trends such that recollection of an early experience with prejudice prompted higher scores on fear, sadness, guilt, shyness, and surprise, whereas envisioning a current situation elicited more anger, disgust, and contempt (Izard, 1972). Depending on the amount of validity one wishes to confer upon retrospective reports, this change in emotion pattern could reflect an adaptive response to aversive aspects of the environment.

Other evidence obliquely points toward developmental differences, too. Basic emotions emerge along a developmental pattern, as dramatically illustrated by studies of infants on the visual cliff (Sorce et al., 1985). Fear, not present in the repertoire of newborns, appears to emerge as the result of maturation and not to require any cognitive precursors (Izard, 1991). Emotions are socialized as they emerge in development; therefore, the possible configurations of any pattern are limited both by what society (and particularly the family) dictates and by which basic emotions are developmentally available. This logic generates hypotheses such as the prediction that fear and interest-excitement initially should be the most prominent emotions in the anxiety responses of young children (Buechler & Izard, 1980). Although this theory has not been tested in a controlled design as yet, the hypothesis fits well with the emergence of both exploratory behavior and occasional "stranger anxiety" at roughly the same time (Izard, 1991).

Studies suggest possible variations in patterns of basic emotions associated with similar contexts and concerns for different age groups or genders. For example, researchers have found that anger was on average more highly elevated in the profile of depressed boys than in the patterns typically found in both nondepressed peers and depressed adults (Blumberg & Izard, 1985, 1986). Such results are consistent with clinical observations that depression in boys may differ from its adult analog in terms of correlation with impulsive, aggressive, and acting-out behaviors (Blumberg & Izard, 1985). the same research also indicates that there may be significant differences across gender in emotion patterning with implications for the identification of the same clinical needs in different populations (consider, for example, the discussion of the different emotional and behavioral correlates of Conduct Disorder in boys and girls included in the DSM-IV).

Finally, there is compelling evidence for traitlike or temperamental individual differences in patterns of emotion expression (e.g. Izard, 1991; Kagan, 1994). Anxiety and negative basic emotions are primarily related to trait neuroticism (Clark & Watson, 1994). Individual differences in temperament and mood may relate directly to the thresholds for activation of basic emotions, which may, in turn, be linked to neurohormonal processes. Although it is increasingly thought that anxiety and panic are distinct phenomena (e.g., Gray & Barlow, this volume), some recent research on panic may address the physiological contribution to emotion activation. Klein (1995) provides data from both pregnant women and sufferers of extreme premenstrual syndrome indicating that phasic endorphinergic deficiency is related to panic. Specifically, pregnant women do not suffer panic during delivery when cognitive models would predict such occurrence, but they may panic afterward when hormone levels are changing dramatically. Similarly, the basic emotions related to depression show the greatest changes over time and the highest average elevation in women over the weeks following delivery, a pattern fitting well with the concept of postpartum depression (see earlier section "Biogenetic-Neurohormonal Processes" and Izard et al., 1993).

Thus even though research specifically targeting anxiety as a pattern of emotions is only beginning, there are good reasons to anticipate differences in the manifestation of emotion feelings in anxiety. Attention needs to be paid to the cultural, gender, developmental, and personal historical contexts surrounding an individual, for all of these factors can shape emotional experience.

CHALLENGES TO THE CONCEPT OF PATTERNING

One of the most prevalent criticisms of an emotions perspective on psychological functioning is that a cognitive conceptualization is more parsimonious and sufficient to explain the evidence. The extreme argument, that emotions are epiphenomenal, has found voice in the assertion that emotion feelings are not important to the mechanism of anxiety any more than fever is the underlying pathological process in malaria (Beck, 1985). Schemas and cognitions are considered to be the root of psychological functioning, and emotions are construed as output from the cognitive system.

This radical view is readily controverted, though. From a theoretical vantage, it is clear that DET acknowledges that cognitions can activate emotions. DET relativizes cognition, placing it in a larger framework that includes three noncognitive pathways in a broader motivational system (Izard, 1993) and that recognizes the unique motivational capacity of emotion feelings.

Research findings also indicate that emotions influence behavior (and pathology) to an equal or greater extent than cognitions. The relation is admittedly complex: attributional style appears to be related to particular basic emotions (Arkin, Detchon, & Maruyama, 1982). Basic emotion feelings help predict the level of depression in both children (Blumberg & Izard, 1985) and college students (Izard, Blumberg, & Oyster, 1985) above and beyond the effect of attributional style. Furthermore, cognitive attributional style accounted for little if any unique variance after controlling for the effects of basic emotion feelings in these studies. It is reasonable to expect that a similar pattern of findings would appear if cognitions and emotion feelings were examined in relation to reports of anxiety.

There is another converging line of evidence that militates against a strictly cognitive conceptualization of fear and anxiety. As mentioned earlier, LeDoux's (LeDoux et al., 1988) groundbreaking work has conclusively demonstrated the existence of at least two neural pathways by which fear can be conditioned: one route involving the neocortex and another in which sensory input is processed in the thalamus and amygdala without any cortical interaction.

This subcortical pathway, or other neural connections similar to it, may be the conduit for "flashbulb memories" or panic attacks (Izard & Ackerman, in press). Emotion circuits swiftly process information, integrate experiences, and strengthen contextual memory—all with varying amounts of cognitive input and structuring. Thus emotionally powerful events can leave a lasting legacy of memories and influence on future behavior without necessarily being available for rational and articulate description. LeDoux's work further suggests that contingencies that are conditioned via the subcortical pathway could prove extremely resistant to cognitive attempts at modification (LeDoux, 1994).

These findings clearly indicate the insufficiency of a solely cognitive approach to emotions and motivation in general and to the phenomenology of fear and anxiety in particular. Izard and Ackerman (in press) speculate that evidence supporting noncognitive pathways to emotion also could have implications for the etiology and maintenance of at least some phobias and posttraumatic stress disorder. This position is already gaining support. Clinical investigations have recently provided parallel evidence for the operation of the subcortical (thalamoamygdaloid) neural mechanisms of fear conditioning in PTSD (Charney, Deutch, Krystal, Southwick, & Davis, 1993).

Most of the evidence from psychopharmacological research points toward discontinuities both within and between diagnostic categories, and this parallels DET's position that anxiety is not a unitary state. For example, Klein (1993) reviewed the relevant literature and concluded that a hypersensitive hypothalamic-pituitary-adreno-cortical system may play a role in fear, chronic anxiety, and anxious surges, but not in panic. He found that panic attacks were ablated by imipramine (an antidepressant that acts on the noradrenergic system), but imipramine had no effect on the emotion experience of fear. Furthermore, the avoidant behavior and chronic anticipatory anxiety that often accompany panic attacks can persist for a long time after the pharmaceuticals have suppressed the panic (Klein, 1993).[1] Other researchers have implicated dysregulation of the seretonergic system in obsessive-compulsive disorder and depression (Kozak and Foa, 1994) and the GABA/endogenous benzodiazepine system in other forms of anxiety and stress, including generalized anxiety disorder (GAD) (Hommer, Skolnick, & Paul, 1987). Similarly, the noradrenergic system (particularly the locus coeruleus and the dorsal ascending noradrenergic bundle) appears to be central in fear and panic disorder (Redmond, 1987), although the correlation with panic has been challenged (Charney et al., 1990).

Although the psychopharmacological findings sometimes appear contradictory, there can be little dispute that the range of anxiety disorders is not a continuum. Instead, anxiety seems to be a composite of phenomena whose phenotypic similarities may belie the diversity of their biological underpinnings. There is still a large gap between current knowledge of the functioning of neurotransmitters and a working neurophysiological model of human emotions, and even the advocates of neuropsychology are growing unimpressed with simpler rheostat models of neurotransmitters and binary conceptions of neurons (Klein, 1995). There is too much complexity at the cellular level, with literally hundreds of different chemicals and receptor sites impinging on single synapses, and too rich a range of human expression at the other end of the system to expect that simple theoretical vehicles will carry us far.

Therefore, emotion feelings serve as a conceptual and empirical bridge between the "bottom-up" approach of materialistic, reductionistic neuropsychology and the subjective, experiential world inhabited by the rest of psychology, including clinical practice. The basic emotions are empirically validated theoretical constructs that have demonstrated relevance at the psychological and behavioral levels through relationships with behavior, motivation, and psychological functioning (as discussed above).

At the same time, there is evidence for the specificity of emotional representation at the neural level for at least some of the emotions. LeDoux (1990; LeDoux et al., 1988) has documented the pathways that mediate the emotion of fear, and he is optimistic about the prospects for charting other emotion pathways. Even though the amygdala, for example, is implicated in a variety of emotion-activating systems, it is a complex structure subserving yet other systems. Studies examining microcircuitry are revealing differential patterns of sensory inputs, outputs, and emotion processes, such as the separate amygdalar circuitry for fear versus appetitive expressions (LeDoux, 1994).

Emotions, and the anxiety pattern of emotion feelings in particular, cannot satisfactorily be accounted for by either cognitive or neurophysiological reductionism. DET acknowledges the contributions of cognitive and biological functions and simultaneously incorporates these perspectives into a more holistic multisystem model of emotion activation and regulation (Izard, 1993; Izard & Ackerman, in press). A differential emotions perspective, particularly a focus on emotion feelings, accounts for aspects of the human experience that otherwise evade contemporary psychological theory.

ISSUES WITH THE MEASUREMENT OF PATTERNS OF EMOTION FEELINGS

A common complaint leveled against studies that examine profiles of emotions in relation to some criterion is that the methodology typically relies on the correlation between the same informant's report on emotions and criterion measures (e.g., Levitt, 1972; Spielberger, 1985). The strong argument is that such correlations demonstrate semantic kinship and not necessarily any deeper psychological relationship (Beck, 1985; Spielberger, 1985). The weaker objection is that any obtained correlations are an artifact of "method variance," reflecting response set, current mood, and other superficial consistencies instead of the presumed relation between variables of interest.

Several studies have rebutted the strong claim that empirical findings represent trivial semantic similarities in the items composing the instruments for assessing emotions and the instruments measuring the criterion variable. One of the simplest designs for testing the hypothesis of semantic similarity between emotion scales and an anxiety criterion measure involved deleting all items judged to have emotional content from the anxiety criterion measure and then examining the extent to which this changed the correlations with the emotion subscales. Blumberg and Izard (1986) did this with two different measures, the Child Depression Inventory (CDI; Kovacs & Beck, 1977) and the State/Trait Anxiety Inventory for Children (STAIC; Spielberger, Edwards, Lushene, Montuori, & Platzek, 1973). Four raters familiar with DET examined the items on the CDI and STAIC and removed all items judged by two or more raters as having overt emotion content, creating "nonaffect" forms of the CDI and STAIC.

No significant differences were found in the pattern of correlation between the emotions assessed on the DES-IV subscales and either the regular or "nonaffect" version of the criterion measures. Additionally, emotions that clearly were not represented on either the CDI or the STAIC, such as guilt and shame, also showed a reliable relation to these measures in regression analysis. These results strongly suggest that the observed relation between measures of emotion feelings and anxiety or depression do not depend on a superficial relation between items with explicitly emotional content on both sets of measures.

Other researchers have addressed the problem of method variance, even more broadly conceptualized, through the use of structured clinical interviews (Wren, 1988) and teacher reports or nominations. These studies demonstrated that groups of children differentiated through means other than self-report still showed significant differences in the patterns of emotion feelings expressed. Furthermore, the observed patterns supported the predictions made by DET (Blumberg & Izard, 1986; Izard et al., 1985): children in the depressed group on average displayed significantly higher levels of sadness, inner-directed hostility, anger, and guilt.

Some supporting evidence can be garnered from the cognitive literature. For example, particular strengths of Wickless and Kirsch's (1988) design include their reliance on structured interviews and behavioral logs (in which subjects monitored daily events that produced emotion feelings and recorded the cognitions experienced proximal to the affective event), rather than depending on self-report on potentially reactive measures. Clark (1986) also advances the argument that instruments such as the Beck Depression Inventory provide some escape from the circularity of method variance inasmuch as they rely on reports of somatic and vegetative symptoms of depression and not simply cognitions and emotion feelings.

In short, the patterns of emotion feelings that are significantly related to anxiety have been validated in studies that use a variety of designs to avoid method variance. The findings of stable patterns with fear as the key emotion have proved robust in studies of anxiety, whereas depression patterns seem to coalesce around sadness, inner-directed hostility, and anger.

ADVANTAGES OF A DET PERSPECTIVE ON ANXIETY AS A PATTERN OF EMOTIONS

DET provides a framework for examining emotions in an evolutionary perspective. Such a view offers insight into how motivational systems that may have been adaptive in the past could become problematic in a modern environment. Our craving for salt and fat served our ancestors well when these nutrients were difficult to obtain. The same craving, which was necessary to galvanize hunter-gatherers, cannot easily adjust to the surfeit of these nutrients in the modern diet (e.g., Konner, 1981).

Similarly, the pattern of emotion feelings involved in anxiety operates as a protective system that may present difficulties in accommodating the social realities of the modern environment (Beck, 1985). In the past, false positives were survivable and false negatives potentially fatal if the emotion alarm system failed to appraise the situation accurately. As mentioned earlier, our appraisals of situations are influenced by our trait emotionality and by our developmental record so there is considerable individual difference in propensity to activate the anxiety pattern of emotion feelings. A broadly conceptual approach that recognizes the history and rootedness of emotions in human evolution will strive to adjust the fit between individual and environment and not misguidedly attempt to ablate the emotion feelings perceived as contributing to a person's distress.

The DET principle of modularity of emotions contradicts current views of cognition and emotion as integral and inseparable and is a more realistic model of psychological functioning as we currently understand it (Izard, 1994a). Many theorists have argued for a continuum of anxiety disorders, ranging from simple, focal phobias to the pervasive distress of GAD (e.g., Lang, 1985; Spielberger, 1985). Besides offering an alluring simplicity of conceptualization, such an anxiety continuum would be consistent with theories that emphasize the role of cognitions (or any other contributing attribute that could vary along a dimension). However, the evidence from both neurophysiological research and clinical practice points toward considerable discontinuity.

Clinical and research implications. The pattern of emotions involved in a given instance of anxiety could have an effect on the differential diagnosis of anxiety versus depression (or other psychological disorders), as well as ramifications for etiology, maintenance, and treatment. While measures of anxiety and depression are typically highly correlated (Beck, 1985; Spielberger, 1985), the discrete emotions approach has consistently found differential patterns of emotion feelings associated with depression and anxiety (e.g., Blumberg & Izard, 1986; Wickless & Kirsch, 1988). There admittedly are indications of differences in emotion profiles across gender (Blumberg & Izard, 1986; Lelwica, 1988; Wren, 1987), age (Izard et al., 1985), and possibly culture or class (unpublished data). The consistencies, such as the nonrelation between feelings of interest-excitement and depression, or the heightened relation between anger and depression versus anger and anxiety, still emphasize the promise of further investigation in this area.

Whereas psychological research has largely avoided the domain of emotion feelings, it has generally been accepted among clinicians that they offer the most direct and useful source of information about how clients believe themselves to be functioning. Reports of emotion feelings help both client and clincian grasp what is important in terms of relations, goals, and assumptions about the world; and it is emotion feelings that motivate most persons to persist in the work of therapy (Lazarus, 1991). Thus an emotions perspective on anxiety has several advantages for the clinician: it focuses on what will often be the most salient aspect of the psychological problem for the client, it automatically calls attention to motivations that can be available for change, and it can help bridge the gap between theory and practice (inasmuch as mental health workers have been practicing with an emotion orientation regardless of the paucity of the research).

A DET approach offers the possibility of more specific therapies, too. In treatment, it is important not only to communicate well and motivate the client but also to anticipate possible reactions of the client during a session. In vivo behavioral treatment has an advantage over imaginal systems, at least in part, because it recruits the fear system more directly, but this also increases the likelihood of activating other emotion systems. The clinician would do well to be aware that interventions targeting fear, such as exposure or systematic desensitization for phobic patients, could often also elicit anger, disgust, and hostility. Good practice requires anticipating these emotions as well as activating and using interest and enjoyment to help propel the client through treatment (Buechler & Izard, 1980).

DET also makes some intriguing predictions with special regard to the assessment and treatment of anxiety. As mentioned earlier, fear and anger have an antagonistic relation with each other. The techniques for relaxation training, sensate focus, and emotion expression as a means of emotion induction are available to help clinician and client exploit this inverse relation as a way of gaining some control over anxiety. A similar beneficial effect has been hypothesized for activating the emotion of interest in persons who are depressed (Izard, 1994b).

Additionally, theorists in this area have begun to generate ideas about how patterns of emotions could interact with each other to produce distinct consequences. Buechler and Izard (1980), for example, have postulated that many people's anxiety patterns are influenced by the developmental process of socializing fear. Shame is often associated with fear, particularly for young men growing up in cultures that value machismo and ridicule any display of fear. There is speculation that strong early experiences of shame could interfere with the establishment of a sense of self-adequacy (Buechler & Izard, 1980). Similarly, it is postulated that many individuals suffer from a fear-sadness bind in which the person becomes afraid of and avoids coping with the source of sadness (Izard, 1991; Tomkins, 1963). This pattern of functioning is expected to relate to a lack of physical courage, panic reactions to pain, and hypochondriasis (Buechler & Izard, 1980; Tomkins, 1963).

Finally, and on a more global level, emotions-oriented research could also do much to clarify the etiological relation between patterns of anxiety and major mood disorders. Reports from a variety of sources indicate that depressive and anxiety disorders may not only be frequently comorbid but actually dynamically related to each other. A cross-sectional study of bereaved spouses found significantly elevated incidence of both panic disorder and generalized anxiety disorders when compared with the community prevalence rates for the same conditions and also established that most of the anxiety cases were not independent of major depression (Jacobs et al., 1990). The substantial overlap between disorders raises questions of whether anxiety is a precursor, concomitant, or residual to major depression.

A differential emotions approach may clarify this issue and show that anxiety as a pattern of feelings is often prodromal to depression. Clark, Watson, and Mineka (1994) assert that depressive symptoms often appear following an unsuccessful or unresolved anxiety response to a stressor. Beck argues that depression may be a dysfunctional expression of an otherwise adaptive system similar to Izard's (1991) conception of the sadness system, designed to conserve resources in response to a failure to master a threat in the environment (Beck, 1985). Passive withdrawal can be an effective coping strategy if it is temporary. Bowlby's (1980) ethological description of the two-stage response to separation or loss is prototypical of this proposed dynamic pattern of basic emotions. The initial isolation provokes active protest, which initially may involve anger and later become a source of fear. This fear response is sometimes equated with the experience of anxiety (e.g., Clark & Watson, 1994; Klein, 1995), and certainly the vigilant and fearful phase is congruent with a differential emotions conception of anxiety. If the attachment figure does not return, eventually the protests are replaced with a passive despair. According to Bowlby (1973), the passive response conserves energy and minimizes the likelihood of attracting predators. This second stage in the separation syndrome is considered an analog of depression. This pattern is mirrored in the typical sequence of human responses to psychological stressors such that fear/anxiety patterns of emotion predominate initially (provided that the stressor cannot be manipulated by means of anger or some other approach) and gradually are accompanied or superseded by sadness and depression if the stressor continues (Akiskal, 1990).

Patterns of Emotion Anxiety: Concluding Remarks

There is now substantial evidence to support the hypothesis that anxiety should be treated in research and clinical practice as a cluster or pattern of emotions. The supporting evidence comes largely from studies of the affective symptomatology of anxiety. In contrast to research using other approaches, the studies congruent with DET discriminate between emotion patterns in anxiety and depression. Current evidence from neurophysiology and neuropharmacology is consistent with DET's emphasis on distinct discrete emotions and their occurrence in interacting patterns in anxiety disorders. Failure to recognize that anxiety consists not simply of fear but of an interacting cluster of discrete emotions could result in incomplete understanding and diagnosis and ineffective therapies.

Examining the pattern of emotion feelings that co-occur in anxiety suggests commonalities and differences across person, circumstance, psychological health, and social context. The constants, such as the prominence of fear in the context of certain other basic emotions, may inform future research and diagnostic procedures and prove to be of relevance in emotion-oriented therapies. Discontinuities and discrepancies are also illuminating because they offer insight into how we, the researcher and the clinician, are encountering a unique individual.

NOTE

1. Some of Klein's observations were questioned by participants at the symposium (Dianne Chambless), and one (Jeffrey Gray) noted that these differential effects of imipramine and other drugs may be dependent on dose.

REFERENCES

Ackerman, B. P., Abe, J. A., & Izard, C. E. (in press). The emotions system and the development of emotion-cognition relations, personality, and psychopathology. In M. F. Mascolo & S. Griffin (Eds.), *What develops in emotional development?* New York: Plenum.

Aggleton, J. P., & Mishkin, M. (1986). The amygdala in emotion. In R. Plutchik & H. Kellerman (Eds.), *Emotion: Theory, research, and experience* (Vol. 3, pp. 281–299). San Diego: Academic.

Akiskal, H. S. (1990). Toward a clinical understanding of anxiety and depression disorders. In J. D. Maser & C. R. Cloninger (Eds.), *Comorbidity of mood and anxiety disorders* (pp. 597–607). Washington DC: American Psychiatric Press.

Altemus, M., & Gold, P. W. (1993). Neurohormones in depression and anxiety. In J. Schulkin (Ed.), *Hormonally induced changes in mind and brain* (pp. 253–286). San Diego: Academic.

Andrew, R. J. (1963). Evolution of facial expression. *Science, 142,* 1034–1041.

Arkin, R. M., Detchon, C. S., & Maruyama, G. M. (1982). Roles of attribution, affect, and cognitive interference in test anxiety. *Journal of Personality and Social Psychology, 43,* 1111–1124.

Bandura, A. (1977). Self-efficacy: Toward a unifying theory of behavioral change. *Psychological Review, 84,* 191–215.

Barlow, D. H. (1988). *Anxiety and its disorders: The nature and treatment of anxiety and panic.* New York: Guilford.

Baron, R. S., Inman, M. L., Kao, C. F., & Logan, H. (1992). Negative emotion and superficial social processing. *Motivation and Emotion, 16,* 323–346.

Bartlett, E. S., & Izard C. E. (1972). A dimensional and discrete emotions investigation of the subjective experience of emotion. In C. E. Izard (Ed.), *Patterns of emotion: A new analysis of anxiety and depression* (pp. 129–173). New York: Academic.

Beck, A. T. (1976). *Cognitive therapy and the emotional disorders.* Madison CT: International University Press.

Beck, A. T. (1985). Theoretical perspectives on clinical anxiety. In A. H. Tuma & J. Maser (Eds.), *Anxiety and the anxiety disorders* (pp. 183–196). Hillsdale NJ: Erlbaum.

Blumberg, S. H., & Izard, C. E. (1985). Affective and cognitive characteristics of depresson in 10- and 11-year-old children. *Journal of Personality and Social Psychology, 49,* 194–202.

Blumberg, S. H., & Izard, C. E. (1986). Discriminating patterns of emotions in 10- and 11-year-old children's anxiety and depression. *Journal of Personality and Social Psychology, 51,* 852–857.

Bower, G. H. (1981). Mood and memory. *American Psychologist, 36,* 129–148.

Bowlby, J. (1973). *Attachment and loss.* New York: Basic Books.

Bowlby, J. (1980). *Attachment and loss: Vol 2. Separation, anxiety and anger.* New York: Basic Books.

Buechler, S., & Izard, C. (1980). Anxiety in childhood and adolescence. In I. L. Kutash & L. B. Schlesinger (Eds.), *Handbook on stress and anxiety: Contemporary knowledge, theory, and treatment* (pp. 285–328). San Francisco: Jossey-Bass.

Cahill, L., Prins, B., Weber, M., & McGaugh, J. L. (1994). B-adrenergic activation and memory for emotional events. *Nature, 371,* 702–704.

Charney, D. S., Deutch, A. Y., Krystal, J. H., Southwick, S. M., & Davis, M. (1993). Psychobiologic mechanisms of posttraumatic stress disorder. *Archives of General Psychiatry, 50,* 294–305.

Charney, D. S., Woods, S. W., Nagy, L. M., Southwick, S. M., Krystal, J. H., Heninger, G. R. (1990). Noradrenergic function in panic disorder. *Journal of Clinical Psychiatry, 51,* 5–11.

Cicchetti, D. (1990). The organization and coherence of socioemotional, cognitive, and representational development: Illustrations through a developmental psychopathology perspective on Down Syndrome and child maltreatment. In R. Thompson (Ed.), *Nebraska Symposium on Motivation* (Vol. 36, pp. 259–366).

Clark, D. A. (1986). Cognitive-affective interaction: A test of the "specificity" and "generality" hypotheses. *Cognitive Therapy and Research, 10,* 607–623.

Clark, L. A., & Watson, D. (1994). Distinguishing functional from dysfunctional affective responses. In P. Ekman & R. Davidson (Eds.), *The nature of emotion: Fundamental questions* (pp. 131–145). New York: Oxford University Press.

Clark, L. A., Watson, D., & Mineka, S. (1994). Temperament, personality, and the mood and anxiety disorders. *Journal of Abnormal Psychology, 103,* 103–116.

Damasio, A. R. (1994). *Descartes' error: Emotion, reason, and the human brain.* New York: Putnam.

Darwin, C. (1965). *The expression of the emotions in man and animals.* Chicago: University of Chicago Press. (Original work published 1872.)

Davis, M. (1992). The role of the amygdala in fear and anxiety. *Annual Review of Neuroscience, 15,* 353–375.

Dawkins, R. (1986). *The blind watchmaker.* New York: Norton.

Easterbrook, J. A. (1959). The effect of emotion on cue utilization and the organization of behavior. *Psychological Bulletin, 66,* 183–201.

Ekman, P., Sorenson, E. R., & Friesen, W. V. (1969). Pan-cultural elements in facial displays of emotion. *Science, 164,* 86–88.

Eysenck, H. J. (1956). The questionnaire measurement of neuroticism and extraversion. *Revista de Psicología, 50,* 113–140.

Finman, R., & Berkowitz, I. (1989). Some factors influencing the effect of depressed mood on anger and overt hostility toward another. *Journal of Research in Personality, 23,* 70–84.

Foa, E. B., Riggs, D. S., Massie, E. D., & Yarczower, M. (1995). The impact of fear activation and anger on the efficacy of exposure treatment for posttraumatic stress disorder. *Behavior Therapy, 26,* 487–499.

Fodor, J. A. (1983). *Modularity of mind: An essay on faculty psychology.* Cambridge MA: MIT Books.

Fridlund, A. J. (1994). *Human facial expression: An evolutionary view.* San Diego: Academic.

Gelernter, D. H. (1994). *The muse in the machine.* New York: Free Press.

Gellhorn, E. (1964). Motion and emotion: The role of proprioception in the physiology and pathology of the emotions. *Psychological Review, 71,* 457–472.

Gould, S. J. (1993). Mozart and modularity. In S. J. Gould (Ed.), *Eight little piggies: Reflections in natural history* (pp. 249–261). New York: Norton.

Gray, J. A. (1982). [Precis of *The neuropsychology of anxiety: An enquiry into the functions of the septo-hippocampal system*]. *Behavioral and Brain Sciences, 5,* 469–534.

Hommer, D. W., Skolnick, P., & Paul, S. (1987). The benzodiazepine/GAPA receptor complex and anxiety. In H. Y. Meltzer (Ed.), *Psychopharmacology: The third generation of progress.* New York: Raven.

Hope, D. A., Heimberg, R. G., & Klein, G. F. (1990). Social anxiety and the recall of interpersonal information. *Journal of Cognitive Psychotherapy, 4*, 185–195.

Insel, T. R. (1993). Oxytocin and the neuroendocrine basis of affiliation. In J. Schulkin (Ed.), *Hormonally induced changes in mind and brain* (pp. 225–251). San Diego: Academic.

Izard, C. E. (1971). *The face of emotion*. New York: Appleton-Century-Crofts.

Izard, C. E. (1972). *Patterns of emotion*. San Diego: Academic.

Izard, C. E. (1977). *Human emotions*. New York: Plenum.

Izard, C. E. (1984). Emotion-cognition relationships and human development. In C. E. Izard, J. Kagan, & R. Zajonc (Eds.), *Emotion, cognition, and behavior* (pp. 17–37). New York: Cambridge University Press.

Izard, C. E. (1989). The structure and functions of emotions: Implications for cognition, motivation, and personality. In I. S. Cohen (Ed.), *The G. Stanley Hall lecture series* (Vol. 9, pp. 35–73). Washington DC: American Psychological Association.

Izard, C. E. (1990). Facial expressions and the regulation of emotions. *Journal of Personality and Social Psychology, 58*, 487–498.

Izard, C. E. (1991). *The psychology of emotions*. New York: Plenum.

Izard, C. E. (1993). Four systems for emotion activation: Cognitive and non-cognitive processes. *Psychological Review, 100*, 68–90.

Izard, C. E. (1994a). Innate and universal facial expressions: Evidence from developmental and cross-cultural research. *Psychological Bulletin, 115*, 288–299.

Izard, C. E. (1994b). What I should remember from my study of emotions, if I were to return to teaching and practicing psychotherapy. In N. H. Frijda (Ed.), *Proceedings of the VIII Conference of the International Society for Research on Emotions* (pp. 149–153). Storrs CT: ISRE Publications.

Izard, C. E. (in press). Emotions and facial expressions: A perspective from differential emotions theory. In J. A. Russell & J. M. Fernandez Dols (Eds.), *The psychology of facial expressions*. New York: Cambridge University Press.

Izard, C. E., & Ackerman, B. P. (in press). Emotion, emotion-cognition relations, and cognitive psychotherapy [Special issue]. *Journal of Cognitive Psychotherapy*.

Izard, C. E., Blumberg, S. H., & Oyster, C. K. (1985). Age and sex differences in the pattern of emotions in childhood anxiety and depression. In J. T. Spence & C. E. Izard (Eds.), *Motivation, emotion, and personality* (pp. 317–324). North Holland: Elsevier.

Izard, C. E., & Harris, P. (1995). Emotional development and developmental psychopathology. In D. Cicchetti & D. J. Cohen (Eds.), *Manual of developmental psychopathology: Vol. 1. Theory and methods* (pp. 467–503). New York: Wiley.

Izard, C. E., Hembree, E. A., & Huebner, R. R. (1987). Infants' emotion expressions to acute pain: Developmental change and stability of individual differences. *Developmental Psychology, 23*, 105–113.

Izard, C. E., Libero, D. Z., Putnam, P., & Haynes, O. M. (1993). Stability of emotion experiences and their relation to traits of personality. *Journal of Personality and Social Psychology, 64*, 847–860.

Izard, C. E., Wehmer, G. M., Livsey, W., & Jennings, J. R. (1965). Affect, awareness, and performance. In S. S. Tomkins & C. E. Izard (Eds.), *Affect, cognition, and personality* (pp. 2–41). New York: Springer.

Jacobs, S., Hansen, F., Kasi, S., Ostfield, A., Berkman, L., & Kim, K. (1990). Anxiety disorders during acute bereavement: Risk and risk factors. *Journal of Clinical Psychiatry, 51*, 269–274.

James, W. (1950). *The principles of psychology* (Vol. 2). New York: Dover. (Original work published 1890.)

Jersild, A. T. (1947). Emotional development. In L. Carmichael (Ed.), *Manual of child psychology* (2nd ed., pp. 833–917). New York: Wiley.

Johnson, M. K., & Weisz, C. (1994). Comments on unconscious processing. In P. M. Niedenthal & S. Kitayama (Eds.), *The heart's eye: Emotional influences in perception and attention* (pp. 145–164). San Diego: Academic.

Kagan, J. (1994). *Galen's prophecy: Temperament in human nature.* New York: Basic Books.

Klein, D. F. (1993). False suffocation alarms, spontaneous panics, and related conditions: An integrative hypothesis. *Archives of General Psychiatry, 50*, 306–317.

Klein, D. F. (1995). *Testing the suffocation false alarm theory of panic disorder.* Unpublished manuscript, Columbia University, New York.

Konner, M. (1981). *The tangled wing: Biological constraints on the human spirit.* New York: Holt Rinehart.

Kovacs, M., & Beck, A. T. (1977). An empirical clinical approach towards a definition of childhood depression. In J. G. Schulterbrandt & A. Raskin (Eds.), *Depression in children: Diagnosis, treatment, and conceptual models.* New York: Raven.

Kozak, M. J., & Foa, E. B. (1994). Obsessions, overvalued ideas, and delusions in obsessive-compulsive disorder. *Behaviour Research and Therapy, 32*, 343–353.

Laird, J. D. (1974). Self-attribution of emotion: The effects of expressive behavior on the quality of emotional experience. *Journal of Personality and Social Psychology, 29*, 475–486.

Lang, P. J. (1985). The cognitive psychophysiology of emotion: Fear and anxiety. In A. H. Tuma & J. D. Maser (Eds.), *Anxiety and the anxiety disorders* (pp. 131–170). Hillsdale NJ: Erlbaum.

Lazarus, R. S. (1991). Cognition and motivation in emotion. *American Psychologist, 46*, 352–367.

LeDoux, J. E. (1987). Emotion. In F. Plum (Ed.), *Handbook of physiology: Section 1. The nervous system* (pp. 410–459). Bethesda MD: American Physiological Society.

LeDoux, J. E. (1989). Cognitive-emotional interactions in the brain. In C. E. Izard (Ed.), *Development of emotion-cognition relations* (pp. 267–289). Hillsdale NJ: Erlbaum.

LeDoux, J. E. (1990). Information flow from sensation to emotion: Plasticity in the neural computation of stimulus value. In M. Gabriel & J. Moore (Eds.), *Learning and computational neuroscience: Foundations of adaptive networks* (pp. 3–51). Cambridge: MIT Press.

LeDoux, J. E. (1994). Emotion-specific physiological activity: Don't forget about CNS physiology. In P. Ekman & R. J. Davidson (Eds.), *The nature of emotion: Fundamental questions* (pp. 248–251). New York: Oxford University Press.

LeDoux, J. E., Iwata, J., Cicchetti, D., & Reis, D. J. (1988). Different projections of the central amygdaloid nucleus mediate autonomic and behavioral correlates of conditioned fear. *Journal of Neuroscience, 4*, 683–698.

LeDoux, J. E., Romanski, L., & Xagoraris, A. (1989). Indelibility of subcortical emotional memories. *Journal of Cognitive Neuroscience, 1*, 238–243.

Lelwica, M. (1988). *Emotional, cognitive, behavioral, and experiential factors*. Unpublished doctoral dissertation, University of Delaware, Newark, Delaware.

Levitt, E. E. (1972). Comments on Dr. Izard's paper. In C. D. Spielberger (Ed.), *Anxiety: Current trends in theory and research* (Vol. 1, pp. 113–114). New York: Academic.

Lewis, M. (1985). Theoretical perspectives on stress and anxiety. In I. L. Kutash & L. B. Schlesinger (Eds.), *Handbook on stress and anxiety*. San Francisco: Jossey-Bass.

Lewis, M. D. (1995). Cognition-emotion feedback and the self-organization of developmental paths. *Human Development, 38*, 78–102.

McNally, R. J. Cognitive bias in the anxiety disorders. This volume.

Mineka, S. (1988). A primate model of phobic fears. In H. Eysenck & I. Martin (Eds.), *Theoretical foundations of behavior therapy* (pp. 81–111). New York: Plenum.

Mineka, S., Davidson, M., Cook, M., & Keir, R. (1984). Observational conditioning of snake fear in rhesus monkeys. *Journal of Abnormal Psychology, 93*, 355–372.

Mineka, S., & Zinbarg, R. E. Fear conditioning and ethological models of anxiety disorder. This volume.

Niedenthal, P. M., & Kitayama, S. (Eds.). (1994). *The heart's eye: Emotional influences in perception and attention*. San Diego: Academic.

Niedenthal, P. M., Setterlund, M. B., & Jones, D. E. (1994). Emotional organization of perceptual memory. In P. M. Niedenthal & S. Kitayama (Eds.), *The heart's eye: Emotional influences in perception and attention* (pp. 87–113). San Diego: Academic.

Ortony, A., Clore, G. L., & Collins, A. C. (1988). *The cognitive structure of emotions*. Cambridge, England: Cambridge University Press.

Panksepp, J. B., Herman, B., Conner, R., Bishop, P., & Scott, J. P. (1978). The biology of social attachments: Opiates alleviate separate distress. *Biological Psychiatry, 13*, 607–613.

Pratto, F. (1994). Consciousness and automatic evaluation. In P. M. Niedenthal & S. Kitayama (Eds.), *The heart's eye: Emotional influences in perception and attention* (pp. 115–143). San Diego: Academic.

Redmond, D. E., Jr. (1987). Studies of the nucleus locus coeruleus in monkeys and hypotheses for neuropsychopharmacology. In H. Y. Meltzer (Ed.), *Psychopharmacology: The third generation of progress* (pp. 967–975). New York: Raven.

Scarr-Salapatek, S. (1976). An evolutionary perspective on infant intelligence: Species patterns and individual variations. In M. Lewis (Ed.), *Origins of intelligence: Infancy and early childhood* (pp. 165–198). New York: Plenum.

Scherer, K. R., & Wallbott, H. G. (1994). Evidence for universality and cultural variation of differential emotion response patterning. *Journal of Personality and Social Psychology, 66,* 310–328.

Schneider, W., Casey, B. J., & Noll, D. (1994). Functional MRI mapping of stimulus rate effects across visual processing stages. *Human Brain Mapping, 1,* 117–133.

Siegel, A., & Demetrikopoulos, M. K. (1993). Hormones and aggression. In J. Schulkin (Ed.), *Hormonally induced changes in mind and brain* (pp. 99–127). San Diego: Academic.

Sorce, J. F., Emde, R. N., Campos, J. J., & Klinnert, M. D. (1985). Maternal emotional signaling: Its effect on the visual cliff behavior of 1-year-olds. *Developmental Psychology, 21,* 195–200.

Spielberger, C. D. (1985). Anxiety, cognition, and affect: A state-trait perspective. In A. H. Tuma & J. Maser (Eds.), *Anxiety and the anxiety disorders* (pp. 171–182). Hillsdale NJ: Erlbaum.

Spielberger, C. D., Edwards, C. D., Lushene, R. F., Montuori, J., & Platzek, D. (1973). *STAIC: Preliminary manual.* Palo Alto CA: Consulting Psychologists Press.

Spielberger, C. D., Gorsuch, R. R., & Lushene, R. E. (1970). *State-trait anxiety inventory test manual for form X.* Pal Alto CA: Consulting Psychologists Press.

Tomkins, S. S. (1962). *Affect, imagery, consciousness: Vol. 1. The positive affects.* New York: Springer.

Tomkins, S. S. (1963). *Affect, imagery, consciousness: Vol. 2. The negative affects.* New York: Springer.

Watson, D., & Clark, L. A. (1992). On traits and temperament: General and specific factors of emotional experience and their relation to the five-factor model. *Journal of Personality, 60,* 441–476.

Watson, D., Clark, L. A., & Tellegen, A. (1988). Development and validation of brief measures of positive and negative affect: The PANAS scales. *Journal of Personality and Social Psychology, 54,* 1063–1070.

Wickless, C., & Kirsch, I. (1988). Cognitive correlates of anger, anxiety, and sadness. *Cognitive Therapy and Research, 12,* 367–377.

Wren, R. W. (1987). *Emotion and family environment characteristics of depressed children.* Unpublished master's thesis, University of Delaware, Newark, Delaware.

Wren, R. W. (1988). *Factors related to depression and distress in children.* Unpublished doctoral dissertation, University of Delaware, Newark, Delaware.

Yule, W., Udwin, O., & Murdoch, K. (1990). The "Jupiter" sinking: Effects on children's fears, depression, and anxiety. *Journal of Child Psychology and Psychiatry, 31,* 1051–1061.

Zajonc, R. B. (1980). Feeling and thinking: Preferences need no inferences. *American Psychologist, 35,* 151–175.

Zajonc, R. B. (1984). On the primacy of affect. *American Psychologist, 39,* 117–123.

Zajonc, R. B., Murphy, S. T., & Inglehart, M. (1989). Feeling and facial efference: Implications of the vascular theory of emotion. *Psychological Review, 96,* 395–416.

Zola-Morgan, S., Squire, L. R., Alvarez-Royo, R., & Clower, R. P. (1991). Independence of memory functions and emotional behavior: Separate contributions of the hippocampal formation and the amygdala. *Hippocampus, 1,* 207–220.

The Neuropsychology of Anxiety: Reprise

Jeffrey A. Gray
Institute of Psychiatry,
University of London

Neil McNaughton
University of Otago

This paper reports on work that is very much in progress; in many cases, indeed, it is still at the point of framing questions rather than proposing answers. The overriding question it addresses is contained in the title: what are the neuropsychological mechanisms whose functioning constitutes the substrate of anxiety? This is not to say that answers have not been offered to this question before: quite apart from the considerable work of many other distinguished workers (e.g., Barlow, 1988; Graeff, 1993; LeDoux, 1987; Miller, 1951; Panksepp, 1982a), including Fowles's (1995) penetrating discussion (at last year's Nebraska Symposium) of the general field to which it belongs, one of us has devoted a long book to it, subjected to intensive peer review (Gray, 1982a, b). We are now in the process of preparing a second edition of that book, taking into account the various developments since it went to press well over a decade ago. During that time some competing theories have fallen by the wayside, but lusty new competitors have emerged. The specific issue we shall address here, therefore, is, How far was the 1982 book on the right lines? As will be seen, we are confident that the core of the argument put forward in 1982 is still valid and in some cases has been strength-

We are extremely grateful to Elizabeth Drawbridge for her care in handling our complicated transcontinental communications and preparing the manuscript for this chapter.

ened by the more recent data. But it is also clear that many additions and changes are necessary if the detailed model is to incorporate all the new data and concepts that have emerged since then. Our purpose here is to outline the most important of these new data and concepts, the issues they raise, and the likely ways they can best be addressed. It will not be possible, however, to address all the issues that emerge, both because to do so would require almost book-length treatment and because it is doubtful that we have yet succeeded in identifying them all.

Emotion and Motivation

Whatever "anxiety" is, it is clearly an emotion; indeed, it occupies such a central place in treatments of this topic that one sometimes wonders if it is not the *only* emotion. It is appropriate therefore to begin with a brief consideration of the relations that hold between emotion and motivation, the latter constituting, of course, the central theme of the series of symposia to which this article contributes.

Although a wide variety of different definitions of "emotion" can be found in the psychological literature, a common thread running through many of them—especially in the tradition that stems, as does the present paper, from animal learning theory—is that emotions are *states of the CNS elicited by reinforcing events*. Before we cash in detail this as-yet blank check, the terms it uses require some further preliminary glosses.

- The term *reinforcing events* carries the familiar Skinnerian meaning (though Skinnerians will surely not approve of the heavily theoretical and neuropsychological context in which we embed it): that is, these are events that an experimental subject will work to obtain or avoid.
- CNS is an abbreviation that we use ambiguously, as did Hebb (1949), to conflate, on the one hand, the conceptual nervous system (that is, the systems that control behavior as inferred from the study of input-output, i.e., stimulus-response, relationships) and, on the other, the central nervous system (that is, the real brain, which carries out the the functions inferred—if they are correctly inferred—of the conceptual nervous system).

- We distinguish between (a) the role of reinforcing events *qua* reinforcers, that is, when they act to encourage or discourage the repetition of behavior that precedes them (their motivational effect); and (b) the role of reinforcers as elicitors of states that follow their presentation (their emotional effects).
- With respect to the latter, emotional effects, we do not assume that the elicited reactions need all arise from activation of some single controlling node in the brain (McNaughton, 1989a); but we do assume that, to a single emotion (once we have properly captured what such a term should encapsulate), there will correspond a relatively unified, single brain system (Gray, 1995a).
- We assume also that the eliciting (as opposed to reinforcing) properties of primary and secondary reinforcers can be, and often are, quite different from each other (Gray, 1975; McNaughton, 1989a, b).

Given the role played by reinforcing events in both motivation and emotion, it is difficult to develop a theory of the one that is not, explicitly or implicitly, a theory also of the other. Thus, although our key concern here is with one of the emotions, we shall first sketch a general outline of the motivational system (Gray, 1995a) of which the emotion of anxiety is, so to speak, part of the other side of the coin. We also see our analysis of anxiety as providing an at least partial paradigm for the analysis of emotion and motivation, and their interrelations, as a whole.

A General Motivational Model: The Limbic System and Basal Ganglia

Gray (1995a; see also Gray, Feldon, Rawlins, Hemsley, & Smith, 1991a) has proposed that the limbic system plus the basal ganglia jointly constitute a general mechanism for the attainment of goals, as illustrated in general terms in Figure 1. The term *goal* here may seem to have anthropomorphic overtones but must be preferred to the idea of a rigid "response programming" mechanism, given the variability of even well-learned behavior. In the sense employed here, the notion of goal-directedness can be applied to as simple a mechanism as the stretch reflex (the goal of which is to maintain muscle length) or be elaborated to cover much more complicated

Goal attainment

Sensory (limbic)

Motor (basal ganglia)

Recognition of goals
as goals

Establishment of
motor programs
directed to goals.

Evaluation of ← Execution of
outcomes of → motor programs
action

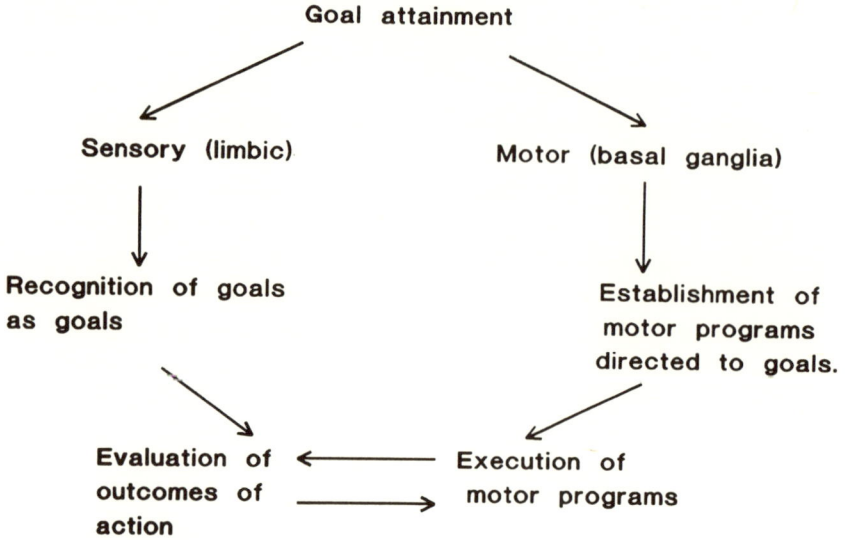

Figure 1. A general system for goal attainment.

motor systems (McNaughton, 1989a, chap. 2). The sensory aspects of this overall function of goal direction (recognition of goals and evaluation of the outcomes of action) are dealt with in the limbic system; the motor aspects (establishment and execution of goal-directed motor programs) in the basal ganglia. The overall coordination of these activities in real time (essentially, working memory) is undertaken by the frontal cortex. To carry out the overall function of goal direction, a number of subsidiary functions must be executed and coordinated. A likely list of such subfunctions and of the major regions of the limbic system and basal ganglia most concerned with them is as follows.

First, goals have to be recognized as goals. The final biological goals of action (positive reinforcers or rewards) are, of course, innate givens (food, water, and the like). An animal cannot, however, wait around until one of these materializes to provide innately recognizable sensory stimulation. It needs to get to where (in both space and time) such a goal is to be found; and, to do that, it needs to establish a series of linked subgoals which will permit it to achieve this "approach behavior." Setting up such a series of linked subgoals depends upon the process described in animal learning theory as establishing a "goal gradient" (Hull, 1943). This process consists of the formation of Pavlovian associations between initially neutral stimuli, or cues, and innate positive reinforcers, the cues now becoming secondary positive reinforcers; followed by the formation of further associations between other cues and those already established as secondary reinforcers (Deutsch, 1964; Gray, 1975). In environments where no such gradients have yet been set up, innate exploratory mechanisms are activated which provide the animal with a means of searching for reinforcers in the absence of prior knowledge of their location. In addition to learning about the spatio-temporal location of desired goals in these ways, an animal must also learn about undesirable outcomes (negative reinforcers or punishments), such as pain or proximity to a predator. This is achieved by a similar process of repeated primary and secondary Pavlovian conditioning, leading to the formation of linked series of secondary negative reinforcers. There is much evidence (LeDoux, 1987; Rolls, 1990) that a key role is played in this process of cue-reinforcer learning, for both positive and negative reinforcement, by neurons in the amygdala.

Once a cue-reinforcer association has been formed (and this can happen very quickly, one trial often being enough), the animal is in a position to do something about the cue: approach it (where the term *approach* includes any behavior that increases proximity in space and time to its occurrence), if it is a secondary positive reinforcer; or escape from or avoid it (performing any behavior that decreases proximity in space and time to its occurrence), if it is a secondary negative reinforcer. This is the function that Gray (1987a) attributes to a "behavioral approach system" and Fowles (1980), to a "behavioral activation system." Much of what follows in this section can be regarded as a description of a proposed neurology for this system (see also Gray, Feldon, Rawlins, Hemsley, & Smith, 1991a).

The complexities of the natural environment are such that, normally, a whole chain of linked secondary reinforcers will be required for effective approach or avoidance behavior. The information concerning this chain, therefore, needs to be transmitted from the amygdala, where it is initially established, to motor systems in the basal ganglia (or in the case of more elementary reactions such as the startle reflex to systems in the brain stem). This step appears to be accomplished by the projection from the amygdala to the ventral striatum, or nucleus (n.) accumbens (Gray et al., 1991a; Rolls & Williams, 1987). The latter structure has been recognized for some time

PERSPECTIVES ON ANXIETY, PANIC, AND FEAR

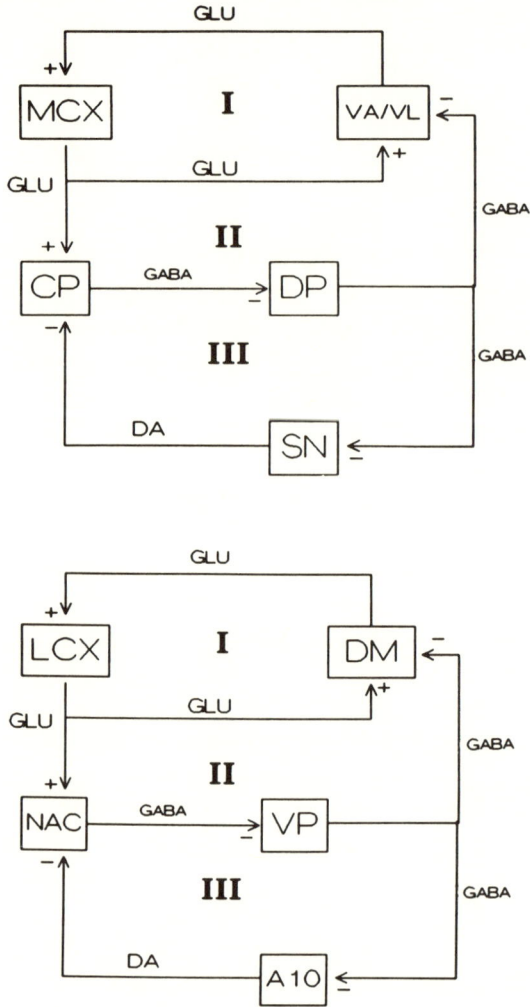

Figure 2. Above. The Caudate Motor System. Nonlimbic cortico-striato-pallido-thalamic-midbrain circuitry making up the "caudate" component of the Behavioral Approach System. MCX: motor and sensorimotor cortex. VA/VL: ventral anterior and ventrolateral thalamic nuclei. CP: caudate-putamen (dorsal striatum). DP: dorsal pallidum. SN: substantia nigra. GLU, GABA, and DA: the neurotransmitters, glutamate, gamma-aminobutyric acid, and dopamine. +, -: excitation and inhibition. I, II, III: feedback loops, the first two positive, the third negative. *Below.* The Accumbens Motor System. Limbic cortico-striato-pallido-thalamic-midbrain circuitry making up the "accumbens" component of the Behavioral Approach System. LCX: limbic cortex, including prefrontal and cingulate areas. DM: dorsomedial thalamic nucleus. NAC: nucleus accumbens (ventral striatum). VP: ventral pallidum. A 10: dopaminergic nucleus A 10 in the ventral tegmental area. Based on Swerdlow and Koob (1987). Reprinted with the permission of Cambridge University Press.

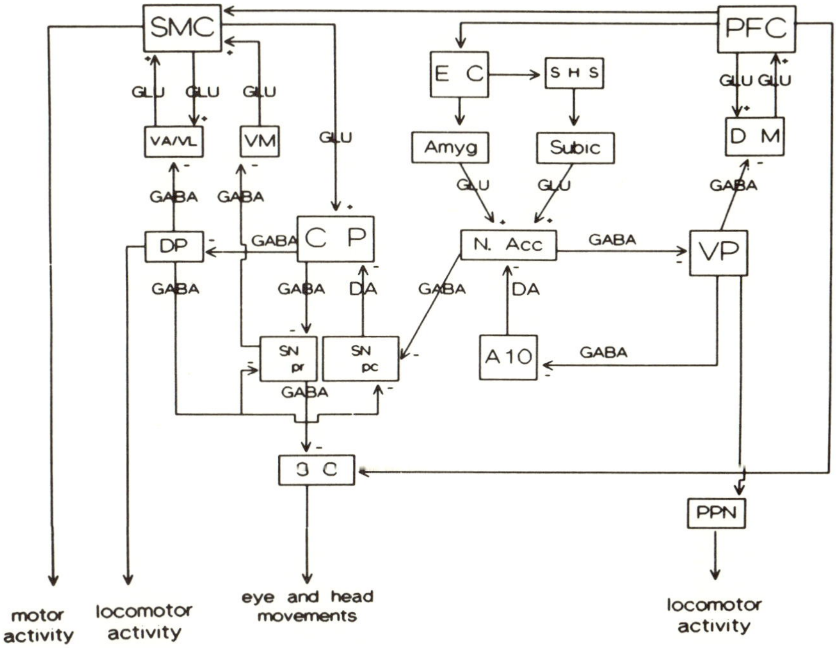

Figure 3. The basal ganglia and their connections with the limbic system. Structures: SMC: sensorimotor cortex; PFC: prefrontal cortex; EC: entorhinal cortex; SHS, septo-hippocampal system; Subic, subicular area; Amyg, amygdala: VA/VL, nucleus (n.) ventralis anterior and ventralis lateralis thalami; VM, n. ventralis medialis thalami; DM, n. dorsalis medialis thalami; DP, dorsal pallidum; VP, ventral pallidum; CP, cau-date-putamen; N. Acc, n. accumbens; SNpr, substantia nigra, pars reticulata; SNpc, substantia nigra, pars compacta; A 10, n. A 10 in ventral tegmental area; SC, superior colliculus; PPN, penduculopontine nucleus. Transmitters: GLU, glutamate; DA, dop-amine; GABA, gamma-aminobutyric acid. From Gray et al., 1991a. Reprinted with the permission of Cambridge University Press.

as a key node in the interface between the limbic system and the basal ganglia (e.g., Mogenson & Nielsen, 1984). There is evidence from sin-gle-unit recording studies that accumbal neurons do indeed receive in-formation about associations between cues and positive reinforcers (Rolls & Williams, 1987), as well as evidence for accumbal release of dopamine in close association with rewarded behavior (Fibiger & Phil-lips, 1988; Hernandez & Hoebel, 1988; Young, Joseph, & Gray, 1992). We have in addition recently demonstrated that cues associated with footshock elicit conditioned dopamine release in n. accumbens (Young, Joseph, & Gray, 1993); thus n. accumbens receives information about secondary negative as well as secondary positive reinforcement.

That neurons receive a certain class of information does not indicate what they do with it. We (Gray et al., 1991a) have proposed that n. accumbens uses information about cue-reinforcer associations to establish the sequence of subgoals and hence run the sequence of motor steps that are required to reach specific overall goals but that the detailed sensorimotor content of each step is contained in the dorsal striatal system, which links the caudate-putamen to sensory and motor cortices, to nn. ventralis anterior and ventralis lateralis of the thalamus, and to the dorsal pallidum. To use a computer analogy, n. accumbens holds a list of subgoals making up a given motor program and is able to switch through the list in an appropriate order, but to retrieve the specific content of each step, it needs to call up the appropriate subroutine by way of its connections to the dorsal striatal system. Drawing upon previous suggestions (Oades, 1985; Swerdlow & Koob, 1987), Gray et al. (1991a, b; see also Weiner, 1991) further proposed that switching from one step to the next in a motor program is achieved by the intra-accumbal release of dopamine at terminals projecting from n. A 10 in the ventral tegmental area. Swerdlow and Koob (1987) have presented a detailed analysis of the way in which the circuitry linking n. accumbens to the limbic cortex (prefrontal and cingulate areas), to the dorsomedial nucleus of the thalamus, and to the ventral pallidum, would allow activation of the A 10 dopaminergic fibers by outputs from n. accumbens itself to achieve this effect (see Figure 2). This circuitry is itself embedded within the complex architecture of the basal ganglia (Figure 3).

What about the detailed sensorimotor content of the motor steps, as executed by the dorsal striatal system (Figures 2 and 3)? Rolls and Williams (1987) and Rolls (1986b) have used the anatomical organization of this system, together with a general theory of random associative networks (Rolls, 1986a), to outline a mechanism by which assemblies of cells with the appropriate connections to motor outputs could be selected. In brief, these authors consider sets of Spiny I striatal cells (the major, GABAergic, output from the caudate-putamen) which, because of the particular pattern of connections that they possess, would receive inputs from both (1) neurons that respond to environmental cues associated with positive reinforcers and (2) other neurons that fire when the animal makes a movement that happens to affect the occurrence of this reinforcer. They show how such cells might initially respond only to the conjunction of cue

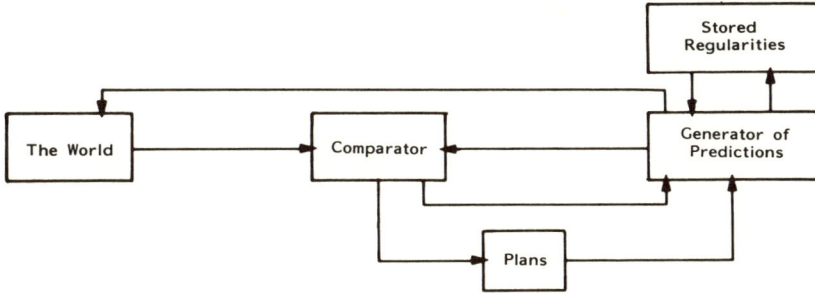

Figure 4. Information processing required for the comparator function of the septo-hippocampal system.

plus movement but could come eventually to be activated by the cue alone, and so to participate in the production of the appropriate movement, given the cue. If we assume that neurons in set (1) receive information from n. accumbens (indirectly, e.g., by way of the dorsomedial nucleus of the thalamus and the prefrontal cortex), Rolls's proposal provides a mechanism by which the list of subgoals held in n. accumbens can be translated into a sequence of detailed sensorimotor steps in the caudate-putamen and its associated thalamic, pallidal, and cortical connections.

In these ways, then, lists of subgoals leading to specific goals (primary and secondary positive reinforcers) can be established and executed. The next requirement is that the outcomes of each step should be monitored to ensure that the intended subgoals are indeed achieved. Our model supposes that this monitoring or "comparator" process (Brooks, 1986; Gray, 1982a; Vinogradova, 1975) is mediated by the septo-hippocampal system (SHS) and the associated Papez circuit, that is, the loop from the subiculum (the major output station for the SHS) via the mammillary bodies, anteroventral thalamus, and cingulate cortex back to the subiculum. The information-processing functions required for such a comparator to work are illustrated in Figure 4. Proposals as to the brain structures that mediate these functions are shown in Figure 5.

Information about the current state of the animal's world is first analyzed in the sensory systems of the neocortex and then fed via the temporal lobe (more specifically, via the perirhinal and parahippocampal cortices) to the hippocampal formation (where it is first received by the entorhinal cortex). The information received by the hippocampal formation in this way has already been heavily pro-

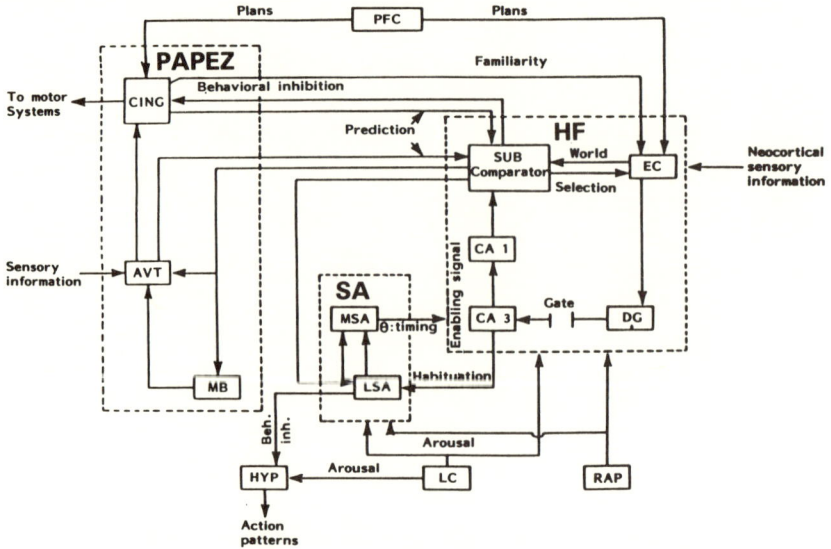

Figure 5. The septo-hippocampal system. The three major building blocks are shown in heavy print: HF, the hippocampal formation, made up of the entorhinal cortex, EC, the dentate gyrus, DG, CA3, CA1, and the subicular area, SUB; SA, the septal area, containing the medial and lateral septal areas, MSA and LSA; and the Papez circuit, which receives projections from and returns them to the subicular area via the mammillary bodies, MB, anteroventral thalamus, AVT, and cingulate cortex, CING. Other structures shown are the hypothalamus, HYP, the locus coeruleus, LC, the raphe nuclei, RAP, and the prefrontal cortex, PFC. Arrows show direction of projection. Words in lower case show postulated functions; beh. inhib., behavioral inhibition. (From Gray, 1982a). Reprinted by permission of Oxford University Press.

cessed, being certainly multimodal and probably highly abstract. O'Keefe and Nadel's (1978) influential hypothesis that this information consists of descriptions of spatial locations within a mapping system is supported by much evidence, but it is clear that the hippocampal formation also handles in addition other, nonspatial kinds of information (Brown 1982; Gray, 1982a; Rawlins, 1985; Rawlins, Lyford, & Seferiades, 1991). Indeed, even for field CA1 of the hippocampus proper, spatial selectivity appears to be a function of the septal rather than the temporal pole of this structure and is not complete even there (Jung, Wiener, & B. McNaughton, 1994).

Whatever their exact form, these descriptions of the current state of the world must be compared to predicted states of the world. As shown in Figure 4, the making of such predictions requires the following data: the last verified current state of the world; the next step in the current motor program; access to stored regularities describing associations between states of the world resembling the last current one and other succeeding states of the world (i.e., stimulus-stimulus associations of the kind set up by Pavlovian conditioning); and access to stored regularities describing associations between the current step in the motor program and succeeding states of the world (i.e., response-stimulus associations of the kind set up by instrumental conditioning).

Our model supposes that the circuit responsible for making predictions is the Papez loop (subicular area–mammillary bodies–anteroventral thalamus–cingulate cortex-subicular area) and that the actual comparison process is accomplished by subicular neurons. Thus the last verified current state of the world is coded by subicular neurons at the outset of a cycle around the Papez circuit; a description of the next subgoal is supplied by way of the projection from frontal cortex (viewed as the location of working memory; Rapoport, 1989) to cingulate cortex; the frontal cortex itself receives information about the list of subgoals from n. accumbens via the dorsomedial nucleus of the thalamus and about specific aspects of past stimuli from other neocortical areas; stimulus-stimulus and response-stimulus regularities are stored in the temporal lobe and other areas of neocortex and accessed by way of the projections from the subicular area and the frontal cortex, respectively, to the entorhinal, perirhinal, and parahippocampal cortices.

Finally, tight synchronization of the passage of information around this circuitry is accomplished by hippocampal theta activity. Theta activity is burst firing at regular intervals in the range approximately 100–200 ms, which in some areas produce a sinusoidal 5–12 Hz gross extracellular rhythm. The notion that hippocampal theta activity quantizes the passage of neural information in this general manner has been proposed by a number of workers (O'Keefe & Nadel, 1978; Vinogradova, 1975; Worden, 1992). These proposals have usually been applied, however, only to the passage of information through the basic hippocampal trisynaptic circuit (entorhinal cortex-dentate gyrus-CA3-CA1), for which a cycle length of c. 80 ms (even at the highest theta frequency) seems unnecessarily long. However, a longer cycle time would be appropriate for recursive hippocampal-neocortical interactions (Miller, 1991; Parmeggiani, Azzaroni, & Lenzi, 1971).

At the end of each such predictive cycle, the subicular neurons responsible for the comparison process make a match-mismatch decision with regard to the input representing the current state of the world derived from neocortical sensory analysis and the input representing the predicted state of the world derived from the Papez predictive circuit. A match decision is followed by initiation of the next predictive cycle coupled with the next analysis of the current state of the world. This analysis is biased toward features that will enter the next prediction, a biasing achieved by feedback from the subicular area to the entorhinal cortex. If, however, there is a mismatch decision (indicating a conflict between the preplanned action and the action required by the actual situation), or if there are conflicting predictions (as when a subgoal has recently been associated with a negative reinforcer, and hence has conflicting approach and avoidance requirements), the current motor program is interrupted. Under these circumstances, biasing of information selection needs to be directed not toward the next predicted state of the world but toward resolution of the problem posed by the mismatch. Such resolution requires exploratory behavior directed toward the novel and/or conflictual aspects of the environment that have led to the mismatch, along with the elaboration of a different, less risky motor program. Thus, the comparator system needs to make comparisons, not only between the predicted and actual states of the perceptual world, but also between the recently prepotent motor program and possible alternatives more suited to current environmental circumstances. It seems likely that these outputs from the subicular comparator are mediated by its projections (Kelley & Domesick, 1982) to n. accumbens. These consequences of a mismatch decision are central to our analysis of the neuropsychology of anxiety; accordingly, we consider them further below.

Match decisions need to be communicated to the motor programming system to confirm that the last intended step in the current program has been successfully completed. This too is accomplished in the model by way of the projection from the subiculum to n. accumbens. This projection terminates upon accumbal GABAergic Spiny I output neurons that also receive dopaminergic inputs from A 10 (Totterdell & Smith, 1989), in the same general caudomedial region where fibers from the amygdala reach n. accumbens (Phillipson & Griffiths, 1985). The model therefore supposes that a match output from the subiculum terminates the current step in the motor program, so permitting the amygdaloid projection, in conjunction with dopaminergic afferents, to switch in the accumbal output neurons corresponding to the next step. This feature of the model was proposed by Gray et al. (1991a). It has recently received strong empirical support from the description by O'Donnell and Grace (1995) of convergence between hippocampal, amygdaloid, and prefrontal cortical afferents upon the same accumbal neurons. Furthermore, as predicted by the model, the hippocampal afferents appear to gate accumbal responses to the afferents from the frontal cortex; indeed, these responses were abolished after section of the fornix-fimbria. Weiner (1991), in a further extension of the model, has proposed a detailed mechanism, utilizing the accumbens projection to the substantia nigra and the circuitry illustrated in Figure 2 (taken from Swerdlow & Koob, 1987), by which such switching between steps within the accumbens can be transmitted to the caudate system that codes for the detailed sensorimotor content of each step.

In this way, then, the model of motivation attempts to give a general account of how the limbic system and basal ganglia are able to establish, run, and monitor goal-directed motor programs.

The Neuropsychology of Anxiety, 1982 Model

In the previous section we considered the integrated action of the limbic system and basal ganglia as this unfolds in the attainment of goals. We now take a second look at these same systems from the point of view of their contribution to the emotion of anxiety. We do this first from the perspective adopted by Gray (1982a, b; Gray & McNaughton, 1983); the remainder of the chapter will then consider what changes may be needed in that perspective. The summary of Gray (1982a) that follows is taken directly, with only minor modifications, from the end of that book. The chapter numbers in this summary refer to the 1982 book; the present tense indicates the state of our theory construction at that date. The summary includes material that has already been presented above, in the section on motivation; but such repetition is likely to be useful in the exposition of what is undoubtedly a complex and multileveled theory.

1. Relying on data from behavioural and psycho-pharmacological experiments, we first postulated a behavioural in-

PERSPECTIVES ON ANXIETY, PANIC, AND FEAR

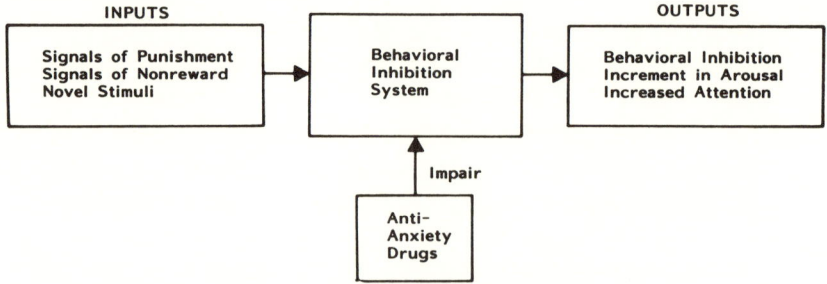

Figure 6. The behavioral inhibition system as defined by its inputs and outputs.

hibition system (Chapters 1 and 2; Figure 6 in the present paper). Activity in this system constitutes anxiety. The anti-anxiety drugs affect anxiety by impairing this activity. The major inputs to the behavioural inhibition system (and thus the adequate stimuli for anxiety) are: stimuli that warn of punishment or non-reward, novel stimuli, and innate fear stimuli (including those that arise during social interaction with conspecifics). The major outputs of the system are: inhibition of ongoing motor behaviour, increased level of arousal and increased attention to the environment, and especially to novel events in the environment. The mode of operation of the behavioural inhibition system has been deduced from a consideration of data on the brain structures presumed to constitute this system (see below).

2. Data obtained in physiological and behavioural experiments (Chapters 3–8) suggest that the neural structures which make up the behavioural inhibition system include: the septal area, the hippocampal formation, and their inter-connections (i.e. the septo-hippocampal system); the "Papez circuit," running from the subicular area in the hippocampal formation to the mammillary bodies, anterior thalamus, cingulate cortex, and back to the subicular area; the neocortical inputs to the septo-hippocampal system from the entorhinal area and prefrontal cortex; the ascending noradrenergic and serotonergic inputs to the septo-hippocampal system; the dopaminergic ascending input to the prefrontal cortex; an ascending cholinergic input to the septo-hippocampal system; the noradrenergic innervation of the hypothalamus; and perhaps (underlying the autonomic outflow of the behavioural inhibition system) the descending nor-

adrenergic fibres of the locus coeruleus (Chapters 10–13). This list is not necessarily exhaustive; nor is it implied that these structures do not participate in other functional systems.

3. Within this overall framework, the septo-hippocampal system, together with the entorhinal area and the "subicular loop" (Papez's circuit), has the task of predicting the next sensory event to which the animal will be exposed and checking whether it actually does occur; of operating the outputs of the behavioural inhibition system either if there is a mismatch between the actual and predicted events or if the predicted event is aversive; and of testing out alternative strategies (including alternative multi-dimensional descriptions of stimuli and/or responses) which may overcome the difficulty with which the animal is faced. Detailed proposals about the neural machinery involved in fulfilling these tasks are made in Chapter 10 (see Figure 5 in the present paper). Among the outputs of the behavioural inhibition system, increased attention to and exploration of the environment are executed via the entorhinal area and cingulate cortex and a descending projection from the lateral septal area to the hypothalamus. The hippocampal theta rhythm quantizes and paces the flow of information around this system.

4. The role of the ascending noradrenergic projection to the septo-hippocampal system is to tag certain stimuli (entering the septo-hippcampal system from the entorhinal area) as "important," i.e. requiring particularly careful checking; that of the ascending serotonergic projection is to add to this "important" tag the information that the stimulus is associated with punishment and/or to bias the operation of the septo-hippocampal system more strongly towards the inhibition of motor behaviour; that of the ascending cholinergic projection is to facilitate stimulus analysis; and that of the noradrenergic projection to the hypothalamus is to mediate the increased arousal output of the behavioural inhibition system by priming hypothalamic motor systems (especially those involved in fight and flight behaviour) for rapid action when required (Chapters 11 and 12).

5. The prefrontal cortex (Chapter 13) plays two roles. It transmits to the septo-hippocampal system information about ongoing motor programmes to be used in the making of pre-

dictions about the next expected sensory events; and, in man, it allows neocortical control, using verbally coded information, of the activities of the septo-hippocampal system. The cingulate cortex may also participate in these functions.

6. The septo-hippocampal system does not store information, but it has access to and may modify information stored elsewhere. The most likely site of storage is in the temporal lobe, to which the septo-hippocampal system has access via the entorhinal area. In man the stored information to which the septo-hippocampal system has access is in part in verbal form. The bidirectional relations between the septo-hippocampal system and neocortical language areas (this and the previous paragraph) allow it to function under certain conditions independently of its ascending inputs. It is this interaction between language areas and the septo-hippocampal system which permits the latter to play a major role in human cognitive function even when this is not emotionally coloured (Chapter 9); in this role the capacity for multidimensional analysis of stimuli and responses (paragraph 3) is particularly important.

7. Under conditions of prolonged stress there are biphasic changes in the functioning of noradrenergic neurons (Chapter 12), a temporary exhaustion being followed by restored or even increased functional capacity. Exhaustion of the noradrenergic arousing input to the hypothalamus (paragraph 4) underlies the phenomena of helplessness in animals and the experience of depression in man. In man individual differences in the reactivity and tendency towards functional exhaustion of central noradrenergic neurons underlie the personality dimension running from susceptibility to anxiety to susceptibility to, successively, neurotic and psychotic depression.

8. The symptoms of anxiety in man (Chapter 14) arise from excessive activity in the behavioural inhibition system as described above. Phobias are most often due to exposure to innate fear stimuli, but secondary aversive stimuli are also sometimes important. Obsessive-compulsive symptoms are due to excessive checking activities in the behavioural inhibition system. The cognitive phenomena of the obsessive-compulsive syndrome arise from the interaction of the septo-hippocampal system and cortical language systems (points 5 and 6 above).

9. The therapeutic action of the anti-anxiety drugs is principally due to a reduction in the activity of ascending monoaminergic projections (noradrenergic and serotonergic to the septo-hippocampal system, noradrenergic to the hypothalamus, and dopaminergic to the prefrontal cortex). This may be secondary to an increase in the activity of GABA-ergic neurons afferent to the monoaminergic systems. A direct action in the hippocampus is also not excluded (Chapters 11–13).

10. Prefrontal and cingulate lesions (Chapter 13) are effective treatments for anxiety which is largely controlled by descending neocortical (linguistic) projections to the septo-hippocampal system (paragraphs 5, 6, and 8). For the same reasons, the conditions in which these lesions are effective are often resistant to pharmacotherapy.

11. Behaviour therapy is effective (Chapter 15) because it permits systematic habituation of the septo-hippocampal response to anxiogenic stimuli. The process of habituation is built in to the circuits described in Chapter 10.

12. Individuals who are especially susceptible to anxiety have highly reactive behavioural inhibition systems (Chapter 16). To allow this simple description of the personality correlates of anxiety, the axes of Eysenck's personality space are rotated so that one dimension runs through high trait anxiety.

This, then, in summary form, was our model of the neuropsychology of anxiety as analyzed in 1982. In the remainder of this chapter we shall consider how, if at all, it now needs changing. We shall do this, first, in a series of specific probes aimed from different angles, and then, at the end, in an overview of how the model stands up to these probes and of how details need to be adjusted or amplified in the light of recent data. Given the scope of the 1982 model, however, it will not be possible here to consider all the aspects summarized above.

The Clinical Phenomena of Anxiety

The first issue we need to consider is the nature of the beast we are trying to explain. How has understanding of the clinical phenomena of anxiety changed since 1982?

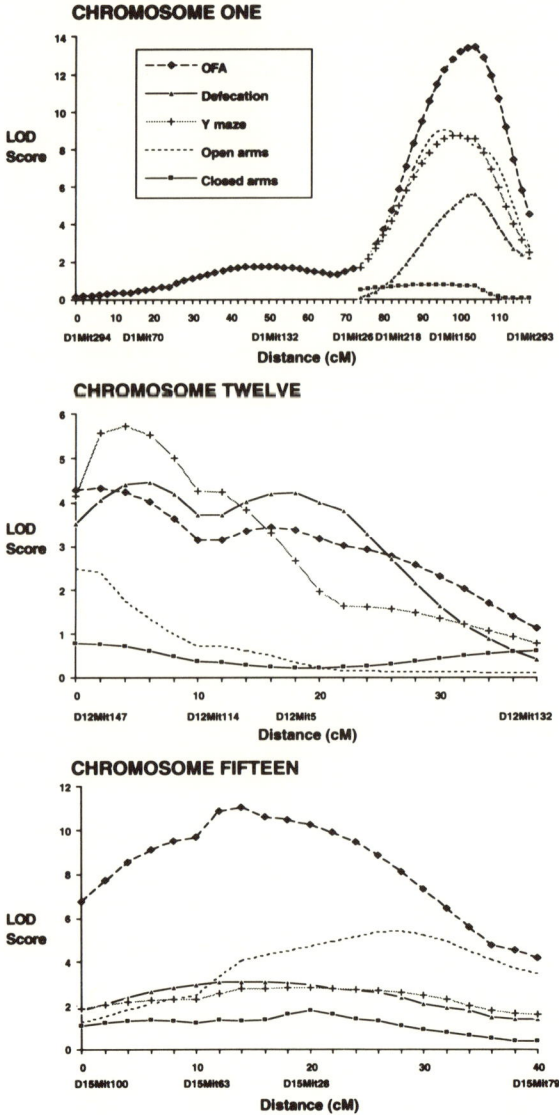

Figure 7. Quantitative trait locus (QTL) analysis of five measures (open-field activity, OFA, defecation in the open field, activity in the Y maze and entry into the open and closed arms of the elevated plus maze, EPM, on chromosones 1, 12, and 15. The LOD score curves were generated by the MAPMAKER-QTL program. The approximate position of markers used is given below the x axis. Reprinted with permission from J. Flint, R. Corley, J. C. De Fries, D. W. Fulker, J. A. Gray, S. Miller, and A. C. Collins, "Chromosomal Mapping of Three Loci Determining Quantitative Variation of Susceptibility to Anxiety in the Mouse," *Science, 268*, 1432–1435. Copyright 1995 American Association for the Advancement of Science.

There is a long-standing and radical difference between (the majority of) psychologists and psychiatrists in the way they approach the classification of psychiatric symptoms: the former tend to think in terms of dimensions of continuous variation in behavior, psychiatric disorder then representing the extremes of these continua, the latter in terms of discrete disease entities. Gray's (1982a) book lay firmly in the psychological tradition, defining (p. 426) anxiety symptoms as "those that are found in individuals whose personality lies in the neurotic introvert portion of the multidimensional personality space described by Eysenck and Eysenck (1969)." From this point of view, the differences between specific conditions that enter, for example, the DSM-IV classification of anxiety disorders are of relatively little significance, representing perhaps the accidents of life history that lead to the formation of a particular cluster of symptoms in a personality that is predisposed to develop one or other such cluster.

This point of view has recently received strong support from studies of the heritability of both symptoms and predisposition. These studies (Andrews, Stewart, Morris-Yates, Holt, & Henderson, 1990; Kendler, Neale, Kessler, Heath, & Eaves, 1992a, b, c) show that what is inherited is a common liability to a variety of different neurotic disorders, including not only those that clearly fall into the anxiety set but also neurotic depression. This liability is well captured by such dimensional analyses of normal personality as that of the Eysencks, which regularly give rise to a major factor of "neuroticism" or "trait anxiety." Moreover, advances in the alliance of molecular and statistical approaches to the analysis of the genetic basis of complex psychological traits (Plomin, Owen, & McGuffin, 1994) are rapidly bringing us closer to the point at which it will be possible to identify the polygenes responsible for such dimensional variation. We have, for example, recently completed a preliminary investigation of the applicability of such techniques to a rodent analogue of trait anxiety ("emotionality"; Gray, 1987a) and have demonstrated the possibility of identifying a number of quantitative trait loci (Haley & Knott, 1992), that is, DNA markers of the chromsomal region where relevant genes are located, that show a pleiotropic effect on several different putative measures of this trait (Flint et al., 1995; Figure 7).

Despite these successes for the dimensional approach, impor-

PERSPECTIVES ON ANXIETY, PANIC, AND FEAR

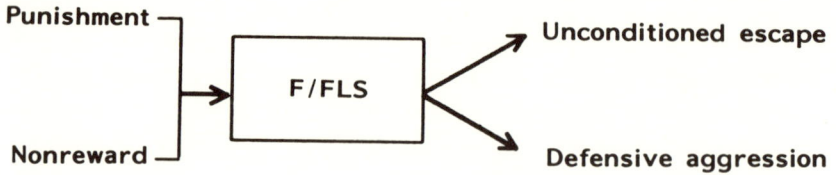

Figure 8. The fight/flight system (F/FLS) as defined by its inputs and outputs.

tant data have also emerged from attempts to differentiate more clearly between different anxiety disorders. These data center upon panic disorder and obsessive-compulsive disorder.

Panic was not seriously discussed by Gray (1982a), being treated simply as one symptom of anxiety, encountered particularly often in agoraphobia. The important work of Klein (1981), however, strongly implies the need to distinguish panic disorder from other conditions involving anxiety. He finds that, whereas standard antianxiety drugs reduce anticipatory anxiety in agoraphobics (including anxiety about possible panic attacks), they do not affect the panic attacks themselves; the latter are, in contrast, reduced by certain antidepressant drugs, especially those that act to block reuptake of the transmitter, serotonin. These clinical observations fit well with experimental observations made by Graeff (1990, 1991, 1993). He points out that the autonomic changes characteristic of panic attacks resemble those that are produced in animals (and indeed in human beings; Nashold, Wilson, & Slaughter, 1969) by electrical stimulation of the central periaqueductal gray of the midbrain and also that drugs that are effective in controlling panic attacks act to block (by potentiating an inhibitory serotonergic input to the periaqeductal gray) the effects of such stimulation. Based on these observations, both Graeff (1991) and Gray (1987a) have proposed that panic attacks reflect, not anxiety mediated by the behavioral inhibition system, but a different form of behavior mediated by what Graeff calls the behavioral aversive system and Gray, the fight/flight system. This system includes, besides nuclei in the central periaqueductal gray, components in the medial hypothalamus and the amygdala. In the model proposed by Gray (1987a; see Figure 8), the fight/flight system is responsible for responses to unconditioned aversive stimuli, as distinct from the conditioned aversive stimuli to which the behavioral inhibition system reacts. It appears, furthermore, that the behavioral inhibition system is capable of acting to inhibit the fight/flight system (acting perhaps by way of the serotonergic afferents to the central periaqueductal gray identified by Graeff).

Deakin and Graeff (1991) provide an illuminating discussion of the significance of these possible interactions between panic, mediated by the central gray, and anticipatory anxiety. They point out that the inhibitory control exercised over the periaqueductal gray by serotonergic afferents (regarded as forming part of the behavioral inhibition system) implies not merely that in panic disorder anticipatory anxiety alternates with panic attacks, but that anxiety actively inhibits panic. This capacity to inhibit panic may provide at least part of the explanation for the gradual spread of anticipatory anxiety, with a concomitant reduction in the frequency of panics, noted by Klein and Klein (1989b). Recent work using in vivo neuroimaging techniques is strongly supportive of such an analysis. Thus studies using positron-emission tomography have demonstrated increased blood flow in the region of the parahippocampal gyrus in patients with panic disorder, associated not with the panic attacks themselves but with the resting state, which, in such patients, is likely to involve elevated anticipatory anxiety (Drevets, Videen, MacLeod, Haller, & Raichle, 1992; Nordahl et al., 1990; Reiman, Raichle, Butler, Herscovich, & Robins, 1984; Reiman et al., 1986); while a study using structural magnetic resonance imaging has demonstrated a substantially elevated rate of abnormalities, including major atrophy, affecting both the hippocampus and the septal area (Dantendorfer et al., in press).

Deakin and Graeff (1991) suggest, furthermore, that similar mechanisms may be involved in the otherwise puzzling phenomena of relaxation-induced (Adler, Craske, & Barlow, 1987) and nocturnal (Craske & Barlow, 1990) panic attacks (see Barlow, Chorpita, & Turovsky, this volume): the restraint on such attacks normally exercised by anticipatory anxiety, according to their hypothesis, is lost during relaxation and sleep. This framework of explanation may also be applicable to patients whose anticipatory anxiety focuses not on panic attacks but on outbursts of anger and aggression and also to the negative relationships between anxiety and aggression noted in studies of childhood conduct disorder by Lahey, McBurnett, Loeber, and Hart (1995) and between fear and pain sensitivity in animal experiments (Bolles & Fanselow, 1980; Fanselow, 1991). As illustrated in Figure 8, the outputs of the fight/flight system include both escape behavior (which is perhaps equivalent to panic) and defensive aggression (perhaps equivalent to anger); furthermore, painful stimuli constitute a major class of inputs to the fight/flight system. This model therefore implies that anxiety and anger should interact in similar manners to anxiety and panic because both equate to interactions between the behavioral inhibition system and the fight/flight system; and similarly for anxiety and pain.

These various developments in relation to panic disorder do not, however, invalidate the approach to anxiety adopted by Gray (1982a, b); they serve rather to delimit more accurately the field of clinical phenomena to which that approach is applicable. For the moment, it would appear that the panic attacks of panic disorder do not lie in this field, but the anticipatory anxiety that normally appears as an additional feature of this disorder does. Conversely, there may well be instances of panic resulting not from some primary disturbance of the panic system itself but simply from the extremity of anxiety. Explanations for panic as a symptom may then occasionally fall within the ambit of anxiety, but explanations of panic disorder proper must be sought elsewhere. Besides the suggestions made by Graeff (1991) and Gray (1987a), indicated above, the hypothesis recently proposed by Klein (1993; Gorman, Laszlo, & Klein, 1990), according to which panic represents overactivity in a specialized "suffocation alarm system," deserves careful attention. Indeed, this hypothesis is fully compatible with the role in panic attributed above to the periaqueductal gray because this region receives information concerning asphyxia via projections from the nucleus tractus solitarius, which in turn receives afferents from carotid and aortic chemoreceptors (Bandler & Törk, 1987). These biologically based approaches to the explanation of panic should not be taken to imply, however, that this condition will be refractory to the cognitive-behavioral methods of treatment that have been so successful with other neurotic disorders. On the contrary, there is already excellent evidence that panic attacks can be substantially reduced by cognitive therapy (Clark et al., 1994). Here, as elsewhere in medicine, there is no straightforward connection between the etiology of a condition and therapies that can alleviate it.

A second condition whose relationship to anxiety has undergone considerable scrutiny in the last few years is obsessive-compulsive disorder (Jakes, in press). The results of this scrutiny are especially relevant to the model of anxiety offered in 1982 because the symptoms of this disorder, especially the cognitive ones (ruminations, worry, intrusive thoughts, impulses, and images), appeared to yield particularly well to an analysis in terms of excessive scanning for threat by the comparator system that lies at the heart of the model (Gray, 1982a, pp. 439–444). Recent data, however, have raised doubts as to whether obsessive-compulsive disorder has anything to do with anxiety at all.

These data tend to show a role for the cingulate cortex and basal ganglia in this condition. The relevant evidence comes, first, from studies showing a familial association between obsessive-compulsive disorder and Tourette's syndrome (Pauls, Towbin, Leckman, Zahner, & Cohen, 1986), a disorder in which tics and other disturbances of motor behavior figure prominently and which probably involves dysfunction in the dopaminergic innervation of the basal ganglia. The observed association is sex-dependent, obsessive-compulsive disorder being relatively more common in female relatives and Tourette's syndrome in the males. The common behavioral elements that link these two conditions may lie in the repetitive and compulsive nature of the symptoms that characterize them (tics in Tourette's syndrome, rituals and ruminations in obsessive-compulsive disorder). These features suggest overactivity in the ascending dopaminergic pathways in the basal ganglia; the dopamine-releasing drug, amphetamine, can produce similarly repetitive and apparently compulsive behavior in animals (Kelly, Seviour, & Iversen, 1975). At least part of the behavior patterns involved in compulsive rituals may be related to grooming behavior observed in animals (Gray, 1982a, p. 443) and perhaps mediated by striatal mechanisms that could become dysfunctional in obsessive-compulsive disorder (Rapoport, 1989; Wise & Rapoport, 1989). This analysis is particularly plausible for that most common of all rituals, hand-washing. A second line of evidence perhaps implicating the basal ganglia in obsessive-compulsive disorder lies in observations of compulsive rituals in individuals with known pathology in this region of the brain (Swedo et al., 1989; Baxter, Schwartz, Guze, Bergman, & Szuba, 1990; LaPlane et al., 1989). In addition, the pharmacology of obsessive-compulsive disorder differs from that of other anxiety disorders in that it responds in a proportion of cases to treatment with serotonin-uptake blockers (Goodman et al., 1990). In this respect, obsessive-compulsive disorder resembles panic disorder, as noted above.

This evidence has led to a view of patients with obsessive-compulsive disorder as suffering from a kind of "mental tic," in which a cognitive routine runs in the brain as automatically as the motor routines that produce tics properly speaking. Thus Rapoport (1989; Rapoport & Wise, 1988; Wise & Rapoport, 1989) suggests that obsessive-compulsive disorder is a distinct dysfunction of the cingulate-basal ganglia circuit. Such a link with the basal ganglia could perhaps provide obsessive-compulsive disorder with a pharmacological sensitivity different from that of anxiety per se. Conversely, the link with the cingulate cortex would differentiate obsessive-compulsive disorder from classical basal ganglia disease. Thus the obsessions might be associated with cingulate involvement, while the related compulsions would provide a closer parallel to motor tics and choreas and would be associated with the basal ganglia involvement.

It is difficult, however, to accept this view as constituting more than part of the truth. Critically, it is possible to identify the stimuli that lead patients with obsessive-compulsive disorder to perform their compulsive rituals and to show that these are indeed anxiogenic. Furthermore, prevention of the rituals leads to increases in anxiety, and performance of the ritual is followed by a decrease in anxiety (Hodgson & Rachman, 1972; Röper & Rachman, 1976). These observations are all as expected if the ritual is a species of active avoidance of a potential source of danger (Gray, 1971a; Rachman & Hodgson, 1978); so that, according to this analysis, obsessive-compulsive disorder would indeed belong with the other anxiety disorders. Furthermore, patients with known basal ganglia pathology fail to show such changes in anxiety when prevented from carrying out their rituals (LaPlane et al., 1989), suggesting that there is only a surface similarity between this behavior and that observed in obsessive-compulsive disorder proper. One possibility is that the diagnosis of obsessive-compulsive disorder is in fact heterogeneous, covering some cases in which anxiety plays a role and others in which it does not. Shafran (1995) has attempted to test this possibility by taking a variety of measures, relating to both the anxiety and the "basal ganglia" hypotheses, in a sample of patients with a diagnosis of obsessive-compulsive disorder and then analyzing the data for evidence of bimodality or different symptom clusters. No such evidence was found.

Rather than seeking to reconcile these different views and databases by the supposition that obsessive-compulsive disorder is etiologically heterogeneous, we might perhaps try the solution adopted above for panic disorder, namely, that this is a *mixed* condition. The mix proposed for panic disorder involved activity in both the fight/flight system (underlying the panic attacks) and the behavioral inhibition system (underlying anticipatory anxiety). The fact that serotonin-uptake blockers have therapeutic effects in both panic disorder (Klein, 1981) and obsessive-compulsive disorder (Goodman et al., 1990) suggests that the two conditions might yield to similar accounts. Our account of panic disorder suggested, with Deakin and Graeff (1991), that the antipanic action of serotonin-uptake blockers might be due to an increase in the inhibition by the behavioral inhibition system of the fight/flight system. A similar analysis for obsessive-compulsive disorder would preserve the analysis of rituals as active avoidance behavior (Gray, 1971a; Rachman & Hodgson, 1979), accomplished by the behavioral approach system. As noted in the section on motivation, above, this system centers upon the basal ganglia and associated cortical areas (frontal, cingulate, and motor), consistent with the evidence that dysfunction in these structures is sometimes linked to obsessive-compulsive disorder. The role of serotonin-uptake blockers would then be to increase the inhibition on such active avoidance behavior exercised by the behavioral inhibition system. One implication of this analysis is that serotonin uptake–blocking drugs might simultaneously reduce rituals but increase (or at least leave unchanged) anxiety levels. Interestingly, a pattern of just this kind has been reported (Apter et al., 1994).

If this treatment of obsessive-compulsive disorder as a variable mixture of outputs from different brain systems is on the right lines, the lack of ritual-associated anxiety in patients with basal ganglia pathology (LaPlane et al., 1989) may not be so atypical as at first appeared. There perhaps exist other people whose obsessions and compulsions are not accompanied by anxiety, at least until these become unmanageable. In the standard clinical case, of course, obsessive-compulsive disorder is accompanied by anxiety—or such patients would not have presented in the clinic in the first place. Thus it might be that (as suggested for panic above) obsessions and compulsions could arise by two different routes. In the first, which might be called "obsessive-compulsive disorder proper," a cingulate-basal ganglia "pathology" would result in repetitive behavior, giving rise to consequent anxiety; in the second, high levels of anxiety would result in compulsive symptoms. A nonpathological example of the latter would be the case of a mother continually checking her child's safety in a threatening environment. Indeed, the necessity for such behavior may well explain why there exists a brain circuit, a possibly minor disturbance in which can lead to cases of obsessive-compulsive disorder.

In sum, the jury is still out on these complex issues; but there is as yet no compelling reason to abandon the view that obsessive-compulsive disorder belongs properly in the group of anxiety disorders.

So far in this section we have, as it were, been defending ourselves against potential attack. We end it, however, on a more positive note. A clear implication of the model of the behavioral inhibition system (Figure 6) is that patients suffering from anxiety should be particularly attentive to threat. This feature of the model was derived entirely from animal experiments, and at the time it was published, there was virtually no clinical evidence to corroborate it; and the view from experimental studies of normal human subjects was that anxiety interfered with attention rather than improving it. Since 1982, however, there has been a spate of reports demonstrating that patients with a variety of anxiety disorders are indeed more attentive to threat, and especially to threatening stimuli that are particularly relevant to their concerns (Mathews & MacLeod, 1994; McNally, this volume; Thrasher, Dalgleish, & Yule, 1994). Given that this was a strong prediction, it is unfortunate that virtually none of these reports have indicated this congruence with the model. Indeed, Eysenck (1992) views the cognitive aspects of these findings as providing evidence directly contrary to the model.

The Ethology of the Behavioral Inhibition System

The behavioral, neurophysiological, and neurochemical effects of the antianxiety drugs, or anxiolytics, constituted a key building block upon which the 1982 model was built. In particular, the behav-

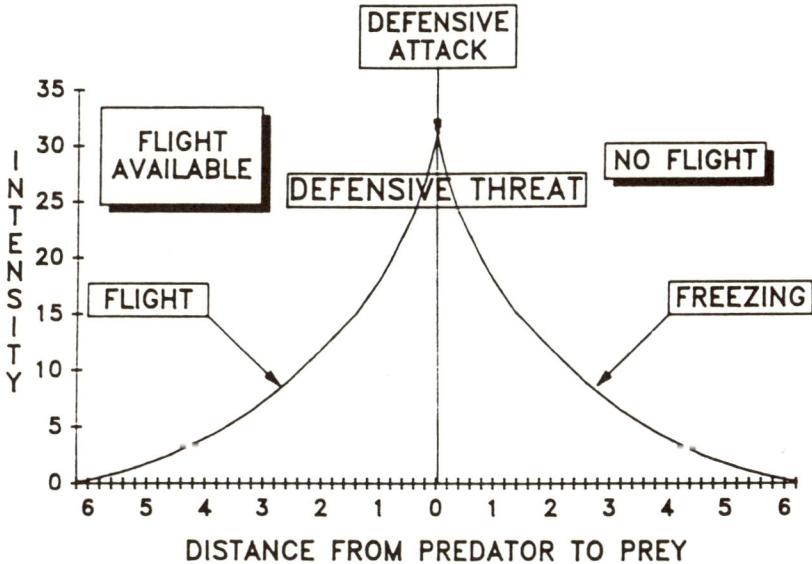

Figure 9. Defensive behavior as a joint function of defensive distance and the availability of escape. From Blanchard and Blanchard, 1990a. Reprinted with the permission of the University of Otago Press.

ioral effects of these compounds were used to construct the input-output analysis of the behavioral inhibition system depicted in Figure 6 (Gray, 1976, 1977). Anxiety is then defined as the state engendered during activation of the behavioral inhibition system (Gray, 1976). Following in the tradition of Miller (1951), Mowrer (1960), and others, a critical feature of this definition was drawn from learning theory, namely, that anxiety is elicited by *conditioned aversive stimuli*, where *aversive* covers both punishment and Amsel's (1962, 1994) concept of frustrative nonreward; *unconditioned aversive stimuli*, in contrast, were seen as acting via the fight/flight system (Figure 8), perhaps eliciting, as noted in the previous section, a state of panic. Recent ethological studies by Caroline and Robert Blanchard (1990a, b) have caused us to refine that distinction. These workers have studied defensive behavior in wild rats in response to two types of predator: human beings and cats. They find that they are able to systematize data obtained in a number of naturalistic settings by distinguishing between the rats' reactions to actual and potential predators, respectively.

In response to an actual predator—an approaching human experimenter, for example—the rat displays a repertoire consisting of flight, freezing, or attack. Which element in this repertoire occurs at any particular moment is determined by a number of environmental factors. If the environment makes flight possible, this is the dominant response, a conclusion consistent with many previous observations. But if the approaching human being comes too close—about 0.5 m in these experiments—flight is replaced by attack. At greater distances from the predator, if flight is not possible, the rat freezes. With decreasing distance from the predator, both flight and freezing increase in intensity until they are replaced by attack. These relationships are summarized in Figure 9. They are fully consistent with our earlier discussions of the fight/flight system, with one important difference: along with these two F-words, we now have a third—freezing.

In Gray's (1982a, 1987a) previous treatments of this topic, freezing was regarded as a manifestation of behavioral inhibition, that is, as an output of the behavioral inhibition system, not the fight/flight system. The Blanchards' analysis, however, finds additional support from recent studies of the central periaqueductal gray. It has long been known that this region contains neurons responsible for organizing fight and flight behavior (Adams, 1979); it is now known that freezing, too, is organized there (Fanselow, 1991). The concept of the fight/flight system therefore needs to be changed to a fight/flight/freezing system, more or less identical to the Blanchards' concept of a system responsible for organizing responses to an actual predator. (As so often, however, terminology becomes a problem here, since the Blanchards regard this system as underlying fear, whereas we have related it above to panic. Furthermore, historically, fear has been used within learning theory to cover responses to *conditioned* aversive stimuli, exactly opposite to the Blanchards' use of the term. We shall therefore continue to speak of the "fight/flight system.") If, however, freezing is an output of the fight/flight system, this poses the problem of distinguishing it from the behavioral inhibition that is an output of the behavioral inhibition system. As a first approximation, we can perhaps regard freezing as a relatively fixed action pattern, organized in the central gray, and behavioral inhibition as a more flexible mode of controlling action, mediated at higher levels.

It is the second aspect of the Blanchards' distinction that is most germane to the subject of this chapter, namely, the set of responses to a *potential* predator. Their introduction to this concept deserves quotation in full.

> Close-in confrontation with a threatening predator is probably a comparatively rare event in the lives of most wild-living animals. What is much more common, in fact virtually ubiquitous, is the potential for the sudden appearance of an attacking predator. The characteristic vigilance shown by most wild mammals attests to the importance of this potential threat, as, indeed, does defensive habituation, a learning mode which functions primarily to reduce orientation and defensive reactivity to stimuli as they prove not to signal threat.
>
> While such potential threat situations necessarily elicit some defensive behaviors, it is important to note that defensive behaviors such as flight and defensive threat/defensive attack which work well to present, discrete, threat stimuli may be useless or even counter-productive in threatening situations in which the actual threatening animal or object has not been localised: Without orientation to the threat source, flight is as likely to result in disaster as in escape. These considerations suggest that such situations may elicit a pattern of defensive behaviors which is intense but very different from the reactions to an approaching and contacting threat stimulus. (Blanchard & Blanchard, 1990a, pp. 128–129)

Blanchard and Blanchard go on to describe the rat's repertoire of reactions to potential predators (e.g., a place that has just contained a cat or an object impregnated with cat odor) and to suggest that these are homologous to the reactions that are characteristic of human anxiety. The essential feature of this repertoire

> appears to be the "risk assessment" pattern which, except for orientation to the predator, does not occur in response to being attacked. The risk assessment pattern involves approach and scanning, stretched attend and low back ambulation, eventually culminating in contact with and manipulation of potential threat stimuli if such specific stimuli are available (e.g., cat odor object, novel object, etc.) and sufficient time is given. This last clause is very important as the latency for risk assessment may range from moments to hours or even days. We interpret

(Blanchard & Blanchard, 1988, 1989) this risk assessment pattern as an essential component in reducing defensiveness by providing information indicating that threat is not imminent. The second function of risk assessment is that it may provide information confirming, identifying, and localizing danger, and thus enable a transition from the "anxiety/defense" pattern to the more effective "fear/defense" pattern. Importantly, when the danger cannot be localized or confirmed, risk assessment continues over a very long period of time. (Blanchard & Blanchard, 1990a, p. 129)

(As noted above, the fear/defense pattern is what we call the output of the fight/flight system.)

Blanchard and Blanchard (1990b) regard human anxiety as being homologous to the set of responses to a potential predator described in their experiments. To test this hypothesis, they adopted a strategy very similar to our own, setting out to show that these responses, but not those to an actual predator, are sensitive to the action of anxiolytic drugs. They used wild rats to study the effects of a number of such compounds; we concentrate here on the results obtained with the benzodiazepine, diazepam (Valium).

Two test batteries were used. The first, a "fear/defense test battery," provided measures of flight, freezing, and defensive threat and attack in response to approaching, and painlessly contacting, threat stimuli (constituted by a human experimenter); in keeping with the terminology adopted here, we shall call this the "fight/flight battery." Diazepam (like two other benzodiazepines tested, chlordiazepoxide and midazolam) had little overall effect, tending only to reduce threat vocalization and ratings by the experimenter of defensiveness to being picked up; avoidance, flight, freezing, and bites were all unaffected.

The second set of tests, an "anxiety/defense test battery," consisted of three short tests, each measuring movement arrest, risk assessment (measured as indicated above), and/or inhibition of non-defensive behavior (e.g., eating or drinking) in response to a situation in which threat had previously been encountered but was no longer present. In the cat odor test, the rat is placed in a runway with a wooden square saturated with cat odor placed at one end of it. In the "light-dark box," the rat is placed in a brightly lit chamber and allowed to enter a darkened one, where it is exposed to a cat behind a wire mesh screen; behavior is then measured after removal of the cat or at retest (no cat) five days later. The "eat-drink box" test is similar: eating and drinking are measured for 20 minutes after removal of a cat that has been briefly exposed behind wire mesh. Of the eight risk assessment measures in the three tasks, six were significantly influenced by diazepam. The direction of change produced by the drug in these measures was a function of the level of risk assessment observed in controls: if this was low (because relatively high levels of threat had caused avoidance and freezing), diazepam increased it; if control risk assessment was high (under relatively low levels of threat), diazepam decreased it.

Blanchard and Blanchard (1990b, p. 198) make the following comment on this final aspect of their findings: "This pattern of results is entirely compatible with analysis of the time course of the risk assessment pattern in the Visible Burrow System (Blanchard & Blanchard, 1989). The analysis indicates that, with the highest levels of defensiveness, risk assessment is suppressed (largely by immobility). As defensiveness declines, it is accompanied by a massive increase in risk assessment, with risk assessment then declining as behavior returns to normal. . . . With highly anxiety-arousing situations . . . anxiolytics should increase risk assessment behaviors. However, in a less potent threat situation . . . anxiolytics should produce a decrease in risk assessment."

The overall pattern of results reported by Blanchard and Blanchard (1990b) calls for further comment from several points of view. First, the relative lack of effect of diazepam in the fight/flight battery, coupled with the substantial effects in the anxiety battery, support the hypothesis that reactions to, respectively, an actual and a potential predator are mediated by different brain systems. Second, the positive results obtained with an anxiolytic in the anxiety battery support the hypothesis that reactions to a potential predator are indeed closely related to human anxiety. Third, diazepam did not affect freezing in the fight/flight battery, supporting the view that this fixed action pattern is indeed mediated by the fight/flight system (see discussion above). Fourth, diazepam did, in contrast, affect measures of behavioral inhibition in the anxiety battery. Thus, in the light-dark and eat-drink box tests, the drug increased the time spent on the "cat" side of the apparatus and transits toward this side. This pattern of results supports the distinction, introduced above, between freezing as a fixed action pattern (anxiolytic-resistant) and behavioral inhibition as a more general mode of controlling action (anxiolytic-sensitive).

There is an obvious similarity between Gray's (1982a) distinction between unconditioned and conditioned aversive stimuli, on the one hand, and the Blanchards' (1990a) distinction between actual and potential predators, on the other. For some cases, indeed, the two distinctions can be applied indiscriminately. One of the Blanchards' manipulations, for example, is to put a cat briefly into an open area adjacent to a burrow system where the rats live, turning this area into "a potential predator"; within the language of learning theory, there would be little hesitation in calling the area a "conditioned aversive stimulus" because of its association with the cat. Since Gray (1982a) and Blanchard and Blanchard (1990) both treat this example as coming under the rubric "anxiety," it would again seem that we have a simple choice of alternative terminologies. There are other cases, however, in which the two distinctions can lead to conflicting decisions. The odor of a cat, for example, is treated by the Blanchards as a potential predator because the cat itself is not present. In learning theory terms, however, the odor (assuming it has been given no associative history) is an unconditioned stimulus. The two vocabularies have their own advantages and disadvantages. The learning theory approach is probably the more rigorous: the experimenter can determine with some certainty whether a stimulus has previously entered into an association, whereas there is a dangerous arbitrariness in deciding, say, that the smell of a cat constitutes a potential predator and the sight of it an actual predator. On the other hand, this very rigor (possible only so long as you stay in the laboratory) can be a handicap when you try to apply it in the messy circumstances of real human life: in the psychiatric clinic, not even the patient usually knows the associative history of relevant stimuli.

If one has to choose either the Blanchards' distinction between actual and potential predators or Gray's (1982a) between unconditioned and conditioned aversive stimuli, the choice will need to be motivated by data, preferably gained in experiments in which a relevant stimulus falls into different categories (related to anxiety or not) depending on which conceptual framework is employed. One implication of the Blanchards' analysis is that anxiety can be generated by innate (e.g., cat odor) as well as learned stimuli. But this point has already been accepted in previous formulations of our model, which include among the adequate inputs to the behavioral inhibition system "innate fear stimuli" (Gray, 1971a, 1987a). By this term we intended to cover such phylogenetically "prepared" (Seligman, 1971) stimuli as snakes and spiders, phobias of which are of course widespread (Marks, 1969). However, a recent experiment based on this approach, in which we attempted to increase snake phobics' approach to a caged snake by giving them diazepam, had a negative outcome (Sartory, MacDonald, & Gray, 1990). The Blanchards' analysis suggests a possible reason for this failure. In their terms, a caged snake is presumably an actual predator, so that reactions to it should be mediated by the fight/flight system. Perhaps, if we measured anxiety in, for example, a mouse phobic in response to a caged mouse or to the odor of a mouse, the former would be unaffected by an anxiolytic but the latter reduced.

A second implication of the Blanchards' analysis is that one should pay more attention to the degree to which a potentially anxiogenic stimulus is discrete or diffuse. As they put it, "defensive behaviors such as flight and defensive threat/defensive attack which work well to present, discrete, threat stimuli may be useless or even counter-productive in threatening situations in which the actual threatening animal or object has not been localised" (Blanchard & Blanchard, 1990a, p. 128). From this point of view, the difference between a cat and a cat odor lies not so much in the presence or absence of the cat as in the clear spatial localization of the cat but not of its odor. This way of thinking of the distinction is consistent with the fact that much of the risk assessment behavior measured by the Blanchards can be seen as aimed at determining the location of the cat. It also fits neatly with the fact that the key structure which, in our model, is linked to anxiety, namely, the septo-hippocampal system, is well-known to play a major role in spatial analysis and exploration (O'Keefe & Nadel, 1978). However, it would be erroneous to suppose that anxiolytics have no effect on behavior elicited by clearly localized stimuli. To take but one example, one of the standard experimental tests of anxiolytic drug action, the Geller-Seifter conflict schedule, requires the animal to desist from pressing a lever, upon pain of footshock, when a sound or light is presented: the lever is clearly localized, the shock comes from the equally well-localized grid floor, and it is hard to see why such diffuse properties as belong to the visual or auditory stimulus should lead to any problems in localizing the "predator" that is presumably (in the Blanchards' terms) constituted by the grid floor. Nonetheless, this aspect of the Blanchards' analysis may well repay further experimental investigation.

The term *predator* that figures so prominently in the Blanchards' analysis is not meant to be fully restrictive. It is intended, for example, also to cover the case in which the threat comes from a conspecific (Blanchard & Blanchard, 1990a), an extension that seems natural enough. One area, however, in which their terminology becomes excessively stretched is that of frustrative nonreward (Amsel, 1962, 1992). There is much evidence (Gray, 1977, 1987a) that anxiolytic drugs impair responses to stimuli associated with nonreward but not to the primary event of non-reward itself. This distinction can be captured readily using the language of learning theory, but the notion of "predator" finds no natural application. This is an important limitation because it is likely that, in human anxiety, concern about failure (non-reward) looms much larger than concern about physical threat.

In sum, the Blanchards' important ethopharmacological observations give rise to a conceptual framework very similar to our own. If one were to draw a diagram of the system that they suppose to mediate anxiety, the inputs would be something like "cues of a potential predator (innate or learned)" and the outputs, "risk assessment and inhibition of other behavior." Such a diagram would differ little from Figure 6 here or from the summary statement that we sometimes employ: the behavioral inhibition system responds to threat with "stop, look, and listen, and get ready for vigorous action."

The Effects of the Anxiolytics

Given the key role played by the behavioral and other actions of the antianxiety drugs in defining our 1982 model, it is clearly important to ask this question: have subsequent studies confirmed the interpretation of the behavioral effects of the anxiolytics summarized in Figure 6? The pharmacological studies conducted by Blanchard and Blanchard (1990b) fit well into that framework, but is this true also

Table 1

Effects of Hippocampal (HIP) and Amygdalar (AMYG) Lesions and of Classical (CLAS) and Novel (NOV) Anxiolytics on Behavior in Various Paradigms

Task	HIP	CLAS	NOV	AMYG
Rewarded running/bar press, CRF	0	0	0	0
Simultaneous discrimination (except olfactory)	0	0	0	0
Shock, skilled escape, active avoidance	0	0		-
Resistance to extinction	+	+	+	+
Two-way active avoidance	+	+		-
Nonspatial active avoidance	+	+		-
Rewarded bar pressing, intermittent RF	+	+	+	0
Passive avoidance	-	-	-	-
Successive discrimination (except olfactory)	-	-	-	-
Spontaneous alternation	-	-		
Rearing	-	-	-		
Differential reinforcement of low rates	-	-	-	0
Discrimination reversal	-	-		-
Water maze, multiple choice mazes (not radial)	-	-	-	
Radial arm maze (spatial)	-	0		
Radial arm maze (cued)	0	-		

0 = no effect

+ = increased

- = decreased

for other studies? Furthermore, the 1982 model depended critically upon the considerable similarities that existed at that time between the profiles of behavioral change observed after, on the one hand, administration of anxiolytics and, on the other, lesions to the septo-hippocampal system. Does that parallel still hold good?

The classes of anxiolytics used to construct the 1982 model comprised the benzodiazepines, barbiturates, and alcohol (collectively termed the "classical" anxiolytics below). Since then, additional compounds have been found to have clinical anxiolytic activity, especially agonists at the 5-hydroxytryptamine type 1a (5HT-1a) receptor, such as buspirone (Rodgers & Cooper, 1991). These novel anxiolytics provide crucial tests of the drug-lesion parallels on which the 1982 theory is based. Unlike classical anxiolytics, they do not increase the effects of the inhibitory transmitter, gamma-aminobutyric acid (GABA). Probably as a result, they do not share with classical anxiolytics their sedative, hypnotic, euphoriant, anticonvulsant, muscle-relaxant, or addictive properties (although they have distinctive side effects of their own). We may reasonably conclude, therefore, that the specifically anxiolytic effects of all these compounds are independent of such side effects. The addition in this way of a novel class of anxiolytics that differ in so many ways from the classical anxiolytics affords a stringent test of the arguments advanced in the 1982 book: does the novel class act in critical experimental paradigms in the same manner as the classes known before? The answer is that in all the crucial paradigms that have been tested, involving both learned and innate behavior, where classical anxiolytics have effects like those of lesions of the septo-hippocampal system, novel anxiolytics (usually buspirone) have the same effects, provided modest doses are used (Table 1).

A particularly important example of the parallel between the effects of the classical and novel anxiolytics is provided by an experiment that appears to tap a specific cognitive aspect of performance. The Morris (Morris, Garrud, Rawlins, & O'Keefe, 1982) water maze is a featureless pool in which a platform is hidden under water that has been rendered opaque, thereby forcing a rat to learn the position of the platform by "spatial navigation." This has become a paradigm test of hippocampal formation damage (e.g., Morris, Hagan, & Rawlins, 1986). Both benzodiazepines and buspirone impair the specifically spatial aspects of acquisition of this water maze task at conventional anxiolytic doses (McNaughton & Morris, 1987, 1992). This result is important because it has sometimes seemed paradoxical that our theory attributes an emotion to a structure to which others generally attribute cognitive functions. We do not ourselves accept the validity of such a sharp distinction between emotion and cognition (Gray & Rawlins, 1986; Gray, 1990a; McNaughton, 1989a). However, whether or not one accepts this distinction, the fact that anxiolytics impair performance in the paradigm test of the cognitive effects of hippocampal system damage—the Morris water maze—would seem to dispose of the paradox.

A second task in which buspirone has effects (Panickar & McNaughton, 1991) that resemble those of both classical anxiolytics and septo-hippocampal lesions is rearing (reduced by all of these treatments; see Gray, 1982a, and Gray & McNaughton, 1983, for reviews) in an open field under relatively low-stress conditions. A lowered level of rearing under these conditions may be regarded as a reduction in risk assessment behavior, as discussed in the previous section in relation to the experiments by Blanchard and Blanchard

(1990a, b). Thus the clearest effects of buspirone, and the clearest similarity to the effects of the classical anxiolytics, are in what might be viewed as the least emotional and most stimulus-oriented measures: spatial navigation in the water maze and rearing in the low-stress open field. The least clear effects and the greatest departure from those of classical anxiolytics are seen, paradoxically, in tasks specifically designed as screens for anxiolytic drugs: the elevated plus maze and tests of social interaction. It is possible that the specific effects of the benzodiazepines played too great a role in the design of these tasks (Gardner, 1988).

Thus the 1982 concept of the behavioral inhibition system, as deduced from the behavioral effects of anxiolytic drugs, emerges largely unscathed from its confrontation with recent psychopharmacological data.

A further foundation of the 1982 model was that, in addition to producing behavioral effects that parallel those of lesions to the septo-hippocampal system, the classical anxiolytics impair the control of the hippocampal theta rhythm and, by implication, the normal functioning of the septo-hippocampal system. Since that time we have shown that all drugs with proven clinical anxiolytic action (classical anxiolytics, buspirone, imipramine) affect the control of theta rhythm in essentially the same way as each other in two separate tests of the control of theta rhythm: thresholds for septal driving of theta rhythm as a function of stimulation frequency (McNaughton et al., 1977) and the frequency of theta rhythm elicited by reticular stimulation (McNaughton, Richardson, & Gore, 1986). The methods involved in these experiments and the key results are presented in Figures 10 and 11. Given the major pharmacological differences between the different classes of anxiolytic drug, it is remarkable that, even with the addition of the novel class of 5ʜᴛ-1a agonists, there continues to be the convergence of effect upon the electro-physiology of the septo-hippocampal system that was first noted, on a much smaller database, by Gray (1970).

The key next step in the 1982 argument (also prefigured much earlier, in Gray, 1970) lay in the similarity, across a large swath of data, between the pattern of behavioral change observed after systemic administration of anxiolytic drugs, on the one hand, and lesions to the septal area and hippocampal formation, on the other. The relevant database is summarized in Table 2, taken from Gray

PERSPECTIVES ON ANXIETY, PANIC, AND FEAR

A

B

C

D

100Hz Stimulation

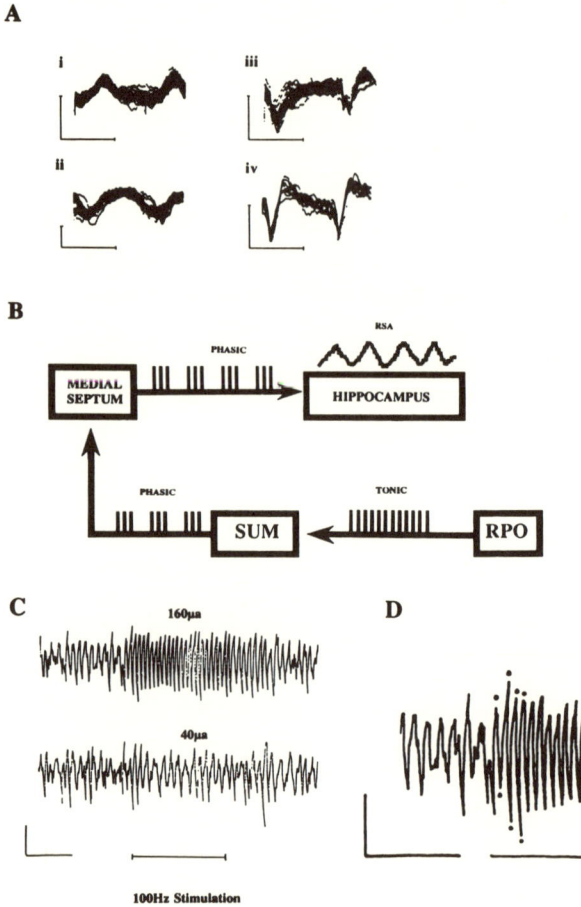

Figure 10. Methods of assessing the control of theta rhythm. As shown in Panel B, tonic impulses from the reticular formation (particularly nucleus reticularis pontis oralis, RPO) are converted to phasic theta activity by the supramammillary nucleus (SUM). These phasic impulses are then relayed by the medial septal nucleus to the hippocampus, where they result in the theta rhythm, also known as rhythmical slow activity (RSA). Theta can be produced by two different kinds of electrical stimulation. First, as shown in Panel A, stimulation of the medial septum at frequencies in the normal theta range produces hippocampal waves phase locked to the stimulation (i, ii). Excessive stimulation or incorrect electrode placements can give rise to other forms of evoked potential (iii, iv). The key feature of tests using this form of stimulation is that they measure the threshold for driving of theta rhythm at a number of frequencies (see Figure 11). Second, as shown in Panel C, high-frequency stimulation of the reticular formation (e.g., in the region of RPO) produces theta rhythm with a frequency that is linearly related to the intensity of stimulation. In this test stimulation strength is set and then the frequency is obtained by measuring the time interval required for the first three elicited waves (Panel D).

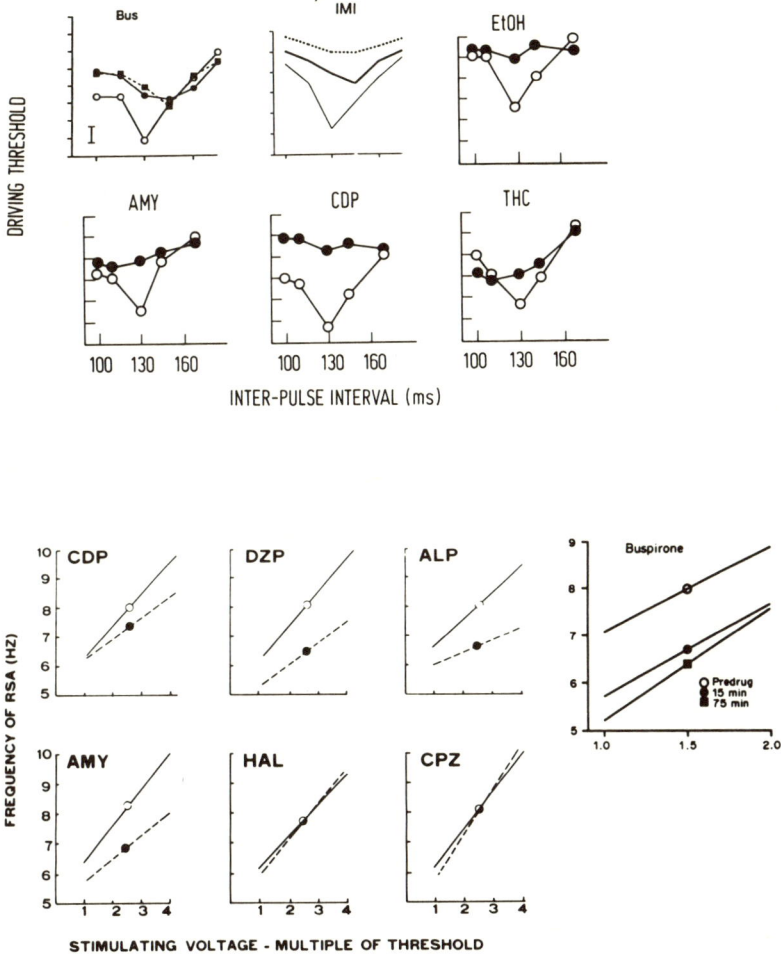

Figure 11. Effects of anxiolytic drugs on the control of theta rhythm. The upper part of the figure shows the effects of novel (BUSpirone, IMIpramine) and classical (AMY-lobarbitone, chlordiazepoxide, CDP) anxiolytics on the threshold for septal driving of theta rhythm (see Figure 10). Ethanol (EtOH) and delta-9-tetrahydrocannabinol (THC) are not used clinically but appear to have anxiolytic effects in humans. Open circles are before drug, filled symbols after drug. The lower part of the figure shows the effects on the frequency of reticular-elicited theta rhythm of the classical benzodiazepine anxiolytics chlordiazepoxide, diazepam (DZP), and alprazolam (ALP), the barbiturate amylobarbitone, and the novel anxiolytic buspirone. Imipramine (not shown) has similar effects to these other anxiolytic drugs. The major tranquilizers, haloperidol (HAL) and chlorpromazine (CPZ), which produce similar reductions in spontaneous movement to the anxiolytics, do not have any effect on frequency. Clinically effective anxiolytic drugs are the only known treatments that produce both of these effects on the control of theta rhythm.

Table 2

Comparison Between the Behavioral Effects of Septal (S) and Hippocampal (H) Lesions and Antianxiety Drugs

Gray (1982a) Chap. 2	Chap. 6	Task	Syndrome common to S and H lesions	Features in S, not H, syndrome	Features in H, not S, syndrome	Effects of Antianxiety drugs
1	1	Rewarded running, CRF	0			0
1	1	Rewarded bar-pressing, CRF	+	+		0
7	1	Rewarded bar-pressing, intermittent reinforcement	+			+[a]
2	2	Passive avoidance	-			-
3	3	Classical conditioning with aversive UCS	0			0
3	3	On-the-baseline conditioned suppression		-		-
3	3	Off-the-baseline conditioned suppression		?	?0	?0
3	3	Taste aversion		?	-	?
4	4	Agonistic escape	+			?
4	4	Skilled escape	0			0
5	5	One-way active avoidance		-		0
5	6	Nonspatial active avoidance	+			+
5	7	Two-way avoidance	+			+
6	8	Threshold of detection of shock	0			0
6	8	Movement elicited by shock	+			?
9, 10, 13		Movement elicited by novel stimuli	+			?
	10	Distraction	-			?
	11	General activity	-	?	+[b]	?
10	12	Exploration of novel stimuli	-[c]			-
10	12	Spontaneous alternation				-
10	12	Open-field ambulation		-/+[d]	+	+/-[d]
10	12	Rearing	-			-
10	13	Habituation rate	?-			?
10	14	Open-field defecation		-		?
10	14	Emergence time		-	?	-

6	15	Shock-induced aggression		+	?-
	15	Hyperreactivity syndrome		+	0
6	15	Social aggression	-		?+e
10	16	Social interaction		+	?+f
7	17	Resistance to extinction	+		+
7	17	Partial reinforcement extinction effect	-		-g
7	17	Partial reinforcement acquisition effect		?0h	-
7	18	Performance on DRL schedule		?	-
7	18	Fixed-interval scallop		-	-
8	19	Simultaneous discrimination	0	?+	0
8	20	Successive discrimination	-i		-
8	20	Single alternation		?	-
8	21	Spatial discrimination	-	?-	?
8	22	Reversal learning	-		-
9	23	Double runway frustration effect	0		0
7	23	Crespi depression effect		?	-

NOTE: This comparison is based on the information in the sections of Chapters 2 and 6 in Gray (1982a) as listed in column 1, together with the more detailed reviews given by Gray (1977) and Gray and McNaughton (1983). +, facilitation; -, impairment; 0, no consistent change; ?, insufficient data. If an entry in columns 4 or 5 is accompanied by a question mark in the other column, the difference between the septal and hippocampal syndromes cannot be established because of insufficient data.

a An exception is the VI schedule, on which rates are not increased by antianxiety drugs but are increased by both lesions.

b The apparent difference between the effects of the two lesions may be an artefact of the available data, since both lesions increase activity in the shuttle-box and decrease activity in the running wheel.

c It is possible that septal lesions increase stimulus perseveration and hippocampal lesions, response perseveration; but this apparent difference has been questioned by McNaughton and Feldon (1980).

d Septal lesions reduce ambulation upon early exposure to the open field but increase ambulation with continued exposure; the pattern of change with antianxiety drugs is the reverse.

e In this case the question mark indicates, not insufficient data, but major inconsistencies in the data (see Gray 1977).

f The antianxiety drugs increase social interaction only if this is suppressed by strong stimulation or environmental novelty (File 1980).

g Antianxiety drugs are relatively ineffective with short intertrial intervals, but the two lesions have very large effects under these conditions (Feldon, Guillamon, Gray, De Wit, & McNaughton, 1979; Feldon and Gray 1979a, b; Rawlins, Feldon, & Gray (1980).

h Feldon and Gray (1979a, b).

i Septal lesions improve successive discrimination with olfactory cues.

(1982a). At that time, no other pattern of change caused by direct intervention in the brain bore so great a resemblance to that seen after anxiolytic drug administration. As we shall see, that generalization is equally strong today. Before we consider this issue further, however, we should first take a look at the roles played by other important structures in defensive behavior considered more generally than just in relation to the action of these drugs. We turn to this topic next.

The Periaqueductal Gray, Medial Hypothalamus, and Amgdala: A Hierarchy of Defensive Control

A major area of recent development has been the analysis of the contributions to defensive behavior of structures to which very little attention was paid in the 1982 book, particularly in the work of Davis (1992), Fanselow (1991), Graeff (1991, 1993, 1994), LeDoux (1987, 1994, 1995), and Panksepp (1982a, 1990). Since these workers often link their analysis to human anxiety, we need to give careful consideration to the nature of the roles played by these structures in defensive behavior. Prominent among the structures concerned are the periaqueductal gray, the medial hypothalamus, and the amygdala.

The picture we shall present in our approach to this topic is of systems that are hierarchically organized at both the motor program and stimulus analysis levels. The hierarchical organization we describe for motor programs follows closely that proposed by Graeff (1994; see especially his Table 1), but with two additions, noted below. Graeff bases his analysis, as we do, on the idea of levels of defense developed by the Blanchards and discussed above. Fight/flight is at the lowest level and results from a contacting or proximal danger, circumstances under which there is little time for analysis of the situation or freedom of action. Directed escape is at the next level and results from a more distal but clearly present danger. Here there is more time for analysis of the situation, a greater variety of possible responses and outcomes, and some room for conditioning. Next, there is active avoidance, resulting from a potential danger that need not be approached. (This is a category omitted by Graeff.) Here analysis and motor programming must reach high levels of abstraction and will often involve conditioning. Finally, there is behavioral

Table 3

The Relationship Among Level of Danger Processing, Behavior, and Neural Substrates

Level of processing	Behavior	Neural substrate
Potential danger (with conflict)	Risk assessment Behavioral inhibition	Septum, hippocampus, amygdala
Potential danger (no conflict)	Avoidance	Amygdala
Distal danger	Escape	Medial hypothalamus
Proximal danger	Freezing Flight Fight	Periaqueductal gray

inhibition (conflated with freezing by Graeff) and risk assessment, resulting from a potential danger that must be approached, circumstances that generate a high level of conflict. This requires not only processing of information by structures that mediate avoidance, as well as processing of information by structures that mediate the competing approach tendency, but also additional complex processing aimed at resolving the discrepancy between the outputs of the structures mediating the avoidance and approach tendencies respectively. It is at this last level that we shall locate the emotion of anxiety. But we need first to consider the levels beneath it.

In agreement with Graeff (1994) we see this logical hierarchy at the psychological level as being mirrored by the hierarchical anatomical and functional organization of the neural systems involved. The relevant proposals are shown in Table 3. (There is one point where Table 3 diverges from the details of Graeff's proposal. In our discussion above of the Blanchards' work, we distinguished behavioral inhibition from freezing. Our divergence from Graeff's scheme, therefore, is that we no longer include the septo-hippocampal system as a structure mediating freezing responses, which are equated by Graeff with behavioral inhibition, to distal danger.) Before we come to the highest level of the hierarchy presented in Table 3, we shall again first consider the levels beneath it.

The separate, but equally hierarchical, organization we describe for stimulus processing is that proposed by LeDoux (1992, 1994). On this view, several levels of sensory processing are connected, independently, to the amygdala. For example, the amygdala receives input from both the visual thalamus and the highest levels of visual cortex. The central underlying principle of this organization is as follows. The lowest levels of stimulus processing provide to the amygdala only partially digested information, but they do so with greater speed than do the higher levels. Having parallel inputs to the amygdala in this manner results in a number of useful properties. It allows extremely fast processing of the simplest and most discriminable danger stimuli. It allows for priming (rather than full-blown activation) of defense circuits by lower levels of processing so as to speed up the subsequent response to input from higher levels of processing. Finally, it allows for receipt, by the defense system, of information about danger from the very highest levels of cognitive analysis, even when such danger cannot be detected by any of the lower levels. "Animals, and humans, need a quick-and-dirty reaction mechanism. . . . Failing to respond to danger is more costly than responding inappropriately to a benign stimulus. . . . Details are irrelevant and, in fact, detrimental to an efficient, speedy and potentially life-saving reaction. The brain simply needs to be able to store primitive cues and detect them. Later, coordination of this basic information with the cortex permits verification" (LeDoux, 1994, p. 38). Such a parallel organization of perceptual inputs, coupled with the capacity for plasticity of synapses in the amygdala, provides a simple basis for the learned association of a wide variety of stimuli with defense systems.

Let us now consider Table 3 in a little more detail. As reviewed by Graeff (1994), and as already noted several times above, explosive escape or flight (which can probably be equated with panic) appears to be controlled largely by the periaqueductal gray. Graeff concludes also that directed escape is probably controlled by the medial hypothalamus, which projects to the periaqueductal gray, and active avoidance, by the amygdala, which in turn projects to the medial hypothalamus. In each of these cases the behavior concerned is that elicited (in the Blanchards' terms) by a predator rather than a potential predator and is insensitive to anxiolytic drugs. In each case also, as we ascend the hierarchy in terms of both behavior and level of central nervous control, we move to more sophisticated versions of

Table 4

Effects of Amygdalar Lesions (AMYG) and Anxiolytic Drugs (ANX) on Behavior in Various Paradigms

Measure	AMYG	ANX
Flight	-	0
Aggression/defense	-	0/+
Cat contact	+	0
Freezing (defensive)	-	0
Corticosterone release	-	-
Rearing	+	-
Eating	0	0
Drinking	0	0
Simultaneous discrimination	0	0
Delayed matching to sample	0	-
One-way avoidance	-	0
Passive avoidance	-	-
Operant conflict	-	-
Two-way avoidance	-	+
Fear potentiated startle	-	-
Startle	0	0
Frustration effect	-	0
Extinction	-	-
Partial reinforcement effect	-	-
Differential reinforcement of low rates	0	-
Fixed interval	0	-
Delayed alternation	-	-
Discrimination reversal	-	-
Negative contrast	-	-
Positive contrast	-	-

0 = no effect

+ = increased

- = decreased

essentially the same flight response (from explosive escape to directed escape to anticipatory active avoidance).

When we reach the amygdalar level of this hierarchy, have we reached the "seat of anxiety"? There are siren calls (see Davis, 1992; LeDoux, 1994, 1995) to say yes to this question. There are two strong reasons to resist them—or, rather, one strong reason that can be viewed from two angles: *the amygdala does too much for it to be the seat of anxiety.*

Putting this reason narrowly, the effects of lesions to the amygdala include some of the effects seen after the administration of anxiolytic drugs, but also far more. Thus, like anxiolytics, amygdalar lesions impair passive avoidance, in which the animal must inhibit a prepotent response to avoid shock, but they also impair active avoidance (in which the animal must produce a specific response to avoid shock) and two-way active avoidance (in which active avoidance and passive avoidance tendencies are both present), whereas anxiolytics largely spare the former and reliably improve the latter (compare Tables 2 and 4).

Putting the same reason more broadly, the amygdala has a better claim to be the seat of emotion generally than of anxiety specifically. Thus, in Blanchard and Blanchard's (1990a, b) terms, amygdalar lesions impair responses to a potential predator, but they also impair responses also to actual predators (Table 4). Such lesions impair unconditioned flight, aggression, and defensive reactions in general. They increase a rat's contacts with a cat, decrease freezing induced by a dominant rat, and produce a general "taming" effect. They decrease the capacity of a novel stimulus to elicit release of adrenocorticotropic hormone (ACTH) and corticosterone, and they decrease stress-induced ulceration. All of this suggests that the role of the amygdala is not specific to conditioned reactions. Neurons in the amygdala are sensitive to associations between initially neutral conditioned stimuli and the aversive unconditioned stimuli by which these are followed (Rolls, 1990, 1992; Ono & Nishijo, 1992); and the amygdala has been shown to be a site at which n-methyl-d-aspartate (NMDA)-receptor dependent plasticity (presumed to be long-term potentiation) occurs to form the associative link between a previously neutral stimulus and avoidance responses (LeDoux, 1994). But amygdalar neurons are also sensitive to associations between conditioned stimuli and *appetitive* unconditioned stimuli (Rolls, 1990). It is not surprising, therefore, that large amygdalar lesions produce the syndrome first described by Klüver and Bucy (1937) in the monkey. The lesioned animals appear no longer to know or to be able to learn what sort of reinforcing event follows upon which stimuli. They try to eat inedible objects or to copulate with sexually inappropriate objects. At the same time, they lose their fear of other animals, of human beings, and of normally dangerous objects such as a hissing snake or a burning match. Similar findings have been made in species other than the monkey. Increased tameness, for example, has been seen in cats, rats, and lynxes (reviewed by Gray, 1987a). The latter finding is consistent with the role in the fight/flight system attributed to the amygdala above. Other findings are consistent with a role in anxiety, for example, observations of amygdala-dependent formation of conditioned reflexes based on aversive unconditioned stimuli (LeDoux, 1994, 1995) or demonstrations that anxiolytic drugs can act directly on the amygdala to reduce fear-potentiated startle (Davis, 1992). But even if we were to put these two roles together and to suppose that there was just one amygdala-dependent system for dealing with all aversive stimuli, this would still not account for the results of experiments, mentioned above, in which appetitive stimuli have been used. Thus, only by recourse to the unattractive hypothesis that mammals have only one emotion system, of which anxiety would be but one manifestation, could one seriously entertain the notion that the amygdala is the seat of anxiety.

Since, nonetheless, the amygdala figures so prominently in contemporary discussions of anxiety (Davis, 1992; LeDoux, 1994, 1995), let us consider what rebuttal there might be to the case we have argued.

First, we have spoken above about the amygdala without considering the very considerable anatomical complexity of this structure, as well as of its connections. Moreover, the amygdala is located within the temporal lobe and closely connected to areas such as the hippocampus and entorhinal cortex. As a result, lesions to it, or stimulation of it, will not only influence these other areas because of its connections with them but can also influence fibers of passage within and at the border of the amygdala. These fibers of passage might often be crucial for temporal lobe functions that are completely independent of the amygdala. The possibility therefore cannot be excluded that, within this overall complexity, there exists a discrete system that discharges only that part of overall emotional behavior which corresponds to the human state of anxiety. If one could target that system selectively, a profile of behavioral change might emerge that corresponds with that of the anxiolytics to an even greater degree than does the septo-hippocampal "syndrome" (Table 2).

Second, the profile of behavioral change produced by the anxiolytics may in any case be the wrong place to start. Perhaps one should start with the fact that "converging evidence now indicates that the amygdala plays a crucial role in the development and expression of conditioned fear" (Davis, 1992, p. 353), a statement that we accept. ("Conditioned fear" in this quotation bears its standard learning theory connotation, e.g., the set of responses elicited by a tone that has been associated with footshock.) This choice of starting point is, of course, crucial for any search for the neural basis of anxiety. The concept of conditioned fear has been the usual starting point within the tradition of learning theory (e.g., Miller, 1951; Mowrer, 1947), and it played a pivotal role in the development of the present model (Gray, 1967). It appeared at one time, indeed, that this concept would serve to bring order into the messy realm of clinical data (Eysenck & Rachman, 1965; Gray, 1971a). However, this approach then encountered such apparently insuperable objections (Eysenck, 1979) that it had to be abandoned even for those cases— the simple phobias—to which it initially appeared to have the most natural application. Mineka and Zinbarg's chapter in this volume offers a new and robust defense of the value of modern conditioning theory (Dickinson, 1980) in the clinical field. Even staying within that theory, however, it is clear that any clinically appropriate account of anxiety must supplement fear of pain (in which the amygdala is clearly implicated) by fear of failure, disappointment, and frustration (in which the amygdala appears not to be implicated; Gray, 1987a).

A further alternative from which to start on the search for anxiety might lie in the observations of clear defensive behavior (flight, defensive aggression, and so on) provoked by stimulation of the central gray and medial hypothalamus (Graeff, 1994). This case has been strongly argued by Panksepp (1982a, b, 1990) and rebutted by Gray (1982c). What is now clear, and was not in 1982, is that any complete account of the clinical phenomena must call upon (at least) two different substrates of negative affective states, one related to panic attacks and the other to anticipatory anxiety (see the discussion of this distinction in the section on clinical phenomena). Given the strong reasons (Graeff, 1990, 1991, 1993) to relate panic to the fight/ flight system, organized in the central gray and medial hypothalamus, with descending control by the amygdala, this system becomes unavailable also to serve as the substrate for anxiety.

Even if there were not these reasons against choosing either conditioned fear or fight/flight behavior as our starting points in the search for the neural substrate of anxiety, we would still argue that the strategy adopted here—to start with the anxiolytic drugs—is the best available. Whatever anxiety is, it is, at least for the time being, best defined by human verbal reports. These reports are reliably changed by a variety of drugs. The fact that these drugs, belonging as they do to several radically different neurochemical classes, produce a common profile of behavioral change in animals, one moreover that has considerable face validity as constituting reduced anxiety (Gray, 1977), provides an unparalleled entry point into the neurology of this emotion. It is encouraging that, using the same strategy but novel experimental methods, Blanchard and Blanchard (1990b) come up with conclusions essentially similar to our own (see above). Thus the arguments in the literature are not about discrepant data or rival methodologies. Once the starting point is chosen, the destinations reached do not substantially differ. Given our starting point, the data—especially those on the behavioral effects of different brain lesions (Tables 2 and 4)—continue to triangulate the septo-hippocampal system.

Nonetheless, it is clear that the amygdala plays a very important role, or roles, in anxiety. How should this role be described?

First, the amygdala appears to act as a high-level detector of threat, both innate and learned. Much progress has been made in understanding how the detection of conditioned threatening stimuli is achieved. Sensory information arrives primarily in the lateral nucleus of the amygdala, which receives gustatory, visceral, auditory, and visual input from the thalamus and also extensive unimodal and polymodal input from sensory neocortex, so obtaining "rather high-level information concerning potentially all aspects of ongoing sensory experiences" (Amaral, Price, Pitkanen, & Carmichael, 1992, p. 55). This information is relayed to the basal nucleus, where an affective component is added by inputs from the parabrachial, insular cortical, and midline thalamic areas, all of which receive nociceptive input. Thus coincidence of conditioned-stimulus input to the lateral nucleus with that of unconditioned-stimulus input to the basal nucleus could provide the basis for long-term potentiation (LeDoux, 1994, p. 36) and hence for the formation of an association between the conditioned and unconditioned stimuli. In addition to learned threat, the lesion evidence indicates that the amygdala also receives information about innate threat. Stimuli of this kind are likely to include threatening conspecific faces; it is relevant, therefore, that Rolls (1992) finds single units in the amygdala that respond to faces.

In addition to these sensory functions, the amygdala also plays an executive role. The sensory information that is processed in the lateral and basal nuclei is passed on to the corticomedial complex. From here, the output is to the thalamus, hypothalamus, brain stem, and spinal cord. The hypothalamic projection makes connection with the anterior hypothalamus, the supraoptic and paraventricular nuclei, and substantially in the ventromedial hypothalamus and the premammillary nuclei. It also makes connections with the lateral hypothalamus as a whole, the paramammillary, tuberomammillary, and supramammillary nuclei. The projection then continues toward and into the spinal cord, while making connections with "a number of structures that have been implicated in autonomic control, including the periaqueductal gray, the parabrachial nucleus, the dorsal vagal nuclei, and the reticular formation" (Amaral et al., 1992, p. 35). Thus it is likely that this output allows the amygdala to influence the operation of the fight/flight system at its hypothalamic and midbrain levels, as indicated by combined lesion studies (Gray, 1987a, pp. 322–324). In addition, the basal nucleus (and accessory basal nucleus) projects to the striatum as a whole: the caudate nucleus, putamen, n. accumbens, olfactory tubercle, and (weakly) to the ventral pallidum; and both the basal and lateral nuclei project to the mediodorsal thalamus, which in turn provides a relay to prefrontal cortex. These connections could, therefore, provide one route for the elicitation and fine-tuning of learned avoidance responses (particularly where the required response is not part of the species-specific defense repertoire). We have already commented on the important role in the elaboration and execution of motor programs that is allotted in our model to the projection from the amygdala to n. accumbens (see the section on motivation and Figures 2 and 3).

In sum, the amygdala plays a crucial role in emotion generally and in behavior dealing with aversive stimuli in particular: it detects learned and innate sources of threat, it represents the highest level of the fight/flight system, and it interacts with the motor programming systems of the basal ganglia in the organization of avoidance behavior. The amygdala might also be a structure through which the autonomic outputs of the behavioral inhibition system are channeled and could, therefore, be one of the sites at which anxiolytic drugs act to reduce this autonomic output. And (see below) we shall also attribute to the amygdala mediation of the "increased arousal" output of the behavioral inhibition system (Figure 6). But it is in the further interaction of the amygdala with the septo-hippocampal system that we should mainly seek the neuropsychology of anxiety. In this continuing search, we should bear in mind that, in anatomical terms, the amygdala provides much more extensive input (from the lateral and basal nuclei) to the hippocampal formation than does the hippocampus to the amygdala (Amaral et al., 1992). There is every reason to suppose that this input conveys to the hippocampal formation information about threat. We move on now to consider what use the hippocampal formation makes of this information.

The Septo-Hippocampal System

Despite the important contributions to defensive behavior of the structures considered in the previous section, the logic of our argument continues then to point to the septo-hippocampal system as the prime candidate for mediation of the human condition of anxiety. A major reason for this conclusion is that the pattern of behavioral change caused by anxiolytic drug administration is closely paralleled by the pattern seen after lesions to this system (Table 2); and damage to no other candidate brain region reproduces this pattern so well. That conclusion is as firm today as it was in 1982. Thus we conclude that the septo-hippocampal system remains a strong candidate for mediating the major behavioral effects in animals of the anxiolytic drugs and therefore for playing a key role in the emotion of anxiety. To those who know the extensive literature on hippocampal function this renewed affirmation of a heterodox belief may simply brand us as unrepentant sinners. For, both before and since 1982, two apparently different views of hippocampal function have dominated the field, namely, that the hippocampus mediates (one or other kind of) memory (Eichenbaum, Otto, & Cohen, 1994; Gaffan, 1977; Milner, 1970; Olton, Becker, & Handelmann, 1979; Rawlins, 1985), or that it mediates spatial cognition (O'Keefe & Nadel, 1978). How are we to resolve these conceptual conflicts?

We start with the memory issue. In contrast to our 1982 model (and also O'Keefe and Nadel's, 1978, model), recent theories of hippocampal function have tended to focus solely on memory, to omit any reference to the known detailed physiology and connections (particularly subcortical) of the hippocampus, and to be based on a limited set of experiments purporting to distinguish between specific types of memory: working/reference, declarative/procedural, spatial/taxon, configural/associative, relational/associative, contextual/discrete (see Eichenbaum et al., 1994, for review). In this list the first member of each pair is the supposed hippocampal-sensitive form. This concentration on memory is not entirely surprising because, first, lesions involving the hippocampus have been reported to produce amnesia (Mayes, 1988) and, second, the hippocampus is the structure of choice for demonstrating long-term potentiation, a putative substrate for memory. In the last ten years, however, abundant reasons have been produced for seeing this concentration on memory as a mistake.

First, it is clear (and all current theorists agree) that the hippocampus is not the final repository even for those types of memory in which it appears to be involved (though few of the theories make clear why, if this is the case, the hippocampus is ever needed). Second, it is clear that long-term potentiation can be obtained in many, if not all, parts of the central nervous system. Indeed, it has been suggested by Graham Goddard (personal communication) that the reason long-term potentiation is so easily seen in hippocampal preparations is because the hippocampus is one of the few places in the brain where it does not occur under normal physiological conditions (other areas show less experimental potentiation because their synapses are already close to saturation). Third, seductive as may have been the lure of the original specific experimental demonstration that gave rise to a particular theory, all theories based on "types of memory" fail at least some crucial tests. For example, water maze learning is affected by hippocampal lesions, despite being a reference memory task rather than a working memory task (Morris et al., 1982); hippocampal lesions affect delayed matching to sample with trial-repetitive but not trial-unique objects (falsifying declarative, spatial, and configural theories; Rawlins, Lyford, Seferiades, Deacon, & Cassaday, 1993); and hippocampal formation lesions do not affect water maze performance if the animal is first trained in a fashion that prevents errors and eliminates competing response strategies (falsifying spatial, contextual, and relational theories; Whishaw, 1995).

The fault with all these theories, in our opinion, is that they are based on the idea that the hippocampus is there to create certain classes of memory. However, this is not consistent even with the phenomenology of amnesia—where errors are frequently intrusions from previous trials (Warrington & Weiskrantz, 1968). This simple observation suggests that the hippocampus is important for proper memory performance, not because it acts to store correct information, but because it prevents the storage (or retrieval) of incorrect information. On our view, then, all memory is a function of plasticity or activity in appropriate neocortical or subcortical areas (e.g., as discussed above, the amygdala for simple fear conditioning), and the apparent "intermediate memory" function of the hippocampus (Rawlins, 1985) derives from the fact that this system prevents confusion during the intermediate stage of consolidation, rather than being a temporary store for information during the intermediate period.

Specifically, we propose that the septo-hippocampal system as a whole is engaged in those memory tasks where there is a high degree of competition between potentially correct alternatives. This hypothesis is essentially the same as the one put forward by Weiskrantz and Warrington (1975), viz, that hippocampal lesions affect tasks that are high in interference. The effect of the processing performed by the hippocampal formation under such conditions is, via its recursive links with many, particularly cortical, structures, actively to suppress the formation of incorrect memories (or to inhibit motor programs that lead to the incorrect goal), principally by increasing negative bias in the evaluation of stimuli. Note that, on this view, the "memorial" functions of the hippocampus are a natural consequence of the non-memorial, conflict-resolving functions which, as suggested by Gray (1982a) and briefly elaborated below, are discharged by the septo-hippocampal system under conditions that provoke anxiety. We believe, therefore, that our model can not only accommodate the same memorial results as classic memory theories of the hippocampus but also can explain the bulk of the cases in which such theories break down, and by using exactly the same principles to account for both the memorial and nonmemorial effects of hippocampal formation lesions. Detailed justification of this claim, however, must wait upon the second edition of *The Neuropsychology of Anxiety*.

It should be noted, incidentally, that this view represents a departure from our earlier positions that, in agreement with Olton et al. (1979), the hippocampus could discharge specifically the function of working memory (Gray, 1982a, p. 284) or that, in agreement with Rawlins (1985), it could act as an intermediate memory buffer (Gray & Rawlins, 1986). Our current view, rather, is that the hippocampus would often be involved in tasks requiring working memory, not because it acts as such a memory itself, but because such tasks are interference-prone so that the hippocampus would be required to suppress inappropriate firing patterns. Similarly, in the intermediate-memory case, the hippocampus would not act as an intermediate store as such, but rather would be required to interact with other, probably neocortical, areas so as to suppress innappropriate connections until such time as the memory trace was sufficiently consolidated.

We turn next to the issue of spatial cognition. The importance of the hippocampus for this function is beyond question. Much evidence in favor of this hypothesis has accumulated since O'Keefe and Nadel (1978) first enunciated it. The recent experiments of Jarrard (1991, 1993) now add to this evidence the important finding that, when excitotoxins are used to destroy the hippocampus proper with a selectivity not hitherto possible, performance on tasks involving spatial analysis is reliably and substantially disrupted, while performance on other tasks, which from earlier findings with larger lesions might have been expected to be disrupted, is left intact.

What *is* still in dispute, however, is the degree to which the hippocampus is devoted *only* to spatial analysis. Over the years, many examples have been offered of tasks that appear to be totally lacking in spatial elements and yet which are sensitive to hippocampal damage. O'Keefe and Nadel have remained resolute in the face of such observations (e.g., Nadel, 1991), and to some extent their contumely has been justified by Jarrard's (1991, 1993) findings, showing, for example, that working memory tasks without spatial components are unaffected by selective hippocampal lesions. Yet the problem posed by such observations for the purely spatial theory has not gone away. Also using selective excitotoxic hippocampal lesions, for example, we have shown, in the rat, impairments in lever-press performance on a schedule of differential reinforcement of low rates of response (Sinden, Rawlins, Gray, & Jarrard, 1986) and in the resistance to extinction of a running response (Jarrard, Feldon, Rawlins, Sinden, & Gray, 1986); and, after combined lesions of the hippocampus and subicular area, we have shown an impairment in the partial reinforcement extinction effect (Sinden, Jarrard, & Gray, 1988). None of these findings is readily explained as a deficiency in spatial analysis. Even more telling, Davidson and Jarrard (1993) have shown that hippocampal lesions impair the rat's capacity to bring its responses under the contextual control of the state of hunger. Similarly, Ridley, Timothy, MacLean, and Baker (1995) have studied marmosets with excitotoxic lesions confined to the CA1 region of the hippocampus and demonstrated impairment in a conditional discrimination in which the spatial element (or, rather, lack thereof) was rigorously controlled. The latter result can probably be generalized to human subjects, in whom we have shown, after large temporal lobe lesions for relief of epilepsy, an impairment in conditional discrimination in a totally nonspatial eyeblink conditioning task (Daum, Channon, Polkey, & Gray, 1991). We can reasonably conclude, therefore: space, yes; only space, no.

It is important also to note that our theory, which has as a central feature the role of the theta rhythm in determining the effects of anxiolytic drugs, deals with the hippocampal formation as a whole. That is, we include the dentate gyrus, hippocampus proper, and entorhinal cortex within the "hippocampal formation." This view not only fits with modern anatomical conclusions but is driven by the fact that all of these areas receive their own independent input from the medial septum and all have their own independent generation of theta rhythm. On our view, therefore, anxiolytic drugs produce a degradation (rather than abolition) of the information-processing functions of all these areas. They should produce, therefore, both less extreme and more widespread effects than total lesions restricted to the hippocampus proper.

There are at this point two possible ways forward. Either the hippocampal formation has two independent functions, one to do with spatial analysis, the other not; or it discharges one unitary function, which is strongly invoked by spatial analysis but which also enters into other transactions with the environment. The comparator hypothesis on which our model is based takes the latter, more parsimonious, route. It supposes that the general comparator functions of detecting unexpected stimuli, establishing predictions for their future occurrence, interacting with motor programs (interrupting those that lead to mismatch, not those that lead to match) and with exploratory systems able to reduce environmental uncertainty (e.g., those that control head and eye movement in the superior colliculus, or locomotor exploration in the midbrain, to both of which access can be gained via the subiculo-accumbens projection; Gray et al., 1991a) can serve *either* to build and modify spatial maps *or* to detect threat and modify motor plans to deal with it. The general lines of this approach are set out in detail in Gray (1982a; see also Gray et al., 1991a), although the new model that we are preparing will develop and expand upon them. Like Eichenbaum et al. (1994), we believe that essentially the same general principles of relational learning and conditional discrimination will prove to be applicable in both the spatial and nonspatial realms.

Parsimony is, of course, the normally preferred scientific option. But, in any case, we do not think it an accident that the hippocampus should be involved in both spatial analysis and anxiety. The Blanchards' work, discussed in detail above, is a good demonstration of the intimate relationship between these two functions, one cognitive, the other emotional. (In general, it is a mistake to draw a rigid line between these two types of cognitive function; Gray, 1990b.) The behavior that proved to be most sensitive to anxiolytic drug action was that of risk assessment, that is, exploration of a spatial environment that might contain, or just had contained, a predator, presumably carried out with the aim of establishing the current whereabouts of the predator. There is no choice to be made here between treating this behavior as one relating to spatial analysis or to anxiety: it is both simultaneously.

More generally, the role of the septo-hippocampal system can be seen as one of troubleshooting: of establishing in which context a particular motor program is appropriate and in which it is inappropriate and of establishing how the significance of particular stimuli varies according to context. For this purpose, as described in Gray (1982a), it can call upon the predictive circuits of the comparator system to compute the likely outcomes of different motor programs in different circumstances, and it can call upon, and modify, memories stored in the temporal lobe or elsewhere in the neocortex to aid in, and benefit from, these computations. Critically, in such computations, specific response-stimulus and stimulus-response associations must be differentiated according to specific contexts, and by far the most important way in which, in the normal ecology of mammals, contexts can be specified is by their geography and its contents—that is, spatially. Thus the link between spatial cognition and the emotion of anxiety is, we believe, phylogenetically ancient and persistent. The capacity of anxiolytic drugs to impair behavior in the Morris water maze, a paradigmatic test of spatial cognition, is consistent with such a link (McNaughton & Morris, 1987, 1992), as is evidence that inbred strains of mice that differ in hippocampal morphology show correlated differences also in behavioral tests of both susceptibility to anxiety and spatial performance (Lipp et al., 1989).

Overall, as emphasized by Graeff (1993, 1994), the septo-hippo-campal system can be seen as the top of a hierarchical system dealing with the various motivations that are generated when an animal is exposed to threat. With immediate, apparently inescapable, threat we get panic controlled by the periaqueductal gray; with escapable threat, we get directed escape controlled by the hypothalamus, in interaction with the periaqueductal gray; with stimuli that warn of impending threat, without complication from other conflicting response tendencies, we get simple conditioned reflexes or active avoidance controlled by the amygdala; finally, where avoidance (active or passive) is compromised by a conflicting approach (or active avoidance) tendency (that is, the two tendencies are of approximately equal intensity), and similarly where the conflict is set up by conditions of mixed reward and nonreward, the hippocampus becomes involved. Its function, under such circumstances, is one of *conflict resolution*: to determine which of the competing response tendencies is more appropriate to the current context and to inhibit the others. This function has a particular application in regard to spatial contexts, as indicated above; and, just as the septo-hippocampal system inhibits temporarily incorrect response tendencies, so it suppresses temporarily inappropriate memories, also as indicated above. The emotional state linked to the operation of this system is that of anxiety. In this context, it is relevant that H.M., the well-known patient with temporal lobe damage, is not only densely amnesic but also fails to control food intake via normal hunger cues (Eichenbaum et al., 1994) and appears to have totally lost any capacity for anxiety (J. Ogden, personal communication, 1993).

The Output to Motor Systems

One of the major puzzles at the time the 1982 book was written concerned the way in which the septo-hippocampal system manages to influence motor behavior. An important contribution to resolving this puzzle came from the report (Kelley & Domesick, 1982) of a major projection from the subicular region (a key output station for the hippocampal formation) to the ventral striatum, or n. accumbens, which plays a nodal role in the motor programming circuitry of the basal ganglia (Figures 2 and 3). Subsequently, it has become clear that a parallel projection connects the entorhinal cortex to the nucleus accumbens (Clark, Feldon, & Rawlins, 1992; Yee, Rawlins, & Feldon, 1995). These connections from the hippocampal system to the basal ganglia play a central role in the model of motivation with which we commenced this chapter and also in the application of an extended version of the model of anxiety to the cognitive aberrations characteristic of acute, positively symptomatic schizophrenia (Gray et al., 1991a; Gray et al., 1995). How do they affect the model of anxiety that forms our present concern?

An important feature of that model is that the behavioral inhibition output of the behavioral inhibition system (Figure 6) is very general: to fulfill its functions it must be capable of suppressing *any* behavior in which the animal is engaged at the time it encounters threat. This feature is illustrated in Figure 12, which divides the inhibited behavior into three classes: fight/flight behavior, consummatory behavior (eating, drinking, copulation, and so on), and rewarded instrumental behavior. Gray (1982a) attributed the inhibition of consummatory behavior to a pathway described by Albert, Brayley, and Milner (1978), which descends to the hypothalamus from the lateral septal area. Inhibition of fight/flight behavior, as discussed in the section on the clinical phenomena of anxiety, appears to be controlled by serotonergic inputs to the central periaqueductal gray (Graeff, 1993, 1994), although it remains unclear how the output of the serotonergic system is coordinated with that of the septo-hippocampal system (Gray, 1982a, pp. 370–371).

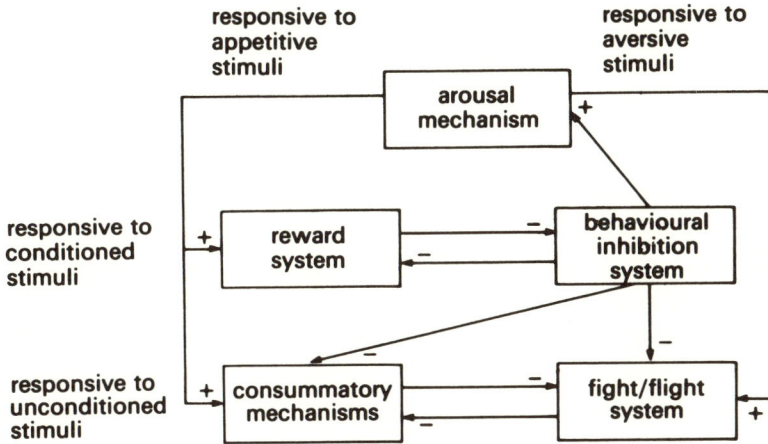

Figure 12. Proposed inhibitory (-) and excitatory (+) interactions between the various components of the conceptual nervous system identified in this chapter. The reward and behavioral inhibition systems respond to conditioned reinforcing stimuli; the fight/flight system and consummatory mechanisms respond to unconditioned reinforcing stimuli. The reward system and consummatory mechanisms respond to appetitive stimuli; the behavioral inhibition and fight/flight systems respond to aversive stimuli.

These two aspects of the 1982 model for behavioral inhibition do not seem at present to require any modification. The inhibition of instrumental behavior, however, calls for additional consideration.

Inhibition of instrumental behavior was attributed in the 1982 book to the output from the subiculum to the cingulate cortex (a region which, together with the prefrontal cortex, appears to play a high-level role in motor programming; see the section on the motivational model, above). The description of the subiculo-accumbens projection (Kelley & Domesick, 1982) suggests an alternative, or perhaps additional, route by which such inhibition of instrumental behavior might be achieved. The nucleus accumbens appears to play a central part in mediating incentive motivation. Inputs to this structure from the amygdala (where, as discussed above, cue-reinforcement associations appear to be formed), together with the mesolimbic dopaminergic pathway that ascends from nucleus A 10 in the ventral tegmental area, are apparently responsible for conveying information concerning the availability of reward. Dorsal striatal neurons (to which n. accumbens has indirect projections), and the thalamic, pallidal, and cortical circuits in which these are embedded (see Figures 2 and 3), are then responsible for carrying out appropriate motor behavior. Thus n. accumbens is a key node within the basal ganglia at which the subicular afferents from the septo-hippocampal system might interrupt the running of motor programs aimed at appetitive goals (reward or, in the case of active avoidance behavior, safety).

Lavin and Grace (1994) have studied what happens to the outputs from the nucleus accumbens further downstream. Using electrophysiological and tract tracing techniques, these workers have demonstrated that the inhibitory GABA-ergic output from the n. accumbens synapses, in the ventral pallidum, upon further GABA-ergic inhibitory neurons that project to the dorsomedial thalamic nucleus. This pathway is likely to be critical in bringing ongoing motor programs to a halt because it is from here that the thalamus projects to the prefrontal and cingulate cortices, which appear to constitute the highest level of the motor programming system. As already noted, the subiculum also projects directly to the cingulate cortex; it may be, therefore, that the behavioral inhibition output of the behavioral inhibition system, insofar as this affects instrumental behavior, is jointly executed by the subicular outputs to cingulate cortex and n. accumbens.

Lavin and Grace's (1994) work has also demonstrated that the ventral pallidum projects to a second nucleus in the thalamus, the nucleus reticularis thalami. This projection may play an important role in another output of the behavioral inhibition system illustrated in Figure 6, viz, increased attention, especially to novel or ambiguous environmental stimuli. The nucleus reticularis thalami is unusual among thalamic nuclei in that it consists mainly of GABA-ergic neurons that project to a number of the surrounding thalamic nuclei whose job is to relay sensory impulses to the appropriate sensory regions of the cerebral cortex (Jones, 1975). Since the pallidal output to these neurons is itself inhibitory, its activation has the effect of disinhibiting these sensory relay pathways, that is, increasing the entry to the cerebral cortex of environmental stimuli (Taylor & Alavi, 1993). Gray (1982a) attributed the increased attention output of the behavioral inhibition system to the projection from the subiculum to the entorhinal cortex, seeing in this also a means of ensuring that the increased attention was selectively linked to any mismatch or threat that had been detected by the comparator system. As noted above,

GLU

+   -
LCX   I   DM ←   Neocortical sensory processing

GLU   +

GABA   +

GLU   II

Sub ERC   +   NAC   -   VP   -   NRT   -   Thalamocortical sensory relay nuclei

GLU   GABA   GABA   GABA

DA   III   GABA

A10

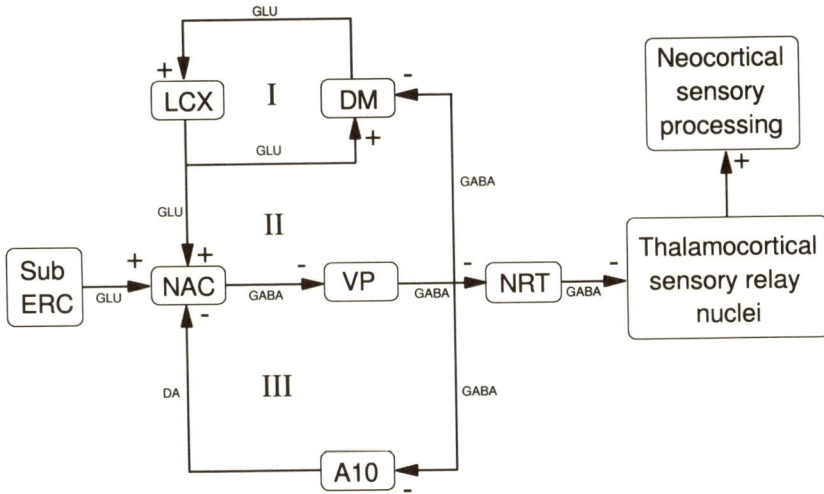

Figure 13. Connections from the subiculum (sub) and entorhinal cortex (ERC) to the n. accumbens (NAC) component of the motor system (Figure 2) and from that system to the nucleus reticularis thalami (NRT) and thalamocortical sensory pathways. For remainder of abbreviations, see Figure 2.

the entorhinal cortex also projects to the nucleus accumbens (Yee et al., 1995). Thus the increased attention output of the behavioral inhibition system may be jointly executed by the subicular projection directly to the nucleus accumbens and indirectly via the entorhinal cortex, with onward transmission via the nucleus reticularis thalami to affect the gating of sensory transmission to the cortex. A further role that may be played by the nucleus accumbens lies in its indirect connections to the superior colliculus (involved in the programming of eye movements) and the midbrain locomotor exploratory region (Somogyi, Bolam, Totterdell, & Smith, 1981; Williams & Faull, 1988); these may mediate the exploratory behavior required to resolve the problem (mismatch or threat) detected by the comparator system.

In sum, the subiculo-accumbens projection (Figure 13), together with the other related pathways indicated above, appears to be well placed to mediate both the inhibition of instrumental motor programs and the accompanying attention and exploratory behavior upon activation of the behavioral inhibition system. These outputs are essentially the same as those described by Blanchard and Blanchard (1990a, b) as risk assessment.

As already concluded by Gray (1982a, pp. 298–299), however, the third output of the behavioral inhibition system (Figure 6), in-

creased arousal, does not appear to be mediated by the septo-hippocampal system. Gray (1982a) suggested that this output might be
mediated by the ascending noradrenergic innervation of the hypothalamus (see paragraph 4 of the summary of the 1982 book, above).
In the light of Davis's (1992) demonstration that the potentiation of
the startle response by conditioned fear stimuli (treated by Gray,
1987a, as a paradigm case of anxious behavior), and the reversal of
this potentiation by anxiolytic drugs, are mediated by the amygdala
(whereas dorsal hippocampal lesions fail to influence potentiated
startle; M. Davis, personal communication), we would now substi-
tute this route as constituting the increased arousal output of the behavioral inhibition system. Given the control exercised by the amygdala over the hypothalamic level of the fight/flight system, this does
not constitute a substantial deviation from the 1982 model. It does,
however, raise the major issue (present in the 1982 model and not
yet resolved) as to how the different components of the behavioral
inhibition system are coordinated. This issue arises not only for the
relations between the septo-hippocampal system and the amygdala
but also for those between both of these forebrain structures and the
ascending monoaminergic pathways by which they and other relevant regions are innervated, and which undoubtedly play key roles
in mediating both anxiety and anxiolytic drug action. Resolving this
and many other still outstanding problems leaves a great deal of further work to do.

Coda: Consciousness

The state of anxiety is one of both the conceptual nervous system
and the central nervous system, and we have tried above to define
these substrates of anxiety in at least a little detail as the behavioral
inhibition system and the septo-hippocampal system (plus a great
deal of other associated circuitry). But anxiety is also a state with
subjective, conscious components. Of this aspect of anxiety, Gray
(1982a, p. 444) wrote, "As to the remainder of the dimension of feeling, that is shrouded in the mystery of how the brain becomes conscious of its own doings (Gray, 1971b), a mystery that is neither more
nor less acute for anxiety than it is for the rest of psychology." At the
risk of being branded "new mysterians" by Dennett (1991), we admit

that this mystery is still intact today and is likely to be so for a long time to come (Gray, 1987b). But it is perhaps worth closing with a pointer to a speculative hypothesis that has emerged, in part, out of our attempt to construct a neuropsychology of anxiety. A development of this kind is not altogether surprising since, phenomenologically, one of the clearest features of anxious feelings and cognitions is their capacity to dominate consciousness, often to the exclusion of all else.

The speculation in question (Gray, 1995b), which is backed up by consideration of a variety of features of the contents of consciousness of which it appears to be able to give a more or less plausible account, is that such contents of consciousness consist of the outputs of the subicular comparator, tagged as "match" or "mismatch" (that is, with a feeling of familiarity or novelty) and fed back so as to reactivate the cortically located sensory inputs that have participated in the most recent match/mismatch decision. It is, as we have seen, the mismatch decision that is most relevant to anxiety. As indicated in Figure 13, the neural events proposed as ensuing from such a decision include activation of a pathway from the subiculum, via the nucleus accumbens, the ventral pallidum, and the nucleus reticularis thalami, which disinhibits passage along all the thalamic sensory relay stations to the neocortex. Such an action should have the effect of greatly increasing general perceptual awareness, as modeled by Taylor and Alavi (1993). Although the general mystery of the links between brain function, behavior, and conscious experience remains, there may nonetheless be fruitful lines of empirical inquiry to which such speculations might lead. It is in that spirit that we bring this work in progress to a temporary halt.

REFERENCES

Adams, D. B. (1979). Brain mechanism for offence, defense and submission. *Behavioral and Brain Sciences, 2*, 201–241.

Adler, C. M., Craske, M. G., & Barlow, D. H. (1987). Relaxation-induced panic (RIP): When resting isn't peaceful. *Integrative Psychiatry, 2*, 94–112.

Albert, D. J., Brayley, K. N., & Milner, J. A. (1978). Connections from the lateral septum modulating reactivity in the rat. *Physiology and Behavior, 21*, 761–767.

Amaral, D. G., Price, J. L., Pitkanen, A., & Carmichael, S. T. (1992). Anatomical organization of the primate amygdaloid complex. In J. P. Aggleton (Ed.), *The amygdala: Neurobiological aspects of emotion, memory and mental dysfunction* (pp. 1–66). New York: Wiley-Liss.

Amsel, A. (1962). Frustrative nonreward in partial reinforcement and discrimination learning: Some recent history and a theoretical extension. *Psychological Review, 69,* 306–328.

Amsel, A. (1992). *Frustration theory.* Cambridge: Cambridge University Press.

Andrews, G., Stewart, G., Morris-Yates, A., Holt, P., & Henderson, S. (1990). Evidence for a general neurotic syndrome. *British Journal of Psychiatry, 157,* 6–12.

Apter, A., Ratzoni, G., King, R. A., Weizman, A., Iancu, I., Binder, M., & Riddle, M. A. (1994). Fluvoxamine open-label treatment of adolescent inpatients with obsessive-compulsive disorder or depression. *Journal of the American Academy of Child and Adolescent Psychiatry, 33,* 342–348.

Bandler, R., & Törk, I. (1987). Midbrain periaqueductal grey region in the cat has afferent and efferent connections with solitary tract nuclei. *Neuroscience Letters, 74,* 1–6.

Barlow, D. H. (1988). *Anxiety and its disorders.* New York: Guilford.

Baxter, L. R., Jr., Schwartz, J. M., Guze, B. H., Bergman, K., & Szuba, M. P. (1990). Neuroimaging in OCD: Seeking the mediating neuroanatomy. In M. A. Jenike, L. Baer, & W. E. Minichiello (Eds.), *OCD theory and management.* St. Louis: Year Book Medical.

Blanchard, D. C., & Blanchard, R. J. (1988). Ethoexperimental approaches to the biology of emotion. *Annual Review of Psychology, 39,* 43–68.

Blanchard, R. J., & Blanchard, D. C. (1989). Antipredator defense behaviours in a visible burrow system. *Journal of Comparative Psychology, 103,* 70–82.

Blanchard, R. J., & Blanchard, D. C. (1990a). An ethoexperimental analysis of defense, fear and anxiety. In N. McNaughton, & G. Andrews (Eds.), *Anxiety* (pp. 124–133). Dunedin, New Zealand: University of Otago Press.

Blanchard, D. C., & Blanchard, R. J. (1990b). Effects of ethanol, benzodiazepines and serotonin compounds on ethopharmacological models of anxiety. In N. McNaughton & G. Andrews (Eds.), *Anxiety* (pp. 188–199). Dunedin, New Zealand: University of Otago Press.

Bolles, R. C., & Fanselow, M. S. (1980). A perceptual defensive-recuperative model of fear and pain. *Behavioral and Brain Sciences, 3,* 291–323.

Brooks, V. B. (1986). How does the limbic system assist motor learning? A limbic comparator hypothesis. *Brain, Behavior and Evolution, 29,* 29–53.

Brown, M. W. (1982). The effect of context on the response of single units recorded from the hippocampal region of behaviourally trained monkeys. In C. Ajmone Marsan & H. Matthies (Eds.), *Neuronal plasticity and memory formation: Proceedings of the Vth International Neurobiological Symposium on Learning Memory.* New York: Raven.

Clark, A. J. M., Feldon, J., & Rawlins, J. N. P. (1992). Aspiration lesions of rat ventral hippocampus disinhibit responding in conditioned suppression or extinction, but spare latent inhibition and the partial reinforcement extinction effect. *Neuroscience, 48*, 821–829.

Clark, D. M., Salkovskis, P. M., Hackman, A., Middleton, H., Anastasides, P., & Gelder, M. (1994). A comparison of cognitive therapy, applied relaxation and imipramine in the treatment of panic disorder. *British Journal of Psychiatry, 164*, 759–769.

Craske, M. G., & Barlow, D. H. (1990). Nocturnal panic response to hyperventilation and carbon dioxide challenges. *Journal of Abnormal Psychology, 99*, 302–307.

Dantendorfer, K., Prayer, D., Kramer, J., Amering, M., Baischer, W., Berger, P., Schoder, M., Steinberger, K., Windhaber, J., Imhof, H., & Katsching, H. (in press). High frequency of EEG and MRI brain abnormalities in panic disorder. *Psychiatry Research Neuroimaging*.

Daum, I., Channon, S., Polkey, C. E., & Gray, J. A. (1991). Classical conditioning after temporal lobe lesions in man: Impairment in conditional discrimination. *Behavioral Neuroscience, 105*, 396–408.

Davidson, T. L., & Jarrard, L. E. (1993). A role for hippocampus in the utilization of hunger signals. *Behavioral and Neural Biology, 59*, 167–171.

Davis, M. (1992). The role of the amygdala in fear and anxiety. *Annual Review of Neuroscience, 15*, 353–375.

Deakin, J. F. W., & Graeff, F. G. (1991). 5-HT and mechanisms of defence. *Journal of Psychopharmacology, 5*, 305–315.

Dennett, D. C. (1991). *Consciousness explained*. Cambridge: Cambridge University Press.

Deutsch, J. A. (1964). *The structural basis of behaviour*. Cambridge: Cambridge University Press.

Dickinson, A. (1980). *Contemporary animal learning theory*. Cambridge: Cambridge University Press.

Drevets, W. C., Videen, T. O., MacLeod, A. K., Haller, J. W., & Raichle, M. E. (1992). PET images of blood flow changes during anxiety: Correction. *Science, 256*, 1696.

Eichenbaum, H., Otto, T., & Cohen, N. J. (1994). The functional components of the hippocampal memory system. *Behavioral and Brain Sciences, 17*, 449–518.

Eysenck, H. J. (1979). The conditioning model of neurosis. *Behavioral and Brain Sciences, 2*, 155–166.

Eysenck, H. J., & Eysenck, S. B. G. (1969). *The structure and measurement of personality*. London: Routledge & Kegan Paul.

Eysenck, H. J., & Rachman, S. J. (1965). *The causes and cures of neurosis*. London: Routledge & Kegan Paul.

Eysenck, M. W. (1992). The nature of anxiety. In A. Gale & M. W. Eysenck (Eds.), *Handbook of individual differences: Biological perspectives* (pp. 157–178). Chichester: Wiley.

Fanselow, M. S. (1991). The midbrain periaqueductal gray as a coordinator of action in response to fear and anxiety. In A. Depaulis & R. Bandler (Eds.), *The midbrain periaqueductal grey matter: Functional, anatomical and immunohistochemical organization*. New York: Plenum.

Feldon, J., & Gray, J. A. (1979a). Effects of medial and lateral septal lesions on the partial reinforcement extinction effect at one trial a day. *Quarterly Journal of Experimental Psychology, 31*, 653–674.

Feldon, J., & Gray, J. A. (1979b). Effects of medial and lateral septal lesions on the partial reinforcement extinction effect at short inter-trial intervals. *Quarterly Journal of Experimental Psychology, 31*, 675–690.

Feldon, J., Guillamon, A., Gray, J. A., De Wit, H., & McNaughton, N. (1979). Sodium amylobarbitone and responses to nonreward. *Quarterly Journal of Experimental Psychology, 31*, 19–50.

Fibiger, H. C., & Phillips, A. G. (1988). Mesocorticolimbic dopamine systems and reward. In P. W. Kalivas & C. B. Nemeroff (Eds.), *The mesolimbic dopamine system* (pp. 206–215). Bethesda MD: New York Academy of Sciences.

Flint, J., Corley, R., DeFries, J. C., Fulker, D. W., Gray, J. A., Miller, S., & Collins, A. C. (1995). Chromosomal mapping of three loci determining quantitative variation of susceptibility to anxiety in the mouse. *Science, 268*, 1432–1435.

Fowles, D. C. (1980). The three arousal model: Implications of Gray's two-factor learning theory for heart rate, electrodermal activity and psychopathy. *Psychophysiology, 17*, 87–104.

Fowles, D. C. (1995). A motivational theory of psychopathology. In W. Spaulding (Ed.), *Nebraska Symposium on Motivation: Integrated views of motivation, cognition and emotion*. Vol. 41. Lincoln: University of Nebraska Press.

Gaffan, D. (1977). Monkeys' recognition memory for complex pictures and the effect of fornix transection. *Quarterly Journal of Experimental Psychology, 29*, 505–514.

Gardner, C. R. (1988). Potential use of drugs modulating 5HT activity in the treatment of anxiety. *General Pharmacology, 19*, 347–356.

Goodman, W. K., Price, L. H., Delgado, P. L., Palumbo, J., Krystal, J. H., Nagy, L. M., Rasmussen, S. A., Heninger, G. R., & Charney, D. S. (1990). Specificity of serotonin reuptake inhibitors in the treatment of obsessive-compulsive disorder: Comparison of fluvoxamine and desipramine. *Archives of General Psychiatry, 47*, 577–585.

Gorman, J. M., Laszlo, P., & Klein, D. F. (1990). Biological models of panic disorder. In G. D. Burrows, M. Roth, & R. Noyes (Eds.), *Handbook of anxiety* (Vol. 3, pp. 59–139). Amsterdam: Elsevier Science Publishers.

Graeff, F. G. (1990). Brain defense systems and anxiety. In G. D. Burrows, M. Roth, & R. Noyes, (Eds.), *Handbook of anxiety* (Vol. 3, pp. 307–354). Amsterdam: Elsevier Science Publishers.

Graeff, F. G. (1991). Neurotransmitters in the dorsal periaqueductal gray and animal models of panic anxiety. In M. Briley & S. E. File (Eds.), *New concepts in anxiety* (pp. 288–312). London: Macmillan.

Graeff, F. G. (1993). Role of 5-HT in defensive behaviour and anxiety. *Reviews in the Neurosciences, 4*, 181–211.

Graeff, F. G. (1994). Neuroanatomy and neurotransmitter regulation of defensive behaviours and related emotions in mammals. *Brazilian Journal of Medical and Biological Research, 27*, 811–829.

Gray, J. A. (1967). Disappointment and drugs in the rat. *Advancement of Science, 23*, 595–605.

Gray, J. A. (1970). Sodium amobarbital, the hippocampal theta rhythm and the partial reinforcement extinction effect. *Psychological Review, 77*, 465–480.

Gray, J. A. (1971a). *The psychology of fear and stress*. London: Weidenfeld & Nicolson; New York: McGraw-Hill.

Gray, J. A. (1971b). The mind-brain identity theory as a scientific hypothesis. *Philosophical Quarterly, 21*, 247–253.

Gray, J. A. (1975). *Elements of a two-process theory of learning*. London: Academic.

Gray, J. A. (1976). The behavioural inhibition system: A possible substrate for anxiety. In M. P. Feldman & A. M. Broadhurst (Eds.), *Theoretical and experimental bases of behaviour modification* (pp. 3–41). London: Wiley.

Gray, J. A. (1977). Drug effects on fear and frustration: Possible limbic site of action of minor tranquillizers. In L. L. Iversen, S. D. Iversen & S. H. Snyder (Eds.), *Handbook of psychopharmacology* (Vol. 8, pp. 433–529). New York: Plenum.

Gray, J. A. (1982a). *The neuropsychology of anxiety: An enquiry into the functions of the septo-hippocampal system*. Oxford: Oxford University Press.

Gray, J. A. (1982b). Précis of "The neuropsychology of anxiety": An enquiry into the functions of the septo-hippocampal system. *Behavioral and Brain Sciences, 5*, 469–484.

Gray, J. A. (1982c). On the classification of the emotions. *Behavioral and Brain Sciences, 5*, 431–432.

Gray, J. A. (1987a). *The psychology of fear and stress* (2nd ed.). Cambridge: Cambridge University Press.

Gray, J. A. (1987b). The mind-brain identity theory as a scientific hypothesis: A second look. In C. Blakemore & S. Greenfield (Eds.), *Mindwaves* (pp. 461–483). Oxford: Blackwell.

Gray, J. A. (1990a). Brain systems that mediate both emotion and cognition. *Cognition and Emotion, 4*, 269–288.

Gray, J. A. (Ed.). (1990b). *Psychological aspects of relationships between emotion and cognition*. (Special issue of *Cognition and Emotion, 4*, 1161–1308). Hove UK: Lawrence Erlbaum Associates.

Gray, J. A. (1995a). A model of the limbic system and basal ganglia: Applications to anxiety and schizophrenia. In M. S. Gazzaniga (Ed.), *The cognitive neurosciences* (pp.1165–1176). Cambridge: MIT Press.

Gray, J. A. (1995b). The contents of consciousness: A neuropsychological conjecture. *Behavioral and Brain Sciences, 18*, 617–680.

Gray, J. A., & McNaughton, N. (1983). Comparison between the behavioural effects of septal and hippocampal lesions: A review. *Neuroscience and Biobehavioral Reviews, 7*, 119–188.

Gray, J. A., & Rawlins, J. N. P. (1986). Comparator and buffer memory: An attempt to integrate two models of hippocampal function. In R. L. Isaacson & K. H. Pribram (Eds.), *The hippocampus* (Vol 4, pp. 159–201). New York: Plenum.

Gray, J. A., Feldon, J. , Rawlins, J. N. P., Hemsley, D. R., & Smith, A. D. (1991a). The neuropsychology of schizophrenia. *Behavioral and Brain Sciences*, 14, 1–20.

Gray, J. A., Hemsley, D. R., Feldon, J., Gray, N. S., & Rawlins, J. N. P. (1991b). Schiz bits: Misses, mysteries and hits. *Behavioral and Brain Sciences*, 14, 56–84.

Gray, J. A., Joseph, M. H., Hemsley, D. R., Young, A. M. J., Warburton, E. C., Boulenguez, P., Grigoryan, G. A., Peters, S. L., Rawlins, J. N. P., Tai, C.-T., Yee, B. K., Cassaday, H., Weiner, I., Gal, G., Gusak, O., Joel, D., Shadach, E., Shalev, U., Tarrasch, R., & Feldon, J. (1995). The role of mesolimbic dopaminergic and retrohippocampal afferents to the nucleus accumbens in latent inhibition: Implications for schizophrenia. *Behavioural Brain Research*, 71, 19–31.

Haley, C. S., & Knott, S. A. (1992). A simple regression method for mapping quantitative trait loci in line crosses using flanking markers. *Heredity*, 69, 315–324.

Hebb, D. O. (1949). *The organization of behaviour*. New York: Wiley; London: Chapman & Hall.

Hernandez L., & Hoebel, B. G. (1988). Food reward and cocaine increase extracellular dopamine in the nucleus accumbens as measured by microdialysis. *Life Sciences*, 42, 1705–1712.

Hodgson, R., & Rachman, S. J. (1972). The effects of contamination and washing in obsessional patients. *Behaviour Research and Therapy*, 10, 111–117.

Hull, C. L. (1943). *Principles of behavior*. New York: Appleton-Century-Crofts.

Jakes, I. C. (in press). *Theoretical approaches to obsessive-compulsive disorder*. New York: Cambridge University Press.

Jarrard, L. E. (1991). On the neural basis of the spatial mapping system: Hippocampus versus hippocampal formation. *Hippocampus*, 2, 236–239.

Jarrard, L. E. (1993). On the role of the hippocampus in learning in memory in the rat. *Behavioral and Neural Biology*, 60, 9–26.

Jarrard, L. E., Feldon, J., Rawlins, J. N. P., Sinden, J. D., & Gray, J. A. (1986). The effects of intrahippocampal ibotenate on resistance to extinction after continuous or partial reinforcement. *Experimental Brain Research*, 61, 519–530.

Jones, E. G. (1975). Some aspects of the organisation of the thalamic reticular complex. *Journal of Comparative Neurobiology*, 162, 285–308.

Jung, M. W., Wiener, S. I., & McNaughton, B. L. (1994). Comparison of spatial firing characteristics of units in dorsal and ventral hippocampus of the rat. *Journal of Neuroscience*, 14, 7347–7356.

Kelley, A. E., & Domesick, V. B. (1982). The distribution of the projection from the hippocampal formation to the nucleus accumbens in the rat: An anterogradeand retrogade-horseradish peroxidase study. *Neuroscience*, 7, 2321–2335.

Kelly, P. H., Seviour, P. W., & Iversen, S. D. (1975). Amphetamine and apomorphine responses in the rat following 6–OHDA lesions of the nucleus accumbens septi and corpus striatum. *Brain Research*, 94, 507–522.

Kendler, K. S., Neale, M. C., Kessler, R. C., Heath, A. C., & Eaves, L. J. (1992a). Generalized anxiety disorder in women: A population-based twin study. *Archives of General Psychiatry, 49*, 267–272.

Kendler, K. S., Neale, M. C., Kessler, R. C., Heath, A. C., & Eaves, L. J. (1992b). The genetic epidemiology of phobias in women: The interrelationship of agoraphobia, social phobia, situational phobia and simple phobia. *Archives of General Psychiatry, 49*, 273–281.

Kendler, K. S., Neale, M. C., Kessler, R. C., Heath, A. C., & Eaves, L. J. (1992c). Major depression and generalized anxiety disorder: Same genes, (partly) different environments? *Archives of General Psychiatry, 49*, 716–722.

Klein, D. F. (1981). Anxiety re-conceptualized. In D. F. Klein & J. Rabkin (Eds.), *Anxiety: New research and changing concepts,* (pp. 235–263). New York: Raven.

Klein, D. F. (1993). False suffocation alarms, spontaneous panics and related conditions. An integrative hypothesis. *Archives of General Psychiatry, 50*, 306–317.

Klein, D. F., & Klein, H. M. (1989a). The definition and psychopharmacology of spontaneous panic and phobia: A critical review. I. In P. J. Tyrer (Ed.), *Psychopharmacology of anxiety* (pp. 135–162). New York: Oxford University Press.

Klein, D. F., & Klein, H. M. (1989b). The nosology, genetics and theory of spontaneous panic and phobia: A critical review. II. In P. J. Tyrer (Ed.), *Psychopharmacology of anxiety* (pp. 163–195). New York: Oxford University Press.

Klüver, H., & Bucy, P. C. (1937). Psychic blindness; and other symptoms following bilateral temporal lobectomy in rhesus monkeys. *American Journal of Physiology, 119*, 352–353.

Lahey, B. B., McBurnett, K., Loeber, R., & Hart, E. L. (1995). Psychobiology of conduct disorder. In G. P. Sholevar (Ed.), *Conduct disorders in children and adolescents: Assessments and interventions.* Washington DC: American Psychiatric Press.

LaPlane, D., Levasseur, M., Pillon, B., Dubois, B., Baulac, M., Mazoyer, B., Tran Dinh, S., Seite, G., Danze, F., & Baron, J. C. (1989). Obsessive-compulsive and other behavioural changes with bilateral basal ganglia lesions. *Brain, 112*, 699–725.

Lavin, A., & Grace, A. A. (1994). Modulation of dorsal thalamic cell activity by the ventral pallidum: Its role in the regulation of thalamocortical activity by the basal ganglia. *Synapse, 18*, 104–127.

LeDoux, J. E. (1987). Emotion. In V. Mountcastle (Ed.), *Handbook of physiology: The nervous system, Vol. 5, Higher functions of the brain* (pp. 419–459). Bethesda MD: American Physiological Society.

LeDoux, J. E. (1992). Brain mechanisms of emotion and emotional learning. *Current Opinion in Neurobiology, 2*, 191–197.

LeDoux, J. E. (1994). Emotion, memory and the brain. *Scientific American, 270*, 32–39.

LeDoux, J. E. (1995). In search of an emotional system in the brain: Leaping from fear to emotion and consciousness. In M. S. Gazzaniga (Ed.), *The cognitive neurosciences* (pp. 1049–1062). Cambridge: MIT Press.

Lipp, H.-P., Schwegler, H., Crusio, W. E., Wolfer, D. P., Leisinger-Trigona, M. C., Heimrich, B., & Driscoll, P. (1989). Using genetically-defined rodent strains for the identification of hippocampal traits relevant for two-way avoidance behavior: A non-invasive approach. *Experientia, 45*, 845–859.

Marks, I. M. (1969). *Fears and phobias*. London: Heinemann.

Mayes, A. R. (1988). *Human organic memory disorders*. Cambridge: Cambridge University Press.

McNally, R. J. (1996). Cognitive bias in the anxiety disorders. This volume.

McNaughton, N. (1989a). *Biology and emotion*. Cambridge: Cambridge University Press.

McNaughton, N. (1989b). Anxiety: One label for many processes. *New Zealand Journal of Psychology, 18*, 51–59.

McNaughton, N., & Feldon, J. (1980). Spontaneous alteration of body turns and place: Differential effects of amylobarbitone, scopolamine and septal lesions. *Psychopharmacology, 68*, 201–206.

McNaughton, N., James, D. T. D., Stewart, J., Gray, J. A., Valero, I., & Drewnowski, A. (1977). Septal driving of hippocampal theta rhythm as a function of frequency in the male rat: Effects of drugs. *Neuroscience, 2*, 1019–1027.

McNaughton, N., & Morris, R. G. M. (1987). Chlordiazepoxide, an anxiolytic benzodiazepine, impairs place navigation in the rat. *Behavioural Brain Research, 24*, 39–46.

McNaughton, N., & Morris, R. G. M. (1992). Buspirone produces a dose-related impairment in spatial navigation. *Pharmacology, Biochemistry and Behaviour, 43*, 167–171.

McNaughton, N., Richardson, J., & Gore, C. (1986). Hippocampal slow waves generated by reticular stimulation: Common effects of anxiolytic drugs. *Neuroscience, 19*, 899–903.

Mathews, A., & MacLeod, C. (1994). Cognitive approaches to emotion and emotional disorders. *Annual Review of Psychology, 45*, 25–50.

Miller, N. E. (1951). Learnable drives and rewards. In S. S. Stevens (Ed.), *Handbook of experimental psychology* (pp. 435–472). New York: Wiley.

Miller, R. (1991). *Cortico-hippocampal interplay and the representation of contexts in the brain*. Berlin: Springer-Verlag.

Milner, B. (1970). Memory and the medial temporal regions of the brain. In K. H. Pribram & D. E. Broadbent (Eds.), *Biology of memory* (pp. 29–50). New York: Academic.

Mineka, S., & Zinbarg, R. E. (1996). Conditioning and ethological models of anxiety disorders. This volume.

Mogenson, G. J., & Nielsen, M. (1984). A study of the contribution of hippocampal-accumbens-subpallidal projections to locomotor activity. *Behavioral and Neural Biology, 42*, 52–60.

Morris, R. G. M., Garrud, P., Rawlins, J. N. P., & O'Keefe, J. (1982). Place navigation is impaired in rats with hippocampal lesions. *Nature, 297,* 681–683.

Morris, R. G. M., Hagan, J. J., & Rawlins, J. N. P. (1986). Allocentric spatial learning by hippocampectomised rats: A further test of the "spatial mapping" and "working memory" theories of hippocampal function. *Quarterly Journal of Experimental Psychology, 38,* 365–395.

Mowrer, O. H. (1960). *Learning and behaviour.* New York: Wiley.

Nadel, L. (1991). The hippocampus and space revisited. *Hippocampus, 1,* 221–229.

Nashold, B. S. Jr., Wilson, W. P., & Slaughter, G. S. (1969). Sensations evoked by stimulation in the midbrain of man. *Journal of Neurosurgery, 30,* 14–24.

Nordahl, T. E., Semple, W. E., Gross, M., Mellman, T. A., Stein, M. B., Goyer, P., King, A. C., Uhde, T. W., & Cohen, R. M. (1990). *Neuropsychopharmacology, 3,* 261–272.

Oades, R. D. (1985). The role of NA in tuning and DA in switching between signals in the CNS. *Neuroscience and Biobehavioral Review, 9,* 261–282.

O'Donnell, P., & Grace, A. A. (1995). Synaptic interactions among excitatory afferents to nucleus accumbens neurons: Hippocampal gating of prefrontal cortical input. *Journal of Neuroscience, 15,* 3622–3639.

O'Keefe, J., & Nadel, L. (1978). *The hippocampus as a cognitive map.* Oxford: Clarendon.

Olton, D. S., Becker, J. T., & Handelmann, G. E. (1979). Hippocampus, space and memory. *Behavioral and Brain Sciences, 2,* 352–359.

Ono, T., & Nishijo, H. (1992). Neurophysiological basis of the Klüver-Bucy syndrome: Responses of monkey amygdaloid neurons to biologically significant objects. In J. P. Aggleton (Ed.), *The amygdala: Neurobiological aspects of emotion, memory, and mental dysfunction* (pp. 167–190). New York: Wiley-Liss.

Panickar, K. M., & McNaughton, N. (1991). Dose-response analysis of the effects of buspirone on rearing in rats. *Journal of Psychopharmacology, 5,* 72–76.

Panksepp, J. (1982a). Towards a general psychobiological theory of emotions. *Behavioral and Brain Sciences, 5,* 407–467.

Panksepp, J. (1982b). Anxiety viewed from the upper brainstem: Though panic and fear yield trepidation, should both be called anxiety? *Behavioral and Brain Sciences, 5,* 495–496.

Panksepp, J. (1990). Gray zones at the emotion/cognition interface: A commentary. In J. A. Gray (Ed.), *Cognition and Emotion.* Special issue: Psychobiological aspects of relationships between cognition and emotion (pp. 289–302). Hove UK: Lawrence Erlbaum Associates.

Parmeggiani, P. L., Azzaroni, A., & Lenzi, P. (1971). On the functional significance of the circuit of Papez. *Brain Research, 30,* 357–374.

Pauls, D. L., Towbin, K. E., Leckman, J. F., Zahner, G. E. P., & Cohen, D. J. (1986). Gilles de la Tourette's syndrome and obsessive-compulsive disorder. *Archives of General Psychiatry, 43,* 1180–1182.

Phillipson, O. T., & Griffiths, A. C. (1985). The topographical order of inputs to nucleus accumbens in the rat. *Neuroscience, 16,* 275–296.

Plomin, R., Owen, M. J., & McGuffin, P. (1994). The genetic basis of complex human behaviors. *Science, 264,* 1733–1738.

Rachman, S. J., & Hodgson, R. (1978). *Obsessions and compulsions.* New York: Prentice-Hall.

Rapoport, J. L. (1989, March). The biology of obsessions and compulsions. *Scientific American,* 63–69.

Rapoport, J. L., & Wise, S. P. (1988). Obsessive-compulsive disorder: Evidence for a basal ganglia dysfunction. *Psychopharmacology Bulletin, 24,* 380–384.

Rawlins, J. N. P (1985). Associations across time: The hippocampus as a temporary memory store. *Behavioral and Brain Sciences, 8,* 479–528.

Rawlins, J. N. P., Feldon, J., & Gray, J. A. (1980). The effects of hippocampectomy and of fimbria section upon the partial reinforcement extinction effect in rats. *Experimental Brain Research, 38,* 273–283.

Rawlins, J. N. P, Lyford, G. L., & Seferiades, A. (1991). Does it still make sense to develop nonspatial theories of hippocampal function? *Hippocampus, 1,* 283–286.

Rawlins, J. N. P, Lyford, G. L., Seferiades, A., Deacon, R. M. J., & Cassaday, H. J. (1993). Critical determinants of nonspatial working memory deficits in rats with conventional lesions of the hippocampal formation or fornix. *Behavioural Neuroscience, 107,* 236–249.

Reiman, E. M., Raichle, M. E., Bauler, F. K., Herscovich, P., & Robins, E. (1984). A focal brain abnormality in panic disorder, a severe form of anxiety. *Nature, 310,* 683–685.

Reiman, E. M., Raichle, M. E., Robins, E., Butler, F. K., Hersovich, P., Fox, P., & Perlmutter, J. (1986). The application of positron emission tomography to the study of panic disorder. *American Journal of Psychiatry, 143,* 469–477.

Ridley, R. M., Timothy, C. J., MacLean, C. J., & Baker, H. F. (1995). Conditonal learning and memory impairments following neurotoxic lesion of the CA1 field of the hippocampus. *Neuroscience, 67,* 263–275.

Rodgers, R. J., & Cooper, S. J. (Eds.). (1991). *5-HT_{1A} agonists, 5-HT_3 antagonists and benzodiazepines: Their comparative behavioural pharmacology.* Chichester UK: Wiley.

Rolls, E. (1986a). Information representation, processing and storage in the brain: Analysis at the single neuron level. In R. Ritter & S. Ritter (Eds.), *Neural and molecular mechanisms of learning.* Stuttgart: Springer-Verlag.

Rolls, E. (1986b). A theory of emotion and its application to understanding the neural basis of emotion. In Y. Oomura, (Ed.), *Emotions: Neural and chemical control.* Japan Scientific Societies. Basel: Karger.

Rolls, E. (1990). A theory of emotion, and its application to understanding the neural basis of emotion. In J. A. Gray (Ed.), *Psychobiological aspects of relationships between emotion and cognition.* Special issue of *Emotion and Cognition* (pp. 161–190). Hillsdale NJ: Erlbaum.

Rolls, E. (1992). Neurophysiology and functions of the primate amygdala. In J. P. Aggleton, (Ed.), *The amygdala: Neurobiological aspects of emotion, memory, and mental dysfunction* (pp. 143–165). New York:Wiley-Liss.

Rolls, E. T., & Williams, G. W. (1987). Sensory and movement-related neuronal activity in different regions of the primate striatum. In J. S. Schneider & T. I. Kidsky (Eds.), *Basal ganglia and behaviour: Sensory aspects and motor functioning* (pp. 37–59). Toronto: Hans Huber.

Röper, G., & Rachman, S. J. (1976). Obsessional compulsive checking: Experimental replication and development. *Behaviour Research and Therapy, 14,* 23–32.

Sartory, G., MacDonald, R., & Gray, J. A. (1990). Effects of diazepam on approach, self-reported fear and psychophysiological responses in snake phobics. *Behaviour Research and Therapy, 28,* 273–282.

Seligman, M. E. P. (1971). Phobias and preparedness. *Behavior Therapy, 2,* 307–320.

Shafran, R. L. (1995). *An investigation into the cognitive-behavioral model of obsessive compulsive disorder: Can this be reconciled with a neurological deficit model?* Ph.D. thesis, University of London.

Sinden, J. D., Jarrard, L. E., & Gray, J. A. (1988). The effects of intra-subicular ibotenate on resistance to extinction after continuous or partial reinforcement. *Experimental Brain Research, 73,* 315–319.

Sinden, J. D., Rawlins, J. N. P, & Gray, J. A. (1986). Selective cytotoxic lesions of the hippocampal formation and DRL performance in rats. *Behavioural Neuroscience, 100,* 320–329.

Somogyi, P., Bolam, J. P., Totterdell, S., & Smith, A. D. (1981). Monosynaptic input from the nucleus accumbens-ventral striatum region to retrogradely labelled nigrostiatal neurones. *Brain Research, 217,* 245–263.

Swedo, S. E., Schapiro, M., Grady, C., Cheslow, D. L., Leonard, H. L., Kumar, A., Friedland, R., Rapoport, S., & Rapoport, J. L. (1989). Cerebral glucose metabolism in childhood onset obsessive-compulsive disorder. *Archives of General Psychiatry, 46,* 518–523.

Swerdlow, N. R., & Koob, G. F. (1987). Dopamine, schizophrenia, mania and depression: Toward a unified hypothesis of cortico-striato-pallidothalamic function. *Behavioral and Brain Sciences, 10,* 197–245.

Taylor, J. G., & Alavi, F. N. (1993). Mathematical analysis of a competitive network for attention. In J. G. Taylor (Ed.), *Mathematical approaches to neural networks* (pp. 341–382). Amsterdam: Elsevier Science Publishers.

Thrasher, S. M., Dalgleish, T., & Yule, W. (1994). Information processing in post-traumatic stress disorder. *Behaviour Research and Therapy, 32,* 247–254.

Totterdell, S., & Smith, A. D. (1989). Convergence of hippocampal and dopaminergic input onto identified neurons in the nucleus accumbens of the rat. *Journal of Chemical Neuroanatomy, 2,* 285–298.

Vinogradova, O. S. (1975). Functional organization of the limbic system in the process of registration of information: Facts and hypotheses. In R. L. Isaacson & K. H. Pribram (Eds.), *The hippocampus, Vol. 2, Neurophysiology and behavior* (pp. 1–70). New York: Plenum.

Warrington, E. K., & Weiskrantz, L. (1968). A study of learning and retention in amnesic patients. *Neuropsychologia, 6*, 283–291.

Weiner, I. (1991). The accumbens-substantia nigra pathway, mismatch and amphetamine. *Behavioral and Brain Sciences, 14*, 54–55.

Weiskrantz, L., & Warrington, E. K. (1975). The problem of the amnesic syndrome in man and animals. In R. L. Isaacson & K. H. Pribram (Eds.), *The hippocampus, Vol. 2, Neurophysiology and behavior* (pp. 411–428). New York: Plenum.

Whishaw I. Q. (1995). Data presented at the 19th Winter Conference on the Neurobiology of Learning and Memory, Park City UT, January 1995.

Williams, M. N., & Faull, R. L. M. (1988). The nigrotectal projection and tectospinal neurons in the rat: A light and electron microscopic study demonstrating a monosynaptic nigral input to identified tectospinal neurons. *Neuroscience, 25*, 533–562.

Wise, S. P., & Rapoport, J. L. (1989). Obsessive-compulsive disorders: Is it basal ganglia dysfunction? In J. L.Rapoport (Ed.), *Obsessive-compulsive disorder in children and adolescents* (pp. 327–346). Washington DC: American Psychiatric Press.

Worden, R. (1992). Navigation by fragment fitting: A theory of hippocampal function. *Hippocampus, 2*, 165–188.

Yee, B. K., Feldon, J., & Rawlins, J. N. P. (1995). Latent inhibition in rats is abolished by NMDA-induced neuronal loss in the retrohippocampal region but this lesion effect can be prevented by systemic haloperidol treatment. *Behavioural Neuroscience, 109*, 227–240.

Young, A. M. J, Joseph, M. H., & Gray, J. A. (1992). Increased dopamine release *in vivo* in nucleus accumbens and caudate nucleus of the rat during drinking: A microdialysis study. *Neuroscience, 48*, 871–876.

Young, A. M. J., Joseph, M. H., & Gray, J. A. (1993). Latent inhibition of conditioned dopamine release in the nucleus accumbens. *Neuroscience, 54*, 5–9.

Conditioning and Ethological Models of Anxiety Disorders: Stress-in-Dynamic-Context Anxiety Models

Susan Mineka
Northwestern University

Richard Zinbarg
University of Oregon

Early in this century two starkly contrasting views regarding the origins of fears, phobias, and anxiety states were put forth, one by Freud (1926/1936) and the other by Pavlov (1927) and Watson (Watson & Rayner, 1920). These two views still represent two of the major different ways psychologists think about the origins of fears and anxiety disorders even today—although now there are also biological as well as cognitive approaches. According to Freud and other theorists of the psychoanalytic tradition, anxiety is viewed as a reaction to, and a signal of, unconscious memories of real or imagined dangers that are often associated with infantile wishes (1926/1936). By contrast, according to Pavlov and Watson, fears and anxiety disorders were seen as arising out of simple classical conditioning of fear when neutral objects

The authors would like to thank the following individuals for their comments on an earlier version of this chapter: Caroline Blanchard, Dianne Chambless, Robert Hendersen, and Steve Maier. We are particularly indebted to Robert Hendersen for suggesting the terms "Stress-in-Total-Isolation Anxiety models" and "Stress-in-Dynamic-Context Anxiety models."

or situations have been paired with trauma. Later theorists in this tradition such as Mowrer (1947, 1960) and Eysenck and Rachman (1965) elaborated on this view and developed an avoidance model of these disorders, in which avoidance responses were seen as motivated by classically conditioned fear, and reinforced by fear or anxiety reduction. As the distinctions between the different anxiety disorders became better understood, the avoidance model was seen as especially compelling for specific and social phobias, agoraphobia, and obsessive-compulsive disorder because of the prominent and persistent avoidance behaviors that characterize these disorders.

One apparent attraction of the psychoanalytic view is that it appears to capture, at least in a post hoc fashion, the richness and diversity of factors that go into the origins and maintenance of people's fears and anxieties. Indeed, this rich interpretive framework that it provides has been part of the continuing source of interest in this theory for many clinicians. But an obvious weakness of this view is that it has not put forth many hypotheses or propositions that are scientifically testable through empirical research. The strengths and weaknesses of the behavioral approach of Pavlov, Watson, and others are in some sense the opposite. Because this approach stems from an empirical tradition, many hypotheses and propositions of the behavioral approach have been tested. Unfortunately, some of this research has revealed what appear to be major weaknesses of the original traditional conditioning approaches (e.g., Rachman, 1978, 1990). These weaknesses can be aptly summarized by stating that the early behavioral approaches do not seem adequately to account for the richness and diversity of factors that go into the development and maintenance of people's fears and anxieties.

In this chapter we argue that the central shortcoming of traditional behavioral models has been their failure to consider the dynamic context in which stressors occur in a person's life. By ignoring the powerful effect of dynamic contextual factors on the impact of those stressors, behavioral models have appeared to be much more simplistic than they need to be and to have far less explanatory power than we know they can have. We refer to the more traditional models as Stress-in-Total-Isolation Anxiety models (SITIA models). We will present an alternative model in which we show that stress must always be considered in a dynamic context rather than in isolation in determining the outcome of exposure to stress. The relevant dynamic contextual factors that we will consider include constitutional factors such as temperament, past experiential history (including general factors such as a history of exposure to uncontrollable life events as well as specific factors such as prior traumatic conditioning events), current contextual factors at the time of a stressor (such as whether there are already reliable predictors of the stressor, or the nature of the conditioned stimulus relative to the nature of the unconditioned stimulus, or whether the stressor can be controlled), and future modification of the impact of the stressor (through processes such as forgetting and other memory modifications, as well as through later experiences with other stressors). We refer to these models as the Stress-in-Dynamic-Context Anxiety models (SIDCA models).

The authors of DSM-III-R and DSM-IV (American Psychiatric Association, 1987, 1994) have identified six different anxiety disorders, which share some overlapping features but also have distinctive characteristics. They are specific phobias, social phobias, panic disorder with or without agoraphobia, generalized anxiety disorder, posttraumatic stress disorder, and obsessive-compulsive disorder. In presenting SIDCA models we will review research and thinking from the contemporary conditioning and ethological literatures—both animal and human—that are relevant to understanding important features of each of these disorders. We are particularly attuned to recent developments in conditioning research and theory that greatly expand the scope and explanatory power of conditioning models because they allow the development of SIDCA models. Although none of the research to be presented provides as yet a full-fledged model of the etiology, symptomatology, therapy, and prevention of these disorders as advocated by theorists such as Seligman (1974) and McKinney (1974), we present many interesting and compelling mini-models that can be useful in illuminating certain aspects of many disorders for which full-fledged animal models are not yet or may never be available. Mini-models may be defined as behavioral or cognitive phenomena studied in animals or humans (where the behaviors are experimentally manipulated through either behavioral or physiological manipulations or are carefully and systematically observed, as done by ethologists) that illuminate certain features of the disorder, such as its etiology, *or* its maintenance, *or* its symptomatology, *or* its prevention, *or* its treatment (Marks, 1977; Mineka, 1985a). Thus mini-models may help us to understand only one or a few prominent or cardinal features of a disorder; however, it is understood that in reality such factors would act in conjunction or interaction with other factors in producing the full-fledged human disorder. Such interactions form the core of SIDCA models, and although the exact nature of the interactions of causal factors that are likely to be involved in the etiology of these disorders are not always understood at the present time, enough is known to present hypotheses for future research.

When discussing animal models it should be acknowledged that the degree of cross-species similarity on these criteria may depend on the level of analysis one adopts. Substantial differences between species should be expected when focusing on either observable behaviors (e.g., rats commonly defecate when confronted by threat but people rarely do) or the physical properties of the stimuli that are involved in the etiology of the syndromes under investigation (e.g., people sometimes develop anxiety after reading about threat, but we doubt that the written word has ever contributed to the development of anxiety in animals). At the same time, one could reasonably argue that these symptoms that differ at a surface level are produced by underlying processes that are similar across the species. Thus it is reasonable to expect that a conditioned fear response in animals that follows direct traumatic experiences with an aversive stimulus could be argued to be mediated by the same mechanism that mediates the development of anxiety in people after reading about threat. In fact, Wagner's (1979, 1981) Standard-Operating-Procedures theory of conditioning suggests a plausible candidate for such a mechanism—the joint rehearsal in short-term or working memory of the representations of stimuli that had previously been affectively neutral with the representation of a highly aversive stimulus.

Clearly, drawing inferences regarding hypothesized constructs or mechanisms that are not directly observable is more difficult and challenging than simple stimulus-response analyses that focus only on observable variables. By definition, the theorist interested in a latent construct implicitly acknowledges imperfection in his or her measures by drawing a distinction between the latent constructs he or she is interested in and his or her observed measures. Inferences about latent constructs and mechanisms can be on firm footing, however, by "triangulating" on them—that is, by employing multiple measures (either across studies or within a single study) that are heterogeneous with respect to their sources of bias/error (Campbell & Fiske, 1959; Cook & Campbell, 1979). Thus in our presentation of mini-models of the anxiety disorders, we emphasize underlying constructs and mechanisms. As more information about other differences between the species involved becomes known, it is possible that these mini-models may even come to be regarded as similar to the human phenomenon on all the criteria suggested by Seligman (1974) and McKinney (1974), which include similarities of symptomatology, etiology, therapy, and prevention.

Specific Phobias

Specific phobias involve intense or irrational fears of various objects or situations, which usually lead to a good deal of avoidance behavior. The traditional view of Pavlov and Watson was that phobias are simply intense, classically conditioned fears that result when a neutral object is paired with a traumatic event. By the 1960s, when it became known that classically conditioned fear in the laboratory does not show the high resistance to extinction seen with phobias, theorists such as Eysenck and Rachman (1965) proposed an avoidance learning model of phobia acquisition and maintenance. According to the then prevailing two-process theory of avoidance learning, classically conditioned fear motivates the learning of avoidance responses, which are reinforced or strengthened by a reduction in fear. The apparent superiority of this model arose from the fact that avoidance responses conditioned in the laboratory are notoriously resistant to extinction, as are phobias. As we have argued elsewhere (Mineka, 1985a; Mineka & Zinbarg, 1991; see also Seligman, 1971), however, there are several problems with the avoidance model of phobias and today most theorists favor a modified version of the simpler classical conditioning model (see "Selective Associations," below).

For the past 20 to 25 years, conditioning models of specific phobias have been severely criticized for a variety of reasons (and similar criticisms would apply to the avoidance models). The major problems with the traditional behavioral approaches stem from their having been de-

Table 1

A Summary of the Shortcomings of Stress-in-Total-Isolation Anxiety (SITIA) Models and How They Are Addressed by Stress-in-Dynamic-Context Anxiety (SIDCA) Models

Shortcomings of SITIA Models	SIDCA Model Responses
1. Many cases of phobias and other anxiety disorders have no known traumatic conditioning history.	1. Fear and anxiety can also be acquired through observational conditioning.
2. Many people who do have a traumatic conditioning history do not develop phobias or other anxiety disorders.	2. Temperament and a multitude of experiential variables occurring before, during, or following a traumatic or an observational conditioning experience affect the amount of fear and anxiety that is experienced at the time and that is acquired and maintained into the future.
3. Fears and phobias do not occur to a random arbitrary group of objects or situations.	3. Primates and humans seem to have a biologically based preparedness to more easily associate aversive events with certain objects or situations that were dangerous to our early ancestors.
4. Phobias and other anxiety disorders often appear to be resistant to extinction and may even overgeneralize with the passage of time.	4. (a) Responses conditioned to fear-relevant objects are more resistant to extinction than responses conditioned to fear-irrelevant objects. (b) Conditioned fears that have been extinguished can be reinstated through exposure to noncontingent traumatic events. (c) Simple mental rehearsal of a US can result in increased CR strength. (d) Generalization gradients around a CS+ flatten over time whereas a CS- often loses its fear inhibitory properties over time. (e) Safety signals and avoidance responses may protect a conditioned fear response from extinction.
5. The cognitive processes associated with some anxiety disorders are more complex than traditional models could explain, e.g., the emo-	5. Compound and contextual cues often affect the amount of anxiety and fear that is acquired or displayed; some stimuli may serve as "occasion

Table 1 Continued

Shortcomings of SITIA Models	SIDCA Model Responses
tional reacton to an anxiety/fear trigger is often dependent on contextual factors, and not all cues present during traumatic events become effective CS+s.	setters" that can turn on or turn off conditioned fear even though the occasion setter does not itself elicit or inhibit conditioned fear.
6. Animal models cannot model symptoms that are dependent on self-report (i.e., worry, obsessions, flashbacks, intrusive thoughts, or nightmares).	6. Although some of the surface-level symptoms of anxiety disorders cannot be modeled in animals, it may be possible to model their underlying mechanisms. For example, interpreted within the framework of Wagner's SOP (1981) model of conditioning, conditioned fear responses can model some of the reexperiencing symptoms of PTSD and important aspects of other reexperiencing symptoms.

veloped in the tradition of SITIA models. This was, in part, because Pavlovian methodology dictated that naive animals be placed in soundproof rooms where they were isolated from the experimenter and from noises, smells, or lights that were extraneous to the conditioning process. Today, however, advances in knowledge about the theoretical and empirical foundations of conditioning demand that conditioning models of fear be viewed as a subset of SIDCA models.

The majority of the criticisms of conditioning models from the SITIA tradition can be placed in one of four categories. The first problem comes from clinical observations that in many cases people with these disorders have no known traumatic conditioning history. If so many individuals with fears and phobias have no known traumatic conditioning history, how can we account for the origins of their fears and phobias? The second problem with SITIA conditioning models of phobias is that they have difficulty accounting for why so many individuals who do undergo traumatic experiences do *not* develop phobias. In other words, why do more people with traumatic conditioning histories not have fears and phobias (Rachman, 1990)? The third problem stems from the failure of these models to account for why fears and phobias do not occur to a random arbitrary group of objects or situations associated with trauma, as clearly

explicated by Seligman (1971) in his well-known paper on preparedness and phobias. Finally, a fourth problem with SITIA conditioning
models is their failure adequately to account for why some fears are
so persistent and why some even increase and overgeneralize with
the passage of time. That is, given the laws of extinction of conditioned responses, why are fears and phobias often so resistant to extinction and why do they often generalize to new objects and situations with the passage of time? We now review contemporary
conditioning research in the tradition of SIDCA models that resolves
each of these problems with SITIA conditioning models. (See Table
1, points 1–4, for a summary of these criticisms.)

VICARIOUS CONDITIONING OF FEARS AND PHOBIAS

How can SIDCA conditioning models account for the origins of fears
and phobias in individuals with no known traumatic conditioning
history? For some years it has been speculated that vicarious or observational conditioning experiences may play an important role in
the origins of some fears and phobias. Numerous studies have
shown that human subjects do acquire conditioned responses simply through observing another human model ostensibly receiving
shock in the presence of some neutral stimulus (see Green & Osborne, 1985, for a review). These studies, however, have all involved
mild conditioning of autonomic responses in single-session laboratory experiments, with no tests for maintenance of the conditioning
days or weeks later. Thus these studies do not answer the question
of whether strong and persistent fears such as occur in full-blown
phobias can also be conditioned observationally. One line of evidence suggesting that they can comes from studies that have asked
phobic subjects detailed questions about how their phobias came
about. Although retrospective recall is certainly not an infallible
measure, the results of several studies provide some support for this
hypothesis. For example, Öst and Hugdahl (1981) found that about
17% of specific phobics (40% of animal phobics) recalled a vicarious
conditioning incident as having been involved in the origins of their
specific phobia. In addition, Merckelbach and associates (1989)
found that 53% of their phobics recalled a combination of direct and

vicarious conditioning processes (rather than either alone) as having contributed to the onset of their phobia. Moreover, there is now good experimental evidence stemming from a primate model of fear conditioning that strong and persistent phobiclike fears can be learned through observation alone.

Mineka and Cook and colleagues conducted a series of experiments which demonstrated rapid, strong, and persistent observational conditioning of snake fear in rhesus monkeys (Cook & Mineka, 1987, 1989, 1990; Cook, Mineka, Wolkenstein, & Laitsch, 1985; Mineka & Cook, 1986, 1993; Mineka, Davidson, Cook, & Keir, 1984b). In most of these experiments laboratory-reared young adult monkeys watched unrelated wild-reared monkeys reacting fearfully in the presence of live and toy snakes and nonfearfully in the presence of neutral objects. The lab-reared monkeys did not show a fear of snakes during an initial pretest, and the majority of them rapidly acquired an intense fear of snakes as a result of the observational conditioning sessions (Cook et al., 1985; Mineka et al., 1984b). Indeed, the observers showed levels of fear on the posttest that were nearly as strong as those of the wild-reared monkeys, who had presumably acquired their fear in the wild many years earlier (Mineka, Keir, & Price, 1980). Furthermore, this acquired fear did not show significant signs of diminution over a three-month interval. One additional experiment showed that lab-reared monkeys could acquire the fear simply through watching a color videotape of a model monkey behaving fearfully in the presence of snakes (Cook & Mineka, 1990, Experiment 1). The latter finding is important because it suggests that humans may also be susceptible to acquiring fears vicariously through movies and television rather than simply through observing live models in vivo.

Thus conditioning models from the SITIA tradition paid insufficient attention to the important role that observational or vicarious conditioning can play in the origins of fears and phobias (see Table 1, point 1). In other words, the context of fear conditioning need not include direct experience with an unconditioned traumatic stimulus. Nevertheless, it is also interesting that the combined results of several of these experiments support the hypothesis that the mechanisms involved in observational conditioning may be very similar to those involved in direct traumatic conditioning (see Mineka & Cook, 1993, for a detailed discussion), rather than involving a separate "pathway" to fear acquisition as has been suggested by Rachman (1978, 1990).

SOURCES OF INDIVIDUAL DIFFERENCES IN THE ACQUISITION OF FEARS AND PHOBIAS

The second problem with SITIA conditioning models is that they fail to account for why not all individuals who undergo traumatic experiences acquire phobias. For example, both Di Nardo, Guzy, and Bak (1988) and Ollendick and King (1991) have noted that many non-phobics have had traumatic experiences in the presence of some potentially phobic objects and yet not acquired a fear or phobia. In addition, Rachman (1978, 1990) argues that conditioning theory cannot account for why so few people acquired lasting fears or phobias during the air raids and bombings of World War II. Although such findings may seem puzzling from the perspective of SITIA conditioning models, they are predicted by SIDCA models (see Table 1, point 2).

Part of the explanation for why only some people who have had traumatic experiences acquire fears and phobias undoubtedly involves genetic and temperamental factors. Theorists ranging from Pavlov to Eysenck and Kagan have noted that personality and temperamental variables affect the dynamics of conditioning and the origins of fear (see Mineka & Zinbarg, 1991, for a review; see also "Social Phobia" section of this chapter). Temperamental variables are incorporated by SIDCA models as part of the dynamic context in which a traumatic or observational conditioning experience occurs but only rarely by SITIA models.

In addition, SIDCA models explicitly acknowledge that much of the variance in the outcome of a traumatic conditioning experience is accounted for by experiential variables that also constitute an important part of the context. Models from the SIDCA tradition note that it is well-known that a multitude of experiential variables occur before, during, or following a traumatic event or an observational fear conditioning experience that can act singly or in combination to affect the amount of fear that is experienced, acquired, or maintained over time (Mineka, 1985a, b; Mineka & Zinbarg, 1991). Thus SIDCA models underscore that to understand why only some people develop fears or phobias, it is important to understand a wide range of experiential variables on which individuals undergoing the same trauma may differ—one very important aspect of the dynamic context in which conditioning occurs. That this point was not acknowledged by SITIA models may not be too surprising given that traditional Pavlovian methodologies dictated that naive animals be studied in isolated conditioning chambers. Although this methodology was initially developed for good reasons (e.g., to study the fundamentals of conditioning without extraneous potentially confounding variables such as prior experiences on which animals might differ), there were profound dangers hidden in extrapolating directly from the results of such studies to how conditioning experiences might affect humans who were neither "naive" nor isolated from the world during conditioning. SIDCA models explicitly acknowledge such complexities.

One important variable affecting fear conditioning is the amount of prior experience the organism has had with the to-be-conditioned stimulus. For example, the well-known phenomenon of latent inhibition demonstrates that prior exposure to a conditioned stimulus (CS) (before the CS and unconditioned stimulus [US] are ever paired together) reduces the amount of subsequent conditioning to the CS (e.g., Lubow, 1973; Mackintosh, 1983). Using their observational conditioning paradigm, Mineka and Cook (1986) explored whether one would see even stronger attenuation of fear conditioning if the prior exposure to a CS had occurred in the context of watching a nonfearful model monkey behaving nonfearfully with snakes (as opposed to the latent inhibition procedure of simply exposing the observer monkey to the snake without a nonfearful model). Their results showed that prior exposure to a nonfearful monkey behaving nonfearfully with snakes prevented the acquisition of fear on subsequent exposure to a fearful model. Such results may help to account for why correlations between parents' fears and children's fears are not as high as one might expect given our results showing how robust the observational conditioning phenomenon seems to be (Emmelkamp, 1982; Marks, 1987). Extensive preexposure to a nonfearful parent or peer behaving nonfearfully to the phobic object or situation of the other parent may immunize a child against the effects of later seeing the fearful or phobic parent behaving fearfully with that object. Or, put in the context of SIDCA models, people will differ in whether they acquire fear of some object during an observational conditioning experience at least partly as a function of their different prior experiences with that object.

A second experiential variable that is of importance in determining individuals' reactions to frightening and traumatic situations is their history of control over important aspects of their environment. Developmental psychologists have long argued that an infant's experience with control over important aspects of its environment promotes secure attachment relationships, exploration of novel events, less fearful reactions to strange or arousing stimuli, and the ability to cope with transient uncontrollable stressful experiences (e.g., Lewis & Goldberg, 1969; Watson, 1979; White, 1959). Evidence supporting this proposition in human infants comes largely from correlational studies. One experiment with infant rhesus monkeys that manipulated control in an experimental fashion over a one-year period, however, supports the importance of early experience with controlling important outcomes in affecting the ability to cope with transient stressful and frightening situations. This study (Mineka, Gunnar, & Champoux, 1986) explored this question by rearing baby monkeys in controllable (Masters) versus uncontrollable (Yoked) environments for the first 10 to 12 months of life. Then the effects of these experiences with control on their reaction to several frightening and novel situations were studied. Their results indicated that Master monkeys who had early experience with control and mastery over appetitive events showed reduced levels of fear, as well as higher levels of exploration in novel situations, relative to Yoked monkeys reared without control. Taken together with the results from the correlational studies with human subjects, these results suggest that individuals with a prior history of control over important events in their environment may show reduced susceptibility to the development of fear and anxiety disorders.

As suggested earlier, experiential variables that occur *during* a conditioning experience, as well as before it, are also an important part of the dynamic context that determines the level of fear that is experienced or conditioned. Historically, Pavlovian or classical conditioning of fear was studied only in paradigms in which the organism had no control over the presentation of the neutral conditioned stimulus or the noxious unconditioned stimulus. The organism was seen as a passive recipient of an essentially involuntary conditioning process. Yet in real life, in many of the everyday events in which

Pavlovian conditioning occurs, organisms do have some control over the US, such as when it will end. And indeed, for some years it has been known that much lower levels of fear are conditioned to neutral stimuli paired with escapable or controllable as opposed to inescapable or uncontrollable shock (e.g., Desiderato & Newman, 1971; Mineka, Cook, & Miller, 1984a; Mowrer & Viek, 1948). In fact, the results of several experiments conducted by Mineka et al. (1984a) indicated that levels of acquired fear in the rats that received uncontrollable shocks were approximately twice as high as levels of acquired fear in rats that received controllable shocks.

There are additional complexities in the dynamics of the conditioning process that overcome some of the problems associated with traditional SITIA conditioning models (see Table 1, point 5). For example, a great deal of recent work has been done on a class of stimuli called "occasion setters" which in and of themselves do not evoke conditioned responding but that may influence behavior in the presence of a CS (Holland, 1983; Rescorla, 1988). That is, the presence or absence of the occasion-setting stimulus can turn on or turn off conditioned fear to a CS even though the occasion setter itself does not evoke fear. In addition, we now know that conditioning does not occur to all stimuli that are present during a traumatic event. Rather, it is the CSs that provide the most reliable and nonredundant information about the occurrence of a US to which conditioning will occur (e.g., Mackintosh, 1983; Rescorla, 1988; Rescorla & Wagner, 1972). Moreover, in a situation where there are multiple potential CSs, the dynamics of which CS has the most strength also vary over time as the relative predictive value of all stimuli present is gradually learned by the organism (Rescorla & Wagner, 1972).

Given these basic facts from contemporary conditioning research, SIDCA models do not lead to the problem of overprediction of fear that Rachman (1977, 1978, 1990) noted in his critique of what we call SITIA conditioning models. For example, Rachman noted that these conditioning models predicted that many people who were subjected to repeated air raids during World War II should have developed intense phobias or other psychiatric casualties. He also noted, however, that air raids in England, Japan, and Germany during World War II did not in fact result in widespread and prolonged panic and terror and quoted Janis (1951, p. 111) as saying "there was a definite decline in overt fear-reactions as the air blitz continued, even though the raids became heavier and more destructive." Rachman (1990) also cited Janis as having noted, "The bombed population displayed increasing indifference towards the air attacks, and warning signals tended to be disregarded unless attacking planes were in the immediate vicinity" (Rachman, 1990, p. 29). Although this evidence contradicted what was expected by earlier SITIA conditioning models, we do not believe it refutes SIDCA models. For example, Janis's account clearly suggests that the bombed population displayed some degree of fear when warning signals were accompanied by the sight or sounds of attacking planes. In other words, there was some conditioned fear, but it was relatively circumscribed because there were clear danger signals (sight or sounds of attacking planes) in the presence of occasion-setting stimuli (warning signals). Alternatively, it may well have been the case that early on many people did have fear of the warning signals but that these signals lost their fear-provoking properties because they were not reliable signals of danger. That is, gradually all the conditioning accrued to the sight and sound of the attacking planes themselves because they were the most reliable signals of danger. This would certainly be in accord with the Rescorla-Wagner (1972) model of the dynamics of the conditioning process.

Rachman also noted that these conditioning models (i.e., SITIA) could not explain why the fear reactions did not generalize to the sights, sounds, and smells of the cities that were bombed. As already noted, SIDCA models take into account the contextual conditioning principle that when multiple cues are present on a conditioning trial, the most reliable predictor of the US will block the formation of conditioned associations to the less reliable predictors of the US (Kamin, 1968; Mackintosh, 1983; Rescorla & Wagner, 1972; see also Sutton & Barto, 1981). Certainly the sights, sounds, and smells of a city were less reliable predictors of danger than were the sight and sound of an attacking plane. Why the fear reactions did not generalize to the sights or sounds of friendly or commercial planes can probably be explained within the SIDCA perspective by the fact that these other planes were probably not accompanied by the occasion setter of the warning signal. Finally, SIDCA conditioning models explicitly incorporate the principles of "belongingness" or "preparedness" based on evolutionary history into their models (see below). These principles suggest that it is not too surprising that air raids did not result in widespread and debilitating fears because "air raids, based as they are on sophisticated modern technology, have no evolutionary history, and for this reason human beings are not predisposed to acquire fears during exposures to bombs released from sky-borne craft" (Rachman, 1978, p. 46).

Next we will examine several phenomena suggesting the importance of what happens following conditioning on the level of fear that is maintained over time—another aspect of the dynamic context considered by SIDCA but not by SITIA models. We will first consider the inflation effect (Rescorla, 1974). Rescorla first conditioned a mild fear to a tone by pairing the tone with weak electric shocks. Later, following conditioning, the subjects were randomly exposed to a more intense traumatic US than was involved in the original conditioning. When subjects were subsequently tested for their fear of the CS that had been originally paired with weak shocks, Rescorla found that the fear conditioned response (CR) had been inflated in the direction that would have been expected if the more intense shock had been involved in the conditioning in the first place. To the extent that parallel effects occur in humans, a person who had a conditioning experience with a mildly traumatic event and acquired a fear of nonphobic intensity might be expected to show an increase in that fear, perhaps to phobic intensity, if a noncontingent, highly traumatic experience occurred at a later point in time. Furthermore, Hendersen (1985) showed that the greater the time interval between the original conditioning experiment and exposure to the higher intensity US, the greater the inflation effect. As Hendersen (1985) noted, it is as if the organism has a memorial representation of the original US that can be altered through later experience with other USs and that the malleability of the fear memory increases with time.

A second variable that affects the persistence of acquired fear is whether the organism has control over the termination of the conditioned stimulus. Starr and Mineka (1977) showed that in the context of an avoidance learning paradigm, fear of the CS declines over the course of avoidance learning (e.g., Kamin, Brimer, & Black, 1963) only if the organism has control over CS and US termination. In their experiment, Yoked animals who were not given the ability to terminate the CS or avoid the US themselves did not show the same decline in fear that the Master animals showed, even though both groups experienced the exact same pattern of nonreinforced CSs as the Master animals' avoidance responses became well learned. This finding underscores the importance of control in producing this attenuation of fear that is seen as an avoidance response becomes well learned (see also Cook, Mineka, & Trumble, 1987, for related results).

We have summarized a number of experiential variables occurring before, during, and after a stressful experience that affect the level of fear that is experienced, conditioned, or maintained over time. These examples illustrate that the second problem with conditioning models from the SITIA tradition is not a problem for SIDCA models. It is true that the factors involved in the origins and maintenance of fears and phobias are considerably more complex than was generally assumed by behavioral learning theorists in the past. Yet these complexities can be understood from the vantage point of contemporary research on conditioning and learning, which points to the crucial importance of SIDCA models. Thus the major problems with SITIA conditioning models in accounting for individual differences in the acquisition of fear are handled simply in SIDCA models by bringing clinical theories about the origins of phobic fears and anxiety states up-to-date with respect to contemporary knowledge about conditioning.

SELECTIVE ASSOCIATIONS IN THE CONDITIONING OF FEARS AND PHOBIAS

The third problem with conditioning models from the SITIA tradition derives from observations that fears and phobias do not tend to occur to a random arbitrary group of objects associated with trauma (see Table 1, point 3). Seligman (1971) and Öhman and colleagues (e.g., 1986; Öhman, Dimberg, & Öst, 1985) have argued that primates and humans may have a biologically based preparedness to associate rapidly certain objects—such as snakes, spiders, water, and enclosed spaces—with aversive events. They have argued that this is because there may have been a selective advantage in the course of evolution for primates and humans who rapidly acquired fears of certain objects or situations that may frequently have been dangerous or posed a threat to our early ancestors (referred to as fear-relevant stimuli). Öhman and his colleagues in Sweden have done an important series of experiments that are generally consistent with this theory. They have found superior conditioning using slides of snakes and spiders as fear-relevant conditioned stimuli and mild shock as an unconditioned stimulus, compared to what is found using more fear-irrelevant CSs such as slides of flowers and mushrooms or geometric figures. The superior conditioning is usually indexed by enhanced resistance to extinction of conditioned electrodermal responses (e.g., Öhman, 1986; Öhman et al., 1985).

More recent studies from Öhman's laboratory have also shown that following conditioning to fear-relevant CSs, even subliminal presentations of these CSs are sufficient to elicit conditioned responses; by contrast, subliminal presentations of fear-irrelevant CSs do not elicit conditioned responses (e.g., Öhman & Soares, 1993). In another experiment it was shown that subjects who were preselected for being highly fearful of snakes or spiders also showed elevated electrodermal responses to masked (subliminal) presentations of slides of their feared object (Öhman & Soares, 1994). Öhman and Soares have argued that such results may provide a theoretical explanation for the irrationality of phobias. "According to this explanation, phobics are unable to control their fear voluntarily because its origin rests in cognitive structures that are not under the control of conscious intentions. This implies that the autonomic arousal, which provides a central component of the phobia, may be already under way when the stimulus information that defines the phobic object reaches conscious, controlled levels of information processing. . . . It is no wonder, therefore, that phobics remain unable to consciously control their fear and revert to escape and avoidance strategies as keys to coping" (Öhman & Soares, 1993, p. 129).

Although the experiments of Öhman and colleagues provide a convincing case that there is differential conditionability of fear to fear-relevant versus fear-irrelevant stimuli, they cannot rule out ontogenetic factors because all subjects had experiences with snakes and spiders before participating in these experiments. To rule out possible ontogenetically based differences in experience with fear-relevant and fear-irrelevant stimuli it is necessary to test for differences in conditionability to fear-relevant versus fear-irrelevant stimuli that are totally novel to the organism.

Cook and Mineka (1989, 1990, 1991) decided to explore this issue with their observational fear-conditioning paradigm—that is, would monkeys who have never had prior exposure to any of the objects to be used as conditioned stimuli in the observational fear-conditioning paradigm acquire a fear of fear-irrelevant stimuli such as flowers as easily as they do a fear of fear-relevant stimuli such as snakes? To address this question it was necessary to equate the model's fear performance in the presence of flowers with his or her fear performance in the presence of snakes because the major determinant of the level of snake fear acquired by the observer monkeys is the level of snake fear shown by the fearful models (Cook et al., 1985; Mineka et al., 1984b; Mineka & Cook, 1993). To accomplish this matching of fear levels, Cook and Mineka used edited videotapes in which the model was in reality reacting fearfully to a snake, but—through elaborate splicing techniques—it looked as if the model was reacting to the flowers.

There were two groups in this experiment (Cook & Mineka, 1990, Experiment 2). The sn + fl- group watched two videotapes of model monkeys reacting fearfully to toy snake stimuli and nonfearfully to flower stimuli. The fl + sn- group watched two videotapes of model monkeys reacting fearfully to flower stimuli and nonfearfully to toy snake stimuli. The fear performance of the models that each group saw was identical; the groups differed only in whether the fear appeared to be elicited by a toy snake or by flowers. Monkeys in the sn + fl- group did indeed acquire a significant fear of snakes but not of flowers. By contrast, monkeys in the fl + sn- group did not acquire a fear of flowers. Cook and Mineka (1989, Experiment 2) found comparable results when using as CSs two animals that differed in fear-relevance or preparedness; that is, observer monkeys acquired a significant fear of a toy crocodile but did not acquire a fear of a toy rabbit in a similar study of discriminative observational conditioning. Finally, another experiment demonstrated that when the flower and snake stimuli were used as discriminative stimuli in a complex operant appetitive discrimination paradigm, there were no differences in the monkeys' abilities to learn about these stimuli (Cook & Mineka, 1990, Experiment 3). This makes it unlikely that the flowers were simply less salient stimuli than were the toy snakes in the fear-conditioning experiments (see also Cook & Mineka, 1991).

Thus these monkey experiments on preparedness are consistent with those of Öhman and others who have used human subjects to demonstrate superior conditioning of electrodermal responses to fear-relevant stimuli paired with mild electric shock. Both monkeys and humans seem selectively to associate certain fear-relevant stimuli with aversive outcomes. Because the monkeys used in these experiments had no prior experience with any of the stimuli used in these experiments, the results of these experiments strongly implicate phylogenetic factors in these selective associations. These findings on selective associations are not surprising, however, because it is well-known among contemporary learning researchers that for a given species certain CS-US combinations are more easily learned about than are other CS-US combinations (e.g., LoLordo, 1979a, b; LoLordo & Droungas, 1989), a point that is incorporated by SIDCA but not SITIA models.

PERSISTENCE OF FEARS AND PHOBIAS

Turning now to the fourth problem for fear-conditioning models from the SITIA tradition, we address the question of why some fears are so persistent and even increase with the passage of time (see Table 1, point 4). One partial answer to this question may derive from research on preparedness and selective associations reviewed above. In their research with human subjects, Öhman and colleagues found that responses conditioned to fear-relevant objects such as snakes and spiders are more resistant to extinction than are responses conditioned to fear-irrelevant objects. Indeed, this seems to be the single most robust finding in the human research on selective associations in fear conditioning (McNally, 1987).

This possibility is also supported by the results of a recent experiment by de Jong, Merckelbach, and Arntz (1995), which used an illusory correlation paradigm adapted from Tomarken, Mineka, and Cook (1989). De Jong and colleagues found that subjects' expectancies that shocks would follow spider slides stayed high over the course of a series of trials in which different categories of slides were randomly followed by different outcomes, in spite of the disconfirming evidence that the subjects were receiving. By contrast, their expectancies that shocks would follow slides of weapons declined over the same series of trials. This provides further support for the idea that expectancies of aversive outcomes (one definition of a fear CR) following phylogenetically fear-relevant stimuli such as spiders are especially resistant to disconfirmation. These findings also extend the results of Öhman and colleagues because de Jong et al. were not using a traditional extinction paradigm in which the CS is repeatedly presented without the US. In the de Jong et al. experiment USs were still occurring but were randomly paired with the different CSs. Extinction of the expectancy for the shock US occurred for the weapons but not for the spiders.

It was not possible to examine the issue of differential extinction to fear-relevant versus fear-irrelevant stimuli in the monkey research on selective associations because one cannot compare extinction to snakes versus flowers or toy crocodiles versus toy rabbits when no conditioning to the fear-irrelevant stimuli occurred in the first place. Nevertheless, other experiments showed that the snake fear seen in our wild-reared monkey models is extraordinarily resistant to extinction (Mineka et al., 1980; Mineka & Cook, unpublished data; Mineka & Keir, 1983). Thus it may be that strong and intense "prepared" fears, such as seen in these monkey experiments, are more resistant to extinction than are fears to fear-irrelevant objects.

DeSilva, Rachman, and Seligman (1977) addressed this issue retrospectively in a study of phobic patients and found no relation between the degree of preparedness of a phobia and the length of time it took to treat the phobia. A retrospective analysis of this issue, however, does not make a compelling case against this hypothesis because the nature and the type of treatment were not controlled. In addition, there was no attempt to equate the subjects with prepared versus unprepared phobias on temperamental variables or on severity of their phobia. What is needed are prospective studies of phobic patients undergoing the same type of exposure therapy whose phobias differ only in their degree of preparedness (and not in severity of the phobia) to see if the phobias to highly prepared stimuli are slower to extinguish than are the phobias to less prepared stimuli; controlling for temperamental variables would also be important.

Another phenomenon that may well contribute to the persistence of fears and phobias over time is the phenomenon of reinstatement of fear (Rescorla & Heth, 1975). This refers to the finding that following extinction of a conditioned fear, the fear can be reinstated simply through exposure to a noncontingent traumatic stimulus. Thus if a person's fear began to extinguish and he or she was accidentally exposed to a nonrelated traumatic event, this might be sufficient to reinstate the original level of fear.

Eysenck (1968) has also argued that fears may incubate, or increase in intensity, with repeated nonreinforced exposures to a CS that elicits fear because he believes that fear itself is a noxious enough state to serve as a US, and a self-perpetuating reinforcement mechanism may thereby cause the fear to incubate rather than extinguish. Although this theory is intuitively appealing and may account for a few anomalous observations in the literature on fear (e.g., the Napakalov effect— see Eysenck, 1968), there are no good studies to support it (see Bersh, 1980, and Mineka, 1985a, for reviews). Two recent studies by Davey and Matchett (1994) do show that human subjects who are either high in levels of trait anxiety or have undergone induced somatic anxiety and are instructed to rehearse the US following conditioning do show transient increases in the strength of their CR. This suggests that simple mental rehearsal of a US can result in increased CR strength, at least under some conditions.

Overgeneralization of fears is also likely to occur with the passage of time after original conditioning. This common clinical observation (e.g., Beck & Emery, 1985) is easily accounted for by research on conditioning conducted in animals that has amply documented that the generalization gradient around a CS+ is much steeper immediately following conditioning than it is some days or weeks later. As reviewed by Riccio, Richardson, and Ebner (1984) and Riccio, Rabinowitz, and Axelrod (1994), this flattening of the generalization gradient is caused not by a decline in fear to the CS+ but rather by an increase in fear to the generalization test stimuli. It seems that with the passage of time, the organism forgets the specific attributes of the CS that was involved in the original conditioning experience and comes to behave fearfully in a wider range of situations than it would have immediately following conditioning. Hendersen (1985) also reviewed evidence that the specific attributes of the US are forgotten with the passage of time, with the similar result that the organism behaves fearfully in a wider range of situations than it would have immediately following conditioning. Mineka and Tomarken have discussed the possibility of a kind of adaptive conservatism to account for such findings (Mineka, 1992; Mineka & Tomarken, 1989; Tomarken, 1988; see also Hendersen, 1985).

In addition, both Hendersen (1978) and Thomas (1979) demonstrated that conditioned inhibitors of fear lose their fear inhibitory properties with the passage of time. That is, although conditioned excitors of fear are not forgotten with the passage of time, conditioned inhibitors of fear (or safety signals) are forgotten. This may also indirectly affect the maintenance and overgeneralization of fears with the passage of time. Assuming that similar phenomena occur in human classical conditioning, this would suggest that shortly after the onset of a phobia through traumatic conditioning, the phobic individual might have safety signals or CS-s (inhibitory CSs) that would facilitate discrimination of dangerous versus safe places. With the passage of time, however, the CS-s may lose their fear inhibitory properties, with a possible consequence being a loss of discrimination between safe and dangerous places or events and a concomitant increase in generalization of fears (see Mineka, 1992).

To summarize, in this review of specific phobias, we have suggested that the factors involved in the origins and maintenance of fears and phobias are considerably more complex than has often been assumed by past conditioning models from the SITIA tradition. However, these complexities are expected from the standpoint of conditioning models in the SIDCA tradition that consider a large variety of dynamic contextual variables and how they affect the outcome of conditioning experiences. For example, many phobic fears may be acquired observationally rather than through direct conditioning. Furthermore, for humans most fears do not originate out of a single or even a few trials of direct or observational fear conditioning or avoidance learning, occurring in a vacuum, as was often assumed by conditioning models from the SITIA tradition. Instead, there appear to be a multitude of experiential variables that can occur before, during, or following a direct or an observational conditioning experience that interact and affect the amount of fear that is experienced, conditioned, or maintained over time. Results indicating that the nature of the stimulus used during observational fear conditioning can have powerful effects on whether fear is acquired were also reviewed. Observer monkeys showed rapid conditioning of fear to fear-relevant stimuli such as snakes but not to fear-irrelevant stimuli such as flowers. Furthermore, following conditioning, a host of other factors occurring after acquisition of a fear, such as inflation and forgetting of CS and US specificity, can promote maintenance or even exacerbation of fears or an increase in the places in which fears are exhibited.

Social Phobia

As described in the DSM-III-R (American Psychiatric Association, 1987) and DSM-IV (American Psychiatric Association, 1994), people with social phobia fear one or more social situations in which they believe they might do or say something to embarrass or humiliate themselves or in which they may be evaluated. Although some degree of social anxiety is normal and nearly universal, in social phobia it reaches such proportions that it is markedly distressing and/or interferes with functioning. We begin our discussion of conditioning and ethological models of social phobia in the SIDCA tradition by considering social phobia in an adaptive/functional framework. Öhman and his colleagues (Öhman, 1986; Öhman et al., 1985) proposed that social fears evolved as a by-product of dominance hierarchies. The competitive encounters between members of a social group that help to establish dominance hierarchies often involve ritualized displays of threat on the part of the dominant animal and of fear and submissiveness on the part of the defeated animal (see Öhman et al., 1985, for an excellent summary). Öhman and his colleagues also noted that the fear displayed by the submissive animal more often leads to a short dash to get out of the immediate reach of the attacker than to total escape from the situation. They summarized a good deal of psychophysiological research consistent with the notion that, in comparison to people with specific phobias, the fear response seen in those with social phobias is "much more loosely and conditionally concocted, with a less prominent and reflexive role for active avoidance behavior" (1985, p. 141). Moreover, they also noted that the typical age of onset for social phobias (adolescence and young adulthood) coincides with the time when dominance conflicts become prominent.

PREPAREDNESS AND CONDITIONING MODELS OF SOCIAL PHOBIA

In the first extension of the preparedness theory of phobias to the understanding of social anxiety and phobias, Öhman and Dimberg (1978) reasoned that prepared stimuli for social anxiety should involve social stimuli signaling dominance and intraspecific aggression if social anxiety evolved as a by-product of dominance hierarchies, as they assumed. Because of the strong facial component, including threat or anger expressions on the part of the dominant animal involved in ritualized displays of dominance and submission, Öhman and Dimberg (1978) hypothesized that angry facial expressions would be prepared or fear-relevant stimuli for social anxiety. Consistent with this hypothesis, they found superior conditioning when slides of angry faces were used as CSs relative to the outcome when slides of happy or neutral faces were used.

A particularly fascinating aspect of this literature is that the studies of preattentive activation of prepared conditioned responses (e.g., Öhman & Soares, 1993; Öhman, Dimberg, and Esteves, 1989) have also been applied to the activation of social anxiety. Öhman (1986) found that, following conditioning, conditioned responses could be elicited to subliminally presented CSs when the CSs were angry faces but not when they were happy or neutral faces. These results may help to account for the irrational quality of social phobia in that the emotional reaction can be activated without conscious awareness of the threat cue (see Mineka & Zinbarg, 1995, for further discussion of these studies and their implications for social phobia).

In summary, the work of Öhman and colleagues on preparedness and social phobias suggests that there is an evolutionarily based predisposition to acquire anxiety to angry, critical, or rejecting faces (see Table 1, point 3). Barlow (1988) further argues that social anxieties will be mild or transient for most individuals, and that full-blown social phobia develops only in individuals who are vulnerable for biological and/or psychological reasons to develop what he calls anxious apprehension about future social situations—as would be expected from the perspective of SIDCA models. The biological sources of vulnerability undoubtedly include the temperamental variables discussed below. Moreover, the psychological vulnerabilities seem to stem from the individual's sense of control (or lack thereof) over the environment, as will also be discussed below, in addition to the experiential variables occurring before, during, and after a conditioning experience (see Table 1, point 2).

Nevertheless, important questions remain about the role of such conditioning in the origins of full-blown social phobia (rather than simply conditioning of electrodermal responses). First, what would determine whether a specific or a social phobia would be conditioned when a traumatic event occured? We hypothesize that social phobia is expected if the US occurred in the presence of salient social stimuli such as eating in public or speaking in front of an audience and specific phobia is expected if the US occurred in the presence of an animal such as a snake or a dog or in the presence of salient inanimate cues such as heights or thunder. Given what we now know about the belongingness principle of associative learning (LoLordo, 1979a, b; LoLordo & Droungas, 1989), we would also expect that USs involving perceived embarrassment or humiliation would be more likely to result in the acquisition of social phobias than USs involving physical danger. The fact that posttraumatic stress disorder, rather than social phobia, is considered to be the most common psychiatric sequel when one perceives one's life to be in danger during a sexual assault, an intraspecific trauma, appears to be consistent with this formulation (Kilpatrick & Resnick, 1993).

All of the previous research on preparedness and phobias has used electric shock as USs. This methodological shortcoming may account, at least in part, for Dimberg's (1986) finding that the CRs acquired to slides of the angry face of one person did not generalize to slides of the angry face of a second person. Such specificity clearly is at odds with the clinical features of social phobia because it is rare for individuals with social phobia to be frightened only of a specific individual. We would predict that generalization to be more likely, however, if an angry voice or some aspect of social humiliation or defeat rather than electric shock were used as the US (see Mineka & Zinbarg, 1995, for a more detailed discussion). Indeed, the animal literature on social defeat, to be discussed in more detail below, is consistent with this prediction. But what evidence do we have that social phobias can indeed occur through direct or observational conditioning of fear in the same way as do many specific phobias? It is to this question that we turn our attention next.

DIRECT TRAUMATIC CONDITIONING, OBSERVATIONAL CONDITIONING, AND SOCIAL PHOBIA

Öst and Hugdahl (1981), in a study cited in the specific phobias section, found that 58% of their sample with social phobia recalled direct traumatic conditioning experiences as having played a role in the onset of their social phobia. More recently, Townsley (1992) reported that 56% of a sample with specific social phobia (fear of one or more specific social situations) recalled direct traumatic conditioning experiences as having been involved in the origins of their phobia, although 20% of a control group had also had similar experiences and did not acquire a phobia (see Table 1, point 2).

Although there are methodological limitations of such studies which rely entirely on retrospective recall, we find the convergence between the results of the two studies to be encouraging. In addition, although the finding that 20% of the normal control group from the Townsley study recalled traumatic conditioning experiences may be problematic for a SITIA conditioning account of the origins of social phobias, it is not problematic from the perspective of SIDCA models. That is, it is well-known among contemporary conditioning researchers that CS-US pairings are neither necessary nor sufficient for the development of conditioned fears; contemporary conditioning research suggests that a host of variables occurring before, during, and after a given conditioning experience affect the amount of fear that is acquired and maintained into the future. Thus we interpret the results reported by Öst and Hugdahl and by Townsley as being consistent with SIDCA models given that a large proportion of people with social phobia report that direct traumatic experiences were involved in the onset of their phobia.

What of the individuals who do not recall direct traumatic experiences before the onset of their social phobia—do they constitute evidence disconfirming a learning theory explanation of the etiology of social phobia? (See Table 1, point 1.) Although the work of Mineka and Cook (Mineka, 1987; Mineka & Cook, 1988; Cook and Mineka, 1991) on the vicarious conditioning of snake fear in rhesus monkeys described earlier has never been extended to the acquisition of social anxiety, ethological studies have produced uncontrolled evidence suggesting that such learning does indeed occur. Certainly, it is clear that dominance hierarchies are passed down from one generation to the next in some species. We are particularly intrigued by de Waal's (1989) observations of the intergenerational transmission of dominance hierarchies in rhesus monkeys that included three instances in which infants were adopted. In all three cases, the infant's rank was based on its adoptive parents rather than its biological parents.

Although this evidence is only indirect (de Waal himself acknowledged that more definitive studies ruling out a genetic contribution are needed), it is consistent with the hypothesis that social behaviors relating to dominance and submissiveness can be acquired through observational learning (see Mineka & Zinbarg, 1995, for further discussion).

There are even fewer data regarding the role of observational conditioning experiences than there are for direct traumatic conditioning experiences in the origins of social phobias in humans. In the only relevant study we are aware of, Öst and Hugdahl (1981) found a smaller percentage of subjects with social phobia who recalled vicarious learning experiences as having played a role in the origin of their social phobia (13%) than recalled direct traumatic conditioning experiences (58%). Independent replications of this finding are required before firm conclusions may be drawn, but these results nevertheless suggest that observational conditioning of social fear and phobia can indeed occur in humans.

TEMPERAMENTAL VARIABLES AND SOCIAL PHOBIA

Temperament is another variable in SIDCA models of social phobia that affects the outcome of a socially traumatic conditioning experience and may help explain why only some individuals who undergo such an experience go on to develop social phobia (see Table 1, point 2). In recent years consensus has grown that behavioral inhibition (e.g., Biederman et al., 1990; Gray, 1982; Kagan, 1994; Kagan, Reznick, & Snidman, 1988) is the temperamental construct that is most relevant for the study of anxiety. The behavioral inhibition system is thought to be responsible for inhibiting behavior in response to novelty and signals for either punishment or frustration. Evidence for the existence of a behavioral inhibition system has been found in several species, including cats (Adamec, 1975), dogs (Scott & Fuller, 1965), humans (Kagan, 1989, 1994), rats (Gray, 1982; Hall, 1941), and rhesus monkeys (Chamove, Eysenck, & Harlow, 1972). Scott and Fuller's (1965) investigations are especially noteworthy in that they permitted the study of the genetic basis of behavioral inhibition and found evidence for a substantial genetic contribution to this trait. Of particular relevance for understanding the origins of social phobia, many of these studies found that behavioral inhibition is related to conspecific stressors in addition to nonsocial stressors (for a more detailed discussion, see Mineka & Zinbarg, 1995). Moreover, there is some evidence that behavioral inhibition is negatively correlated with copulation frequency (Hall, 1941). This evidence is particularly intriguing because social anxiety in people is also negatively correlated with sexual experience (Leary & Dobbins, 1983) and male sexual dysfunction has been conceptualized as a form of social phobia (Barlow, 1986; Barlow, Chorpita, & Turovsky, this volume; Heimberg & Barlow, 1988). Thus it could be argued that the parallels between behaviorally inhibited animals and people with social phobia may even extend to heterosexual interactions.

This brief review of the behavioral inhibition literature suggests the following two hypotheses: social anxiety should covary significantly with nonsocial forms of anxiety, and behavioral inhibition may be the temperamental vulnerability factor common to most if not all of the anxiety disorders, including social phobia. Zinbarg and Barlow's (1992) study of the structure of anxiety and the anxiety disorders produced evidence consistent with these two hypotheses. These analyses revealed a second-order general factor that was loaded on by each of 23 measures tapping various forms of anxiety, including social anxiety as well as several nonsocial manifestations of anxiety. Moreover, discriminant function analysis revealed that each of the six anxiety disordered groups included in the study (representing each of the DSM-III-R anxiety disorder principal diagnoses except posttraumatic stress disorder) obtained significantly higher scores than a no mental disorder control group on the second-order general factor described above and there were few significant differences among the patient groups on this same factor. Certainly, these results provide unambiguous support for the hypothesis that social anxiety covaries significantly with nonsocial anxiety. In addition, although other alternative explanations are plausible, these results are consistent with the hypothesis that the second-order general factor was tapping a core vulnerability common to all the anxiety disorders, including social phobia.

Finally, extrapolating from animal evidence suggesting an inherited basis for behavioral inhibition (Scott & Fuller, 1965), we would expect to find a genetic contribution to the etiology of social phobia. More specifically, we would predict that the genetic di-athesis for social phobia would be common to most, if not all, of the anxiety disorders. This prediction is consonant with Barlow's (1988) conclusion, based on a review of the available genetic evidence, that "what seems to be inherited is a 'vulnerability' to develop *an* [em-phasis added] anxiety disorder, rather than a specific clinical syn-drome itself" (p. 176) and with recent findings of Kendler and col-leagues (1992a).

UNCONTROLLABILITY AND SOCIAL PHOBIA

Numerous studies have demonstrated that uncontrollable stress, but not controllable stress, reduces aggressiveness and increases submissiveness using several different measures, including shock-elicited aggression and competition for limited food resources (e.g., Maier, Anderson, & Lieberman, 1972; Powell, Francis, Francis, & Schneiderman, 1972; Rapaport & Maier, 1978). Williams and his col-leagues (1982; Williams & Lierle, 1986) have found similar results using the colony-intruder test, which they argue provides a more ecologically valid measure of social submissiveness. The colony-in-truder test involves placing naive intruder rats in an established col-ony of rats, where they are typically attacked by the dominant male colony resident (see also Blanchard, Takahashi, & Blanchard, 1977). Given that the colony-intruder test involves interactions between strangers, one could also argue that it provides a more ecologically valid analogue to human social phobia because interacting with strangers is a common anxiety trigger in people with social phobia (Scholing & Emmelkamp, 1990).

   Although the above studies all used electric shock as the stressor and it seems evident that neither electric shock nor physical pain is involved in the etiology of social phobia, the literature on the effects of social defeat—a more ecologically valid line of research—provides converging evidence implicating uncontrollability in the onset of social phobia. Repeated social defeat, but not repeated vic-tories, leads to increased submissiveness and lowering of position in a dominance hierarchy (e.g., Ginsburg & Allee, 1942; Kahn, 1951; Scott, 1948; Scott & Marston, 1953; Uhrich, 1938). Interestingly, the defeated animals do not appear to learn to be submissive to specific animals; rather, they appear to display submissiveness in response to the "general deportment of an aggressive individual" (Ginsburg & Allee, 1942, p. 492). Similarly, Uhrich (1938) concluded that "the subordinates do not recognize the dominant (as an individual) but merely flee from any mouse that happens to attack them or assumes a threatening attitude" (p. 402). In this respect, the social defeat literature would appear to offer a better model of human social phobia than the research performed to date examining conditioning to angry faces using electric shock as the US because in those experiments conditioned responses were elicited only by the specific faces used during conditioning (Dimberg, 1986; Öhman et al., 1985).

Not only does repeated social defeat lead to increased submissiveness, as one might expect, but it also appears to produce many of the effects produced by inescapable shock. First, Williams and Lierle (1988) found that repeated social defeat, but not repeated victories, is associated with a similar escape deficit as was reported in the original demonstrations of the "learned helplessness" effect (e.g., Maier, Seligman, & Solomon, 1969; Overmier & Seligman, 1967; Seligman & Maier, 1967). Second, repeated social defeat, relative to repeated victories, also appears to be associated with potentiated conditioned fear responses similar to those associated with inescapable shock relative to escapable shock. Williams and Scott (1989) found that rats that had been defeated and later tested for fear in the presence of odors from an aggressive colony showed significantly more fear than rats that were either defeated and tested with nonaggressive colony odors, undefeated and tested with aggressive colony odors, or undefeated and tested with nonaggressive colony odors. These results have since been replicated by Williams, Worland, and Smith (1990) and were interpreted as indicating that the odors from the aggressive colonies became conditioned fear stimuli for the defeated animals. Williams, Rogers, and Adler (1990) also showed that the defeated animals' fear responses to aggressive colony odors could be extinguished through prolonged exposure to the odors. (See Mineka & Zinbarg, 1995, for further parallels between the effects of social defeat and exposure to uncontrollable shocks.)

Earlier in our discussion of specific phobias, we cited a study by Mineka et al. (1986) demonstrating that extensive experience with controlling appetitive events can have beneficial consequences, serving at least partially to immunize the organism against the effects of various stressors. One feature of that study that seems particularly relevant for social phobia was the results of separation tests conducted with monkeys from the replication sample. One set of these tests involved taking the monkeys out of their own group one by one and placing them in with another group for several days (intruder separations). In this situation, the Master subjects coped better when serving as intruders in the Yoked group than vice versa. The Yoked host groups also showed more fear/submissive behavior toward the Master intruders than vice versa. These results suggest that an early history of control over appetitive events can not only immunize the organism against inanimate stressors (such as a toy monster and a large novel playroom), as discussed earlier, but also can immunize against social stressors such as interacting with strangers during a time of stress (separation from one's peer group).

The animal evidence reviewed above strongly suggests that perceptions of uncontrollability play a role in the etiology and maintenance of social anxiety. There is some correlational evidence suggesting an association between perceptions of uncontrollability and social phobia in humans. Cloitre, Heimberg, Liebowitz, and Gitow (1992) found that, in comparison to a group of control subjects, both a group of individuals with social phobia and a group with panic disorder had significantly less belief in their ability to influence events in their lives. More specific analyses revealed that this diminished sense of personal control among the group with social phobia was primarily accounted for by beliefs that control over the significant events in their lives is primarily determined by "powerful others." These results have been replicated by Leung and Heimberg (submitted). Although it is impossible to infer the direction of causality on the basis of this correlational data, they are consistent with the animal data from studies that more directly suggest that uncontrollability plays a causal role in the acquisition of heightened levels of social anxiety.

In summary, simplistic SITIA models suggesting that direct traumatic experiences are the only causal factors in the origins of social fears and phobias are inadequate and outdated. SIDCA learning models of social phobia, consistent with the advances in knowledge about the theoretical and empirical foundations of conditioning that have developed over the past 25 years, on the other hand, are capable of accounting for the complexities and individual differences in-

volved in the etiology of social phobia. SIDCA learning models of social phobias take into account the powerful role of experiential variables occurring before, during, and after both direct and vicarious
conditioning experiences in determining the outcome of those direct
or vicarious learning experiences. These models also address the
role of the preparedness of certain cues for social anxiety and acknowledge the role of temperamental variables in putting certain individuals at higher risk than others. Finally, SIDCA learning models
of social phobia also include the role of perceptions of uncontrollability over important life events in influencing the development or
maintenance of the symptoms of social phobia. (See Table 1 for a
summary.)

Panic Disorder and Agoraphobia

People with panic disorder experience recurrent unexpected panic
attacks, usually associated with worry or persistent concern about
having another attack—a phenomenon called anticipatory anxiety.
Most, but not all, people with panic disorder go on to develop some
degree of agoraphobic avoidance; that is, they learn to avoid situations in which, if they had a panic attack, escape might be either difficult or embarrassing. Over the years a variety of conditioning
models of panic disorder and agoraphobia have been proposed.
One of the most widely cited models is that of Goldstein and Chambless (1978), who implicated conditioning both in the development
of agoraphobic avoidance ("these clients begin to avoid situations
where they fear panic attacks may occur"; p. 54) and in precipitating
panic attacks themselves ("Having suffered one or more panic attacks, these people become hyperalert to their sensations and interpret feelings of mild to moderate anxiety as signs of oncoming panic
attacks and react with such anxiety that the dreaded episode is almost invariably induced"; p. 55). The conditioning involved in the
initiation of panic attacks themselves is *interoceptive conditioning* as
described by Razran (1961) in that the conditioned and unconditioned stimuli are both internal bodily sensations and physiological
symptoms of intense arousal ("a client's own physiological signs of
arousal become the conditioned stimuli for the powerful conditioned response of a panic attack"; p. 55). More recent variants on

this model include Reiss and McNally's expectancy and anxiety sensitivity model (1985; McNally, 1990, 1994; Reiss, 1987) and van den Hout's (1988) interoceptive fear model. Although these models have some important differences, they share in common the idea that people with panic disorder are characterized by fears of interoceptive bodily sensations.

Conditioning models of panic disorder have been criticized for not accounting for the complexity of the cognitive processes associated with panic disorder (see Table 1, point 5). For example, Clark (1988) criticized interoceptive conditioning models of panic disorder on the basis of the observation that contextual factors may prevent individuals from making catastrophic interpretations of bodily sensations and thereby prevent panic. He argued that conditioning models overpredict panic responses because they would seem to have to predict panic attacks every time the initial symptoms of anxiety (the interoceptive CSs) are experienced.

Although Clark's criticism is applicable to SITIA conditioning models, it is less applicable to SIDCA models. Since the seminal work of Rescorla and Wagner (1972; Wagner & Rescorla, 1972), leading theories of conditioning explicitly incorporate compound and contextual conditioning phenomenon (see also Balsam & Tomie, 1985). The key insight of the Rescorla-Wagner model was that the expectation or emotional significance of a given stimulus configuration is based on the aggregate associative strength of all cues present. For example, the summation test for inhibition is based on the premise that conditioned responding to a conditioned stimulus will be less when that stimulus is presented in compound with a conditioned inhibitor. Thus, when a conditioned excitor of fear (such as bodily sensations of anxiety) is presented in compound with a discrete safety signal or in a context that has acquired safety value, less conditioned fear is observed than would be otherwise and this decrement in fear responding is proportional to the strength of the safety association developed in connection with the safety signal or context. This could easily account for why many panic patients are less likely to panic when in the presence of a "safe" or trusted companion or when in a safe place. Recent empirical support for this observation came from a study by Carter, Hollon, Carson, and Shelton (1995), who found that panic patients showed fewer panic symptoms (less self-rated affective distress, fewer catastrophic cognitions, and less physiological arousal) in response to a CO_2 panic provocation challenge if a safe person they brought with them was present than if they were alone with the experimenter.

As noted earlier, a great deal of recent work has been done on a class of stimuli called occasion setters, which in and of themselves do not evoke conditioned responding but which may influence behavior in the presence of a CS (e.g., Holland, 1983; Rescorla, 1988). That is, the presence or absence of the occasion-setting stimulus can turn on, or turn off, conditioned fear to a CS even though the occasion setter itself does not evoke fear. To use a human analogy, if a panic patient just ran up three flights of stairs and noticed his or her heart racing, the setting (running up stairs) may turn off the conditioned fear to the sensations of heart palpitations.

In addition, van den Hout (1988) notes that a potential problem for conditioning models of panic disorder is that they would seem to predict that panic attacks should extinguish given that the internal bodily sensations that constitute the CSs for panic are encountered or experienced more frequently than are panic attacks (see Table 1, point 4). These seemingly nonreinforced "trials" should result in extinction, he argues. But it is important to remember that panic patients often engage in subtle forms of avoidance behavior (such as holding on to a shopping cart when dizzy), which may effectively protect the CS (dizziness) from extinction (Chorazyna, 1962; Salkovskis, 1988).

Recently some attention has been devoted to developing a primate model of panic disorder through the use of biological challenges, including the injection of sodium lactate, which have been found to provoke panic attacks in humans with panic disorder (e.g., Friedman, Sunderland, & Rosenblum, 1988; Sunderland, Friedman, & Rosenblum, 1989). For example, several studies found that lactate produced "temporally circumscribed episodes of agitation, wariness, and motor responses, normally elicited under stressful or threatening conditions" (Friedman et al., 1988, p. 65). Although the paradigms used in such studies have the potential for studying a conditioning model of panic, as of yet this has not happened. Sunderland et al. (1989) did make incidental observations that over the course of the study, the monkeys began to show signs of behavioral disturbance while being restrained and injected, as if they had developed conditioned distress to these warning cues. Unfortunately, however, the observations were not made in a systematic enough fashion to assure that this was really the result of classical conditioning. Moreover, no attempt has been made using such paradigms to study the possibility of interoceptive conditioning of these paniclike responses.

The second basic research area that may be of relevance for understanding various features of panic disorder and agoraphobia is the literature on the effects of unpredictable and uncontrollable aversive events. When given a choice, animals and people in general prefer predictable to unpredictable aversive events and generally find predictable aversive events to be less stressful (see Mineka & Hendersen, 1985, for a review). Because panic attacks are highly aversive events for most people with panic disorder, one might expect that people with predicted panic attacks would show lower overall levels of anxiety than people with unpredicted panic attacks. A study by Craske, Glover, and Decola (1995) provided partial support for these predictions. They found that for a subgroup of panic patients who experienced a mixture of predicted and unpredicted attacks, anxiety and worry decreased on the day following a predicted panic attack and increased on the day following an unpredicted attack. They noted that these findings are in keeping with some of the animal literature on experimental neurosis as reviewed by Mineka and Kihlstrom (1978), suggesting that the deleterious effects of lack of predictability may be exacerbated for those who have a history of predictability (see also Rapee, Mattick, & Murell, 1986, for additional evidence regarding the role of predictability in mediating the affective reaction to the physical sensations of panic attacks).

The literature on uncontrollable aversive events also has great potential relevance for understanding various features of panic disorder and agoraphobia. As discussed earlier, it is well-known that controllable aversive events result in much lower levels of conditioned fear than do uncontrollable aversive events. Because panic attacks are highly aversive, one would expect that the degree of perceived uncontrollability that a person has over panic attacks would be positively related to the person's levels of agoraphobic avoidance and anticipatory anxiety. In keeping with this prediction, Telch and colleagues (1989) found that a measure of perceived inability to cope with panic attacks predicted levels of agoraphobic avoidance. A related hypothesis is that perceived control over the initial symptoms of a panic attack may reduce the likelihood that these symptoms will spiral into a full-blown attack. Sanderson, Rapee, and Barlow (1989) reported a very important experiment demonstrating support for this latter prediction. They had 20 patients with panic disorder undergo a CO_2 panic provocation procedure. Half the patients were told that if a light came on while they were inhaling the CO_2, they could turn a dial and the rate of CO_2 infusion would decrease—this was the perceived control group. The other half of the patients were told the same thing, but for this group the light never came on—the no perceived control group. Although none of the patients exercised control, patients in the perceived control group showed lower levels of physiological arousal and were less likely to panic than were those in the no perceived control group. These two studies by Craske et al. (1995) and Sanderson et al. (1989) point to the fruitfulness of pursuing ideas from the research literature on unpredictable and uncontrollable aversive events in further study of panic disorder and agoraphobia, as would be expected from the perspective of SIDCA models.

Generalized Anxiety Disorder

Generalized anxiety disorder (GAD) is characterized by chronic excessive anxiety and worry about a number of events or activities. This state was traditionally described as free-floating anxiety because it was not anchored to a specific object or situation as are specific or social phobias. DSM-IV criteria specify that the anxiety or worry must occur more days than not for at least six months and that it must be experienced as difficult to control. The subjective experience of excessive anxiety or worry must also be accompanied by at least three of the following six symptoms: restlessness or feelings of being keyed up or on edge; a sense of being easily fatigued; difficulty concentrating or mind going blank; irritability; muscle tension; and sleep disturbance. Because we cannot have access to the content of an animal's thoughts, some might argue that animal models of GAD are not feasible (see Table 1, point 6). Many of the other symptoms of GAD, however, have clearly been seen in animal models, and so we do not dismiss their utility simply because we cannot gain access to the animal's thoughts.

Many of the best examples of symptoms resembling GAD come from the old experimental neurosis literature from the 1930s and 1940s—long before there were separate anxiety disorders—and so this resemblance went unnoticed until Mineka and Kihlstrom's (1978) review of the experimental neurosis literature. Pavlov, Gantt, Liddell, and Masserman all consistently found patterns of behavior in their animals characterized by extreme agitation, hypersensitivity, rapid respiration and heartbeat, restlessness, piloerection, muscular tension, distractibility, and inability to perform previously learned responses. These symptoms were often apparent outside of the experimental situation in which the "neurotic behavior" was induced—in other words, it was generalized, and it was also often very persistent—sometimes even worsening with the passage of time. Thus they seemed to show many of the symptoms of GAD (see also Mineka, 1985a).

In humans there are undoubtedly genetic and temperamental contributions to GAD (e.g., Barlow, 1988; Kendler et al., 1992b), and we have already reviewed evidence in the social phobia section showing that close analogues of the behavioral inhibition phenomenon exist in animals, with the evidence clearly suggesting that reactivity to nonsocial and social stressors is highly correlated. Thus the temperamental diathesis for a variety of the anxiety disorders is probably relatively nonspecific. But what of experiential contributions to GAD?

As discussed by Mineka (1985a), classical and instrumental conditioning models—mostly from the SITIA tradition—do not fare very well, with the possible exception of interoceptive classical conditioning, which long ago was postulated by Russian investigators to be involved in free-floating anxiety, the earlier term for GAD (Razran, 1961). The idea was that various interoceptive CSs could be paired with unpleasant, anxiety-producing USs and thereby elicit anxiety, even though the person was not aware of the occurrence of the CS. Such interoceptive conditioning is known to be highly stable and resistant to extinction compared to exteroceptive conditioning, and because such CSs (and USs) are part of everyday living, their opportunity for playing a role in GAD is reasonable.

Nevertheless, as would be expected from the perspective of

SIDCA models, there are better animal models for GAD, and they derive once again from the literature on unpredictable and uncontrollable aversive events. For the past 30 years numerous theorists have suggested that uncertainty and helplessness are implicated in generalized anxiety. For example, Mandler (e.g., 1972; Mandler & Watson, 1966) argued that anxiety and arousal occur when a response sequence is interrupted and the person has no perceived control over the interruption. Lazarus (1966; Lazarus & Averill, 1972) argued that anxiety occurs when a person perceives a threat whose source is unknown or ambiguous, leaving no clear response options available. Finally, Seligman (1975) argued that unpredictability over important life events—especially negative ones—led to anxiety.

It may seem surprising to some to refer to helplessness as a model of anxiety when 20 years ago Seligman presented it as a model of depression (1974, 1975). Over the past decade several investigators have proposed that it may be a better model of anxiety than of depression (e.g., Maier, personal communication, 27 May 1995; Mineka, 1985a; Barlow, 1988), although given the high comorbidity between the two, this may not be so surprising. For example, Maier and his colleagues have shown that benzodiazepines—antianxiety drugs—administered before a helplessness induction phase prevent helplessness effects from occurring 24 hours later (Drugan, Ryan, Minor, & Maier, 1984; Sherman, Allers, Petty, & Henn, 1979). These results strongly implicate the induction of anxiety as necessary for learned helplessness effects to be observed. Maier has also shown that following a helplessness induction phase the animals show symptoms of anxiety for several days in totally novel environments. In other words, the anxiety generalizes outside the experimental situation and is not tied to the context in which inescapable shock occurred (Peterson, Maier, & Seligman, 1993).

One prominent theory is that exposure to unpredictable events leads to feelings of chronic fear or anxiety because in the absence of a signal for the aversive event, there is also no safety signal telling the organism when he or she can relax and feel safe (Seligman, 1968; Seligman & Binik, 1977). This certainly seems to parallel the uncertainty theme in the anxiety literature, and the helplessness ideas seem to parallel the response unavailability theme in the anxiety literature. It is also of interest to consider the experimental neurosis literature referred to above in this context. Mineka and Kihlstrom (1978) reviewed that literature and concluded that the two most prominent themes that ran through the myriad paradigms that all seemed to produce this common set of symptoms—many of which are similar to those seen in GAD—are that important life events become unpredictable or uncontrollable or both. That is, buried within each of the experimental neurosis paradigms is evidence that environmental events of vital importance to the organism (food for a hungry animal or shock for a restrained animal) become unpredictable or uncontrollable or both. Thus, as would be expected from SIDCA models, recent empirical and theoretical work on the effects of uncontrollable and/or unpredictable aversive events has clearly had an important impact on our thinking about GAD.

Posttraumatic Stress Disorder

In DSM-IV, the symptoms of PTSD are arranged into three categories labeled reexperiencing, avoidance, and increased arousal. Reexperiencing symptoms include intrusive recollections of the trauma, nightmares, flashbacks, and emotional distress and/or physiological reactivity at exposure to reminders of the trauma. Foa, Zinbarg, and Olasov-Rothbaum (1992) suggested that the avoidance category can be further subdivided into avoidance of trauma-related situations or thoughts and numbing of emotional responsiveness, including restricted range of affect, detachment from others, and decreased interest in activities. Interestingly, findings that Vietnam veterans with PTSD show reduced pain sensitivity when exposed to reminders of combat suggests that numbing may have a literal manifestation as analgesia (Pitman, van der Kolk, Orr, & Greenberg, 1990; van der Kolk, Pitman, & Orr, 1989). Arousal symptoms include disturbed functioning (difficulty sleeping or concentrating), generalized anxiety (exaggerated startle, hypervigilance), and irritability.

It should be readily apparent, even from the brief description above, that the symptom profile for PTSD is the most complex of all the anxiety disorders. Although there is a great deal of symptom overlap between PTSD and the other anxiety disorders (e.g., heightened arousal, hypervigilance, avoidance) and between PTSD and depressive disorders (e.g., decreased interest in activities, difficulties sleeping, problems concentrating), other features of PTSD appear to be more distinctive. Certainly the numbing symptoms appear to be distinctive vis-à-vis the other anxiety disorders, and several authors have suggested that a biphasic alternation between episodes of intrusions and numbing may be the hallmark feature of PTSD (e.g., Foa et al., 1992; Horowitz, 1986; van der Kolk, 1987).

Earlier simple conditioning models of PTSD from the SITIA tradition did not fare very well, in part because they failed to model the complexity of the PTSD symptom profile (e.g., Foa et al., 1989). Despite this complexity of the symptom profile, however, several authors have proposed that the animal literature on unpredictable and uncontrollable aversive events may provide mini-models for PTSD from the SIDCA category that can shed light on some of the mechanisms involved in the development of PTSD symptoms (Foa et al., 1992; Kolb, 1987; van der Kolk, 1987; van der Kolk, Greenberg, Boyd, & Krystal, 1985; Başoğlu & Mineka, 1992). These authors suggested numerous parallels between the effects of uncontrollable and unpredictable stress and PTSD. First, Başoğlu and Mineka (1992) argued that the intense physical stressors used in the animal literature (e.g., electric shocks, near drowning from cold water swims, defeats in physical fighting) closely resemble those in at least one form of human traumatization that often leads to PTSD—torture. In addition, we also note that intense physical harm is often present, or at least threatened, in several other forms of human traumatization associated with elevated rates of PTSD, including child abuse, spouse abuse, and both sexual and nonsexual assault. A second similarity is that the persistent course of the disturbances associated with unpredictable and/or uncontrollable aversive events in animals parallels the chronic course of untreated PTSD (e.g., Başoğlu & Mineka, 1992; Foa et al., 1992; Mineka & Kihlstrom, 1978).

Foa et al. (1992) and Başoğlu and Mineka (1992) argued that a third parallel is that there appear to be compelling similarities between the symptoms of PTSD and the behavioral and physiological disturbances observed in animals exposed to unpredictable and/or uncontrollable aversive stimulation. The most obvious of these similarities is the heightened generalized anxiety and arousal characteristic of both PTSD and animals exposed to unpredictable or uncontrollable aversive stimulation. As noted earlier, the arousal symptoms of PTSD as defined in the DSM-IV include indices of both disturbed physiological functioning (such as difficulty sleeping) and generalized anxiety (such as hypervigilance and exaggerated startle). In addition, psychophysiological studies have repeatedly shown PTSD to be associated with elevated baseline levels of heart rate and blood pressure (e.g., Blanchard, 1990; Blanchard, Kolb, Gerardi, Ryan, & Pallmeyer, 1986; Davidson & Baum, 1986). These symptoms and characteristics of PTSD appear to be analogous to the potentiated levels of contextual anxiety and disturbed physiological functioning associated with uncontrollable and unpredictable shock reviewed elsewhere (see the section on specific phobias earlier in this chapter; for more detailed discussions see Başoğlu & Mineka, 1992; Foa et al., 1992; Mineka & Hendersen, 1985).

There also appears to be a relatively clear analogy between the avoidance symptoms characteristic of PTSD and the patterns of avoidance behavior displayed by animals subjected to uncontrollable and unpredictable shock. This analogy may not be obvious at first glance given that the most widely known sequelae of uncontrollable, unpredictable shock are deficits in escape and *active* avoidance—the classic "learned helplessness" effect (Overmier & Seligman, 1967; Seligman & Maier, 1967; Maier, Albin, & Testa, 1973). An analysis of avoidance learning would be incomplete, however, without considering passive avoidance in addition to active avoidance. In passive avoidance paradigms, the contingencies are arranged such that the organism must withhold a designated response to avoid punishment, in contrast to active avoidance paradigms in which the organism must emit a designated response to avoid punishment. As we have reviewed elsewhere (Foa et al., 1992; Rush, Mineka, & Suomi, 1982; Zinbarg, Barlow, Brown, & Hertz, 1992), a less widely known effect produced by uncontrollable shock is that it appears to be associated with superior learning of passive avoidance. Thus to restate this analogy more clearly and precisely, the enhanced passive avoidance behavior displayed by animals exposed to uncontrollable shock appears to resemble the avoidance symptoms of PTSD sufferers in which they *passively* avoid entering situations where they might encounter reminders of their trauma.

It is also interesting that child abuse survivors are not only at increased risk for the development of PTSD following adult victimization but are also at increased risk for being victimized as adults (e.g., Feuer & Zinbarg, 1995; Bolstadt & Zinbarg, 1995). Although the mechanisms mediating this tendency toward revictimization are unclear, one possibility is that this tendency may reflect deficits at escape and active avoidance. That is, when a risky situation is encountered despite passive attempts to avoid danger, the survivor of child abuse may differ from the person who did not suffer child abuse in terms of the motivational or cognitive sets that might facilitate escaping the situation unharmed. Although this hypothesis is admittedly highly speculative at this time, it will be important to test in the future because it suggests another parallel between the symptoms of PTSD and the disturbances associated with the uncontrollability/unpredictability model.

Given the findings demonstrating stress-induced analgesia in PTSD sufferers noted earlier, there also may be an animal analogue of the numbing symptoms of PTSD. As reviewed elsewhere (Başoğlu & Mineka, 1992; Foa et al., 1992; Maier, 1986, 1989), both escapable and inescapable shock produce stress-induced analgesia. In comparison to the analgesia produced by escapable shock, however, that produced by inescapable shock is opiate-mediated, and although it dissipates fairly rapidly, it is reinstatable at least 24 hours later by exposure to several shocks. In addition, inescapable shock leads to hyperactivity to the analgesic effects of morphine not observed after escapable shock, suggesting that inescapable shock sensitizes the opioid system. That there may also be an opioid-mediated analgesia in PTSD was demonstrated in a Vietnam veteran with PTSD who showed analgesia while watching a video of a combat scene; the analgesia was blocked by naloxone—an opioid antagonist (Pitman et al., 1990). This suggests that the numbing experienced by PTSD sufferers may resemble the analgesia associated with inescapable shock in being mediated by endogenous opioid systems. Torture victims also often report analgesia ("feeling numb all over") (Başoğlu & Mineka, 1992). "For example, one survivor said the difficult part of electrical torture was the beginning; after a while he felt numb all over his body and completely dissociated from the situation" (pp. 207–208)—exactly what would be expected based on the animal literature.

Reexperiencing symptoms would appear to be more problematic to model in animals because several of these symptoms (nightmares, flashbacks, intrusive recollections) are dependent on self-report (see Table 1, point 6). However, only one of the five reexperiencing symptoms listed in the DSM-IV is required for the diagnosis of PTSD, and two of these symptoms are emotional distress at exposure to reminders of the trauma and physiological reactivity at exposure to such reminders. Thus nightmares, flashbacks, and intrusive recollections are not necessary for the diagnosis.

Given the considerations outlined above, Foa et al. (1992) argued that distress at exposure to reminders of trauma is central to the construct of reexperiencing. These authors went on to suggest that emotional distress or physiological reactivity at exposure to reminders of trauma, which are not necessarily dependent on self-report, can be reconceptualized as conditioned fear responses. That is, reminders of trauma can be seen as a CS which, viewed from the perspective of contemporary conditioning models, may be seen as a reminder of the US. This interpretation appears to be particularly consistent with Wagner's (1979, 1981) standard-operating-procedures model of conditioning that suggests that a conditioned fear response is a sign that the CS has associatively primed the representation of the US. In other words, Wagner's model suggests that a conditioned fear response results when the US is being reprocessed or reexperienced. Thus, Foa et al. propose that a conditioned fear response can model some of the reexperiencing symptoms and important aspects of the processes underlying reexperiencing. As discussed earlier in the specific phobias section, numerous studies have shown that a CS for inescapable shock produces greater conditioned fear than does a CS for escapable shock, suggesting that, in comparison to controllable stress, uncontrollable stress is associated with greater reexperiencing symptoms.

Before exploring some of the implications that can be derived from the uncontrollable/unpredictable stress model for the understanding of PTSD, it is important to acknowledge that this model has been considered as relevant to several different anxiety and mood disorders. Indeed, we ourselves have suggested that perceptions of uncontrollability and unpredictability play a role in many of the anxiety disorders discussed in this chapter. This may indicate that the uncontrollability/unpredictability model has been overextended. An alternative perspective emerges, however, when we consider the substantial comorbidity and symptom overlap among the anxiety disorders (Moras, Di Nardo, Brown, & Barlow, 1995; Zinbarg & Barlow, 1992) and between anxiety and depression (Alloy, Kelly,

Mineka, & Clements, 1990; Clark & Watson, 1991a and b). Given this overlap, it may be that the literature on uncontrollability and unpredictability illuminates variables relevant to the core features common to the full spectrum of disorders of negative affect.

Acknowledging that this model may have some relevance for many of the anxiety and depressive disorders does not rule out the possibility that it is more relevant for some disorders than for others or that it is relevant in somewhat different ways for the different disorders. Indeed, it has been suggested that this model is most directly relevant for the study of PTSD (Başŏglu & Mineka, 1992; Foa et al., 1992). The claim of special relevance for PTSD has been based on arguments that the entire syndrome produced by uncontrollable or unpredictable stress, including opioid-mediated analgesia, appears most closely to resemble the PTSD syndrome (Başŏglu & Mineka, 1992; Foa et al., 1992) and the physical stressors most used in the animal literature most closely resemble those involved in the onset of at least some cases of PTSD (Başŏglu & Mineka, 1992).

Having now reviewed evidence regarding the similarity of symptoms of PTSD and those produced by uncontrollable and unpredictable stress, what are the implications of the uncontrollability, unpredictability model for understanding other aspects of PTSD? A number of findings that have emerged from the studies on uncontrollable and unpredictable aversive events allow for the generation of more specific hypotheses regarding human PTSD. First, the experience of trauma survivors can be roughly divided into three broad phases: the pretrauma phase, the traumatization phase, and the posttrauma phase (Başŏglu & Mineka, 1992). Accordingly, the literature on the effects of uncontrollable and unpredictable aversive events can be divided into three broad categories that correspond to each of these three phases (see Table 1, point 2). The analogue of the pretrauma phase in the experimental literature involves studies of the pretreatment variables that either immunize or sensitize the organism to the deleterious effects of subsequent exposure to uncontrollable and unpredictable aversive events. The analogue of the traumatization phase in the experimental literature concerns questions of what are the acute reactions to uncontrollable and unpredictable aversive events. Finally, the analogue of the posttrauma phase in the experimental literature involves the study of both the long-term consequences of uncontrollable and unpredictable stress

and the variables that occur following the experience of uncontrollable and unpredictable stress that influence the intensity and duration of the emotional and behavioral disturbances maintained into
the future (Başoğlu & Mineka, 1992).

Starting with the traumatization phase, this model suggests the
hypothesis that the degree to which traumas are perceived to be uncontrollable and unpredictable is related to the likelihood that a survivor will develop PTSD symptoms, as well as the entire PTSD syndrome. Alternatively, it may be that the more traumas are perceived
to be uncontrollable and unpredictable, the more intense and persistent the PTSD symptoms will be. Ethical considerations obviously
prohibit studies attempting to manipulate directly perceptions of
uncontrollability and unpredictability of traumatic events in humans; therefore, tests of these hypotheses must rely on correlational
designs. Although we are not aware of any prospective studies that
have examined the ability of perceptions of uncontrollability and
unpredictability to predict the later development or maintenance of
PTSD symptoms, there is some cross-sectional evidence that the severity of PTSD symptoms is associated with diminished perceptions
of controllability. Kushner, Riggs, Foa, and Miller (1993) found that
sexual and nonsexual assault survivors who scored lowest on a scale
measuring belief in their ability to influence events in their lives received the highest scores on a clinician-rated composite measure of
PTSD symptom severity. Bolstadt and Zinbarg (1995) reported similar results using the Rotter Locus of Control Scale. In this study, survivors of a single sexual assault in adulthood who showed the most
diminished perceptions of their ability to influence the events in
their lives received the highest scores on a self-report version of the
composite measure of PTSD symptom severity used by Kushner et
al. (1993).

Given the cross-sectional nature of the studies conducted by
Kushner et al. (1993) and Bolstadt and Zinbarg (1995), they are in
need of replication using longitudinal designs such as assessing perceptions of uncontrollability over trauma and PTSD symptoms
shortly after the experience of a trauma (Time 1) and examining the
utility of the perception of uncontrollability measure to predict PTSD
symptom severity at a later time after statistically controlling for
PTSD symptom severity at Time 1. These cross-sectional results sug-

gest that more rigorous tests of the uncontrollability and unpredictability model of PTSD are warranted.

Regarding the traumatization phase, there is one additional particularly intriguing set of findings that may have implications for our understanding of variables during the traumatization phase that can mitigate against the deleterious effects of trauma. Weiss, Glazer, and Pohorecky (1976) found that the expression of aggression may moderate the stress produced by uncontrollable shock. In this study, rats exposed to uncontrollable shock that were allowed to fight with conspecifics during the shocks showed reduced levels of ulceration relative to yoked rats not given the opportunity to fight or display aggressiveness during the shocks. Furthermore, rats exposed to uncontrollable shock and simply allowed to show aggressive postures toward a conspecific even though they were prevented from actual fighting by the presence of a barrier also showed reduced levels of ulceration. Extrapolating from this finding to stress responses to human torture, Başoğlu and Mineka (1992) hypothesized that the amount of trauma inflicted during torture "per se may be less predictive than is the victim's psychological state of resistance and fighting back versus giving up and conceding defeat" (1992, p. 193). In addition, at least one study found that rape victims who physically fight their attacker adapt better following the rape (Chambless, personal communication, 23 April 1995).

Some of the findings from the social defeat literature, discussed earlier in the social phobia section, appear to be consistent with those reported by Weiss et al. (1976). In particular, several studies showed that the analgesia induced by extensive exposure to attack from conspecifics is more highly correlated with the extent to which the animal assumes the characteristic postures of defeat than with the number of bites actually received (Miczek, Thompson, & Shuster, 1982; Rodgers & Hendrie, 1983). These findings converge with those reported by Weiss et al. in suggesting the hypothesis that the trauma survivor's attitude of resistance versus defeat may be an important determinant of the intensity of posttraumatic stress reactions.

As noted above, the experimental literature not only has implications for understanding the traumatization phase itself, but this literature also suggests pretrauma and posttrauma variables that may influence the development or maintenance of PTSD. There are studies showing that prior experiences with uncontrollable stressors sensitize the organism toward the deleterious effects of a subsequent experience with uncontrollable trauma (e.g., Drugan, Moye, & Maier, 1982; Moye, Hyson, Grau, & Maier, 1983). These findings led Foa et al. (1992) to predict that repeated childhood abuse would predispose survivors to developing PTSD following later traumatization. Consistent with these hypotheses derived from the animal literature, a history of childhood abuse has been found to be associated with greater PTSD severity in response to sexual and non-sexual assault in adulthood (Dancu, Shoyer, Riggs, & Foa, 1991, cited in Foa et al., 1992). Bolstadt and Zinbarg (1995) extended this finding by showing that abuse is particularly associated with greater severity of PTSD symptoms in response to sexual assault in adulthood when the childhood abuse was experienced repeatedly.

By contrast, there are also findings that suggest that immunization against the effects of uncontrollable stress is possible, at least under some circumstances. Numerous studies have shown that a prior history of control can immunize against the deleterious effects of subsequent uncontrollable stress (e.g., Hannum, Rosellini, & Seligman, 1976; Joffe, Rawson, & Mulick, 1973; Mineka et al., 1986; Moye, Cook, Grau, & Maier, 1981; Moye et al., 1983; Seligman & Maier, 1967; Volpicelli, Ulm, Altenor, & Seligman, 1983; Williams & Maier, 1977; see Başoğlu & Mineka, 1992, for a more detailed review). Indeed, experimental work with animals has shown that immunization procedures not only prevent behavioral indices of learned helplessness but can even prevent physiological changes such as opiate-mediated analgesia that occur following exposure to uncontrollable shocks. In addition, early studies by Seligman (1968) and Weiss (1968) showed that predictable stressors often have significantly less aversive impact than do unpredictable stressors, and more recent studies by Overmier (1985) have shown that exposure to predictable but uncontrollable shocks often does not result in the associative deficit of learned helplessness.

In keeping with such findings, Başoğlu and Mineka (1995) tested the idea that prior psychological preparedness for trauma would relate to less perceived distress during torture. In two previous papers, Başoğlu and colleagues (Başoğlu et al., 1994a; Başoğlu, Paker, Tasdemir, Ozmen, & Sahin, 1994b) reported that only 33% of a sample of 55 carefully studied torture survivors who had been political activists in Turkey before being imprisoned and tortured had ever qualified for a diagnosis for PTSD (based on the lifetime Structured Clinical Interview for DSM-III-R). At the time of the interview—which was an average of five years following their last experience with torture—only 18% qualified for a diagnosis of PTSD. This low rate of PTSD seemed very surprising at first glance given that these torture survivors had experienced an average of 23 different forms of torture and a mean total number of exposures to various kinds of torture of 291. Nevertheless, this was an unusual sample because they were all political activists and it seemed that their political activism was likely to have led them to be more psychologically prepared and better immunized in the sense of having greater perceived control over their environment than a random criminal who had been imprisoned and tortured. To test this hypothesis, Başoğlu and Mineka (1995) developed a psychological preparedness scale that was a combined index of experience exercising control over important life issues and of predictability of being imprisoned and tortured. Results revealed that psychologically more prepared subjects had experienced a greater variety of forms of torture ($r = .29, p < .05$) and had more exposures to torture events ($r = .27, p < .05$). Yet there was a trend for the more prepared subjects to have given *lower* global overall distress ratings for their entire torture experience ($r = -.23, p < .10$). So these results do provide some support for the proposition that psychological preparedness (again, a combined index of experience exercising control over important life issues and of predictability of being imprisoned and tortured) does relate to lower global distress rating. It will still be important, however, to compare these results with those from a sample of prisoners who are not political activists but who have had comparable experiences with torture. Rates of PTSD should be much higher in such a sample, according to the present theory.

Nevertheless, the literature regarding prior experiences with control appears to be complex because other studies have found that having prior experience with control can make the subsequent reaction to uncontrollable stress more severe when control is taken away, relative to what is seen in animals with no prior experience with control (e.g., Hanson, Larson, & Snowdon, 1976; Staub, Tursky, & Schwartz, 1971; Weiss, 1971). These sensitization effects may be related to the superconditioning effect in which greater conditioned fear accrues to a CS if it is presented in compound with a conditioned inhibitor of fear during acquisition training (Rescorla, 1971). This finding suggests that violation of previously held safety associations, such as previously held perceptions of control over one's environment, the beneficial effects of which may be mediated, at least in part, by the safety signal properties associated with the controlling response (Cook et al. 1987; Mineka et al., 1984a), can have particularly deleterious effects on the organism.

There has not yet been a completely satisfactory resolution of the apparent inconsistencies in when prior experience with control has beneficial as opposed to deleterious consequences. Mineka and Kelly (1989) speculated, however, that contextual factors may be critical in mediating the effects of prior control. On the one hand, these authors proposed that prior control may sensitize the organism to the subsequent effects of uncontrollability experienced in the same context where the organism previously had control (maximizing the sense of loss of control). On the other hand, they proposed that prior control may immunize the organism against the effects of future uncontrollable experiences in contexts dissimilar to the context in which the organism previously had control (see Mineka & Kelly, 1989, for a more detailed discussion). Foa et al. (1992) further speculated that if the resolution suggested by Mineka and Kelly (1989) is valid, the underlying mediating mechanism when sensitization is produced may be that prior safety associations are more likely to be violated because the context in which uncontrollability is experienced is the same as the context in which the organism previously experienced control.

The reinstatement effect discussed earlier in this chapter is one example of a posttrauma experience that may influence the course of PTSD symptoms. An interesting study by Rosellini, Widman, Abrahamsen, and Bassuk (1990) suggested that issues of controllability may interact with potentially reinstating events to influence posttrauma emotional reactions. These investigators found that animals with a prior history of uncontrollable, unpredictable shock appear to be predisposed to show an exaggerated reinstatement of anxiety to a CS when a noncontingent US is presented following extinction training with the CS. Clinical observations suggest that processes similar to reinstatement also occur in people with PTSD. For example, Foa and Dancu (1994) described a case in which a woman who had achieved considerable symptom reduction in therapy for PTSD related to a sexual assault experienced a relapse in her assault-related symptoms after being involved in a car accident. In this case, it appears that the car accident reinstated her assault-related PTSD symptoms. Extrapolating from the results of Rosellini et al., we would expect that trauma victims who most strongly perceive an initial trauma to be uncontrollable and unpredictable would be at greatest risk for experiencing reinstatement of emotional distress after experiencing another trauma not related to the original trauma.

In addition, recent evidence from the animal laboratory suggests that the reexperiencing symptoms of PTSD might be involved in mediating the often persistent course of this disorder. In particular, Maier (27 May 1995, personal communication) has found that the usual time course of some of the classic learned helplessness effects in rats such as the shuttlebox escape deficit (typically 2–3 days) can be prolonged if the rats are simply exposed at 2–3-day intervals to the context in which they had previously experienced uncontrollable stress. That is, simple reminders of the original trauma through exposure to the context in which it occurred seem sufficient to prolong the time period during which learned helplessness deficits can be observed. Currently, results show the effect can be prolonged to at least 12 days. By analogy, such findings suggest that humans who exhibit many reexperiencing symptoms (e.g., flashbacks, nightmares, or simple reexposure to cues for trauma) may be expected to show a more persistent time course for the disorder relative to those with fewer reexperiencing symptoms.

In summary, there appear to be some compelling similarities between the often persistent behavioral disturbances produced by uncontrollable and unpredictable shock in animals and the chronic symptoms of PTSD in humans. In addition, intense physical stressors and stressors such as social defeat used in the animal literature resemble those in at least some forms of human traumatization that often lead to PTSD, including torture, child abuse, spouse abuse, and both sexual and nonsexual assault. These similarities suggest that perceptions of uncontrollability and unpredictability may influence the development and maintenance of PTSD symptoms. Initial studies at the human level have produced evidence that is largely consistent with this hypothesis (Bolstadt & Zinbarg, 1995; Kushner et al., 1993). The animal literature on predictability and immunization may also help explain why some people seem to be at reduced risk for PTSD. For example, it may help explain why torture survivors who were political activists showed such low rates of PTSD. Conversely, the animal literature on pretreatment variables that sensitize the organism to the deleterious effects of subsequent exposure to uncontrollable and unpredictable aversive events may help to illuminate why some people are at greater risk for PTSD than others. In addition, several studies reviewed by Clark, Watson, and Mineka (1994) show that conduct disorder or antisocial personality disorder may increase risk for PTSD by increasing exposure to traumatic stressors—possibly through a sensitization process (e.g., Helzer, Robins, & McEvoy, 1987; Kulka et al., 1990). This may be because individuals with conduct disorder or antisocial personality disorder often grow up in chaotic environments that expose them to multiple stressors. Finally, studies of the effects of uncontrollability on the later reinstatement of conditioned anxiety may help to explain relapses of PTSD symptoms related to a prior trauma after experiencing another trauma in the future, and studies of how exposure to reminders of trauma may prolong learned helplessness effects may help to explain some aspects of the persistent course of this disorder.

Obsessive-Compulsive Disorder

Obsessive-compulsive disorder (OCD) is defined in DSM-IV by the occurrence of unwanted and intrusive obsessive thoughts, impulses, or distressing images; these are usually accompanied by compulsive behaviors designed to neutralize the obsessive thoughts or images or to prevent some dreaded event or situation. The compulsive behaviors are repetitive behaviors such as hand-washing, ordering, or checking, or mental acts, such as praying or counting, that the person feels driven to perform in response to an obsession. Conditioning and ethological models of obsessive-compulsive disorder are perhaps more limited in scope than those of some of the other anxiety disorders we discuss here. This is in part because it is probably difficult if not impossible to develop an animal model of obsessions because we do not have access to the content of animals' thought processes. Thus it is more difficult to understand the nature of the particular compulsive behavior analogues the animals engage in because the nature of the particular compulsive behaviors engaged in is so often closely tied to the content of the obsessions (see Table 1, point 6). In spite of this limitation, a good deal has been written about conditioning and ethological models of obsessive-compulsive disorder, and we will briefly review some of the major findings that are thought to be of relevance.

ANIMAL MODELS OF COMPULSIVE BEHAVIORS

At the most basic level of symptom similarity to human compulsive behaviors, at least five different phenomena in the literature have been proposed as animal models. From the animal learning literature, similarities between well-trained avoidance responses and compulsive behaviors have long been noted (e.g., Mineka, 1985a; Solomon, Kamin, & Wynne, 1953). With extensive training, avoidance responses (to avoid electric shock) become stereotyped in nature and highly resistant to extinction. In addition, Maier's (1949) classic studies of frustration and fixation in rats showed that compulsive, ritualistic behavior could be elicited when rats were repeatedly frustrated as they were faced with insoluble discrimination problems (see Mineka, 1985a, for more extensive discussion).

In the animal behavior literature, it has long been observed that animals subjected to a variety of stressful conditions (such as abnormal rearing conditions or confinement such as in a zoo or animal laboratory) often engage in stereotypic behavior, which is generally defined as any repetitive locomotor behavior involving patterned and rhythmic movement. Relatedly, ritualistic behaviors involve idiosyncratic nonlocomotor stereotyped behaviors such as strumming the mesh of a cage or picking at one's teeth for prolonged periods of time. Such stereotyped and ritualistic behaviors are particularly elevated during times of stress such as during repeated social separations in monkeys (Mineka, Suomi, & Delizio, 1981).

Ethologists have also observed that many species of animals engage in displacement activities under situations of high arousal or conflict; in essence, when a motivated behavior is thwarted or blocked, an animal may suddenly engage in some seemingly unrelated behavior, which is usually highly stereotyped in nature and is called a displacement activity. Some have argued that these activities bear some resemblance to the compulsive rituals seen in OCD. For example, Holland (1974) observed that two of the most common displacement activities are grooming and nesting and went onto suggest that these may be functionally related to grooming and tidying rituals seen in OCD (see also Pitman, 1989; Stein, Shoulberg, Helton, & Hollander, 1992). That compulsive rituals in OCD tend to be provoked by the anxiety, discomfort, or distress brought on by obsessive thoughts parallels the occurrence of displacement activities during situations of high arousal or conflict. It is also of interest that in Goodall's (1986) extensive observations of the chimpanzees of Gombe, she noted that social grooming occurs frequently (although not exclusively) during periods when the chimpanzees are frightened, tense, or anxious and that it seemed to help them relax during such periods.

Most recently, Rapoport (1989) argued that compulsive rituals may be fixed action patterns that have been released inappropriately, noting that "the behaviors in OCD resemble misplaced grooming and/or protective rituals" (p. 193) (see also Swedo, 1989). This is a more general argument than the displacement activity argument because fixed action patterns can be triggered by appropriate releasing stimuli at nearly any time—not just during periods of conflict or high arousal. The appeal of this more general model may be that it is better able to account for why the occurrence of compulsive rituals is not always associated with emotional states such as anxiety, frustration, or distress (e.g., Rachman & Hodgson, 1980). But it does not help account for why an emotional reaction often seems to be involved in triggering rituals. Nor have researchers yet been able to identify the key releasing stimuli for such fixed action patterns (Swedo, 1989). In addition, compulsive rituals in OCD are not as fixed and invariant across members of a species as are the fixed action patterns traditionally studied by ethologists. Although rituals may become very stereotyped, there seems to be a greater ontogenetic component to their development than is true for fixed action patterns in lower animals, which may not be too surprising given input from our highly developed neocortex.

ANXIETY REDUCTION THEORY

As reviewed elsewhere (e.g., Mineka, 1985a), for years the anxiety-reduction theory was the dominant alternative to the psychoanalytic theories of OCD (e.g., Dollard & Miller, 1950; Metzner, 1963; Nemiah, 1967; Rachman & Hodgson, 1980; Teasdale, 1974). The essential argument, which is based on Mowrer's (1947) two-process theory of avoidance learning, is that obsessive thoughts or images elicit anxiety or discomfort and therefore motivate the performance of what becomes a compulsive ritual; the ritual is reinforced and strengthened by the reduction in anxiety that ensues. At a descriptive level, this theory, which could be said to derive from what we call the SITIA tradition, does seem to describe what goes on in a majority of cases (see Rachman & Hodgson, 1980, for results supporting the theory).

This theory seems, however, more compelling as a theory of the maintenance of OCD than as a theory of etiology. First, there is little if any evidence that a traumatic conditioning history (direct or vicarious) is involved in the origins of OCD in most cases (Mineka, 1985a; Rachman & Hodgson, 1980). Moreover, there is increasing evidence for a biological basis to this disorder (e.g., Baxter, Schwartz, & Guze, 1991; Baxter, Schwartz, Guze, & Szuba, 1992; Insel, 1990, 1992; Liebowitz & Hollander, 1991; Rapoport & Wise, 1988; Swedo, Leonard, & Rapoport, 1992). By contrast, as a model of the maintenance of the disorder it has considerable heuristic value in accounting for many of the features of day-to-day fluctuations in obsessive-compulsive symptoms.

Two findings from the avoidance learning literature have often been cited as relevant to understanding the high frequency of occurrence of compulsive rituals. Avoidance responses occur more frequently with unsignaled (Sidman) than with signaled avoidance paradigms (Mineka, 1985a; Teasdale, 1974). In unsignaled avoidance the contingencies are arranged such that the aversive stimulus will occur at regular intervals (e.g., once every minute) unless the organism emits a designated response during the intervening time interval; there are no external signals that the aversive stimulus is imminent (as in signaled avoidance) other than the passage of time. One can consider compulsive rituals to be avoidance behavior that is under poor or minimal stimulus control because the provoking stimuli are not easily discriminated as reliable danger signals (e.g., how can one tell if a germ is present, or how does one tell the difference between safe and dangerous dirt?). Relatedly, it is well-known that avoidance learning and efficient avoidance maintenance are facilitated by the presence of safety signals or feedback stimuli when the avoidance response is made (e.g., Bolles, 1970; Denny, 1971; Mineka, 1979; Mowrer, 1960; Weisman & Litner, 1969, 1972). These feedback stimuli are thought to acquire fear inhibitory properties and to become sources of positive reinforcement for the avoidance response. Several theorists have argued that such findings are of relevance to understanding the high rate of occurrence of compulsive behaviors because many compulsive rituals can be characterized as having poor feedback or safety-signal properties (e.g., Mineka, 1985a; Rachman & Hodgson, 1980; Teasdale, 1974). In particular, if, as noted above, the particular stimuli provoking the response are poorly defined, it follows that accurate and convincing feedback about their removal will also be difficult to obtain (e.g., if you cannot detect whether germs are present, it is also difficult to determine whether they are gone). Moreover, the dangers that often precipitate checking rituals are often invisible, or intangible, future events, and so it is inherently difficult to know whether one has been successful in avoiding them. As Rachman and Hodgson noted, the obsessive-compulsive "has no assurance that the task is finished (i.e., that the perceived danger has been removed). At best the risks are diminished" (1980, p. 134).

Two more phenomena that have been studied in the avoidance learning literature may also help explain why the frequency of compulsive rituals sometimes shows temporary increases. First, it is well known that CS+s for fear when presented in an unsignaled avoidance situation will cause an increase in the rate of avoidance responding (e.g., Rescorla & LoLordo, 1965). Thus one might expect that rates of ritualizing would increase over baseline levels when novel objects or situations (other than the usual ones) that provoke anxiety or distress are encountered. This is in keeping with clinical observations (Chambless, personal communication, 23 April 1995). Because fear inhibitory phenomena are much more fragile than are fear excitatory effects (Hendersen, 1978, 1985; LoLordo, 1967; Mineka, 1992), however, and because obsessive-compulsives may not have good safety signals for reasons noted above, one may be less likely to see rates of ritualizing decrease from baseline levels, as can be observed when effective CS-s are presented during unsignaled avoidance responding (e.g., Rescorla & LoLordo, 1965). In other words, there may be a much wider range of frightening or distressing situations that could increase rates of ritualizing compared to a relative paucity of inhibitory stimuli or situations that might reduce their rates of occurrence.

The second related phenomenon from the avoidance learning literature of relevance to understanding temporary increases in the frequency of compulsive rituals (Mineka, 1985a; Teasdale, 1974) stems from observations that punishment of avoidance responding very often causes an increase in rate of responding or enhances resistance to extinction of the avoidance response rather than facilitating its extinction (e.g., Brown, 1969; Dean & Pitman, 1991). One popular explanation of this phenomenon starts with the premise that the punishing shocks or free shocks serve to increase the animal's fear or anxiety level. Because the animal has already learned to make the avoidance response in order to reduce the fear of the CS, it continues automatically to make the same response because this response has been strongly reinforced by anxiety reduction in the past. Thus one would expect that presentation of noxious stimulation (USs) could serve to increase the rate of performance of compulsive rituals. The noxious stimuli that could potentially have this effect could range from aversive consequences of excessive performance of the ritual itself (e.g., painful, bleeding hands) to criticism and intolerance expressed by family members. Consistent with such predictions, Steketee and Chambless (1995) have found that high levels of expressed emotion in the families of OCD patients undergoing behavioral treatment predicted a poor treatment outcome.

This also raises an important point about the wide variety and generality of the situations in which compulsive behaviors tend to be elicited. Avoidance models of obsessive-compulsive behavior from the SITIA tradition have sometimes been criticized on the grounds that they cannot account for this broad generalization of contexts in which compulsive rituals occur (see Table 1, point 4). Although it is true that most of the literature on avoidance learning has focused on training one response in one context, there are several important findings considered in the context of SIDCA models which effectively counter this criticism. First, it has been shown that independently established CS+s for fear (conditioned in a different context than the avoidance training context) can immediately acquire control over previously established avoidance responses when the CS+ is delivered for the first time in the avoidance context (e.g., Rescorla & LoLordo, 1965; Solomon & Turner, 1962). Second, and even more important, are several examples in the literature in which highly idiosyncratic responses (such as jumping over barriers or engaging in idiosyncratic running rituals) trained to reduce fear or frustration in one situation are spontaneously exhibited in a totally different situation when a similar emotional state is elicited through different means (e.g., Fonberg, 1956; Ross, 1964; see Amsel, 1971, and Mineka, 1985a, for extended discussions). Taken together, these experiments provide a model for demonstrating that ritualized behaviors can occur across a wide variety of situations given that a similar emotional state is elicited in each when, and if, a particular response has previously been conditioned to occur in the presence of that state. Similarly, the same displacement activities observed by ethologists can occur in a wide variety of situations that create tension or conflict.

PREPAREDNESS AND THE NONRANDOM DISTRIBUTION OF OBSESSIVE THOUGHTS AND COMPULSIVE BEHAVIORS

The concept of preparedness and selective associations has been applied not only to understanding specific and social phobias but also to obsessive-compulsive disorder (e.g., DeSilva, Rachman, & Seligmen, 1977). The basic observation leading to the extension of this hypothesis to OCD was that the themes of obsessive thoughts and images, as well as the nature of the most commonly observed compulsive rituals, seems to be nonrandom (as for the stimuli and situations that provoke specific and social phobias) (see Table 1, point 3). Moreover, this may be because there had been some evolutionarily based predisposition to have such thoughts and to engage in such behaviors. For example, thoughts about dirt and contamination associated with compulsive washing are so common as to make their occurrence seem nonrandom. DeSilva et al.'s (1977) rating system for the preparedness of phobias was extended to obsessive thoughts and compulsive behaviors. As expected, the investigators found that the content of a great majority of obsessions (as well as of phobias) was rated as prepared. Moreover, the preparedness ratings for the compulsive behaviors for the OCD patients were the highest of all.

DeSilva et al. (1977) also tried to determine whether there was any relationship between the preparedness of the content and behavior of the obsessions and compulsions and any other clinical features of the disorder, such as speed of onset or resistance to treatment. As noted in the specific phobia section, there were numerous problems with drawing firm conclusions from such a retrospective study that produced null results. Moreover, there are even problems with the rationale behind the hypotheses of this study. This part of the study was predicated on important features of Seligman's original preparedness theory (1970, 1971), which postulated that prepared associations should not only be selective in nature (i.e., certain CS-US combinations condition especially well together) but also share other common features, such as speed of learning, and resistance to extinction.

In spite of Seligman's claims that his theory will be of little utility unless it can be shown that prepared or selective associations share these other common features (such as high resistance to extinction and ease of acquisition), others have argued that it is not reasonable to expect this kind of covariance (e.g., Cook & Mineka, 1991; Mineka, 1985a; Rozin & Kalat, 1971; Shettleworth, 1972). For example, there is no reason to think that it would always be adaptive to have all associations that are easily acquired always be difficult to extinguish. For example, it may be adaptive to learn easily the location of a new food source but also easily to forget it in an environment where food sources are frequently changing (Rozin & Kalat, 1971). So, as argued elsewhere, the important insight in Seligman's original preparedness theory of phobias probably centers simply on the concept of selective associability (Mineka, 1985a; Cook & Mineka, 1991). That is, primates and humans seem to be biologically prepared to acquire rapidly fears of certain objects or situations that may once have posed a threat to our early ancestors. Extending the argument to OCD, they may also be biologically prepared to obsess or ruminate about certain topics related to situations that may also have posed a threat to our early ancestors. Moreover, they may also be biologically prepared to perform certain responses (and not others) to reduce emotional states of distress.

What evidence is there for this aspect of preparedness theory? There is ample evidence that animals are predisposed to acquire certain escape or avoidance responses to reduce fear or anxiety. For example, years ago, Bolles (1970) systematized observations about avoidance learning in animals and developed what he called a species-specific defense response theory of avoidance learning. According to this theory, animals can easily acquire as learned escape or avoidance responses only ones that resemble those that they would exhibit in the wild under conditions of threat—what he called species-specific defense responses. Other, more arbitrary responses are learned with greater difficulty or sometimes not at all.

With regard to the proposition that fear or anxiety is more easily conditioned to certain stimuli that may have posed a threat to our early ancestors, we have already reviewed evidence that this is the case for specific and social phobias. Although there are no exactly parallel experiments providing a model for OCD, the findings of de Silva et al. (1977) regarding the content and behavior of OCD falling predominantly in the "prepared" range, along with similar observations of Rapoport (1989), provide a solid basis for speculating that very similar arguments may apply. Particularly striking in this regard are Goodall's (1986) observations of the chimpanzees of Gombe, who are "quite fastidious, and if their bodies become soiled with dirt (feces, urine, mud, and so forth) they often use leaves to wipe themselves. They also use leaf napkins to dab at bleeding wounds" (p. 545). In addition, she noted, "The Gombe chimpanzees, in fact, seem to have an almost instinctive horror of being soiled with excrement and only very rarely have been seen to touch feces (their own or another's) with their bare hands. If a chimpanzee accidentally becomes smeared with the feces of another, the offending substance is wiped off carefully with leaves. . . . Mothers usually clean themselves at once if they are accidentally dirtied by the excrement of their infants. . . . If a chimpanzee is accidentally sprinkled with urine (by a companion above him, for example), it too may be wiped off with leaves, but the behavior is not so frantic. . . . Chimpanzees often dab at bleeding wounds with leaves, which they then lick; they may repeat the process many times" (pp. 545–547). These careful observations of the Gombe chimpanzees over many years provide ample documentation that humans' obsessions with dirt and contamination did not arise out of a vacuum but rather have deep evolutionary roots.

In summary, as stated at the outset, there are limitations inherent in animal models of OCD because we cannot know the specific content of animals' thoughts, as would be necessary to determine if they experience anything resembling human obsessive thoughts or images. As reviewed above, however, there are many examples of compulsive behavior in animals that bear significant resemblance to compulsive rituals in humans. Moreover, although the anxiety-reduction model of OCD may have little bearing on understanding the actual etiology of the disorder, there are nonetheless many findings from the avoidance learning literature that may help to explain important features of the course of the disorder, in particular the fluctuations in intensity of symptoms that is commonly seen. Finally, the literature on selective associability for certain stimuli and for certain avoidance responses helps to illuminate why the content of obsessive compulsives' obsessions usually center around only a few common themes and why their compulsive rituals also usually center around behaviors that closely resemble the fixed action patterns and displacement activities that are commonly seen throughout much of the animal kingdom.

Conclusions

In this chapter we have reviewed conditioning and ethological research from animals and humans that we believe is highly relevant to understanding each of the six different anxiety disorders. Many of the criticisms that have been made of conditioning models in the past have been based on long outmoded contiguity views of conditioning that considered only the effects of stress in isolation in producing anxiety and anxiety disorders—what we have called SITIA (Stress-in-Total-Isolation Anxiety) models. By contrast, contemporary conditioning theory is actually quite cognitive and views conditioning as involving the development of expectancies about the nature of the US. Moreover, there are many dynamic contextual variables that affect the outcome of exposure to stressful life events. The role of such variables is explicitly acknowledged by what we have called SIDCA (Stress-in-Dynamic-Context Anxiety) models. These include temperamental variables, the controllability of the US, the relative predictive value of different CSs in a given situation, prior experiences with a conditioned stimulus, subsequent memory modifications that occur with the passage of time, and others. Evolutionary principles of belongingness or selective associability also tell us a good deal about the nonrandom content of people's phobias, obsessive thoughts, and compulsive behaviors. Finally, findings from the vast animal literature on unpredictable and uncontrollable aversive events have considerable relevance to understanding most of the anxiety disorders, with their relevance for PTSD being especially strong. We urge clinical theorists interested in anxiety and the anxiety disorders to abandon their critiques of outmoded SITIA models and to explore the many promising hypotheses for further understanding of the anxiety disorders that stem from the SIDCA models we have presented here and elsewhere (e.g., Cook & Mineka, 1991; Mineka, 1985a; Mineka, 1992; Mineka & Zinbarg, 1991, 1995).

REFERENCES

Adamec, R. (1975). The behavioral bases of prolonged suppression of predatory attack in cats. *Aggressive Behavior, 1*, 297–314.

Alloy, L. B., Kelly, K. A., Mineka, S., & Clements, C. M. (1990). Comorbidity in anxiety and depressive disorders: A helplessness/hopelessness perspective. In J. D. Maser & C. R. Cloninger (Eds.), *Comorbidity in anxiety and mood disorders* (pp. 499–544). Washington DC: American Psychiatric Press.

American Psychiatric Association. (1987). *Diagnostic and statistical manual of mental disorders* (3rd ed. revised). Washington DC: American Psychiatric Press.

American Psychiatric Association. (1994). *Diagnostic and statistical manual of mental disorders* (4th ed.). Washington DC: American Psychiatric Press.

Amsel, A. (1971). Frustration, persistence and regression. In H. Kimmel (Ed.), *Experimental psychopathology: Recent research and theory* (pp. 51–69). New York: Academic.

Balsam, P., & Tomie, A. (Eds.) (1985). *Context and learning*. Hillsdale NJ: Erlbaum.

Barlow, D. H. (1986). Causes of sexual dysfunction: The role of anxiety and cognitive interference. *Journal of Consulting and Clinical Psychology, 54*, 140–145.

Barlow, D. H. (1988). *Anxiety and its disorders: The nature and treatment of anxiety and panic*. New York: Guilford.

Başoğlu, M., & Mineka, S. (1992). The role of uncontrollable and unpredictable stress in post-traumatic stress responses in torture survivors. In M. Başoğlu (Ed.), *Torture and its consequences: Current treatment approaches*. Cambridge: Cambridge University Press.

Başoğlu, M., & Mineka, S. (1995). Perceived distress during torture and its relationship to post-traumatic stress responses. Unpublished manuscript.

Başoğlu, M., Paker, M., Paker, O., Ozmen, E., Marks, I. M., Incesu, C., Sahin, D., & Sarimurat, N. (1994a). Psychological effects of torture: A comparison of tortured with nontortured political activists in Turkey. *American Journal of Psychiatry, 151*, 76–81.

Başoğlu, M., Paker, M., Tasdemir, O., Ozmen, E., & Sahin, D. (1994b). Factors related to long term traumatic stress responses in survivors of torture in Turkey. *Journal of the American Medical Association, 272*, 357–363.

Baxter, L. R., Jr., Schwartz, J. M., & Guze, B. H. (1991). Brain imaging: Toward a neuroanatomy of OCD. In J. Zohar, T. Insel, & S. Rasmussen (Eds.), *The psychobiology of obsessive-compulsive disorder* (pp. 101–125). New York: Springer.

Baxter, L. R., Schwartz, J. M., Guze, B. H., Szuba, M. P. (1992). Neuroimaging in obsessive-compulsive disorder: Seeking the mediating neuroanatomy. In M. A. Jenike, L. Baer, & W. E. Minichiello (Eds.), *Obsessive-compulsive disorders: Theory and management* (pp. 167–188). Chicago: Year Book Medical Publishers.

Beck, A. T., & Emery, G. (1985). *Anxiety disorders and phobias: A cognitive perspective*. New York: Basic Books.

Bersh, P. (1980). Eysenck's theory of incubation: A critical analysis. *Behaviour Research and Therapy, 18*, 11–17.

Biederman, J., Rosenbaum, J. F., Hirshfeld, D., Farone, S., Bolduc, E., Gersten, M., Meminger, S., Kagan, J., Snidman, N., & Reznick, J. S. (1990). Psychiatric correlates of behavioral inhibition in young children of parents with and without psychiatric disorders. *Archives of General Psychiatry, 47*, 21–26.

Blanchard, E. B. (1990). Elevated basal levels of cardiovascular responses in Vietnam veterans with PTSD: A health problem in the making? *Journal of Anxiety Disorders, 4*, 233–237.

Blanchard, E. B., Kolb, L. C., Gerardi, R. J., Ryan, D., & Pallmeyer, T. P. (1986). Cardiac response to relevant stimuli as an adjunctive tool for diagnosing post-traumatic stress disorder in Vietnam veterans. *Behavior Therapy, 17*, 592–606.

Blanchard, R. J., Takahashi, L. K., & Blanchard, D. C. (1977). The development of intruder attack in colonies of laboratory rats. *Animal Learning and Behavior, 5*, 365–369.

Bolstadt, B., & Zinbarg, R. E. (1995). *Locus of control and self-reported symptoms of post-traumatic stress following sexual assault*. Unpublished manuscript.

Bolles, R. C. (1970). Species-specific defense reactions and avoidance learning. *Psychological Review, 77*, 32–48.

Brown, J. S. (1969). Factors influencing self-punitive locomotor behavior. In B. A. Campbell & R. M. Church (Eds.), *Punishment and aversive behavior* (pp. 467–514). New York: Appleton-Century-Crofts.

Campbell, D. T., & Fiske, D. W. (1959). Convergent and discriminant validation by the multitrait multimethod matrix. *Psychological Bulletin, 56,* 81–
105.

Carter, M. M., Hollon, S. D., Carson, R., & Shelton, R. C. (1995). Effects of a
safe person on induced distress following a biological challenge in panic
disorder with agoraphobia. *Journal of Abnormal Psychology, 104,* 156–163.

Chamove, A. S., Eysenck, H. J., & Harlow, H. F. (1972). Personality in monkeys: Factor analyses of rhesus social behavior. *Quarterly Journal of Experimental Psychology, 24,* 496–504.

Choraznya, H. (1962). Some properties of conditioned inhibition. *Acta Bio-
logica Experimentalis, 22,* 5.

Clark, D. M. (1988). A cognitive model of panic attacks. In S. Rachman & J.
D. Maser (Eds.), *Panic: Psychological perspectives* (pp. 71–89). Hillsdale NJ:
Erlbaum.

Clark, L. A., & Watson, D. (1991a). Theoretical and empirical issues differentiating depression from anxiety. In J. Becker & A. Kleinman (Eds.), *Advances in mood disorders, Vol. 1: Psychological aspects* (pp. 39–65). Hillsdale
NJ: Erlbaum.

Clark, L. A., & Watson, D. (1991b). Tripartite model of anxiety and depression: Psychometric evidence and taxonomic implications. *Journal of Abnormal Psychology, 100,* 316–336.

Clark, L. A., Watson, D., & Mineka, S. (1994). Temperament, personality,
and the mood and anxiety disorders. *Journal of Abnormal Psychology, 102,*
103–116.

Cloitre, M., Heimberg, R. G., Liebowitz, M. R., & Gitow, A. (1992). Perceptions of control in panic disorder and social phobia. *Cognitive Therapy and
Research, 16,* 569–577.

Cook, E., Hodes, R., & Lang, P. J. (1986). Preparedness and phobia: Effects
of stimulus content on human visceral conditioning. *Journal of Abnormal
Psychology, 95,* 195–207.

Cook, M., & Mineka, S. (1987). Second-order conditioning and over-
shadowing in the observational conditioning of fear in monkeys. *Behaviour Research and Therapy, 25,* 349–364.

Cook, M., & Mineka, S. (1989). Observational conditioning of fear to fear-
relevant versus fear-irrelevant stimuli in rhesus monkeys. *Journal of Abnormal Psychology, 98,* 448–459.

Cook, M., & Mineka, S. (1990). Selective associations in the observational
conditioning of fear in monkeys. *Journal of Experimental Psychology: Animal Behavior Processes, 16,* 372–389.

Cook, M., & Mineka, S. (1991). Selective associations in the origins of phobic
fears and their implications for behavior therapy. In P. Martin (Ed.),
Handbook of behavior therapy and psychological science: An integrative approach
(pp. 413–434). New York: Pergamon.

Cook, M., Mineka, S., & Trumble, D. (1987). The role of response produced
and exteroceptive feedback in the attenuation of fear over the course of
avoidance learning. *Journal of Experimental Psychology: Animal Behavior
Processes, 13,* 239–249.

Cook, M., Mineka, S., Wolkenstein, B., & Laitsch, K. (1985). Observational conditioning of snake fear in unrelated rhesus monkeys. *Journal of Abnormal Psychology, 94*, 591–610.

Cook, T. D. & Campbell, D. T. (1979). *Quasi-experimentation: Design and analysis issues for field settings.* Boston: Houghton Mifflin.

Craske, M. G., Glover, D., & DeCola, J. (1995). Predicted versus unpredicted panic attacks: Acute versus general distress. *Journal of Abnormal Psychology, 104*, 214–223.

Dancu, C. V., Shoyer, B., Riggs, D. S., & Foa, E. B. (1991). [Childhood sexual abuse and crime-related PTSD]. Unpublished raw data.

Davey, G. C. L., & Matchett, G. (1994). Unconditioned stimulus rehearsal and the retention and enhancement of differential "fear" conditioning: Effects of trait and state anxiety. *Journal of Abnormal Psychology, 103*, 708–718.

Davidson, L. M., & Baum, A. (1986). Chronic stress and post-traumatic stress disorders. *Journal of Consulting and Clinical Psychology, 54*, 303–308.

Dean, S., & Pittman, C. (1991). Self-punitive behavior: A revised analysis. In M. R. Denny (Ed.), *Fear, avoidance and phobias: A fundamental analysis* (pp. 259–284). Hillsdale NJ: Erlbaum.

de Jong, P. J., Merckelbach, H., & Arntz, A. (1995). Covariation bias in phobic women: The relationship between a priori expectancy, on-line expectancy, autonomic responding, and a posteriori contingency judgement. *Journal of Abnormal Psychology, 104*, 55–62.

Denny, R. (1971). Relaxation theory and experiments. In F. R. Brush (Ed.), *Aversive conditioning and learning* (pp. 235–295). New York: Academic.

Desiderato, O., & Newman, A. (1971). Conditioned suppression produced in rats by tones paired with escapable or inescapable shock. *Journal of Comparative and Physiological Psychology, 96*, 427–431.

De Silva, P., Rachman, S. J., & Seligman, M. E. P. (1977). Prepared phobias and obsessions: Therapeutic outcome. *Behaviour Research and Therapy, 15*, 65–77.

de Waal, F. (1989). *Peacemaking among primates.* Cambridge MA: Harvard University Press.

Dimberg, U. (1986). Facial expressions as excitatory and inhibitory stimuli for conditioned autonomic responses. *Biological Psychology, 22*, 37–57.

Di Nardo, P. A., Guzy, L. T., & Bak, R. M. (1988). Anxiety response patterns and etiological factors in dog-fearful and non-fearful subjects. *Behaviour Research and Therapy, 26*, 245–252.

Dollard, J., & Miller, N. E. (1950). *Personality and psychotherapy.* New York: McGraw-Hill.

Drugan, R. C., Moye, T. B., & Maier, S. F. (1982). Opioid and nonopioid forms of stress induced analgesia: Some environmental determinants and characteristics. *Behavioral and Neural Biology, 35*, 251–264.

Drugan, R. C., Ryan, S. M., Minor, T. R., & Maier, S. F. (1984). Librium prevents the analgesia and shuttlebox escape deficit typically observed following inescapable shock. *Pharmacology, Biochemistry, and Behavior, 21*, 749–754.

Emmelkamp, P. (1982) *Phobic and obsessive-compulsive disorders: Theory, research, and practice.* New York: Plenum.

Eysenck, H. J. (1968). A theory of the incubation of anxiety/fear response. *Behaviour Research and Therapy, 6,* 309–321.

Eysenck, H. J., & Rachman, S. J. (1965). *Causes and cures of neurosis.* London: Routledge & Kegan Paul.

Feuer, C., & Zinbarg, R. E. (1995, March). *Gender differences in the experience of childhood sexual abuse.* Poster presented at the 1995 Nebraska Symposium on Motivation, Lincoln NE.

Foa, E. B., & Dancu, C. (1994, November). *Cognitive behavioral treatments for women with PTSD following sexual assault.* Workshop presented at the 28th Annual Convention of the Association for the Advancement of Behavior Therapy, San Diego CA.

Foa, E. B., Steketee, G., & Rothbaum, B. (1989). Behavioral/cognitive conceptualization of post-traumatic stress disorder. *Behavior Therapy, 20,* 155–176.

Foa, E., Zinbarg, R. E., & Olasov-Rothbaum, B. (1992). Uncontrollability and unpredictability in post-traumatic stress disorder: An animal model. *Psychological Bulletin, 112,* 218–238.

Fonberg, E. (1956). On the manifestation of conditioned defensive reactions in stress. *Bulletin of the Society of Science and Letters of Fodz. Class III. Science, Mathematics and Nature, 7,* 1.

Freud, S. (1936). *The problem of anxiety.* New York: Norton. (Original work published, 1926).

Friedman, S., Sunderland, G. S., & Rosenblum, L. A. (1988). A nonhuman primate model of panic disorder. *Psychiatry Research, 23,* 65–75.

Ginsburg, B., & Allee, W. C. (1942). Some effects of conditioning on social dominance and subordination in inbred strains of mice. *Physiological Zoology, 15,* 485–506.

Goldstein, A. J., & Chambless, D. L. (1978). A reanalysis of agoraphobia. *Behavior Therapy, 9,* 47–59.

Goodall, J. (1986). *The chimpanzees of Gombe.* Cambridge MA: Harvard University Press.

Gray, J. A. (1982). *The neuropsychology of anxiety: An enquiry into the functioning of the septo-hippocampal system.* Oxford: Oxford University Press.

Green, G., & Osborne, J. (1985). Does vicarious instigation provide support for observational learning theories? A critical review. *Psychological Bulletin, 97,* 3–17.

Hall, C. S. (1941). Temperament: A survey of animal studies. *Psychological Bulletin, 38,* 909–943.

Hannum, R., Rosellini, R., & Seligman, M. (1976). Retention of learned helplessness and immunization in the rat from weaning to adulthood. *Developmental Psychology, 12,* 449–454.

Hanson, J. P., Larson, M. E., & Snowdon, C. T. (1976). The effects of control over high intensity noise on plasma control levels in rhesus monkeys. *Behavioral Biology, 16,* 333–340.

Heimberg, R. G., & Barlow, D. H. (1988). Psychosocial treatments for social phobia. *Psychosomatics, 29*, 27–37.

Helzer, J. E., Robins, L. N., & McEvoy, L. (1987). Posttraumatic stress disorder in the general population. *New England Journal of Medicine, 317*, 1630–1634.

Hendersen, R. (1978). Forgetting of conditioned fear inhibition. *Learning and Motivation, 8*, 16–30.

Hendersen, R. (1985). Fearful memories: The motivational significance of forgetting. In F. R. Brush & J. B. Overmier (Eds.), *Affect, conditioning and cognition: Essays in the determinants of behavior* (pp. 43–53). Hillsdale NJ: Erlbaum.

Holland, H. (1974). Displacement activity as a form of abnormal behaviour in animals. In H. Beech (Ed.), *Obsessional states* (pp. 161–173). London: Metheun.

Holland, P. (1983). "Occasion-setting" in Pavlovian feature positive discriminations. In M. L. Commons, R. J. Herrnstein, & A. R. Wagner (Eds.), *Quantitative analyses of behavior: Vol. 4. Discrimination processes* (pp. 183–206). Cambridge MA: Ballinger.

Horowitz, M. J. (1986). *Stress response syndromes.* Northvale NJ: Aronson.

Insel, T. R. (1989). Animal models of compulsive behavior. *Biological Psychiatry, 26*, 189–198.

Insel, T. R. (1990). Serotonin in obsessive compulsive disorder. *Psychiatric Annals, 20*, 560–564.

Insel, T. R. (1992). Toward a neuroanatomy of obsessive-compulsive disorder. *Archives of General Psychiatry, 49*, 739–744.

Janis, J. L. (1951). *Air war and emotional stress.* New York: McGraw-Hill.

Joffe, J., Rawson, R., & Mulick, J. (1973). Control of their environment reduces emotionality in rats. *Science, 180*, 1383–1384.

Kagan, J. (1989). The concept of behavioral inhibition to the unfamiliar. In J. S. Reznick (Ed.), *Perspectives on behavioral inhibition* (pp.1–23). Chicago: University of Chicago Press.

Kagan, J. (1994). *Galen's prophecy.* New York: Basic Books.

Kagan, J., Reznick, J. S., & Snidman, N. (1988). Biological bases of childhood shyness. *Science, 240*, 167–171.

Kahn, M. W. (1951). The effect of severe defeat at various age levels on the aggressive behavior of mice. *Journal of Genetic Psychology, 79*, 117–130.

Kamin, L. J. (1968). "Attention like" processes in classical conditioning. In M. R. Jones (Ed.), *Miami Symposium on the Prediction of Behavior: Aversive Stimulation* (pp. 9–33). Miami: University of Miami Press.

Kamin, L. J., Brimer, C. J., & Black, A. H. (1963). Conditioned suppression as a monitor of fear of the CS in the course of avoidance training. *Journal of Comparative and Physiological Psychology, 56*, 497–501.

Kendler, K. S., Neale, M. C., Kessler, R. C., Heath, A. C., & Eaves, L. J. (1992a). The genetic epidemiology of phobias in women: The interrelationship of agoraphobia, social phobia, situational phobia, and simple phobia. *Archives of General Psychiatry, 49*, 273–281.

Kendler, K. S., Neale, M. C., Kessler, R. C., Heath, A. C., & Eaves, L. J. (1992b). Generalized anxiety disorder in women: A population based twin study. *Archives of General Psychiatry, 49*, 267–272.

Kilpatrick, D. G., & Resnick, H. S. (1993). Posttraumatic stress disorder associated with exposure to criminal victimization in clinical and community populations. In J. R. T. Davidson & E. B. Foa (Eds.), *Posttraumatic stress disorder: DSM-IV and beyond* (chap. 7, pp. 113–146). Washington DC: American Psychiatric Press.

Kolb, L. C. (1987). A neuropsychological hypothesis explaining posttraumatic stress disorders. *American Journal of Psychiatry, 144*, 989–995.

Kulka, R. A., Schlenger, W. E., Fairbank, J. A., Hough, R. L., Jordan, B. K., Marmar, C. R., & Weiss, D. S. (1990). *Trauma and the Vietnam War generation: Report of findings from the National Vietnam Veterans Readjustment Study.* New York: Brunner/Mazel.

Kushner, M. G., Riggs, D. S., Foa, E. B., & Miller, S. M. (1993). Perceived controllability and the development of posttraumatic stress disorder (PTSD) in crime victims. *Behaviour Research and Therapy, 31*, 105–110.

Lazarus, R. S. (1966). *Psychological stress and the coping process.* New York: McGraw-Hill.

Lazarus, R. S., & Averill, J. (1972). Emotion and cognition: With special reference to anxiety. In C. Spielberger (Ed.), *Anxiety: Current trends in theory and research* (Vol. 2, pp. 241–283). New York: Academic.

Leary, M. R., & Dobbins, S. E. (1983). Social anxiety, sexual behavior and contraceptive use. *Journal of Personality and Social Psychology, 45*, 1347–1354.

Leung, A. W., & Heimberg, R. G. (Submitted). Perceptions of control, homework compliance, and outcome of cognitive-behavioral treatment for social phobia.

Lewis, M., & Goldberg, S. (1969). Perceptual-cognitive development in infancy: A generalized expectancy model as a function of mother-infant interaction. *Merrill-Palmer Quarterly, 15*, 81–85.

Liebowitz, M. R., & Hollander, E. (1991). Obsessive-compulsive disorder: Psychobiological integration. In J. Zohar, T. Insel, & S. Rasmussen (Eds.), *The psychobiology of obsessive-compulsive disorder* (pp. 227–255). New York: Springer.

LoLordo, V. (1967). Similarity of conditioned fear responses based upon different aversive events. *Journal of Comparative and Physiological Psychology, 64*, 154–158.

LoLordo, V. (1979a). Constraints on learning. In M. Bitterman, V. LoLordo, J. Overmier, & M. Rashotte, (Eds.), *Animal learning: Survey and analysis* (pp. 473–504). New York: Plenum.

LoLordo, V. (1979b). Selective associations. In A. Dickinson & R. Boakes (Eds.), *Mechanisms of learning and motivation: A memorial to Jerzy Konorski* (pp. 367–398). Hillsdale NJ: Erlbaum.

LoLordo, V., & Droungas, A. (1989). Selective associations and adaptive specializations: Food aversion and phobias. In S. Klein & R. Mowrer (Eds.), *Contemporary learning theories: Instrumental conditioning theory and* the impact of biological constraints on learning (pp. 145–179). Hillsdale NJ: Erlbaum.

Lubow, R. E. (1973). Latent inhibition. *Psychological Bulletin, 79*, 398–407.

Mackintosh, N. (1983). *Conditioning and associative learning*. New York: Oxford University Press.

Maier, N. R. F. (1949). *Frustration: The study of behavior without a goal*. New York: McGraw-Hill.

Maier, S. F. (1986). Stressor controllability and stress-induced analgesia. In D. D. Kelley (Ed.), *Annals of the New York Academy of Sciences* (Vol. 467, pp. 55–71). New York: Academy of Sciences.

Maier, S. F. (1989). Determinants of the nature of environmentally induced hypoalgesia. *Behavioral Neuroscience, 103*, 131–143.

Maier, S. F., Albin, R. W., & Testa, T. J. (1973). Failure to learn to escape in rats previously exposed to inescapable shock depends on nature of escape response. *Journal of Comparative and Physiological Psychology, 85*, 581–592.

Maier, S. F., Anderson, C., & Lieberman, D. (1972). Influence of control of shock on subsequent shock-elicited aggression. *Journal of Comparative and Physiological Psychology, 81*, 94–100.

Maier, S. F., Seligman, M. E. P., & Solomon, R. L. (1969). Pavlovian fear conditioning and learned helplessness: Effects on escape and avoidance behavior of a) the CS-US contingency and b) the independence of the US and voluntary responding (pp. 299–342). In B. A. Campbell & R. M. Church (Eds.), *Punishment*. New York: Appleton-Century-Crofts.

Mandler, G. (1972). Helplessness: Theory and research in anxiety. In C. Spielberger (Ed.), *Anxiety: Current trends in theory and research* (Vol. 1 pp. 359–374). New York: Academic.

Mandler, G., & Watson, D. (1966). Anxiety and the interruption of behavior. In C. Spielberger (Ed.), *Anxiety and behavior* (pp. 263–288). New York: Academic.

Marks, I. M. (1977). Phobias and obsessions: Clinical phenomena in search of a laboratory model. In J. Maser & M. Seligman (Eds.), *Psychopathology: Experimental models* (pp. 174–213). San Francisco: Freeman.

Marks, I. M. (1987). *Fears, phobias, and rituals: Panic, anxiety, and their disorders*. New York: Oxford University Press.

McKinney, W. T. (1974). Animal models in psychiatry. *Perspectives in Biology and Medicine, 17*, 529–541.

McNally, R. J. (1987). Preparedness and phobias: A review. *Psychological Bulletin, 101*, 283–303.

McNally, R. J. (1990). Psychological approaches to panic disorder: A review. *Psychological Bulletin, 108*, 403–419.

McNally, R. J. (1994). *Panic disorder: A critical analysis*. New York: Guilford.

Merckelbach, H., de Ruiter, C., van den Hout, M. A., & Hoekstra, R. (1989). Conditioning experiences and phobias. *Behaviour Research and Therapy, 27*, 657–662.

Metzner, R. (1963). Some experimental analogues of obsession. *Behaviour Research and Therapy, 1*, 231–236.

Miczek, K., Thompson, M., & Shuster, L. (1982). Opioid-like analgesia in defeated mice. *Science, 215,* 1520–1522.

Mineka, S. (1979). The role of fear in theories of avoidance learning, flooding and extinction. *Psychological Bulletin, 86,* 985–1010.

Mineka, S. (1985a). Animal models of anxiety-based disorders: Their usefulness and limitations. In J. Maser & A. Tuma (Eds.), *Anxiety and the anxiety disorders* (pp. 199–244). Hillsdale NJ: Erlbaum.

Mineka, S. (1985b). The frightful complexity of the origins of fears. In F. R. Brush & J. B. Overmier (Eds.), *Affect, conditioning, and cognition: Essays on the determinants of behavior* (pp. 55–73). Hillsdale NJ: Erlbaum.

Mineka, S. (1987). A primate model of phobic fears. In H. Eysenck & I. Martin (Eds.), *Theoretical foundations of behavior therapy.* New York: Plenum.

Mineka, S. (1992). Evolutionary memories, emotional processing and the emotional disorders. In D. Medin (Ed.), *The psychology of learning and motivation* (Vol. 28, pp. 161–206). New York: Academic.

Mineka, S., & Cook, M. (1986). Immunization against the observational conditioning of snake fear in rhesus monkeys. *Journal of Abnormal Psychology, 95,* 307–318.

Mineka, S., & Cook, M. (1988). Social learning and the acquisition of snake fear in monkeys. In T. Zentall & G. Galef (Eds.), *Comparative social learning* (pp. 51–73). Hillsdale NJ: Erlbaum.

Mineka, S., & Cook, M. (1993). Mechanisms involved in the observational conditioning of fear. *Journal of Experimental Psychology: General, 122,* 23–38.

Mineka, S., & Cook, M. (unpublished data). High resistance to extinction of snake fear in wild-reared monkeys undergoing exposure alone vs watching a nonfearful model.

Mineka, S., Cook, M., & Miller, S. (1984a). Fear conditioned with escapable and inescapable shock: The effects of a feedback stimulus. *Journal of Experimental Psychology: Animal Behavior Processes, 10,* 307–323.

Mineka, S., Davidson, M., Cook, M., & Keir, R. (1984b). Observational conditioning of snake fear in rhesus monkeys. *Journal of Abnormal Psychology, 93,* 355–372.

Mineka, S., Gunnar, M., & Champoux, M. (1986). Control and early socioemotional development: Infant rhesus monkeys reared in controllable versus uncontrollable environments. *Child Development, 57,* 1241–1256.

Mineka, S., & Hendersen, R. (1985). Controllability and predictability in acquired motivation. *Annual Review of Psychology, 36,* 495–530.

Mineka, S., & Keir, R. (1983). The effects of flooding on reducing snake fear in rhesus monkeys: 6 month follow-up and further flooding. *Behaviour Research and Therapy, 21,* 527–535.

Mineka, S., Keir, R., & Price, V. (1980). Fear of snakes in wild- and lab-reared rhesus monkeys. *Animal Learning and Behavior, 8,* 653–663.

Mineka, S., & Kelly, K. A. (1989). The relationship between anxiety, lack of control and loss of control. In A. Steptoe, & A. Appels (Eds.), *Stress, personal control and health* (pp. 163–191). Brussels: Wiley.

Mineka, S., & Kihlstrom, J. (1978). Unpredictable and uncontrollable aversive events. *Journal of Abnormal Psychology, 87*, 256–271.

Mineka, S., Suomi, S. J., & Delizio, R. (1981). Multiple peer separations in adolescent monkeys: An opponent process interpretation. *Journal of Experimental Psychology: General, 110*, 56–85.

Mineka, S., & Tomarken, A. J. (1989). The role of cognitive biases in the origins and maintenance of fear and anxiety disorders. In T. Archer & L.-G. Nilsson (Eds.), *Aversion, avoidance, and anxiety: Perspectives on aversively motivated behavior* (pp. 195–221). Hillsdale NJ: Erlbaum.

Mineka, S., & Zinbarg, R. E. (1991). Animals of experimental psychopathology. In C. E. Walker (Ed.), *Clinical psychology: Historical and research foundations* (pp. 51–86). New York: Plenum.

Mineka, S. & Zinbarg, R. E. (1995). Animal-ethological models of social phobia. In R. Heimberg, M. Liebowitz, D. Hope, & F. Schneier (Eds.), *Social phobia: Diagnosis, assessment and treatment* (pp. 134–162). New York: Guilford.

Moras, K., Di Nardo, P. A., Brown, T. A., & Barlow, D. H. (1995). *Comorbidity, functional impairment, and depression among the DSM-III-R anxiety disorders.* Manuscript in preparation.

Mowrer, O. H. (1947). On the dual nature of learning: A reinterpretation of "conditioning" and "problem-solving." *Harvard Educational Review, 17*, 102–148.

Mowrer, O. H. (1960). *Learning theory and behavior.* New York: Wiley.

Mowrer, O. H., & Viek, P. (1948). An experimental analogue of fear from a sense of helplessness. *Journal of Abnormal and Social Psychology, 43*, 193–200.

Moye, T. B., Cook, D., Grau., J., & Maier, S. F. (1981). Therapy and immunization of long-term analgesia in rats. *Learning and Motivation, 12*, 133–148.

Moye, T. B., Hyson, R., Grau, J., & Maier S. F. (1983). Immunization of opioid analgesia: Effects of prior escapable shock on subsequent shock-induced and morphine-induced antinociception. *Learning and Motivation, 4*, 238–251.

Nemiah, J. (1967). Obsessive compulsive neurosis. In A. M. Freedman and H. I. Kaplan (Eds.), *A comprehensive textbook of psychiatry* (pp. 912–928). Baltimore: Williams and Wilkens.

Öhman, A. (1986). Face the beast and fear the face: Animal and social fears as prototypes for evolutionary analyses of emotion. *Psychophysiology, 23*, 123–145.

Öhman, A., & Dimberg, U. (1978). Facial expressions as conditioned stimuli for electrodermal responses: A case of "preparedness"? *Journal of Personality and Social Psychology, 36*, 1251–1258.

Öhman, A., Dimberg, U., & Esteves, F. (1989). Preattentive activation of aversive emotions. In T. Archer & L.-G. Nilsson (Eds.), *Aversion, avoidance and anxiety: Perspectives on aversively motivated behavior* (pp. 169–199). Hillsdale NJ: Erlbaum.

Öhman, A., Dimberg, U., & Öst, L.-G. (1985). Animal and social phobias: Biological constraints on the learned fear response. In S. Reiss &

R. Bootzin (Eds.), *Theoretical issues in behavior therapy* (pp. 123–175). New York: Academic.

Öhman, A., & Soares, J. J. F. (1993). On the automatic nature of phobic fear: Conditioned electrodermal responses to masked fear-relevant stimuli. *Journal of Abnormal Psychology, 102*, 121–132.

Öhman, A., & Soares, J. J. F. (1994). "Unconscious anxiety": Phobic responses to masked stimuli. *Journal of Abnormal Psychology, 103*, 231–240.

Ollendick, T. H., & King, N. J. (1991). Origins of childhood fears: An evaluation of Rachman's theory of fear acquisition. *Behaviour Research and Therapy, 29*, 117–123.

Öst, L.-G., & Hugdahl, K. (1981). Acquisition of phobias and anxiety response patterns in clinical patients. *Behaviour Research and Therapy, 16*, 439–447.

Overmier, J. B. (1985). Toward a reanalysis of the causal structure of the learned helplessness syndrome. In F. R. Brush & J. B. Overmier (Eds.), *Affect, conditioning and cognition: Essays on the determinants of behavior* (pp. 211–228). Hillsdale NJ: Erlbaum.

Overmier, J. B., & Seligman, M. E. P. (1967). Effects of inescapable shock upon subsquent escape and avoidance responding. *Journal of Comparative and Physiological Psychology, 63*, 28–33.

Pavlov, I. (1927). *Conditioned reflexes.* London: Oxford University Press.

Peterson, C., Maier, S. F., Seligman, M. E. P. (1993). *Learned helplessness: A theory for the age of personal control.* New York: Oxford University Press.

Pitman, R. K. (1989). Animal models of compulsive behavior. *Biological Psychiatry, 26*, 189–198.

Pitman, R. K., van der Kolk, B. A., Orr, S. P., & Greenberg, M. S. (1990). Naloxone reversible analgesic response to combat-related stimuli in posttraumatic stress disorder. *Archives of General Psychiatry, 47*, 541.

Powell, D. A., Francis, M. J., Francis, J., & Schneiderman, N. (1972). Shock-induced aggression as a function of prior experience with avoidance, fighting, or unavoidable shock. *Journal of the Experimental Analysis of Behavior, 18*, 323–332.

Rachman, S. J. (1977). The conditioning theory of fear acquisition: A critical examination. *Behaviour Research and Therapy, 15*, 375–388.

Rachman, S. J. (1978). *Fear and courage.* San Francisco: Freeman.

Rachman, S. J. (1990). *Fear and courage.* New York: Freeman.

Rachman, S. J., & Hodgson, R. J. (1980). *Obsessions and compulsions.* Englewood Cliffs NJ: Prentice-Hall.

Rapaport, P., & Maier, S. F. (1978). Inescapable shock and food-competition dominance in rats. *Animal Learning and Behavior, 6*, 160–165.

Rapee, R. M., Mattick, R., & Murrell, E. (1986). Cognitive mediation in the affective component of spontaneous panic attacks. *Journal of Behavior Therapy and Experimental Psychiatry, 17*, 245–253.

Rapoport, J. L. (1989). *The boy who couldn't stop washing: The experience and treatment of obsessive-compulsive disorder.* New York: Penguin.

Rapoport, J. L., & Wise, S. P. (1988). Obsessive-compulsive disorder: Evidence for basal ganglia dysfunction. *Psychopharmacology Bulletin, 24*, 380–384.

Razran, G. (1961). The observable unconscious and the inferable conscious in current Soviet psychophysiology: Interoceptive conditioning, semantic conditioning, and the orienting reflex. *Psychological Review, 68*, 81–147.

Reiss, S. (1987). Theoretical perspectives on the fear of anxiety. *Clinical Psychology Review, 7*, 585–596.

Reiss, S., & McNally, R. J. (1985). Expectancy model of fear. In S. Reiss & R. R. Bootzin (Eds.), *Theoretical issues in behavior therapy* (pp. 107–121). San Diego: Academic.

Rescorla, R. A. (1971). Variation in the effectiveness of reinforcement and nonreinforcement following prior inhibitory conditioning. *Learning and Motivation, 2*, 113–123.

Rescorla, R. A. (1974). Effect of inflation of the unconditioned stimulus value following conditioning. *Journal of Comparative and Physiological Psychology, 86*, 101–106.

Rescorla, R. A. (1988). Pavlovian conditioning: It's not what you think it is. *American Psychologist, 43*, 151–160.

Rescorla, R. A., & Heth, C. (1975). Reinstatement of fear to an extinguished conditioned stimulus. *Journal of Experimental Psychology: Animal Behavior Processes, 104*, 88–96.

Rescorla, R. A., & LoLordo, V. M. (1965). Inhibition of avoidance behavior. *Journal of Comparative and Physiological Psychology, 59*, 406–412.

Rescorla, R. A., & Wagner, A. R. (1972). A theory of Pavlovian conditioning: Variations in the effectiveness of reinforcement and nonreinforcement. In A. Black & W. Prokasy (Eds.), *Classical conditioning II* (pp. 64–99). New York: Appleton-Century-Crofts.

Riccio, D., Rabinowitz, V., & Axelrod, S. (1994). Memory: When less is more. *American Psychologist, 49*, 917–926.

Riccio, D., Richardson, R., & Ebner, D. (1984). Memory retrieval deficits based upon altered contextual cues: A paradox. *Psychological Bulletin, 96*, 152–165.

Rodgers, R. J., & Hendrie, C. A. (1983). Social conflict activates status-dependent endogenous analgesic and hyperalgesic mechanisms in male mice. *Physiology and Behavior, 30*, 775–780.

Rosellini, R., Widman, D., Abrahamsen, G., & Bassuk, A. (1990). *Reinstatement of fear following uncontrollable and/or unpredictable stress.* Unpublished manuscript.

Ross, R. R. (1964). Positive and negative partial-reinforcement extinction effects carried through continuous reinforcement, changed motivation, and changed response. *Journal of Experimental Psychology, 68*, 492–502.

Rozin, P., & Kalat, J. W. (1971). Specific hungers and poison avoidance as adaptive specializations of learning. *Psychological Review, 78*, 459–487.

Rush, D. K., Mineka, S., & Suomi, S. J. (1982). The effects of control and lack of control on active and passive avoidance in rhesus monkeys. *Behaviour Research and Therapy, 20*, 135–152.

Salkovskis, P. M. (1988). Phenomenology, assessment, and the cognitive model of panic. In S. Rachman & J. D. Maser (Eds.), *Panic: Psychological perspectives* (pp. 111–136). Hillsdale NJ: Erlbaum.

Sanderson, W. C., Rapee, R. M., & Barlow, D. H. (1989). The influence of an illusion of control on panic attacks induced via inhalation of 5.5% carbon dioxide-enriched air. *Archives of General Psychiatry, 46*, 157–162.

Scholing, A., & Emmelkamp, P. M. G. (1990). Social phobia: Nature and treatment. In H. Leitenberg (Ed.), *Handbook of social and evaluation anxiety* (pp. 217–246). New York: Plenum.

Scott, J. P. (1948). Studies on the early development of social behavior in puppies. *American Psychologist, 3*, 7.

Scott, J. P., & Fuller, J. L. (1965). *Genetics and the social behavior of the dog*. Chicago: University of Chicago Press.

Scott, J. P., & Marston, M. (1953). Nonadaptive behavior resulting from a series of defeats in fighting mice. *Journal of Abnormal and Social Psychology, 48*, 417–428.

Seligman, M. E. P. (1968). Chronic fear produced by unpredictable shock. *Journal of Comparative and Physiological Psychology, 66*, 402–411.

Seligman, M. E. P. (1970). On the generality of the laws of learning. *Psychological Review, 77*, 408–418.

Seligman, M. E. P. (1971). Phobias and preparedness. *Behavior Therapy, 2*, 307–320.

Seligman, M. E. P. (1974). Depression and learned helplessness. In M. Friedman & M. Katz (Eds.), *The psychology of depression* (pp. 83–113). Washington DC: Winston.

Seligman, M. E. P. (1975). *Helplessness: On depression, death, and development*. San Francisco: Freeman.

Seligman, M. E. P., & Binik, Y. (1977). The safety signal hypothesis. In H. Davies & H. Hurwitz (Eds.), *Operant-Pavlovian interactions* (pp. 165–187). Hillsdale NJ: Erlbaum.

Seligman, M. E. P., & Maier, S. F. (1967). Failure to escape traumatic shock. *Journal of Experimental Psychology, 74*, 1–9.

Sherman, A. D., Allers, G. L., Petty, F., & Henn, F. A. (1979). A neuropharmacologically-relevant animal model of depression. *Neuropharmacology, 18*, 891–893.

Shettleworth, S. (1972). Constraints on learning. In D. S. Lehrman, R. A. Hinde, and E. Shaw (Eds.), *Advances in the study of behavior, Vol. 4* (pp. 1–68). New York: Academic.

Solomon, R. L., Kamin, L. J., & Wynne, L. C. (1953). Traumatic avoidance learning: The outcomes of several extinction procedures with dogs. *Journal of Abnormal and Social Psychology, 48*, 291–302.

Solomon, R. L., & Turner, L. H. (1962). Discriminative classical conditioning in dogs paralyzed by curare can later control discriminative avoidance responses in the normal state. *Psychological Review, 69*, 202–219.

Starr, M. D., & Mineka, S. (1977). Determinants of fear over the course of avoidance learning. *Learning and Motivation, 8*, 332–350.

Staub, E., Tursky, B., & Schwartz, G. E. (1971). Self-control and predictability: Their effects on reactions to aversive stimulation. *Journal of Personality and Social Psychology, 18*, 157–162.

Stein, D. J., Shoulberg, N., Helton, K., & Hollander, E. (1992). The neuroethological approach to obsessive-compulsive disorder. *Comprehensive Psychiatry, 33*, 274–281.

Steketee, G., & Chambless, D. (1995). *Expressed emotion in anxiety disorders.* Unpublished manuscript.

Sunderland, G. S., Friedman, S., & Rosenblum, L. A. (1989). Imipramine and alprazolam treatment of lactate-induced acute endogenous distress in nonhuman primates. *American Journal of Psychiatry, 146*, 1044–1047.

Sutton, R. S. & Barto, A. G. (1981). Toward a modern theory of adaptive networks: Expectation and prediction. *Psychological Review, 88*, 135–170.

Swedo, S. E. (1989). Rituals and releasers: An ethological model of obsessive-compulsive disorder. In J. L. Rapoport (Ed.), *Obsessive-compulsive disorder in children and adolescents* (pp. 269–288). Washington DC: American Psychiatric Press.

Swedo, S. E., Leonard, H. L., Rapoport, J. L. (1992). Childhood-onset obsessive-compulsive disorder. In M. A. Jenike, L. Baer, & W. E. Minichiello (Eds.), *Obsessive-compulsive disorders: Theory and management* (pp. 28–38). Chicago: Year Book Medical Publishers.

Teasdale, J. D. (1974). Learning models of obsessional-compulsive disorder. In H. R. Beech (Ed.), *Obsessional states* (pp. 197–229). London: Methuen.

Telch, M. J., Brouillard, M., Telch, C. F., Agras, W. S., & Taylor, C. B. (1989). Role of cognitive appraisal in panic-related avoidance. *Behaviour Research and Therapy, 27*, 373–383.

Thomas, D. (1979). Retention of conditioned inhibition in a bar-press suppression paradigm. *Learning and Motivation, 10*, 161–177.

Tomarken, A. J. (1988). *Fear-relevant selective associations and covariation bias.* Unpublished doctoral dissertation, University of Wisconsin-Madison.

Tomarken, A. J., Mineka, S., & Cook, M. (1989). Fear-relevant selective associations and covariation bias. *Journal of Abnormal Psychology, 98*, 381–394.

Townsley, R. (1992). *Social phobia: Identification of possible etiological factors.* Unpublished doctoral dissertation, University of Georgia.

Uhrich, J. (1938). The social hierarchy in albino mice. *Journal of Comparative Psychology, 25*, 373–413.

van den Hout, M. A. (1988). The explanation of experimental panic. In S. Rachman & J. D. Maser (Eds.), *Panic: Psychological perspectives* (pp. 237–257). Hillsdale NJ: Erlbaum.

van der Kolk, B. A. (1987). *Psychological trauma.* Washington, DC: American Psychiatric Press.

van der Kolk, B. A., Greenberg, M. S., Boyd, H., & Krystal, J. H. (1985). Inescapable shock, neurotransmitters, and addiction to trauma: Toward a psychology of post-traumatic stress. *Biological Psychiatry, 20*, 314–325.

van der Kolk, B. A., Pitman, R. K., & Orr, M. S. (1989). Endogenous opioids, stress-induced analgesia and post-traumatic stress disorder. *Psychopharmacology Bulletin, 25*, 108–112.

Volpicelli, J. R., Ulm, R. R., Altenor, A., & Seligman, M. E. P. (1983). Learned mastery in the rat. *Learning and Motivation, 14*, 204–222.

Wagner, A. R. (1979). Habituation and memory. In A. Dickinson & R. A. Boakes (Eds.), *Mechanisms of learning and motivation* (pp. 53–82). Hillsdale NJ: Erlbaum.

Wagner, A. R. (1981). SOP: A model of automatic memory processing in animal behavior. In N. Spear & R. Miller (Eds.), *Information processing in animals: Memory mechanisms* (pp. 5–47). Hillsdale NJ: Erlbaum.

Wagner, A. R., & Rescorla, R. A. (1972). Inhibition in Pavlovian conditioning: Application of a theory. In R. Boakes & M. Halliday (Eds.), *Inhibition and learning* (pp. 301–336). New York: Academic.

Watson, J. B., & Rayner, R. (1920). Conditioned emotional reactions. *Journal of Experimental Psychology, 3*, 1–14.

Watson, J. S. (1979). Perception of contingency as a determinant of social responsiveness. In E. Thomas (Ed.), *Origins of infant's social responsiveness* (pp. 33–64). New York: Erlbaum.

Weisman, R. G., & Litner, J. S. (1969). Positive conditioned reinforcement of Sidman avoidance behavior in rats. *Journal of Comparative and Physiological Psychology, 68*, 597–603.

Weisman, R. G., & Litner, J. S. (1972). The role of Pavlovian events in avoidance training. In R. A. Boakes & M. S. Halliday (Eds.), *Inhibition and learning* (pp. 253–270). New York: Academic.

Weiss, J. M. (1968). Effects of coping response on stress. *Journal of Comparative and Physiological Psychology, 65*, 251–260.

Weiss, J. M. (1971). Effects of coping behavior in different warning signal conditions on stress pathology in rats. *Journal of Comparative and Physiological Psychology, 77*, 1–13.

Weiss, J. M., Glazer, H. I., & Pohorecky, L. A. (1976). Coping behavior and neurochemical changes: An alternative explanation for the original "learned helplessness" experiments. In A. Serban & A. Kling (Eds.), *Animal models in human psychobiology* (pp. 141–173). New York: Plenum.

White, R. (1959). Motivation reconsidered: The concept of competence. *Psychological Bulletin, 66*, 317–330.

Williams, J. L. (1982). Influence of shock controllability by dominant rats on subsequent attack and defensive behaviors toward colony intruders. *Animal Learning and Behavior, 10*, 240–252.

Williams, J. L., & Lierle, D. M. (1986). Effects of stress controllability, immunization, and therapy on the subsequent defeat of colony intruders. *Animal Learning and Behavior, 14*, 305–314.

Williams, J. L., Lierle, D. M. (1988). Effects of repeated defeat by a dominant conspecific on subsequent pain sensitivity, open-field activity, and escape learning. *Animal Learning and Behavior, 16*, 477–485.

Williams, J. L., & Maier, S. (1977) Transsituational immunization and ther-apy of learned helplessness in the rat. *Journal of Experimental Psychology: Animal Behavior Processes, 3*, 240–252.

Williams, J. L., Rogers, A. G., & Adler, A. P. (1990). Exposure to conspecific and predatory odors on defensive burying and freezing. *Animal Learning and Behavior, 18*, 453–461.

Williams, J. L. & Scott, D. K. (1989). Influence of conspecific and predatory stressors and the associated odors on defensive burying and freezing. *Animal Learning and Behavior, 17*, 383–393.

Williams, J. L., Worland, P., & Smith, M. G. (1990). Defeat-induced hypo-algesia in the rat: Effects of conditioned odors, naltrexone and extinction. *Journal of Experimental Psychology: Animal Behavior Processes, 16*, 345–357.

Zinbarg, R. E., & Barlow, D. H. (1992, November). *The construct validity of the DSM-III-R anxiety disorders: Empirical evidence*. Presented at the 26th An-nual Meeting of the Association for the Advancement of Behavior Ther-apy, Boston.

Zinbarg, R. E., Barlow, D. H., Brown, T. A., & Hertz, R. M. (1992). Cogni-tive-behavioral approaches to the nature and treatment of anxiety disor-ders. *Annual Review of Psychology, 43*, 235–267.

Cognitive Bias in the Anxiety Disorders

Richard J. McNally
Harvard University

Clinical psychologists have traditionally considered cognition as equivalent to conscious thought and have accordingly used questionnaires and interviews to study the cognitive aspects of anxiety disorders. But limitations of introspective self-report have prompted investigators to apply the concepts and methods of experimental cognitive psychology to elucidate information-processing biases that may figure in the maintenance, and perhaps the etiology, of these syndromes. Two types of studies have predominated. *Content-independent* studies require subjects to process information that varies in complexity but not in emotional valence. Research in this tradition has clarified the relation between anxiety and cognitive deficits by showing, for example, that anxiety-related reductions in capacity impair performance only on complex, strategic tasks (for a review, see Eysenck, 1992). In contrast, *content-dependent* studies require subjects to process information having emotional significance and have revealed that patients with anxiety disorders are characterized by biases favoring the processing of threatening information. The focus of this chapter is on content-dependent cognitive research.

Clinicians have long recognized that cognition is disturbed in people with anxiety disorders. But only recently have researchers used methods capable of discriminating between cognitive processes that are dysfunctional from those that are not. In contrast to early theories that implied biased processing throughout the system (e.g., Beck, Emery, & Greenberg, 1985; Bower, 1981), recent theories state that biases are not pervasive (e.g., Eysenck, 1992; Williams, Watts, MacLeod, & Mathews, 1988). Williams et al., for example, believe that anxiety is associated with emotion-congruent biases in attention and interpretation but not in (explicit) memory. But general statements about which biases are associated with which emotions are difficult to sustain in patients who commonly suffer from both anxiety and depressive symptoms. Complicating matters further, some biases occur in certain syndromes (e.g., panic disorder) but not in others (e.g., generalized anxiety disorder, GAD; McNally, 1994a).

Cognitive psychopathologists who study anxiety have been agnostic about how information-processing biases are instantiated at the neural level of analysis, and most have assumed that cognitive bias need not imply brain disease. Just as an error in a software program need not imply a defect in the computer itself, cognitive biases need not imply organicity. Cognition is instantiated in the brain, but it is not reducible or translatable into its neural underpinnings. Nevertheless, neuropsychological methods may clarify conflicting findings at the cognitive level (Otto, McNally, Pollack, Chen, & Rosenbaum, 1994), suggesting that cross-fertilization between cognitive and neuroscience perspectives may prove fruitful (McNally, 1994b, pp. 212–218).

The purpose of this chapter is to provide a survey and analysis of cognitive bias research in the anxiety disorders. I review studies concerning disturbances in interpretation, attention, memory, and interoception and consider how these findings bear on the crucial distinction between automatic and strategic processing. I concentrate on research with clinical populations but address studies on people with high trait anxiety when pertinent to vulnerability for developing anxiety disorders. I conclude by elucidating clinical implications of cognitive bias research.

Interpretive Bias

People encounter many situations in everyday life whose meaning is ambiguous. Sudden chest pain may signify heart disease or merely a pulled muscle. A phone call in the middle of the night may portend bad news about distant relatives or merely be a wrong number. People whose default option is to interpret ambiguous stimuli as threatening ought to be especially prone to experience episodes of anxiety (Beck et al., 1985; Mathews, 1990). Conversely, people who often experience episodes of anxiety may be characterized by a bias for interpreting ambiguous stimuli as threatening.

Butler and Mathews (1983) were the first to study interpretive bias in anxiety disorders. They developed a booklet containing a series of ambiguous scenarios and had GAD patients, depressed patients, and control subjects write down the first interpretation that came to mind for each scenario. Subjects then turned the page and ranked three experimenter-provided interpretations for their likelihood of coming to mind in a similar situation. For each scenario, only one interpretation was threatening. The results revealed that GAD patients, relative to control subjects, exhibited a bias for interpreting ambiguous scenarios as threatening. Depressed subjects, however, responded like GAD subjects, perhaps because they were as anxious as GAD subjects.

To investigate interpretive bias in panic disorder, McNally and Foa (1987) modified Butler and Mathews's booklet so that it contained equal numbers of ambiguous scenarios involving external stimuli (e.g., "You wake with a start in the middle of the night, thinking you heard a noise, but all is quiet. What do you think woke you up?") and internal stimuli (e.g., "You feel discomfort in your chest area. Why?"). They reasoned that interpretive bias ought to be especially pronounced for ambiguous internal stimuli in light of the marked anxiety sensitivity associated with panic disorder (McNally & Lorenz, 1987). To test whether treatment abolishes interpretive bias, McNally and Foa administered the task to recovered agoraphobics as well as to symptomatic agoraphobics and healthy control subjects. The results indicated that symptomatic agoraphobics exhibited biases for interpreting both external and internal scenarios as threatening, whereas recovered agoraphobics and control subjects did not.

Other researchers have reported interpretive biases in patients with panic disorder and agoraphobia. Harvey and her associates replicated McNally and Foa's findings and observed similar, but less pronounced, biases in social phobics whose Anxiety Sensitivity Index (Reiss, Peterson, Gursky, & McNally, 1986) scores were as high as those of their panic patients (Harvey, Richards, Dziadosz, & Swindell, 1993). Using a Portuguese translation of the Butler and Mathews booklet, Baptista and his colleagues found that panic patients with varying degrees of agoraphobia provided threatening interpretations for more of the ambiguous scenarios than did healthy control subjects (Baptista, Figueira, Lima, & Matos, 1990).

Modifying McNally and Foa's booklet, Clark, Salkovskis, Koehler, and Gelder (cited in Clark, 1988) found that panic patients without agoraphobia interpreted only ambiguous scenarios involving bodily sensations having a sudden onset (e.g., skipped heartbeat) as threatening but did not do so for ambiguous scenarios involving general events, social events, or symptoms not having a sudden onset (e.g., spot on one's hand). Taken together, these studies imply that panic patients with and without agoraphobia exhibit biases for interpreting ambiguous internal stimuli as threatening, but only those who develop agoraphobia also exhibit biases for interpreting external stimuli as threatening.

Devising another procedure for studying interpretive bias, Stoler and McNally (1991) had agoraphobics, recovered agoraphobics, and healthy control subjects complete a series of sentence stems with the first thought that came to mind and then had them jot down a few additional sentences elaborating on their initial response. The sentence stems were either related or unrelated to threat and were either ambiguous or unambiguous. Thus interpretation of the stem "Knowing that entering the store would produce a sure fit, I . . ." could involve disambiguation of "fit" as referring either to clothes or to a panic attack.

Stoler and McNally found that agoraphobics exhibited biases for interpreting stems as threatening, relative to healthy control subjects, and that the interpretations of recovered agoraphobics resembled those of symptomatic agoraphobics more than those of control subjects, suggesting that interpretive bias may persist after recovery. Although the initial reaction to ambiguous information did not distinguish between recovered and symptomatic agoraphobics, the additional sentences written by recovered agoraphobics suggested an acquired tendency to cope adaptively with threat, whereas those of the symptomatic agoraphobics did not. Accordingly, behavioral treatment may not abolish biases as much as provide patients with skills to counteract them.

The aforementioned studies suggest that pathological anxiety states, such as GAD and panic disorder, are associated with a bias for interpreting ambiguity as threatening. One potential limitation of these procedures is their vulnerability to experimenter demand effects. Symptomatic patients may provide responses they believe are consistent with their diagnosis rather than providing the first response that comes to mind. Similarly, patients who have recovered may provide responses that they believe are consistent with mental health.

Attempting to avoid this problem, Mathews, Richards, and Eysenck (1989b) devised another method for triangulating interpretive bias. They had GAD patients, recovered GAD patients, and healthy control subjects listen to a series of homophones that could be disambiguated in either a threatening (e.g., *die*) or a nonthreatening (e.g., *dye*) fashion and write down the words they heard. If pathological anxiety is associated with an interpretive bias, GAD patients ought to select the threatening spellings more often than the nonthreatening ones, relative to control subjects. The results revealed that GAD subjects produced more threatening spellings than did healthy control subjects, whereas recovered GAD subjects did so to an intermediate degree.

Noting that homophones do not constitute an especially ecologically valid form of ambiguity, these researchers developed another paradigm that involves ambiguous sentences (Eysenck, Mogg, May, Richards, & Mathews, 1991). Eysenck et al. had GAD subjects, recovered GAD subjects, and healthy control subjects listen to an audiotaped series of sentences (e.g., "The doctor examined little Emma's growth") before showing subjects a series of sentences that were either threatening (e.g., "The doctor looked at little Emma's cancer") or nonthreatening (e.g., "The doctor measured little Emma's growth") disambiguations of the sentences they had heard earlier. Subjects were asked to identify which sentences had the same meaning as the audiotaped ambiguous ones. The results revealed that GAD subjects endorsed threatening and nonthreatening disambiguated sentences to an approximately equal extent, whereas both healthy control subjects and recovered GAD subjects exhibited biases for endorsing nonthreatening disambiguated sentences as having the same meaning as the original ones. A second experiment produced similar results (Eysenck et al., 1991).

Although ambiguous homophones and sentences are probably less subject to experimental demand than are ambiguous scenarios, the findings do not necessarily confirm that anxious patients differ from healthy controls in their interpretive style; the effects might arise from an anxiety-linked response bias rather than from an anxiety-linked interpretive bias (Mathews & MacLeod, 1994). Regardless of any desire to satisfy implicit experimental demands, anxious subjects may entertain both meanings of ambiguous input, but because of a characteristic bias to respond in an anxiety-relevant fashion, they might tend to select the anxiety-relevant option. Therefore, it would be desirable to test for interpretive bias in a paradigm that did not require subjects to select an anxiety-related response and thus avoid any possible experimental demands.

MacLeod and Cohen (1993) developed an ingenious text comprehension paradigm that avoids the aforementioned limitations associated with previous paradigms. In this experiment, college students with either high or low trait anxiety read pairs of sequentially presented sentences on a computer screen. For each pair, the first sentence had either a threatening, a nonthreatening, or an ambiguous meaning; the second sentence provided a plausible continuation of the first sentence and had either a threatening or a nonthreatening meaning. Subjects pushed a button to advance from the first to the second sentence and pushed it again to advance from the second sentence to the first member of the next pair. MacLeod and Cohen were thus able to measure the time subjects took to read sentences. Because comprehension latency for the second sentence is inversely related to its plausibility as a continuation of the preceding sentence, MacLeod and Cohen reasoned that comprehension latencies for second sentences that follow ambiguous first sentences can reveal patterns of interpretive bias. For example, if subjects impose a threatening interpretation on the first sentence, they should exhibit shorter comprehension latencies for the second sentence if it constitutes an unambiguous threatening continuation rather than an unambiguous nonthreatening continuation. Because subjects were merely asked to read the sentences and to push buttons, this paradigm seems unlikely to be influenced by experimental demand or by response bias.

The results revealed different patterns of interpretive bias for high and low trait anxious students. Comprehension latency patterns indicated that subjects with high trait anxiety dispropor-tionately imposed threatening meanings on the ambiguous sen-tences, whereas subjects with low trait anxiety did the opposite.

In summary, early studies indicated that panic and GAD patients are characterized by a bias for interpreting ambiguous scenarios as threatening, whereas later studies concerning homophones and ambiguous sentences indicated that anxious patients lack a "pos-itivity" bias possessed by control subjects. Regardless of whether anxiety disorders are characterized by a pathogenic interpretive bias, the absence of a protective positivity bias, or both, vul-nerability to anxiety episodes would be the consequence.

Attentional Bias

Because the human information-processing system has limited ca-pacity, individuals can attend only to certain stimuli at any given time, and any bias for selectively allocating attention to potentially threatening stimuli ought to increase the frequency of anxiety epi-sodes. The ability to detect threat rapidly would seem to be adaptive in that it would enable preparation for defensive action (Gray, 1982, p. 458). Yet a low threshold for shifting into a defensive mode would result in episodes of unnecessary anxiety and perhaps increase risk for full-blown anxiety disorders (Williams et al., 1988).

If the cognitive system associated with pathological anxiety is, in-deed, biased toward ready detection of threat, people with anxiety dis-orders ought to be characterized by an attentional bias favoring the se-lective processing of threat cues. To investigate this issue, researchers have devised detection, interference, and facilitation paradigms.

DETECTION PARADIGMS

Burgess and his colleagues employed dichotic listening methods to investigate attentional bias for threat in agoraphobics, social pho-bics, and control subjects (Burgess, Jones, Robertson, Radcliffe, & Emerson, 1981). They presented subjects with two different prose passages, one to each ear, and had them repeat aloud (shadow) one passage while ignoring the other and to push a button whenever they detected threat (e.g., shopping alone) and neutral (e.g., pick) targets that occurred out of context in either passage. The results revealed that both agoraphobic and social phobic subjects, but not control subjects, detected more threat targets than neutral targets in the unattended passage, thereby implying an attentional bias for threat.

Similar results have been obtained by others. Foa and McNally (1986) administered a dichotic listening task to obsessive-compulsive disorder (OCD) patients before and after intensive behavior therapy (in vivo exposure plus response prevention). Patients attempted to detect neutral (e.g., pick) and threat targets (e.g., urine) embedded out of context in both attended and unattended prose passages. Skin conductance responses (SCRS) were measured during dichotic listening. The results indicated that patients detected more threat than neutral targets and exhibited SCRS of greater magnitude to the former than to the latter, before, but not after, treatment. Behavior therapy, accordingly, may attenuate attentional bias for threat.

Using a nondichotic listening detection paradigm, McNally, Luedke, Besyner, Peterson, Bohm, and Lips (1987) measured skin conductance while combat veterans with posttraumatic stress disorder (PTSD), combat veterans with heroin dependence, and noncombat veterans with heroin dependence attempted to identify threat and nonthreat targets embedded in white noise of varying volumes. Although all groups were especially adept at identifying threat targets (e.g., firefight) relative to other targets (e.g., fingertips), only the PTSD group exhibited enhanced SCR magnitudes to threat targets.

Detection paradigms have provided data consistent with the attentional bias hypothesis. Unfortunately, however, patients may be characterized by an especially low threshold for affirming the presence of threat targets (MacLeod, 1991). Such a guessing bias would produce data similar to that arising from a genuine attentional bias. Needless to say, a response bias for affirming the presence of threat would have considerable clinical significance, but it would not indicate dysfunction in attentional mechanisms.

INTERFERENCE PARADIGMS

In another approach to triangulating attentional bias, researchers have employed interference paradigms that require subjects to ignore extraneous stimuli while performing a task unrelated to the detection of threat. Selective processing of threat is inferred from performance decrements produced by the presence of threat distractors.

The most frequently used interference task has been the emotional Stroop color-naming paradigm. In this paradigm, subjects are shown words of varying emotional valence and are asked to name the colors in which the words are printed while ignoring the meanings of the words (Mathews & MacLeod, 1985; Watts, McKenna, Sharrock, & Trezise, 1986). Delays in color-naming, or Stroop interference, occur when the meaning of the word attracts the subject's attention despite the subject's effort to attend to the color of the word.

If anxious patients are characterized by an attentional bias for processing threatening stimuli, they ought to take longer to name the colors of threat words than to name the colors of nonthreat words. This hypothesis has been confirmed for every anxiety disorder category including specific (spider) phobia (e.g., Watts et al., 1986), social phobia (e.g., Hope, Rapee, Heimberg, & Dombeck, 1990), GAD (e.g., Mathews & MacLeod, 1985), PTSD (e.g., McNally, Kaspi, Riemann, & Zeitlin, 1990a), OCD (e.g., Foa, Ilai, McCarthy, Shoyer, & Murdock, 1993), and panic disorder (e.g., Ehlers, Margraf, Davies, & Roth, 1988a; McNally, Riemann, & Kim, 1990b).

Most studies have revealed content-specificity effects. That is, the closer a word relates to the patient's chief concerns, the more likely it will be to produce delayed color naming. Thus Vietnam veterans with PTSD exhibit interference for words related to combat trauma (e.g., *body bags*) but not for negative words related to the contamination concerns of OCD patients (e.g., *feces*; McNally et al., 1990a). Social phobics display more interference for social threat words (e.g., *stupid*) than for physical threat words (e.g., *fatal*), whereas panic patients exhibit the opposite pattern (Hope et al., 1990). Similarly, rape victims with PTSD exhibit greater interference for words directly related to their trauma (e.g., *rape*) than to words less directly related to their trauma (e.g., *crime*; Cassiday, McNally, & Zeitlin, 1992), and GAD patients who worry more about social than physical threat (and vice versa) exhibit corresponding patterns of interference (Mogg, Mathews, & Weinman, 1989).

Although these studies appear to confirm that patients with

anxiety disorders are characterized by an attentional bias for threat, Martin, Williams, and Clark (1991) have interpreted these results as indicating that patients are merely hyperresponsive to any personally emotionally significant material, irrespective of its valence. They noted that many studies failed to include positively valenced control stimuli, and when investigators have attempted to control for emotionality by including positive words, patients often rate the positive words as less emotional overall, relative to negative words (e.g., McNally et al., 1990a).

Subsequent research, however, suggests that emotionality per se is not the crucial determinant of interference. McNally, Riemann, Louro, Lukach, and Kim (1992) reported that panic patients rated positive words (e.g., *cheerful*) as more emotional than catastrophe words (e.g., *collapse*) but took longer to color-name the latter than the former. Mathews and Klug (1993) reported that a mixed sample of anxious patients exhibited interference for words that raters had deemed relevant to anxiety disorders, regardless of whether the words were positive (e.g., *relaxed*) or negative (e.g., *dying*). But positive words (e.g., *humor*) unrelated to threat did not produce interference. McNally et al. (1994a), however, found that even positive words 180 degrees conceptually removed from threat (e.g., *relaxed*) did not produce interference in panic patients, and Lavy, van Oppen, and van den Hout (1994) also found that positive antonyms (e.g., *clean*) related to threat failed to produce interference in OCD patients. Finally, Kaspi, McNally, and Amir (1995), using an idiographic stimulus selection procedure, determined that Vietnam veterans with PTSD exhibited far more interference for trauma-related words than positive words receiving nearly identical emotionality ratings. Taken together, these studies suggest that positive material uncommonly produces interference except, perhaps, when it is directly related to the patient's chief concerns.

But Stroop interference is not confined to anxious patients, or to processing of cues either directly or indirectly related to threat. Using an idiographic stimulus selection procedure with college student subjects, Riemann and McNally (1995) selected material related to each subject's positive (e.g., a new romantic relationship) and negative (e.g., financial worries) current concerns. The results revealed that words strongly related to both types of current concern produced more interference than did words either weakly related or unrelated to these concerns. In another idiographic Stroop study, Riemann, Amir, and Louro (1995) found that panic patients exhibited interference not only for threat material but also for positive and negative current concerns unrelated to panic.

Emotional Stroop studies do, indeed, show that anxious patients selectively process threat cues, but only because these stimuli are directly relevant to their current concerns. Indifferent to the threat-related preoccupations of anxious patients, healthy control subjects do not exhibit interference for threat words but do so for material related to their own concerns, irrespective of its valence. Therefore, interference for threat words in anxious patients is apparently a special case of a general phenomenon: attention is captured by cues of either positive or negative valence as long as it is directly related to the person's current concerns.

Despite its widespread use, the Stroop paradigm has limitations as a measure of attentional bias. As Mathews (1990) observed, color-naming might be slowed by threat cues capturing attention, by threat cues producing emotional distress that hampers task performance, or by capacity consumption arising from patients' attempting to avoid processing of meaning. Moreover, although the Stroop provides a measure of selective processing in general, it does not provide a measure of selective attention (Fox, 1993). That is, both semantic and color cues occupy the same physical space, and one must separate the cues spatially to test whether attention selectively shifts to threat cues.

To overcome limitations associated with the Stroop, Mathews, May, Mogg, and Eysenck (1990) had normal control subjects, symptomatic GAD subjects, and recovered GAD subjects search for a target that could appear in various locations on a computer screen. They found that the presence of *any* distractors, irrespective of valence, slowed reaction times to the target for symptomatic GAD subjects but not for recovered GAD or normal control subjects. Threat distractors, however, slowed reaction times for recovered as well as for symptomatic GAD subjects. Because both groups of GAD subjects were slower to search for targets among threat distractors than among positive distractors, Mathews et al. concluded that attention is captured specifically by threat cues rather than by any emotional cue and that symptomatic GAD is associated not only with an attentional bias for threat but also by general distractibility.

Mathews and his colleagues modified their conclusions, however, after analyzing data from a longitudinal study of cognitive bias (Mathews, Mogg, Kentish, & Eysenck, 1995). Using the attentional search paradigm, they tested GAD patients both before and immediately after successful behavior therapy and again at a three-month follow-up. Although symptomatic GAD patients exhibited attentional capture by threat distractors as in the previous study (Mathews et al., 1990), recovered GAD patients did not. That is, there was no evidence of residual cognitive bias for threat.

FACILITATION PARADIGMS

Interference tasks provide evidence for attentional bias by showing that the presence of threat cues disrupts performance on a primary task. If threat cues do, indeed, capture attention in pathological anxiety, they ought to facilitate performance on tasks involving attention shifts to threat cues. One such task is the dot-probe attention deployment paradigm (MacLeod, Mathews, & Tata, 1986). This paradigm requires subjects to perform a neutral response (a button press) to a neutral visual stimulus (a dot) that replaces either member of a pair of words that appear on a computer screen. Subjects read the top word of each pair and press a button whenever they detect a dot. On some trials, one of the words has a threatening meaning. Using this procedure, MacLeod et al. found that GAD patients, relative to depressed and healthy volunteers, were faster at responding to dots that replaced threat words and slower at responding to dots that replaced neutral words. These findings indicate that an attentional bias for threat in GAD patients facilitated performance when dots replaced threat words but impaired performance when dots replaced neutral words. That is, attention of GAD patients had shifted to threat cues, thereby shortening reaction times when the target replaced these cues. Mogg, Mathews, and Eysenck (1992) replicated these results in another group of GAD patients.

Using this paradigm, Asmundson and Stein (1994) reported that patients with generalized social phobia responded faster to probes that followed social threat words than to probes that followed neutral and physical threat words. Similarly, Asmundson and his colleagues found that panic patients responded faster to dots that replaced physical threat words than to dots that replaced social threat words (Asmundson, Sandler, Wilson, & Walker, 1992). In neither of these studies, however, was there evidence of patients *shifting* attention to threat cues. Moreover, Asmundson and Stein (1994/1995) have been unable to replicate their findings in a fresh sample of panic patients despite their use of bodily sensation threat words (e.g., *suffocating*) that ought to have provoked more bias than the general physical threat words they had used before (e.g., *cancer*).

Employing a modification of the MacLeod et al. paradigm, Beck and her colleagues reported that panic patients selectively attend to positive as well as physically threatening words, whereas healthy volunteers do not (Beck, Stanley, Averill, Baldwin, & Deagle, 1992). Like Asmundson and his colleagues, Beck et al. were unable to demonstrate attention shifts to threat cues in panic patients. Because the MacLeod et al. and Beck et al. procedures differ in several ways, and because MacLeod et al. did not include positive emotional control words, it is difficult to interpret these conflicting findings.

In summary, converging evidence from diverse paradigms indicates that patients with anxiety disorders exhibit an attentional bias favoring the processing of threat cues. Healthy control subjects do not exhibit a bias for the cues that disturb anxious patients, but they do attend, at least in the Stroop paradigm, to positive and negative cues related to their current concerns. Therefore, the pathology associated with anxiety disorders does not lie in attentional bias per se, but rather in the sorts of cues that capture attention. People without these disorders are not disturbed by themes problematic for anxious patients (e.g., bodily sensations, spiders, social evaluation). It remains to be seen, however, whether current concern effects occur with healthy subjects in paradigms that constitute the best measures of attentional bias (e.g., dot-probe attention deployment paradigm).

Memory Bias

People with anxiety disorders are plagued by unbidden, disturbing thoughts. Panic patients experience terrifying thoughts about impending insanity, heart attacks, and so forth, especially under conditions of arousal. Those with PTSD suffer from involuntary retrieval of traumatic memories in the form of intrusive thoughts, nightmares, and flashbacks. Thus the phenomenology of at least some anxiety disorders suggests that information about threat is characterized by its ease of accessibility. If so, then pathological anxiety ought to be associated with a memory bias for threatening information. Moreover, it is not unreasonable to expect that anxious patients ought to exhibit enhanced memory for threatening information which they selectively encode.

Most memory bias research has concerned explicit rather than implicit memory. Explicit memory is revealed when task performance requires conscious recollection of previous experiences; it is typically assessed by direct tests such as free recall, cued recall, and recognition. Implicit memory is revealed when previous experiences facilitate performance on a task that does not require conscious or deliberate recollection of these experiences; it is typically assessed by indirect tests, such as word-stem completion, tachistoscopic word identification, and lexical decision (Schacter, 1987). Implicit memory is presumably more automatic than explicit memory and less subject to strategic influence.

EXPLICIT MEMORY

Although some theorists hold that depression, but not anxiety, is associated with emotion-congruent explicit memory biases (e.g., Williams et al., 1988), findings vary across diagnostic categories. Results suggestive of memory bias for threat have been most often reported in panic disorder (McNally, 1990). McNally, Foa, and Donnell (1989) had panic patients and healthy control subjects rate the self-descriptiveness of adjectives related to anxiety (e.g., *nervous*) and adjectives unrelated to anxiety (e.g., *polite*) before performing either a high-arousal (i.e., exercise step-test) or a low-arousal (i.e., relaxation) task. Following the arousal manipulation, subjects received a surprise free recall test for the previously rated words. The results revealed that panic patients recalled more anxiety than nonanxiety words, whereas control subjects recalled more nonanxiety words than anxiety words. This bias was nonsignificantly ($p < .11$) exacerbated for panic patients in the high arousal condition. Additional analyses confirmed that these findings could not be attributed merely to a self-descriptive recall bias or to a response bias for guessing anxiety-related words.

Other researchers have found memory biases for threat in panic disorder. Relative to healthy control subjects, panic patients exhibited a free recall bias for words related to panic (e.g., *madness*) but not for positive words (e.g., *sweet*) or for generally negative words unrelated to panic (e.g., *murder*; Becker, Rinck, & Margraf, 1994). Cloitre and Liebowitz (1991) reported that panic patients displayed better free recall for panic-related threat words (e.g., *collapse*) than for positive (e.g., *pleasure*) and neutral (e.g., *magazine*) words. Further analyses ruled out a possible response bias interpretation of these results. Healthy control subjects did not exhibit differential recall as a function of word type.

Using a word-pair association procedure, Cloitre, Shear, Cancienne, and Zeitlin (1994) exposed panic patients, clinicians who treat panic disorder, and healthy control subjects to pairs of words that were either related or unrelated and of either negative, positive, or neutral valence. An example of a related threat word pair is *breathless-suffocate*, and an example of an unrelated positive word pair is *cheerful-bureau*. Subjects read word pairs aloud and rated their relatedness. A cued recall test showed that panic patients recalled more threat than neutral or positive word pairs and more neutral than positive word pairs. The control groups exhibited no such superior memory for threat.

Heiber, Chambless, and Peynircioglu (1995) found that panic patients exhibited greater recall for threat words than for safety or neutral words, whereas normal control subjects did not. Enhanced memory for threat in the panic group remained even after Heiber et al. controlled for the effects of depression.

Norton and his colleagues investigated memory for threat material in nonclinical panickers (Norton, Schaefer, Cox, Dorward, & Wozney, 1988). To prime different memory structures, they had subjects read a paragraph about a person experiencing either hunger, anger, or a panic attack. Immediately thereafter, subjects were asked to memorize anxiety/threat, anger, and neutral words. The results revealed that nonclinical panickers displayed a recall bias for anxiety/danger words, especially after having read the panic paragraph. Norton et al. concluded that the panic paragraph primed a danger schema in nonclinical panickers that facilitated retrieval of threat information.

Nunn, Stevenson, and Whalan (1984) had agoraphobics and

healthy control subjects read phobia-relevant (e.g., about a woman shopping) and phobia-irrelevant (e.g., about a woman having breakfast) prose passages. After a distractor task, subjects received a surprise recall test for material contained in the passages. Both groups recalled a similar number of propositions from the neutral passages, but agoraphobics recalled more propositions from phobia-relevant passages than did control subjects. In the second part of the study, Nunn et al. had subjects attempt to memorize and recall phobia-relevant (e.g., *travel*) and neutral (e.g., *letter*) nouns. Agoraphobics exhibited a memory bias for phobia-relevant words, whereas control subjects exhibited the opposite pattern. This study, however, has been criticized because certain consensually neutral words (e.g., *travel*) are likely to have different emotional meanings for agoraphobic and nonagoraphobic people (Mathews & MacLeod, 1994).

Although standard recognition paradigms have revealed no memory bias for threat in panic disorder (Beck et al., 1992; Ehlers et al., 1988a), panic patients exhibit better recognition memory for threat words relative to positive and neutral words when test items appear for very short durations (35 minutes; Cloitre & Liebowitz, 1991). Accordingly, panic patients may be characterized by enhanced recognition memory for threat only under conditions of stimulus impoverishment.

There have been several failures to demonstrate an explicit memory bias for threat in panic disorder (Otto et al., 1994; Pickles & van den Broek, 1988; Rapee, 1994a). Procedural differences may account for discrepancies across studies. For example, self-descriptive threat words (e.g., *fearful*), physiological arousal, and free recall tests may have fostered recall for negative material in the McNally et al. (1989) study. In contrast, nonself-descriptive threat words (e.g., *coronary*), no arousal, and cued recall tests may have undercut any memory bias for threat in the Otto et al. (1994) study. Alternatively, certain individual difference variables might influence whether biases emerge. Thus Otto et al. found that auditory perceptual asymmetries associated with relative left hemisphere activation strongly predicted cued recall for threat words in panic patients but not in healthy control subjects. Left hemisphere biases may be linked to a verbal processing advantage for personally relevant material (i.e., threat words in panic disorder) that becomes apparent during recall.

Finally, perhaps panic patients are either unable or unwilling to engage in strategic avoidance of elaborative processing, as Mathews (1990) believes GAD patients are capable of doing, and therefore exhibit enhanced recall for threat items.

Explicit memory biases for threat have been studied in other anxiety disorders as well, but with generally negative results. Researchers have consistently failed to obtain biases for threat in GAD (Mathews, Mogg, May, & Eysenck, 1989a; Mogg & Mathews, 1990; Mogg, Mathews, & Weinman, 1987; Otto et al., 1994). Investigators have also reported no biases for threat in either social phobia (Rapee, McCallum, Melville, Ravenscroft, & Rodney, 1994) or specific (spider) phobia (Watts & Coyle, 1993). In contrast, Vrana, Roodman, and Beckham (1995) found that Vietnam combat veterans with PTSD exhibited enhanced explicit memory for emotional words related to their traumatic experiences.

Appealing to Mandler's (1980) distinction between *integration* and *elaboration*, Mathews et al. (1989a) suggested that anxiety states might be characterized by implicit, if not by explicit, memory biases for threat. According to Mandler, implicit memory results from activation of a cognitive representation that strengthens its internal structure (i.e., integration), thereby increasing its accessibility but not necessarily its retrievability. In contrast, explicit memory results from an individual connecting the activated representation to other representations during encoding (i.e., elaboration). By establishing links to multiple retrieval cues, elaborative processing increases the likelihood of subsequent retrieval. Mathews et al. (1989a) proposed that GAD patients may readily encode threat material, but their avoidance of subsequent elaborative processing would impair its memorability on explicit tests. On the other hand, because activation and integration are presumably automatic, GAD patients might exhibit enhanced implicit memory for threat.

To study implicit memory in anxious patients, psychopathologists have typically employed the word-stem completion paradigm (Mathews et al., 1989a). In this paradigm, subjects study words that vary in valence (e.g., *coffin, charm*) and subsequently complete word stems (e.g., *cof*) with the first word that comes to mind. Implicit memory is revealed when subjects complete stems with words that were previously presented (e.g., *coffin*) more often than with words that were not previously presented (e.g., *coffee*). An implicit memory bias for threat occurs if this priming effect is greater for threat than for nonthreat stems.

Researchers have reported mixed results when applying this paradigm in anxiety disordered populations. Mathews and his associates reported an implicit memory bias for threat in GAD in one study (Mathews et al., 1989a), but not in another (Mathews et al., 1995).

Otto et al. (1994), however, failed to observe an implicit memory bias for panic-related material in panic patients in a word-stem completion paradigm. Heiber et al. (1995) also failed to obtain an implicit memory bias for threat in panic disorder. Cloitre and her associates, however, obtained evidence for both implicit and explicit memory biases for threat in panic patients (Cloitre et al., 1994). Using the word-pair association procedure described above, Cloitre et al. found that panic patients exhibited more completions for threat than for positive (but not neutral) word pairs, whereas clinicians did not exhibit differential completions as a function of pair type. Normal control subjects completed more neutral than threat or positive pairs. The groups did not differ in their completion of neutral word pairs, but panic patients completed more threat pairs than did clinician or normal control subjects.

Because they purportedly reflect automatic processing, implicit memory paradigms have captured the attention of experimental psychopathologists. Regrettably, it now appears that word-stem completion and related procedures may be irrelevant to the theoretical concerns of anxiety researchers. For example, priming effects in the word-stem completion paradigm are markedly influenced by the physical properties of the stimuli rather than by their semantic properties. Thus, if the word *coffin* is presented in lowercase letters during the study phase, but its stem is later presented in uppercase letters (COF) during testing, priming effects are much less than if the stem were presented in lowercase letters (*cof*). Therefore, this paradigm seems a better test of *perceptual* implicit memory than *conceptual* implicit memory (e.g., Schacter, 1992). Because anxiety researchers are interested in the automatic processing of emotional meaning, not orthographics, tests that primarily tap perceptual implicit memory are less relevant than those that primarily tap conceptual implicit memory. Indeed, if meaning is largely irrelevant to most implicit memory tasks, it becomes difficult to understand why anxiety patients might exhibit an "implicit memory bias" favoring threat words; contemporary implicit memory research suggests that these tests, if truly tapping implicit memory, ought to be insensitive to semantic and emotional variables. When "implicit memory" tests (e.g., word-stem completion) display sensitivity to emotional meaning, one might suspect that the test is contaminated by explicit memory processing.

Anxiety researchers have scarcely begun to investigate the possibility of conceptual implicit memory biases in panic and related disorders. In an effort to investigate this issue, Amir, McNally, Riemann, and Clements (1996) adapted Jacoby's "white noise" paradigm (Jacoby, Allan, Collins, & Larwill, 1988). This procedure may be more sensitive to conceptual processing of threat cues than are word-stem completion tasks. In this experiment, panic patients and healthy control subjects first heard a series of threat (e.g., "The anxious woman panicked in the supermarket") and neutral (e.g., "The shiny apple sat on the table") sentences. Subjects subsequently heard these old sentences intermixed with previously unheard threat and neutral sentences; each was accompanied by white noise that varied in volume. Subjects were told to judge the volume of white noise that accompanied each sentence. In this paradigm, implicit memory for old sentences is revealed when subjects judge the noise accompanying these sentences as less loud than the noise accompanying new sentences, and an implicit memory bias for threat is confirmed if the difference between noise ratings for new minus old sentences is greater for threat sentences than for neutral sentences. Although the findings did not always achieve significance, Amir et al. found that panic patients exhibited greater priming for panic sentences than for neutral sentences, whereas control subjects exhibited the opposite pattern.

Using the white noise paradigm, Amir, McNally, and Wiegartz (in press) reported similar findings in patients with combat-related PTSD. Vietnam veterans with PTSD, but not healthy combat veterans, exhibited marked priming effects for trauma sentences but not for neutral sentences. On a perceptual identificaton task that strongly taps perceptual but not conceptual implicit memory, McNally and Amir (in press) found no enhanced priming for trauma words in Vietnam combat veterans with PTSD.

Not all psychopathologists agree, however, that conceptual implicit memory is most relevant to pathological anxiety. After finding an anxiety-related memory bias for threat in a tachistoscopic identification task that taps perceptual implicit memory, MacLeod and McLaughlin (1995) argued that perceptual, not conceptual, processing is more central for understanding anxiety disorders. Appealing to evolutionary considerations, they stated, "For example, it may well be more adaptive to ascertain the physical location and trajectory of an attacking predator's teeth and claws than to discriminate the particular genus to which that species of predator belongs" (MacLeod & McLaughlin, 1995, p. 12). This may be true, but it is unclear what the evolutionary significance of perceptual processing of *verbal* representations of threatening stimuli might be.

In summary, data are mixed concerning the presence of implicit memory biases in anxiety disorders. Although psychopathologists agree that tests of automatic memory are theoretically compatible with the phenomenology of pathological anxiety, debate persists about whether conceptual or perceptual memory tests are most appropriate.

AUTOBIOGRAPHICAL MEMORY

Most studies on memory bias and anxiety disorders have involved standardized materials, such as word lists that vary in their emotional significance. Another approach concerns testing of autobiographical memory. For example, GAD patients retrieve a disproportionately large number of negative memories when prompted to retrieve a memory in response to a neutral cue word (Burke & Mathews, 1992). On the one hand, this implies that failures to obtain explicit memory biases for threat in GAD might have been attributable to the artificiality of the typical word list approach. On the other hand, GAD patients might merely have more negative experiences stored in memory relative to control subjects. Unfortunately, it is difficult to disentangle these two interpretations.

Autobiographical cuing paradigms have revealed disturbances other than just mood-congruent recall in clinical populations (e.g., Williams & Dritschel, 1988). While studying mood-congruent memory in depressed individuals, Williams (1996) and his colleagues discovered that these patients had difficulty retrieving specific personal memories in response to cue words. In contrast to control subjects, depressed patients tended to retrieve "overgeneral" memories, especially to positive cues. For example, in response to the cue *happy*, control subjects easily retrieved specific events (e.g., "the day we left to go on holiday"), whereas depressed patients often retrieved a summary memory that did not reference any specific event (e.g., "when I play squash"; Evans, Williams, O'Loughlin, & Howells, 1992).

Difficulties in retrieving specific personal memories may contribute to emotional disturbance in multiple ways (Williams, 1996). Problems in retrieving specific memories may make it difficult for patients to benefit from cognitive therapy; indeed, overgeneral memory strongly predicts failure to recover from depression (Brittlebank, Scott, Williams, & Ferrier, 1993). An inability to retrieve specific positive memories may attenuate positive affect and undermine problem solving.

Several studies suggest that overgeneral memory is associated with disorders other than depression (McNally, Litz, Prassas, Shin, & Weathers, 1994b; McNally, Lasko, Macklin, & Pitman, 1995). McNally et al. (1994b) reported that Vietnam combat veterans with PTSD exhibited difficulties retrieving specific personal memories in response to positive and neutral cue words, especially after having been exposed to reminders of traumatic events (i.e., a combat videotape). Intrusive memories of combat may deplete cognitive capacity, rendering it especially difficult for PTSD patients to use memory in effortful, specific ways. In a follow-up study, McNally et al. (1995) found that Vietnam combat veterans with PTSD exhibited difficulties retrieving personal memories exemplifying traits denoted by positive (e.g., *loyal*) and negative (e.g., *guilty*) cue words; in contrast, healthy combat veterans easily retrieved specific memories exemplifying positive traits. These deficits were markedly pronounced in PTSD subjects who wore Vietnam War regalia (e.g., medals, fatigues, loaded guns) to the laboratory. Wearing regalia in everyday life may be emblematic of psychological fixation to a war that ended more than two decades ago. Perhaps the overgeneral memory problems so evident in veterans who are "still in Vietnam" may partly underlie difficulties envisioning the future, as reflected in the PTSD symptom of "future foreshortening." Indeed, the inability to remember the past (specifically) may underlie the inability to envision the future.

Finally, Kuyken and Brewin (1995) found that depressed women with histories of childhood sexual abuse (but not depressed women without such histories) exhibited deficits in retrieving specific auto-biographical memories in response to cue words. Taken together, these findings suggest that overgeneral memory may arise when-ever individuals are preoccupied with distressing intrusive cogni-tion that consumes the cognitive capacity needed to use memory in effortful and specific ways. Moreover, autobiographical memory deficits in traumatized patients are consistent with data document-ing reduced hippocampal volume in Vietnam veterans with combat-related PTSD (Gurvits et al., 1995).

INTEROCEPTIVE ACUITY

Panic patients are markedly fearful of bodily sensations associated with anxiety and panic (Chambless, Caputo, Bright, & Gallagher, 1984; McNally & Lorenz, 1987). But are they also characterized by en-hanced interoceptive acuity? That is, are they especially adept at de-tecting subtle autonomic changes? Enhanced interoceptive acuity might increase the likelihood of patients noticing feared bodily sen-sations, thereby increasing the likelihood of panic attacks.

Tyrer, Lee, and Alexander (1980) reported that anxiety neurotics (panic patients?) and hypochondriacs were better at estimating their heart rate than were phobic patients. But Ehlers and her colleagues (Ehlers, Margraf, Roth, Taylor, & Birbaumer, 1988b) found no differ-ences in the ability to estimate heart rate between agoraphobics and normal control subjects. Unfortunately, in these studies subjects could have based their estimates on knowledge of their typical heart rate, hence the results do not clearly test for interoceptive acuity.

To avoid this methodological limitation, Asmundson and his as-sociates employed the Whitehead heartbeat discrimination para-digm to determine whether college student panickers were better than nonpanickers at discriminating signals that pulsed either syn-chronously or dysynchronously with their heart rate (Asmundson, Sandler, Wilson, & Norton, 1993). This task is exceptionally difficult; most people perform no better than chance at determining which signal corresponds to their heart rate. Perhaps because of task difficulty, Asmundson et al. found no differences between panickers and control subjects regardless of whether subjects were tested at rest or after a hyperventilation challenge. In any event, they concluded that self-reported perceptual sensitivity for cardiac sensations in panic disorder may merely reflect the importance these patients confer on bodily sensations rather than any enhanced acuity for detecting them.

Pauli et al. (1991) reached similar conclusions after conducting a 24-hour ambulatory EKG monitoring study. They had panic patients and healthy controls record their level of anxiety in response to cardiac events (e.g., acceleration in heart rate). Although patients detected no more cardiac events than did controls, they became more anxious in response to detected accelerations. Moreover, only patients regularly experienced further acceleration in response to these events; control subjects experienced decelerations. Pauli et al. concluded that panickers are afraid of cardiac perturbations but are no better than control subjects at detecting them.

In contrast to the aforementioned studies, Ehlers and Breuer (1992) obtained evidence of enhanced interoceptive acuity by employing a "mental tracking" paradigm. They recorded subjects' EKGs while having them count their heartbeats during intervals of 35, 25, and 45 seconds. The results showed that panic patients were more accurate than healthy control subjects but not more accurate than GAD patients. These data suggest that both panic and GAD patients are characterized by enhanced interoceptive acuity but that this ability increases the risk of panic attacks only in people who fear the cardiac sensations that are detected with such ease.

Rapee (1994b), however, has questioned whether interoceptive acuity may be confined to the paradigm used by Ehlers and Breuer (1992). Rapee exposed panic patients and normal control subjects to inhalations of 5, 10, and 20% carbon dioxide or room air. Carbon dioxide produces a broad range of dose-dependent, physiologic sensations. Inconsistent with the interoceptive acuity hypothesis, patients were no better than control subjects at detecting increasing concentrations of carbon dioxide.

In summary, there is some evidence that panic and GAD patients may be characterized by enhanced interoceptive acuity relative to healthy control subjects. But this acuity persists following recovery

(Antony, Meadows, Brown, & Barlow, 1994), thus suggesting that the meaning patients assign to physiological perturbations, rather than their ability to notice them, is what is most important.

Automatic versus Strategic Cognitive Processing Biases

In their efforts to characterize the nature of cognitive bias, psychopathologists have invoked the distinction between automatic and strategic (a.k.a. effortful, controlled) processing (McNally, 1995a). According to most experimental psychologists, an automatic process does not require cognitive capacity (i.e., effort, resources, energy), does not require awareness (i.e., can occur unconsciously), and does not involve volition (i.e., is obligatory or involuntary). Hence a modal instance of automaticity is capacity-free, unconscious, and involuntary (e.g., Shiffrin & Schneider, 1977). In contrast, most psychologists hold that a strategic process requires cognitive capacity, requires conscious attention, and is subject to voluntary control. Some theorists view purely automatic and purely strategic processes as end points on a continuum of automaticity (e.g., Hasher & Zacks, 1979), whereas others view them dichotomously but stress that most tasks involve both types of process in varying degrees (e.g., Jacoby, 1991).

The rationale for studying automaticity arises from the "ego-dystonic" phenomenology of pathological anxiety. Panic attacks, obsessions, intrusive traumatic recollections, and so forth seem involuntary, hence implying that the underlying mechanisms are automatic, not strategic. Automaticity, moreover, may have implications for clinical intervention. If certain biases are automatic, they may be difficult to eradicate through strategic means such as verbal psychotherapy.

Experimental psychologists who employ tasks devoid of emotional significance believe automatic processes are capacity-free, often unconscious, and involuntary and that the unitary nature of automaticity is what distinguishes it from each of its defining attributes. But these properties do not always covary, especially when individuals process emotionally relevant information, as in social cognition experiments (Bargh, 1989). Therefore, it is reasonable to ask in what sense of automaticity cognitive biases are "automatic." Are they capacity-free, unconscious, involuntary, or some combination thereof?

AUTOMATICITY AS CAPACITY-FREE PROCESSING

Standard conceptions of automaticity maintain that automatic processes do not require cognitive capacity (e.g., Shiffrin & Schneider, 1977). In contrast to strategic ones that consume resources, automatic processes proceed effortlessly and do not disrupt other concurrent processes. If this attribute of automaticity applies to the anxiety disorders, processing of threat cues ought not to interfere with other concurrent tasks.

But as is apparent from the foregoing review, this hallmark characteristic of automaticity does not apply to pathological anxiety. Indeed, emotional Stroop experiments demonstrate that processing of threat cues is anything but capacity-free. If processing of these stimuli were capacity-free, anxiety patients would be no slower in color-naming threat words than words devoid of emotional significance.

Acknowledging the automaticity of the standard Stroop task, Hasher and Zacks (1979) hypothesized that interference arises from response competition rather than from capacity consumption. Subsequent studies, however, have indicated that a response competition hypothesis is insufficient to explain interference (for a review, see C. M. MacLeod, 1991). Therefore, enhanced interference produced by threat cues may be automatic in one sense (i.e., involuntary) without being automatic in another sense (i.e., capacity-free).

Mathews and MacLeod (1986) further confirmed that processing threat cues in anxiety states is not capacity-free. Using a dual-task procedure, they found that threat words occurring on the unattended channel during dichotic listening disproportionately slowed response times to concurrently presented visual probes for GAD patients but not for healthy control subjects. A subsequent recognition test, moreover, revealed that subjects were incapable of identifying the words that had been presented on the unattended channel. Therefore, processing of threat words was automatic in one sense (i.e., unconscious) but was not automatic in another sense (i.e., capacity-free).

AUTOMATICITY AS UNCONSCIOUS PROCESSING

Most psychologists believe that automatic processes can operate outside of awareness, a characteristic potentially relevant to certain anxiety-related phenomena. Free-floating anxiety in GAD may result from automatic, unconscious processing of threat cues (Mathews & MacLeod, 1986), and "spontaneous" panic may be triggered by patients unconsciously processing certain bodily sensations as indicants of imminent catastrophe (e.g., heart attack; Clark, 1988). Although difficult to test empirically, unconscious catastrophic processing of bodily sensations might initiate sleep panics as well (Clark, 1988). Just as sleepers appear to monitor their external environment for significant stimuli, as evinced by how easily they awaken when someone speaks their name (Oswald, 1974, pp. 32–35), so might they monitor their bodies for significant stimuli (e.g., irregular heartbeats). "If this is the case, then an individual who is concerned about his or her heart might have a panic attack triggered by a palpitation which was detected and misinterpreted during sleep" (Clark, 1988, p. 75).

Despite a common emphasis on the unconscious determinants of emotion, cognitive and psychodynamic theorists hold very different views of the phenomenon. Cognitive psychologists view the unconscious as comprising structures and processes that operate outside of awareness which support relatively basic, unintelligent functions. Psychodynamic psychologists, in contrast, view the unconscious as possessing most of the attributes of the conscious mind (e.g., feelings, wishes, creative potential) except consciousness itself. Therefore, the cognitive and psychodynamic versions of the unconscious are far more different than alike.

Cognitive psychologists typically study the unconscious through their use of resource-limited and data-limited paradigms (Norman & Bobrow, 1975). Resource-limited paradigms stress cognitive capacity, typically by requiring concurrent processing of multiple inputs. Although the inputs could potentially be registered in consciousness, capacity overload forces some inputs beyond the perimeter of awareness. Data-limited paradigms, in contrast, require processing of physically impoverished inputs incapable of conscious registration. Psychopathologists have applied both types of paradigm in an effort to study unconscious automatic processing of threat cues in anxiety patients.

As noted above, Mathews and MacLeod (1986) employed a dual-task dichotic listening paradigm to study unconscious processing of threat in GAD. They found that GAD patients exhibited disproportionate slowing of manual reaction time responses to neutral probes when threat words simultaneously occurred outside awareness. Because patients were unable to identify what words had occurred on the unattended channel, these findings seem to qualify as instances of unconscious automaticity.

Dichotic listening procedures, however, have been criticized as inadequate for demonstrating unconscious semantic processing (Holender, 1986). According to Holender, dichotic listening, especially of prose, does not prevent brief attention shifts to the unattended channel that permit momentary word identification followed by immediate forgetting. Thus, GAD patients in the Mathews and MacLeod (1986) study might have been aware of threat words but forgot them by the time of the postexperimental recognition test. Holender's standards for unconscious processing in resource-limited paradigms are extremely strict and border on demanding researchers to prove the null hypothesis that no awareness could have possibly occurred. Nevertheless, Holender's critique has discouraged psychopathologists from pursuing dichotic listening as a means of testing hypotheses about unconscious processing.

As an alternative, researchers have adopted data-limited procedures, such as the subliminal emotional Stroop task, that involve physically impoverished stimuli (MacLeod & Hagan, 1992; MacLeod & Rutherford, 1992; Mogg, Bradley, Williams, & Mathews, 1993). In this paradigm, subjects are shown colored emotional words that occur too briefly to be consciously identified which are often followed by a mask of the same color. Their task is to name the color of the stimulus that flashes on the screen. Using this procedure, MacLeod and his associates found that subjects with elevated trait anxiety exposed to either a medical or an academic stressor exhibited Stroop interference for subliminal threat words even though they were unable to tell whether any words had been presented (MacLeod & Hagan, 1992; MacLeod & Rutherford, 1992). On the other hand, McNally, Amir, and Lipke (1996) did not obtain subliminal Stroop effects for trauma material in Vietnam combat veterans with PTSD, although they used procedures similar to those of MacLeod and Rutherford.

Using similar procedures, Mogg et al. (1993) found that GAD patients exhibited interference effects for subliminal negative words that were as large as those exhibited for supraliminal negative words. Therefore, in contrast to the supraliminal emotional Stroop (e.g., McNally et al., 1990a), the subliminal one does not appear specific to content, although it is specific to valence in general. Mathews and MacLeod (1994) interpreted this to suggest that the earliest stages of (automatic) stimulus analysis appear sensitive only to global valence (positive versus negative), whereas supraliminal presentations permit additional semantic analysis and therefore are sensitive to personally relevant concerns of the patient. This interpretation, however, is not wholly in accord with subliminal processing research in basic cognitive psychology. In a lexical decision paradigm involving nonemotional words, Marcel (1983) demonstrated that subliminal primes influenced responses to targets. Because these effects depend on the semantic relation between the prime and the target, subjects must have semantically processed the specific content of the prime rather than just a global feature such as valence.

The majority of cognitive bias studies have concerned the processing of visual and auditory verbal cues. Verbal threat stimuli, therefore, function as proxies for the genuine threat cues processed by anxious patients in everyday life. Thus, for example, investigators have assumed that biased attentional mechanisms implicated in panic patients' Stroop interference for the written word *heartbeat* are the same as those implicated in enhanced interoceptive acuity for genuine heartbeats. Needless to say, this assumption deserves further justification.

Working in the preparedness and phobias tradition, Öhman and Soares (1994) have provided data that suggest unconscious processing is not confined to verbal representations of threat. They found that snake and spider phobics exhibited unconscious, involuntary processing of pictorial cues depicting their feared animal, as indexed by physiologic and self-report measures of fear. Öhman and Soares presented subjects who were afraid of one animal but not the other with masked and unmasked brief slide presentations of spiders, snakes, mushrooms, and flowers. The results indicated that subjects exhibited fear only to slides of their phobic object, regardless of whether it was masked (subliminal) or unmasked (supraliminal). These data are generally consistent with subliminal Stroop findings except that Öhman and Soares found content-specificity effects, whereas Stroop researchers have not (Mathews & MacLeod, 1994).

AUTOMATICITY AS INVOLUNTARY PROCESSING

Anxiety disorders are syndromes of unwanted thought. Panic patients experience terrifying thoughts about imminent insanity, death, and loss of control in the midst of their attacks; OCD patients suffer from intrusive thoughts about violence, contamination, and other upsetting themes; and GAD patients ruminate about a variety of possible misfortunes. These phenomenologic observations strongly suggest that processing biases in pathological anxiety are most fundamentally automatic in the sense of being involuntary rather than being capacity-free or necessarily unconscious. Anxious patients experience considerable difficulty preventing the occurrence of emotionally disturbing thoughts, and they seemingly cannot help but process information in ways that exacerbate their emotional state. Processing of threat may occur outside of awareness and therefore qualify as automatic under this criterion. But initiation outside of awareness may be insufficient to produce pathologically prolonged emotional distress. Rather, the inability to terminate fear-generating processing that has begun without the patient's intent constitutes the hallmark of pathological anxiety. Indeed, it is the involuntary, obligatory quality of these processes that prompt the characterization of panic attacks, phobias, and so forth, as being "irrational."

Emotional Stroop experiments have provided the best examples of involuntary processing of threat. Despite instructions to attend to word color, patients cannot help but attend to word meaning, especially for material directly relevant to their current concerns. Although the Stroop task has traditionally been considered as the prototype of obligatory processing (e.g., Hasher & Zacks, 1979; Posner & Snyder, 1975), one might doubt its suitability for providing an index of automaticity because stimulus presentation times that permit conscious identification also permit strategic processing to occur (MacLeod & Rutherford, 1992). That is, subjects could conceivably disobey instructions and deliberately ruminate on the meanings of threat words, thereby exacerbating interference arising from automatic processes. This reasoning suggests that the subliminal Stroop may constitute a better index of automaticity than the supraliminal Stroop (MacLeod & Rutherford, 1992).

On the other hand, if being involuntary is an attribute of automaticity more central to pathological anxiety than is being unconscious, then interference effects in the supraliminal Stroop are more impressively automatic than those in the subliminal Stroop. Because subjects are unaware of word content in the subliminal version, they are helpless to counteract biased processing. But in the supraliminal version, subjects could, in principle, counteract these effects because they are aware of word content. Yet awareness notwithstanding, they are incapable of neutralizing cognitive bias. Accordingly, supraliminal interference provides a more impressive demonstration of involuntary automaticity than does subliminal interference.

Motivational Implications of Cognitive Bias

What is the motivational significance of cognitive biases for selectively processing threat? Certainly a capacity for rapidly allocating attention to threatening stimuli would increase the likelihood of appropriate defensive behavior and thus promote survival. Moreover, all else being equal, any tendency to interpret ambiguous cues as threatening would seem to do so as well. On the other hand, selective processing of minimally threatening cues would merely increase anxiety unnecessarily. Accordingly, attention to threat is adaptive in that it serves the motivationally significant goal of survival but is dysfunctional when the system shifts into defensive mode under circumstances when it is unwarranted.

The studies by Riemann and colleagues (Riemann et al., 1995; Riemann & McNally, 1995), however, suggest that people in general may exhibit attentional biases for cues having positive as well as negative personal significance. It is not entirely clear *why* people would be biased toward *rapidly* attending to positive cues. From the standpoint of evolution, rapid response to threat clearly makes sense. Why rapid attentional capture by cues for reward would be adaptive is less obvious. Further work is needed to determine how pervasive is the bias toward processing information of current positive concern.

Any adaptationist interpretations of memory and interoceptive biases would be unconvincing. Certainly the ability to monitor internal states (e.g., pain) clearly has motivational significance, as does the ability to learn from experience (e.g., memory). But exaggerated attention to internal states and enhanced retrieval of threatening information serve no obvious purpose. Accordingly, they constitute instances of dysfunction.

When considering the motivational significance of cognitive biases and other aspects of anxiety disorders, psychopathologists need to remember that merely because a psychobiological attribute has survived the vicissitudes of evolution does not mean that it has done so because it has enhanced survival (McNally, in 1995b; McNally, 1994b, pp. 202–205). Although adaptation through natural selection is, indeed, the chief mechanism of evolution, it is not the only one (Gould & Lewontin, 1984). Characteristics may evolve and persist through genetic drift, through being part of another structure that does confer a selection advantage, and through genetic linkage. Thus, for example, if genes predisposing to panic disorder, depression, phobias, and so forth reside on the same chromosome near genes controlling a vital adaptive function, selection pressures will favor the persistence of the psychopathological attribute even if it confers no adaptive advantage whatsoever. That is, because of genetic linkage, evolution can result in selection *of* a characteristic without selection *for* it.

Therapeutic Implications of Cognitive Bias Research

Research suggests that when cognitive biases are automatic in the anxiety disorders, they are automatic in the sense of being involuntary (and sometimes unconscious), but not in the sense of being capacity-free. Given that automaticity primarily denotes obligatory processing of threat, what implications can we draw for clinical intervention? If these biases are not under voluntary control, how can therapists help patients counteract them?

One approach might be to teach patients strategies for suppressing the conscious products of automatic biases, as in traditional "thought-stopping" techniques. But there are reasons to suspect that strategic thought-suppression attempts may backfire. Wegner (1994) has shown that attempts to suppress neutral thoughts (e.g., of a white bear) may succeed temporarily but often result in a subsequent increase in the frequency of the thought. Negative thoughts may be especially difficult to suppress. Becker, Roth, and Margraf (1993) found that GAD patients had no problems suppressing thoughts of white bears but experienced considerable difficulty suppressing thoughts related to their chief worries. Finally, Salkovskis and Westbrook (1989) have shown that efforts to suppress obsessions often result in an increase in their frequency. Taken together, these findings suggest that strategic attempts to suppress the conscious products of automatic cognitive biases may be counterproductive.

Öhman and Soares (1994) have suggested that systematic exposure in vivo that engenders habituation may correct involuntary, unconscious cognitive biases governing the expression of phobic fear. They argued that verbal attempts to disabuse patients of their automatic biases are unlikely to succeed.

In accord with Öhman and Soares's conjecture, studies have shown that cognitive biases are often responsive to treatment. Foa and McNally (1986) found that behavior therapy significantly reduced attentional and psychophysiologic responsivity to threat cues in OCD patients. Stroop studies have shown that recovery is associated with attenuation or elimination of attentional bias for threat in spider phobia (Lavy, van den Hout, & Arntz, 1993; Watts et al., 1986), GAD (Mathews et al., 1995), and PTSD (Foa, Feske, Murdock, Kozak, & McCarthy, 1991). Mattia, Heimberg, and Hope (1993) demonstrated that social phobics who had recovered following either cognitive-behavioral or phenelzine treatment no longer exhibited Stroop interference for social threat cues, whereas nonresponders continued to exhibit interference. Although Mattia et al. have shown that medication-induced recovery can abolish cognitive bias, a single dose of diazepam is insufficient to do so in GAD (Golombok et al., 1991). Other attentional paradigms also indicate that bias either diminishes (dot-probe; Mogg et al., 1992) or disappears (attentional search; Mathews et al., 1995) after successful behavioral treatment.

Data are mixed concerning the elimination of interpretive bias and nonexistent concerning the elimination of memory bias. Some studies indicate that reduction or elimination of interpretive bias accompanies recovery (Eysenck et al., 1991; Mathews et al., 1989b; McNally & Foa, 1987), but others do not (Stoler & McNally, 1991). No systematic change occurs in interoceptive acuity; some panic patients become less accurate after recovery, whereas others become more accurate (Antony et al., 1994).

In summary, cognitive biases are sensitive indicators of clinical state, and most diminish after successful treatment. Further research is needed to determine whether biases constitute cognitive risk factors for the development of anxiety disorders or whether they constitute, instead, the cognitive manifestations of the syndromes themselves.

Psychopathologists have traditionally assumed that mental health is characterized by a lack of cognitive bias and that the task of therapy is to eradicate those (negative) biases that characterize emotional disorders. But social psychologists have now convincingly demonstrated that well-adjusted people are hardly bias-free (Taylor & Brown, 1988). Instead, mental health is characterized by a skewed tendency to see the world, and oneself in particular, through rose-colored glasses.

Indeed, cognitive bias research indicates that healthy control subjects are often characterized by biases in the opposite direction to those exhibited by anxious patients. Thus MacLeod and Rutherford (1992) found that elevated state anxiety increased subliminal Stroop interference for threat cues relative to nonthreat cues in subjects with high trait anxiety but produced the opposite pattern in subjects with low trait anxiety. In their white noise study, Amir et al. (1996) found that healthy control subjects tended to exhibit greater priming effects for neutral relative to threat sentences, whereas panic patients exhibited the opposite effect. Studies on interpretive bias have often shown that GAD patients are best characterized by a lack of bias, whereas healthy control subjects are characterized by a bias for favoring nonthreatening interpretations.

Taken together, these results imply that mental health may be associated with (automatic?) cognitive biases opposite to those associated with pathological anxiety. Positivity biases may protect people against developing anxiety disorders. It remains to be seen whether clinicians can inculcate positive biases in their patients or whether their therapeutic achievements will be limited to the neutralization or elimination of negative biases.

REFERENCES

Amir, N., McNally, R. J., Riemann, B. C., & Clements, C. M. (1996). Implicit memory bias for threat in panic disorder: Application of the "white noise" paradigm. *Behaviour Research and Therapy*.

Amir, N., McNally, R. J., & Wiegartz, P. D. (in press). Implicit memory bias for threat in posttraumatic stress disorder. *Cognitive Therapy and Research*.

Antony, M. M., Meadows, E. A., Brown, T. A., & Barlow, D. H. (1994). Cardiac awareness before and after cognitive-behavioral treatment for panic disorder. *Journal of Anxiety Disorders, 8*, 341–350.

Asmundson, G. J. G., Sandler, L. S., Wilson, K. G., & Norton, G. R. (1993). Panic attacks and interoceptive acuity for cardiac sensations. *Behaviour Research and Therapy, 31*, 193–197.

Asmundson, G. J. G., Sandler, L. S., Wilson, K. G., & Walker, J. R. (1992). Selective attention toward physical threat in patients with panic disorder. *Journal of Anxiety Disorders, 6*, 295–303.

Asmundson, G. J. G., & Stein, M. B. (1994). Selective processing of social threat in patients with generalized social phobia: Evaluation using a dot-probe paradigm. *Journal of Anxiety Disorders, 8*, 107–117.

Asmundson, G. J. G., & Stein, M. B. (1994/1995). Dot-probe evaluation of cognitive processing biases in patients with panic disorder: A failure to replicate and extend. *Anxiety, 1*, 123–128.

Baptista, A., Figueira, M. L., Lima, M. L., & Matos, F. (1990). Bias in judgement in panic disorder patients. *Acta Psiquiátrica Portuguesa, 36*, 25–35.

Bargh, J. A. (1989). Conditional automaticity: Varieties of automatic influence in social perception and cognition. In J. S. Uleman & J. A. Bargh (Eds.), *Unintended thought* (pp. 3–51). New York: Guilford.

Beck, A. T., Emery, G., & Greenberg, R. L. (1985). *Anxiety disorders and phobias*. New York: Basic Books.

Beck, J. G., Stanley, M. A., Averill, P. M., Baldwin, L. E., & Deagle, E. A., III. (1992). Attention and memory for threat in panic disorder. *Behaviour Research and Therapy, 30*, 619–629.

Becker, E., Rinck, M., & Margraf, J. (1994). Memory bias in panic disorder. *Journal of Abnormal Psychology, 103*, 396–399.

Becker, E., Roth, W. T., & Margraf, J. (1993, September). *"Don't worry and beware of white bears": Thought suppression in anxiety patients*. Paper presented at the Congress of the European Association for Behavioural and Cognitive Therapies, London.

Bower, G. H. (1981). Mood and memory. *American Psychologist, 36*, 129–148.

Brittlebank, A. D., Scott, J., Williams, J. M. G., & Ferrier, I. N. (1993). Auto-biographical memory in depression: State or trait marker? *British Journal of Psychiatry, 162*, 118–121.

Burgess, I. S., Jones, L. M., Robertson, S. A., Radcliffe, W. N., & Emerson, E. (1981). The degree of control exerted by phobic and non-phobic verbal stimuli over the recognition behaviour of phobic and non-phobic subjects. *Behaviour Research and Therapy, 19*, 233–243.

Burke, M., & Mathews, A. (1992). Autobiographical memory and clinical anxiety. *Cognition and Emotion, 6*, 23–25.

Butler, G., & Mathews, A. (1983). Cognitive processes in anxiety. *Advances in Behaviour Research and Therapy, 5*, 51–62.

Cassiday, K. L., McNally, R. J., & Zeitlin, S. B. (1992). Cognitive processing of trauma cues in rape victims with post-traumatic stress disorder. *Cognitive Therapy and Research, 16*, 283–295.

Chambless, D. L., Caputo, G. C., Bright, P., & Gallagher, R. (1984). Assessment of fear of fear in agoraphobics: The Body Sensations Questionnaire and the Agoraphobic Cognitions Questionnaire. *Journal of Consulting and Clinical Psychology, 52*, 1090–1097.

Clark, D. M. (1988). A cognitive model of panic attacks. In S. Rachman & J. D. Maser (Eds.), *Panic: Psychological perspectives* (pp. 71–89). Hillsdale NJ: Erlbaum.

Cloitre, M., & Liebowitz, M. R. (1991). Memory bias in panic disorder: An investigation of the cognitive avoidance hypothesis. *Cognitive Therapy and Research, 15*, 371–386.

Cloitre, M., Shear, M. K., Cancienne, J., & Zeitlin, S. B. (1994). Implicit and explicit memory for catastrophic associations to bodily sensation words in panic disorder. *Cognitive Therapy and Research, 18*, 225–240.

Ehlers, A., & Breuer, P. (1992). Increased cardiac awareness in panic disorder. *Journal of Abnormal Psychology, 101*, 371–382.

Ehlers, A., Margraf, J., Davies, S. O., & Roth, W. T. (1988a). Selective processing of threat cues in subjects with panic attacks. *Cognition and Emotion, 2*, 201–219.

Ehlers, A., Margraf, J., Roth, W. T., Taylor, C. B., & Birbaumer, N. (1988b). Anxiety induced by false heart rate feedback in patients with panic disorder. *Behaviour Research and Therapy, 26*, 1–11.

Evans, J., Williams, J. M. G., O'Loughlin, S., & Howells, K. (1992). Auto-biographical memory and problem-solving strategies of parasuicide patients. *Psychological Medicine, 22*, 399–405.

Eysenck, M. W. (1992). *Anxiety: The cognitive perspective.* Hillsdale NJ: Erlbaum.

Eysenck, M. W., Mogg, K., May, J., Richards, A., & Mathews, A. (1991). Bias in interpretation of ambiguous sentences related to threat in anxiety. *Journal of Abnormal Psychology, 100*, 144–150.

Foa, E. B., Feske, U., Murdock, T. B., Kozak, M. J., & McCarthy, P. R. (1991). Processing of threat-related information in rape victims. *Journal of Abnormal Psychology, 100*, 156–162.

Foa, E. B., Ilai, D., McCarthy, P. R., Shoyer, B., & Murdock, T. B. (1993). Information processing in obsessive-compulsive disorder. *Cognitive Therapy and Research, 17,* 173–189.

Foa, E. B., & McNally, R. J. (1986). Sensitivity to feared stimuli in obsessive-compulsives: A dichotic listening analysis. *Cognitive Therapy and Research, 10,* 477–485.

Fox, E. (1993). Attentional bias in anxiety: Selective or not? *Behaviour Research and Therapy, 31,* 487–493.

Golombok, S., Stavrou, A., Bonn, J., Mogg, K., Critchlow, S., & Rust, J. (1991). The effects of diazepam on anxiety-related cognition. *Cognitive Therapy and Research, 15,* 459–467.

Gould, S. J., & Lewontin, R. C. (1984). The spandrels of San Marco and the Panglossian Paradigm: A critique of the adaptationist programme. In E. Sober (Ed.), *Conceptual issues in evolutionary biology* (pp. 252–270). Cambridge: MIT Press.

Gray, J. A. (1982). *The neuropsychology of anxiety.* Oxford: Oxford University Press.

Gurvits, T. V., Shenton, M. E., Hokama, H., Ohta, H., Lasko, N. B., Orr, S. P., Kilkinis, R., Jolesz, F. A., McCarley, R. W., & Pitman, R. K. (1995). *Reduced hippocampal volume on magnetic resonance imaging in chronic post-traumatic stress disorder.* Manuscript submitted for publication.

Harvey, J. M., Richards, J. C., Dziadosz, T., & Swindell, A. (1993). Misinterpretation of ambiguous stimuli in panic disorder. *Cognitive Therapy and Research, 17,* 235–248.

Hasher, L., & Zacks, R. T. (1979). Automatic and effortful processes in memory. *Journal of Experimental Psychology: General, 108,* 356–388.

Heiber, P. G., Chambless, D. L., & Peynircioglu, Z. (1995). *Cognitive processing of safety, threat and neutral cues by individuals with panic disorder and normals.* Manuscript in preparation.

Holender, D. (1986). Semantic activation without conscious identification in dichotic listening, parafoveal vision, and visual masking: A survey and appraisal. *Behavioral and Brain Sciences, 9,* 1–66.

Hope, D. A., Rapee, R. M., Heimberg, R. G., & Dombeck, M. J. (1990). Representations of the self in social phobia: Vulnerability to social threat. *Cognitive Therapy and Research, 14,* 177–189.

Jacoby, L. L. (1991). A process dissociation framework: Separating automatic from intentional uses of memory. *Journal of Memory and Language, 30,* 513–541.

Jacoby, L. L., Allan, L. G., Collins, J. C., & Larwill, L. K. (1988). Memory influences subjective experience: Noise judgments. *Journal of Experimental Psychology: Learning, Memory, and Cognition, 14,* 240–247.

Kaspi, S. P., McNally, R. J., & Amir, N. (1995). Cognitive processing of emotional information in post-traumatic stress disorder. *Cognitive Therapy and Research, 19,* 433–444.

Kuyken, W., & Brewin, C. R. (1995). Autobiographical memory functioning in depression and reports of early abuse. *Journal of Abnormal Psychology, 104,* 585–591.

Lavy, E., van den Hout, M. A., & Arntz, A. (1993). Attentional bias and spider phobia: Conceptual and clinical issues. *Behaviour Research and Therapy, 31,* 17–24.

Lavy, E., van Oppen, P., & van den Hout, M. A. (1994). Selective processing of emotional information in obsessive compulsive disorder. *Behaviour Research and Therapy, 32,* 243–246.

MacLeod, C. (1991). Clinical anxiety and the selective encoding of threatening information. *International Review of Psychiatry, 3,* 279–292.

MacLeod, C., & Cohen, I. L. (1993). Anxiety and the interpretation of ambiguity: A text comprehension study. *Journal of Abnormal Psychology, 102,* 238–247.

MacLeod, C., & Hagan, R. (1992). Individual differences in the selective processing of threatening information, and emotional responses to a stressful life event. *Behaviour Research and Therapy, 30,* 151–161.

MacLeod, C., Mathews, A., & Tata, P. (1986). Attentional bias in emotional disorders. *Journal of Abnormal Psychology, 95,* 15–20.

MacLeod, C., & McLaughlin, K. (1995). Implicit and explicit memory bias in anxiety: A conceptual replication. *Behaviour Research and Therapy, 33,* 1–14.

MacLeod, C., & Rutherford, E. M. (1992). Anxiety and the selective processing of emotional information: Mediating roles of awareness, trait and state variables, and personal relevance of stimulus materials. *Behaviour Research and Therapy, 30,* 479–491.

MacLeod, C. M. (1991). Half a century of research on the Stroop effect: An integrative review. *Psychological Bulletin, 109,* 163–203.

Mandler, G. (1980). Recognizing: The judgment of previous occurrence. *Psychological Review, 87,* 252–271.

Marcel, A. J. (1983). Conscious and unconscious perception: Experiments on visual masking and word recognition. *Cognitive Psychology, 15,* 197–237.

Martin, M., Williams, R. M., & Clark, D. M. (1991). Does anxiety lead to selective processing of threat-related information? *Behaviour Research and Therapy, 29,* 147–160.

Mathews, A. (1990). Why worry? The cognitive function of anxiety. *Behaviour Research and Therapy, 28,* 455–468.

Mathews, A., & Klug, F. (1993). Emotionality and interference with color-naming in anxiety. *Behaviour Research and Therapy, 31,* 57–62.

Mathews, A., & MacLeod, C. (1985). Selective processing of threat cues in anxiety states. *Behaviour Research and Therapy, 23,* 563–569.

Mathews, A., & MacLeod, C. (1986). Discrimination of threat cues without awareness in anxiety states. *Journal of Abnormal Psychology, 95,* 131–138.

Mathews, A., & MacLeod, C. (1994). Cognitive approaches to emotion and emotional disorders. *Annual Review of Psychology, 45,* 25–50.

Mathews, A., May, J., Mogg, K., & Eysenck, M. W. (1990). Attentional bias in anxiety: Selective search or defective filtering? *Journal of Abnormal Psychology, 99,* 166–173.

Mathews, A., Mogg, K., Kentish, J., & Eysenck, M. W. (1995). Effect of psychological treatment on cognitive bias in generalized anxiety disorder. *Behaviour Research and Therapy, 33*, 293–303.

Mathews, A., Mogg, K., May, J., & Eysenck, M. W. (1989a). Implicit and explicit memory bias in anxiety. *Journal of Abnormal Psychology, 98*, 236–240.

Mathews, A., Richards, A., & Eysenck, M. W. (1989b). Interpretation of homophones related to threat in anxiety states. *Journal of Abnormal Psychology, 98*, 31–34.

Mattia, J. I., Heimberg, R. G., & Hope, D. A. (1993). The revised Stroop color-naming task in social phobics. *Behaviour Research and Therapy, 31*, 305–313.

McNally, R. J. (1990). Psychological aspects of panic disorder: A review. *Psychological Bulletin, 108*, 403–419.

McNally, R. J. (1994a). Cognitive bias in panic disorder. *Current Directions in Psychological Science, 3*, 129–132.

McNally, R. J. (1994b). *Panic disorder: A critical analysis.* New York: Guilford.

McNally, R. J. (1995a). Automaticity and the anxiety disorders. *Behaviour Research and Therapy, 33*, 747–754.

McNally, R. J. (1995b). Preparedness, phobias, and the Panglossian paradigm. *Behavioral and Brain Sciences, 18*, 303–304.

McNally, R. J., & Amir, N. (in press). Perceptual implicit memory for trauma-related information in post-traumatic stress disorder. *Cognition and Emotion.*

McNally, R. J., Amir, N., & Lipke, H. J. (1996). Subliminal processing of threat cues in posttraumatic stress disorder? *Journal of Anxiety Disorders, 10*, 115–128.

McNally, R. J., Amir, N., Louro, C. E., Lukach, B. M., Riemann, B. C., & Calamari, J. E. (1994a). Cognitive processing of idiographic emotional information in panic disorder. *Behaviour Research and Therapy, 32*, 119–122.

McNally, R. J., & Foa, E. B. (1987). Cognition and agoraphobia: Bias in the interpretation of threat. *Cognitive Therapy and Research, 11*, 567–581.

McNally, R. J., Foa, E. B., & Donnell, C. D. (1989). Memory bias for anxiety information in patients with panic disorder. *Cognition and Emotion, 3*, 27–44.

McNally, R. J., Kaspi, S. P., Riemann, B. C., & Zeitlin, S. B. (1990a). Selective processing of threat cues in posttraumatic stress disorder. *Journal of Abnormal Psychology, 99*, 407–412.

McNally, R. J., Lasko, N. B., Macklin, M. L., & Pitman, R. K. (1995). Autobiographical memory disturbance in combat-related posttraumatic stress disorder. *Behaviour Research and Therapy, 33*, 619–630.

McNally, R. J., Litz, B. T., Prassas, A., Shin, L. M., & Weathers, F. W. (1994b). Emotional priming of autobiographical memory in post-traumatic stress disorder. *Cognition and Emotion, 8*, 351–367.

McNally, R. J., & Lorenz, M. (1987). Anxiety sensitivity in agoraphobics. *Journal of Behavior Therapy and Experimental Psychiatry, 18*, 3–11.

McNally, R. J., Luedke, D. L., Besyner, J. K., Peterson, R. A., Bohm, K., & Lips, O. J. (1987). Sensitivity to stress-relevant stimuli in posttraumatic stress disorder. *Journal of Anxiety Disorders, 1*, 105–116.

McNally, R. J., Riemann, B. C., & Kim, E. (1990b). Selective processing of threat cues in panic disorder. *Behaviour Research and Therapy, 28,* 407–412.

McNally, R. J., Riemann, B. C., Louro, C. E., Lukach, B. M., & Kim, E. (1992). Cognitive processing of emotional information in panic disorder. *Behaviour Research and Therapy, 30,* 143–149.

Mogg, K., Bradley, B. P., Williams, R., & Mathews, A. (1993). Subliminal processing of emotional information in anxiety and depression. *Journal of Abnormal Psychology, 102,* 304–311.

Mogg, K., & Mathews, A. (1990). Is there a self-referent mood-congruent recall bias in anxiety? *Behaviour Research and Therapy, 28,* 91–92.

Mogg, K., Mathews, A., & Eysenck, M. W. (1992). Attentional bias to threat in clinical anxiety states. *Cognition and Emotion, 6,* 149–159.

Mogg, K., Mathews, A., & Weinman, J. (1987). Memory bias in clinical anxiety. *Journal of Abnormal Psychology, 96,* 94–98.

Mogg, K., Mathews, A., & Weinman, J. (1989). Selective processing of threat cues in anxiety states: A replication. *Behaviour Research and Therapy, 27,* 317–323.

Norman, D. A., & Bobrow, D. G. (1975). On data-limited and resource-limited processes. *Cognitive Psychology, 7,* 44–64.

Norton, G. R., Schaefer, E., Cox, B. J., Dorward, J., & Wozney, K. (1988). Selective memory effects in nonclinical panickers. *Journal of Anxiety Disorders, 2,* 169–177.

Nunn, J. D., Stevenson, R. J., & Whalan, G. (1984). Selective memory effects in agoraphobic patients. *British Journal of Clinical Psychology, 23,* 195–201.

Öhman, A., & Soares, J. J. F. (1994). "Unconscious anxiety": Phobic responses to masked stimuli. *Journal of Abnormal Psychology, 103,* 231–240.

Oswald, I. (1974). *Sleep* (3rd ed.). Harmondsworth: Penguin.

Otto, M. W., McNally, R. J., Pollack, M. H., Chen, E., & Rosenbaum, J. F. (1994). Hemispheric laterality and memory bias for threat in anxiety disorders. *Journal of Abnormal Psychology, 103,* 828–831.

Pauli, P., Marquardt, C., Hartl, L., Nutzinger, D. O., Holzl, R., & Strian, F. (1991). Anxiety induced by cardiac perceptions in patients with panic attacks: A field study. *Behaviour Research and Therapy, 29,* 137–145.

Pickles, A. J., & van den Broek, M. D. (1988). Failure to replicate evidence for phobic schemata in agoraphobic patients. *British Journal of Clinical Psychology, 27,* 271–272.

Posner, M. I., & Snyder, C. R. R. (1975). Attention and cognitive control. In R. L. Solso (Ed.), *Information processing and cognition: The Loyola Symposium* (pp. 55–85). Hillsdale NJ: Erlbaum.

Rapee, R. M. (1994a). Failure to replicate a memory bias in panic disorder. *Journal of Anxiety Disorders, 8,* 291–300.

Rapee, R. M. (1994b). Detection of somatic sensations in panic disorder. *Behaviour Research and Therapy, 32,* 825–831.

Rapee, R. M., McCallum, S. L., Melville, L. F., Ravenscroft, H., & Rodney, J. M. (1994). Memory bias in social phobia. *Behaviour Research and Therapy, 32,* 89–99.

Reiss, S., Peterson, R. A., Gursky, D. M., & McNally, R. J. (1986). Anxiety sensitivity, anxiety frequency and the prediction of fearfulness. *Behaviour Research and Therapy, 14,* 1–8.

Riemann, B. C., Amir, N., & Louro, C. E. (1995). *Cognitive processing of personally relevant information in panic disorder.* Manuscript submitted for publication.

Riemann, B. C., & McNally, R. J. (1995). Cognitive processing of personally relevant information. *Cognition and Emotion, 9,* 325–340.

Salkovskis, P. M., & Westbrook, D. (1989). Behaviour therapy and obsessional ruminations: Can failure be turned into success? *Behaviour Research and Therapy, 27,* 149–160.

Schacter, D. L. (1987). Implicit memory: History and current status. *Journal of Experimental Psychology: Learning, Memory, and Cognition, 13,* 501–518.

Schacter, D. L. (1992). Understanding implicit memory: A cognitive neuroscience approach. *American Psychologist, 47,* 559–569.

Shiffrin, R. M., & Schneider, W. (1977). Controlled and automatic human information processing: II. Perceptual learning, automatic attending, and a general theory. *Psychological Review, 84,* 127–190.

Stoler, L. S., & McNally, R. J. (1991). Cognitive bias in symptomatic and recovered agoraphobics. *Behaviour Research and Therapy, 29,* 539–545.

Taylor, S. E., & Brown, J. D. (1988). Illusion and well-being: A social psychological perspective on mental health. *Psychological Bulletin, 103,* 193–210.

Tyrer, P. J., Lee, I., & Alexander, J. (1980). Awareness of cardiac function in anxious, phobic and hypochondriacal patients. *Psychological Medicine, 10,* 171–174.

Vrana, S. R., Roodman, A., & Beckham, J. C. (1995). Selective processing of trauma-relevant words in post-traumatic stress disorder. *Journal of Anxiety Disorders, 9,* 515–530.

Watts, F. N., & Coyle, K. (1993). Phobics show poor recall of anxiety words. *British Journal of Medical Psychology, 66,* 373–382.

Watts, F. N., McKenna, F. P., Sharrock, R., & Trezise, L. (1986). Colour naming of phobia-related words. *British Journal of Psychology, 77,* 97–108.

Wegner, D. M. (1994). Ironic processes of mental control. *Psychological Review, 101,* 34–52.

Williams, J. M. G. (1996). Depression and the specificity of autobiographical memory. In D. Rubin (Ed.), *Remembering: Studies in autobiographical memory* (pp. 271–296). Cambridge: Cambridge University Press.

Williams, J. M. G., & Dritschel, B. H. (1988). Emotional disturbance and the specificity of autobiographical memory. *Cognition and Emotion, 2,* 221–234.

Williams, J. M. G., Watts, F. N., MacLeod, C., & Mathews, A. (1988). *Cognitive psychology and the emotional disorders.* Chichester UK: Wiley.

Fear, Panic, Anxiety, and Disorders of Emotion

David H. Barlow, Bruce F. Chorpita, and Julia Turovsky

State University of New York at Albany

In previous reports we have sketched out, in general terms, a model of anxiety and mood disorders developed originally from clinical data that acknowledges that these disorders are fundamentally emotional disorders (Barlow, 1988; Barlow, 1991a, b). This model was based in part on the accumulated wisdom of emotion theory and included new and exciting developments in the area of cognitive science. During the past five to eight years our knowledge of emotional disorders from the points of view of psychopathology, pathophysiology, and treatment has increased. In this fast-moving area, these advances have superseded most models of emotional disorders constructed before 1990. The purpose of this chapter is to examine, selectively, some recent advances in our knowledge of panic, anxiety, depression, and related emotions and to integrate this knowledge, insofar as possible, into a more updated model of emotional disorders.

We begin with a discussion of the construct of anxiety followed by a discussion of the emotion of fear and the phenomenon of panic. After describing how these emotions may interact to produce various anxiety disorders, we turn to a discussion of emotional disorders encompassing the emotional reactions of depression, anger, and excitement (mania).

It is very difficult to discuss the construct of anxiety and related concepts such as fear because theorists use a variety of terms, often with different shades of meaning. As noted elsewhere in more detail (Barlow, 1988, 1991b), among the terms in common use in the English language today are *anxiety, fear, phobia, fright, panic,* and *apprehension*. Placing qualifiers in front of these words such as *acute, morbid, generalized, diffuse,* and so on provides very different shades of meaning. The German word *Angst* also enters into any discussion of psychopathology because this was the word used by both Kierkegaard and Freud, and it does not clearly map onto the English term *anxiety*. Even in the English language, the word *anxiety* is used imprecisely. For example, it has been used to refer to emotional states such as doubt, boredom, mental conflict, disappointment, bashfulness, and feelings of unreality. In addition, various cognitive deficits such as lack of concentration are also labeled "anxiety" from time to time. Descriptors specific to anxiety in the language of psychopathology include *unconscious, conscious, cognitive, somatic, free-floating, bound,* and *signal*. Authors of various chapters in this volume have noted before that we have often used different terms to describe the same process (e.g., Barlow, 1991b; Gray, 1991). Thus it is important to identify and define our terms carefully.

Our own thinking follows the traditions of Kierkegaard and Freud, as well as that of some modern psychopathologists who clearly differentiate the terms *fear* and *anxiety*. For Freud (1926/1959), *Angst* communicated a vague apprehension about the future (although he believed the theoretical significance of this anxiety was found in the past). When Freud described a specific reaction such as escape combined with a sense of terror in the presence of a specific object, he preferred the word *Furcht* (fear). Our conception of fear, as will be made clear below, emphasizes the response, rather than merely the stimulus characteristics of the emotion, although an object or cue is most often present to trigger the emotions. A fear response occurs when we are threatened with a dangerous, perhaps life-threatening event. In our view, these reactions represent Cannon's (1929) emergency reaction characterized by the compelling action tendencies of fight or flight. This conception of fear dates back to Darwin (1872), has been elaborated over the decades by theorists of emotion such as Izard (1977), and provides the basis for our own working definition.

Anxiety

Elsewhere (e.g., Barlow, 1988) we have developed evidence supporting a conceptualization of anxiety as a coherent cognitive-affective structure. This structure is composed primarily of high negative affect, of which the most prominent component is a sense of uncontrollability focused on possible future threat, danger, or other upcoming, potentially negative, events. Thus this negative affective state could be characterized roughly as a state of helplessness because of a perceived inability to predict, control, or obtain desired results in certain upcoming situations or contexts. This negative affective state is accompanied by a shift in attention to what would be primarily a self-focus or a state of self-preoccupation in which evaluation of one's (inadequate) capabilities to deal with the threat is prominent. Accompanying this negative affective state is a strong physiological or somatic component that seems to be characterized by chronic central nervous system (CNS) tension and arousal (e.g., Borkovec, Shadick, & Hopkins, 1991; Fridlund, Hatfield, Cottam, & Fowler, 1986; Hoehn-Saric & McLeod, 1988). This somatic state may be the physiological substrate of "readiness," which may underlie a state of preparation to counteract helplessness. Vigilance (hypervigilance) is another characteristic of anxiety that suggests readiness and preparation to deal with potentially negative events. If one were to put anxiety into words, one might say, "That terrible event could happen again and I might not be able to deal with it, but I've got to be ready to try." For these reasons we have suggested that a better and more precise term for anxiety might be *anxious apprehension*. This conveys the notion that anxiety is a *future-oriented* mood state in which one is ready or prepared to attempt to cope with upcoming negative events. The process of anxiety as described above is presented in Figure 1.

It is important to remember that we consider the construct shown in Figure 1 to be comprised of a number of coherent, closely related affective and cognitive components. In this model, a variety of cues or propositions, to use the terms of Peter Lang (1985; 1994a, b), would be sufficient to evoke anxious apprehension. Importantly, this process could occur without the necessity of a conscious, rational appraisal. For example, one might experience a fear response without realizing the specific trigger or cue, such as an object or situ-

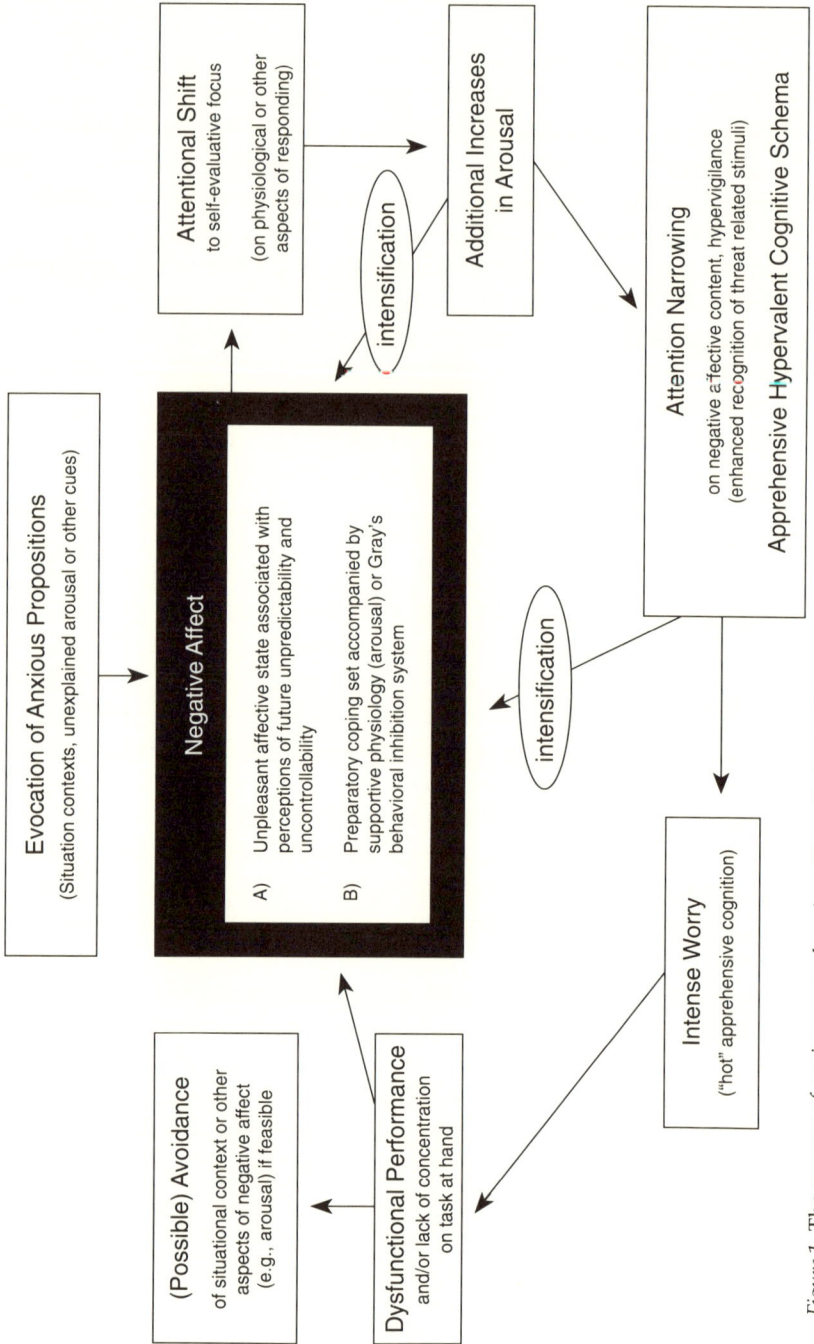

Figure 1. The process of anxious apprehension. (From Barlow 1988.)

ation that "represents" an earlier trauma, or an internal somatic sensation. These cues may be broad based or very narrow. An example of a narrow set of cues would be the case of test anxiety or sexual dysfunction which cues signaling the necessity of imminent performance would evoke a state of negative affect with its associated heightened tension and arousal and negative valence. This state, in turn, is associated with a shift in attention to a self-evaluative focus (or a rapidly shifting focus of attention from external sources to internal self-evaluative content). Evidence suggests that this shift to a self-focused attention further increases arousal and negative affect, thus forming its own small positive feedback loop. This subsystem is also represented in Figure 1.

Continuing on in the larger system or feedback loop, attention narrows to sources of threat or danger, setting the stage for additional distortions in the processing of information either through attentional or interpretive biases reflecting preexisting hypervalent cognitive schemata. In any case, one becomes hypervigilant for cues or stimuli associated with sources of anxious apprehension. This process in humans is analogous to, and may represent, Gray's (1987) "stop, look, and listen" state of behavioral inhibition, although the actual state of inhibition is not so readily apparent in clinical examples of human anxiety as it would be in animals. The next step in the system is arousal-driven worry that (at intense levels) is very difficult to control (Brown, Dowdall, Côté, & Barlow, 1994). In DSM-IV, lack of control over the worry process is a defining feature of generalized anxiety disorder (Brown, Barlow, & Liebowitz, 1994).

At sufficient intensity, this process results in disruption of concentration and performance and, ultimately, avoidance of sources of threat or apprehension if this method of coping is available. Arousal-driven anxious apprehension will, of course, only interfere with any performance that is required. In situations that do not require immediate performance, but in which perceptions of loss of control or other negative affective content have become associated with important life events, the process of worry will predominate. Once again, this process characterizes the severe clinical state of generalized anxiety disorder. In this condition, attempts are often made to avoid the worry process itself or cues that trigger worry (Borkovec et al., 1991; Brown, O'Leary, & Barlow, 1993). In any case, the intensity of the worry will increase or decrease depending on the situational context, the amount of underlying arousal that is available at the time for emotional transfer (Zillmann, 1983), and/or the presence of other "propositions" capable of calling forth this cognitive-affective structure. It is important to understand that this is an illustration of the process of anxious apprehension, not a description of the etiology of anxiety.

Whatever the etiology, philosophers and psychologists have speculated on the fundamental purpose of anxiety in the human condition. We have known for over 80 years that organisms become more vigilant, learn more quickly, and perform better both motorically and intellectually if they are "anxious" (Yerkes & Dodson, 1908). We also know that benzodiazepines and relaxation interfere with effective performance (Barlow, 1988). From this point of view, anxiety can be very adaptive to a point, and its adaptive purpose would seem to be planning and preparing to meet a challenge or threat. As Liddell (1949) noted,

> The planning function of the nervous system, in the course of evolution, has culminated in the appearance of ideas, values, and pleasures—the unique manifestations of man's social living. Man, alone, can plan for the distant future and can experience the retrospective pleasures of achievement. Man, alone, can be happy. But man, alone, can be worried and anxious. Sherrington once said that posture accompanies movement as a shadow. I have come to believe that anxiety accompanies intellectual activity as its shadow and that the more we know of the nature of anxiety, the more we will know of intellect. (p. 185)

It is also well-known that anxiety distributes as a trait (Eysenck, 1967, 1981) and is expressed more or less by most individuals in certain situations. Therefore, it is only very intense anxiety or, perhaps, anxiety with an inappropriate focus that comes to the attention of clinicians.

We will now consider, briefly, recent evidence bearing on some of the components of our model of anxiety or anxious apprehension. Specifically, we will examine recent developments in self-focused attention as it contributes to anxiety, the construct of controllability, and new evidence on neurobiological substrates of anxious apprehension.

Self-Focused Attention: Research on Sexual Dysfunction

Much of the empirical data underlying the development of our conceptions of anxiety or anxious apprehension come from research on sexuality and sexual dysfunction conducted over the years at our clinic (e.g., Barlow, 1986). Through years of programmatic research we have examined the early assumption that anxiety was a contributing cause of sexual dysfunction. We will review our work in this area briefly before presenting our most recent results on self-focused attention.

The assumption that anxiety causes sexual dysfunction is an example of a situation common to our clinical science in which facts that have been available for years simply did not support these assumptions (Barlow, 1988). For example, systematic observations of both humans (Ramsey, 1943; Sarrel & Masters, 1982) and animals (Barfield & Sachs, 1968) reported a facilitating effect of anxiety on simultaneous or subsequent sexual arousal. Social psychologists (e.g., Dutton & Aron, 1974; Riordan, 1979) also noted in a number of analogue situations that experimentally induced anxiety could increase interpersonal or sexual attraction. Following some preliminary experiments (Hoon, Wincze, & Hoon, 1977), this notion was tested more rigorously with sexual arousal in normal male volunteers in our laboratory (Barlow, Sakheim, & Beck, 1983). The purpose of this early experiment was to determine, under controlled laboratory conditions, the effects of inducing anxiety simultaneous with sexual arousal. Anxiety was manipulated by threat of shock during an explicit erotic film. Subjects were told they would see one of three lights while watching the film. The first light signaled that no shock would occur during the erotic film. A second light communicated that there was a 60% chance that they would receive a shock while they watched the film (noncontingent shock). The third light indicated that there was a 60% chance they would receive a shock if they did not achieve at least as large an erection as the average male in our laboratory (contingent shock). The results showed, somewhat surprisingly, that contingent shock produced the highest arousal in these normal males. This result was in line with previous experimental observations but seemingly contradictory to theorizing on the psychological basis of sexual dysfunction. The fact that substantial performance demand actually *increased* sexual arousal in normals made an investigation of the reaction of sexually dysfunctional men to the same paradigm all the more important. Indeed, results from other early reports suggested that dysfunctional males did more poorly under shock threat (e.g., Beck, Barlow, Sakheim, & Abrahamson, 1984; Beck, Barlow, Sakheim, & Abrahamson, 1987; Bruce & Barlow, 1990). In an important replication, Palace and Gorzalka (1990) demonstrated this differential responding in sexually functional and dysfunctional women using a paradigm similar to the Hoon et al. (1977) procedure.

Since emotion seemed to have "transferred" (Zillmann, 1983) between anxiety and sexual arousal in sexually functional subjects, the question remained, What was happening to our sexually dysfunctional patients? It did seem that something was interfering with the transfer of emotion, although the nature of this interference was not immediately obvious. This problem led to preliminary studies on cognitive processes in these two groups. In another early experiment we examined the effects of neutral distraction on sexual arousal in functional and dysfunctional groups (Abrahamson, Barlow, Sakheim, Beck, & Athanasiou, 1985). Both groups achieved adequate and equivalent levels of penile responding under a no distraction condition, and the normal volunteers, as expected, evidenced significant detumescence during distraction. But in a surprising development, the sexually dysfunctional patients were not affected by distraction and maintained tumescence.

Interestingly, other experiments from our laboratory indicated that alternative performance demand conditions produced additional differential response between functional and dysfunctional subjects (e.g., Beck, Barlow, & Sakheim, 1983). For example, Abrahamson, Barlow, Beck, Sakheim, and Kelley (1985) found that a film of a highly aroused woman produced *lowered* arousal in dysfunctional patients but *increased* arousal in normal volunteers compared with levels when viewing a woman who was minimally aroused. It appeared that these differences arose from performance-related concerns that distracted dysfunctionals viewing the highly aroused woman. Thus, while neutral distraction interfered with erectile responding of functionals, it did not affect dysfunctionals, presumably because they were already focusing attention on nonerotic, performance-related concerns.

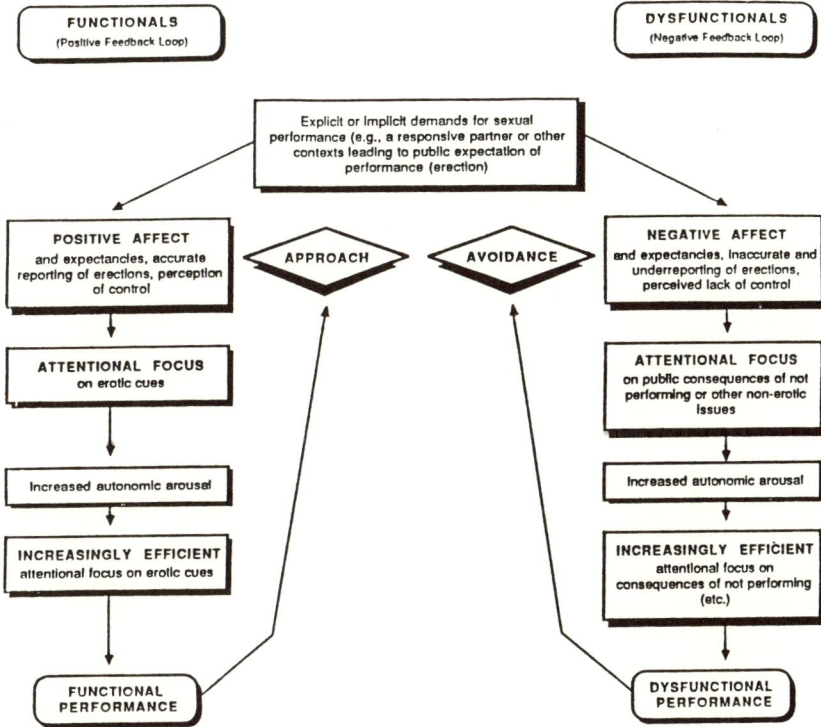

Figure 2. Model of inhibited sexual excitement. Copyright © 1986 by the American Psychological Association. Reprinted with permission.

An additional network of data (e.g., Beck et al., 1987) was integrated with the above findings to suggest a model of sexual dysfunction highlighting the roles of arousal and cognitive distraction. This model is presented in Figure 2 and follows closely our model of anxiety presented in Figure 1, for which it was the source. Basically, this model suggests that perception of a sexual context associated with the possibility of having to perform elicits negative affective responding including perceptions of a lack of control or inability to obtain desired results (in this case, potential inability to achieve or maintain an erection). At this point, a critical shift of attention occurs from an external focus (on erotic material in this instance) to a more internal self-evaluative focus on performance capabilities as well as the autonomic signs and symptoms of arousal itself. Since increasing arousal ensures an increasingly efficient focus or "narrowing" of attention, the negative affective content becomes even more salient or "hot." At this point, these patients may become distracted from what they are doing, which, at extremes, interferes with performance. Fuller descriptions of the data supporting these assertions can be found in Bruce and Barlow (1990) and Cranston-Cuebas and Barlow (1990).

An important component of this model relies on concepts of attentional capacity (Baddeley, 1986). Specifically, we theorized that increasing threat serves to narrow attention and increase concentration on a particular focus. We hypothesized that in the sexual context the focus for dysfunctionals was on performance concerns, such as "I'm not getting aroused." This internal focus of attention and the resulting increases in anxiety-related arousal lead to decreased tumescence (because erotic material is not processed). For functionals, in contrast, attention is more efficiently focused externally on the erotic material. Although this hypothesis regarding differential attentional allocation was originally only inferential (i.e., no measures of attention were taken), post hoc examination of thought content in a replication of Abrahamson et al. (1985) suggested that distraction *did* increase off-task thinking for functional subjects but *not* for dysfunctional subjects (Bruce & Barlow, 1990).

Thus, by inference, dysfunctional subjects maintain a pathological attentional process that is focused internally on concern about performance-related failure. Neutral distraction somehow redirects attention *away* from this self-focus and thereby allows a somewhat greater processing of on-task stimuli (in this case, erotic material). On the other hand, negative affect in this model, as induced by the shock threat experiments, serves to increase arousal and thus to narrow the focus of attention either internally or externally, ultimately interfering with information-processing resources.

These findings have parallels in the literature on anxiety and depression (Ingram, 1990), which emanated originally from the laboratories of social psychology (Barlow, 1988; Duval & Wicklund, 1972; Scheier, Carver, & Matthews, 1983; Schwarzer & Wicklund, 1991). Musson and Alloy (1988) suggested, after reviewing a large body of literature, that there is a strong relationship between self-directed attention and the affective, behavioral, and cognitive characteristics of depression and that distraction *reduces the negative consequences of both depression and self-focus.* For example, Miller (1975) reviewed a variety of evidence demonstrating that external distraction leads to improvement in the performance of depressed individuals on motor and speed tests. This finding seemed to parallel the effects of distraction on arousal in our sexually dysfunctional patients. More recently, Ingram (1990), after reviewing the literature on self-focused attention, extended the conceptualization of self-focused attention as a vulnerability to increased anxiety and depression.

One subsequent study, however, seemed to contradict attentional allocation hypotheses concerning the deleterious effects of self-focused attention. Abrahamson, Barlow, and Abrahamson (1989) used a genital feedback paradigm developed in our laboratory to examine self-focused attention. Sexually dysfunctional and sexually functional subjects each viewed erotic film segments during three conditions that differed in that an adjacent video monitor showed either live genital feedback (obtained from a video camera focused on the subjects' genitals), a variable length straight line, or no stimulus. The feedback condition required each subject to give a rating of the percent of full erection he had at the moment based on the feedback and to indicate whether the erection was sufficient for sexual intercourse and was, in a sense, the ultimate extension of the prototypical "mirror" manipulation used in self-focused attention paradigms in which viewing oneself increases self-focus (e.g., Ingram, 1990; Scheier et al., 1983). During the neutral distracting condition, the subject was instructed to give a rating of the length of the line as a percent of a standard line and whether the presented line was the same width or narrower than a standard line shown previously. This task was intended to control for the amount of "cognitive work" performed in the feedback condition.

The data, which are shown in Figure 3, demonstrated that the distracting condition involving self-focused attention (focusing on one's genitals) had a markedly different effect on the two groups, in contrast to a neutral distracting condition requiring about the same amount of cognitive effort. That is, self-focused attention produced the highest overall penile circumference levels for functional subjects. Dysfunctionals, on the other hand, demonstrated their lowest level of arousal during the self-focused attention condition. Neutral distraction had very little effect in either group, unlike the results from the distraction paradigm discussed above, probably because the distraction stimulus was insufficiently demanding. Thus the inference from these results was that the process of self-focused atten-

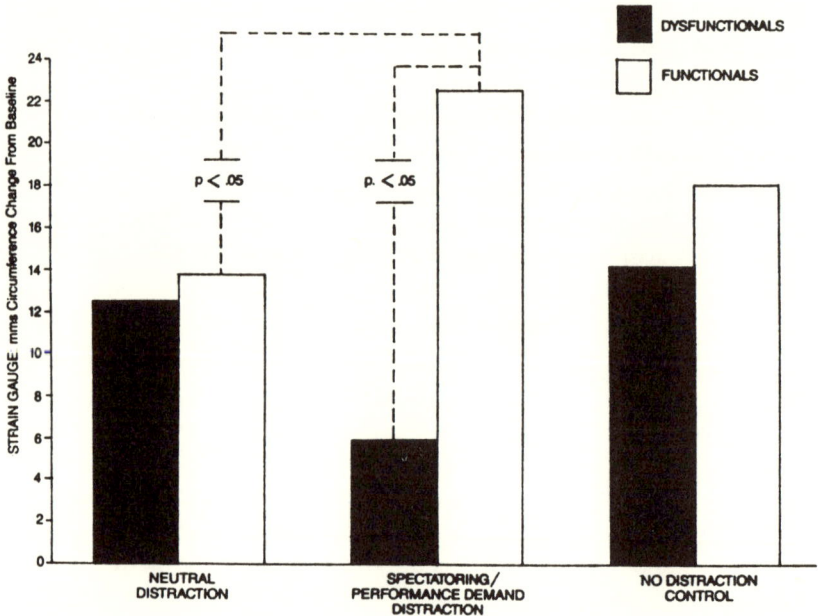

Figure 3. Average maximum penile circumference change from baseline: Group x Condition. Copyright © 1989 by the American Psychological Association. Reprinted with permission.

tion seems specifically associated with erectile dysfunction, but the effects may not be owing to a fully occupied attentional capacity associated with self-focused attention. We suggest some other possibilities below.

These results on self-focused attention also contradict another set of data suggesting that sexually dysfunctional subjects are *not* focusing attention inward or internally. For example, in one paradigm used in years past in our laboratory, subjects were required to monitor continuously their erectile response using a "cognitive lever" (e.g., Wincze, Venditti, Barlow, & Mavissakalian, 1980). Subjects were trained to move this cognitive lever at points between 0 and 100 based on their own estimates of their percentage of full erection. Rather than focus closely on their genital (non) response at the expense of attending to external erotic cues, a consistent and strong set of results from our laboratory (e.g., Sakheim, Barlow, Abrahamson, & Beck, 1987) demonstrated that at the same levels of erectile responding, sexually dysfunctional subjects underestimated their erections, while functional subjects were more accurate. Other studies also evidence this effect very clearly (Abrahamson et al., 1985, 1989). Interestingly, in the latter study, dysfunctionals characteristically reported lower arousal when their erection levels were more substantial; when erection levels were near 0, functionals reported adequately, but dysfunctionals inaccurately reported the presence of some erectile response. In fact, the correlation between our continuous subjective measure and genital responding for functionals was .61 compared with only .32 for dysfunctional subjects (Abrahamson et al., 1989). The fact that dysfunctionals are inaccurate in judging their erectile response suggests that, although preoccupied with their performance, dysfunctionals are either not allocating attention to their genital functioning or possibly are somehow distorting information from an attentional focus on genital functioning. Thus we are faced with seemingly conflicting data sets suggesting that self-focused attention on erectile performance is associated specifically with dysfunctional sexuality but that dysfunctionals are less accurate in monitoring their performance. This quandary suggests that self-focused attention and interoceptive awareness, though frequently conflated, may actually represent different constructs. It is this notion that our most recent research is addressing.

MISATTRIBUTION

We have recently produced and replicated one of the more remarkable findings in the history of our sexuality research program (Cranston-Cuebas & Barlow, 1994; Cranston-Cuebas, Barlow, Mitchell, & Athanasiou, 1993). To provide some background, in a classic experiment, Storms and Nisbett (1970) produced a reverse placebo effect in insomniacs by providing them with placebo pills at bedtime, describing the pills as either increasing or decreasing arousal. Subjects fell asleep faster after receiving the placebo pill with instructions that it would increase arousal. Conversely, subjects fell asleep more slowly after receiving a pill they thought would decrease their arousal. Brockner and Swap (1983) suggested that this reverse placebo effect was most likely to occur in subjects who were more interoceptively aware, through their comparison of sensations with the externally provided information about the pill's effects.

That is, subjects finding themselves less aroused than they expected fell asleep more quickly, and vice versa. A replication of Storms and Nisbett's (1970) original investigation, using additional measures of private body consciousness (Miller, Murphy, & Buss, 1981) and private self-consciousness (Fenigstein, Scheier, & Buss, 1975), confirmed this relationship between high private body consciousness and a reverse placebo (Brockner & Swap, 1983).

We have used this paradigm with our sexually functional and dysfunctional subjects (Cranston-Cuebas et al., 1993). In this paradigm, functional and dysfunctional males viewed sexually explicit films following ingestion of three placebo pills in a repeated measures design. The pills were described to subjects as an erection "enhancement" pill, erection "detraction" pill, and "placebo" pill. Consistent with predictions made by a misattribution hypothesis, functional subjects' erectile responding evidenced a clear reverse placebo effect. That is, erectile responding in the detraction condition was significantly greater than responding in either the enhancement or placebo conditions. The latter conditions did not differ significantly from each other. Interestingly, analysis of subjective ratings of arousal indicated no significant differences among conditions. Therefore, these data do not represent the classic misattribution effect for functionals since previous reports in the social psychology literature illustrated changes in reports of emotional state through provision of alternative labels for physiological arousal. In our experiment, changes were effected in actual physiological responding through a similar manipulation. Sexually dysfunctional subjects, however, rather than demonstrating a reverse placebo effect, evidenced a clear direct placebo effect. That is, dysfunctional subjects evidenced significantly lower erectile responding under the detraction condition although there were no significant differences under enhancement and placebo conditions. Once again, dysfunctionals evidenced no effects on self-reports of arousal as a result of pill manipulation.

Thus, according to Brockner and Swap's interpretation, our dysfunctional subjects may have evidenced a direct placebo effect as a result of their being relatively unaware of their internal bodily sensations. This lack of internal awareness would have precluded a discovery of the discrepancy between internally and externally provided information upon which the reverse placebo effect is presumably predicated. This, of course, is in agreement with data from our lab indicating that dysfunctional males are relatively unaware of their erectile response and provide low or inaccurate estimates of their erectile response on the cognitive lever. But it seems, on the face of it, contradictory to the literature on self-focused attention mentioned above.

We have recently completed an important replication of these findings with functional males (Cranston-Cuebas & Barlow, 1994; see Figure 3). Fifty sexually functional men viewed three sexually explicit films following ingestion of a placebo pill described as either an erection enhancement pill or an erection detraction pill. The first was a control condition that replicated Cranston-Cuebas et al.'s (1993) investigation but used a between-subjects design. The second and third conditions (presented in counterbalanced order) were attentional focus task conditions: erotic focus required that subjects tally (by pushing a button) specified erotic elements appearing in the film; nonerotic focus required that subjects tally specified nonerotic elements. Results from the first (control) condition replicated the reverse placebo effect observed by Cranston-Cuebas et al. (1993), with significantly greater erectile responding for subjects in the detraction relative to the enhancement pill group. More important, the current study added prestimulus reports concerning subjects' expectations for how they would be affected by the pills, thus allowing a causal relationship to be drawn between subjects' misattribution to the pills and their patterns of erectile response. Subjects' expectations were in line with the experimental manipulation and could not account for the results. These manipulations were aided by elaborate pretrial procedures, including "instant" urinalysis. As in the previous investigation, there were no effects of groups or conditions on either subjects' feelings of sexual arousal (as measured by the cognitive lever) or their reported levels of erection. Thus our manipulation directly affected erectile response while bypassing perception of arousal.

Contrary to expectation, the attentional focus tasks employed did not sufficiently redirect subjects' attentional focus so as to reverse patterns of erectile response. Questionnaire analyses revealed that while subjects scoring high on the Private Body Consciousness Scale and those having high strain gauge/cognitive lever correlations (reflecting accurate estimates of erectile response) followed the group pattern (i.e., reverse placebo effect), those subjects scoring higher on a small group of items reflecting a more general state of negative affect regarding bodily concerns that we have labeled "hypochondriasis" evidenced a direct placebo effect. These subjects' erectile response patterns were more similar to those of dysfunctional men than they were to functionals. This finding may shed some light on the discrepancy between the seeming lack of self-focused attention in our dysfunctional groups (as reflected in the lack of a reverse placebo effect and inaccurate estimates of erectile response) and the hypothesized increase in self-focused attention among other groups with high negative affect (Ingram, 1990). To summarize, it may be that a negatively affective worry process focusing on self-evaluative concerns, combined with a tendency to avoid direct observation of one's functioning (lack of interoceptive awareness or interoceptive focus), may characterize psychopathology associated with negative affect. In other words, self-focused attention as reflected in a pathological and affectively laden worry process may be fundamentally an avoidant technique (Borkovec, 1994; Brown et al., 1994; Roemer & Borkovec, 1993) that is orthogonal to interoceptive awareness or focus. In any case, these results are consistent with recent data from our laboratory indicating that our sexually dysfunctional patients score significantly lower in private body self-consciousness than do functional patients.

INTEROCEPTIVE AWARENESS IN ANXIOUS PATIENTS

We are just beginning to examine these constructs more directly in anxious patients. Clinical observations over the years have indicated that patients with anxiety disorders, particularly panic disorder, seem to evidence greater awareness of internal bodily states and are constantly vigilant for any somatic changes that might signal the beginning of the next panic attack. Thus it has been assumed that patients with anxiety can more accurately perceive their bodily state than other subjects (e.g., Tyrer, 1973; 1976). Ehlers and Breuer (1992) tested this assumption by having patients with anxiety disorders as well as normal control subjects estimate their heart rate. Ehlers and Breuer (1992) compared 65 patients with panic disorder,

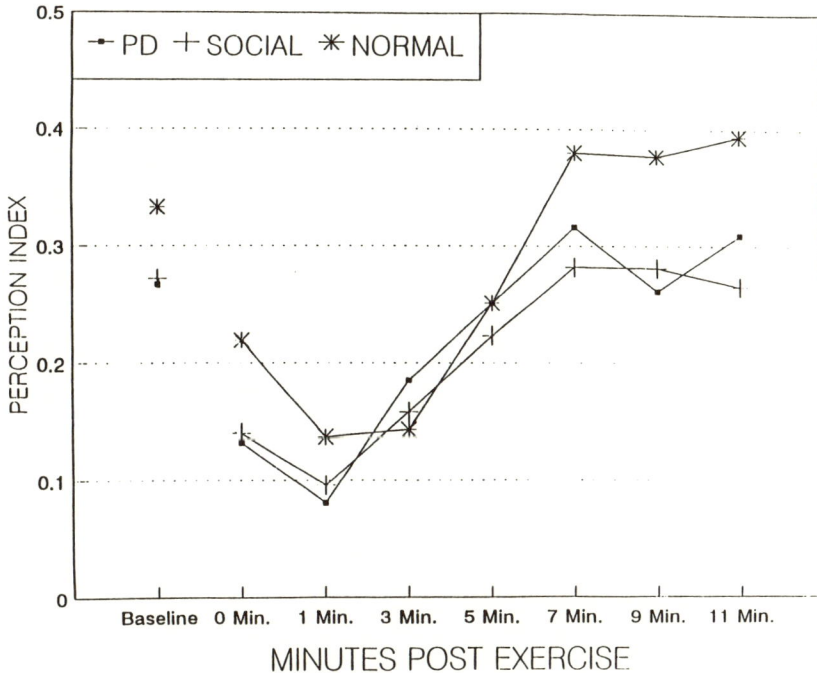

Figure 4. Accuracy of heartbeat estimations: baseline (average across trials) and post-exercise phase 1 (lower values indicate greater accuracy). Reprinted from *Journal of Anxiety Disorders* (1995), Antony, Brown, Craske, Barlow, Mitchell, & Meadows, "Accuracy of heart beat perception in panic disorder, social phobia, and non-anxious subjects," with kind permission from Elsevier Science Ltd., The Boulevard, Langford Lane, Kidlington ox5 1GB, UK.

50 patients with infrequent panic who did not meet criteria for panic disorder, and 27 patients with a simple phobia to 46 normal control subjects. Generally, the results indicated that patients with panic disorder were more accurate in perceiving their heartbeats than were patients with simple phobias, infrequent panickers, or control subjects. In a related replication that included groups of patients with generalized anxiety disorder and depression, patients with panic disorder were once again better at perceiving their heartbeats than were patients with depression. But patients with generalized anxiety disorder were also more accurate and did not differ from patients with panic disorder. This result would seem to suggest that increased interoceptive awareness to the extent that it exists is a component of more generalized anxiety, as reflected in Figure 1.

These results have been difficult to replicate. Antony et al. (1995)

PERSPECTIVES ON ANXIETY, PANIC, AND FEAR

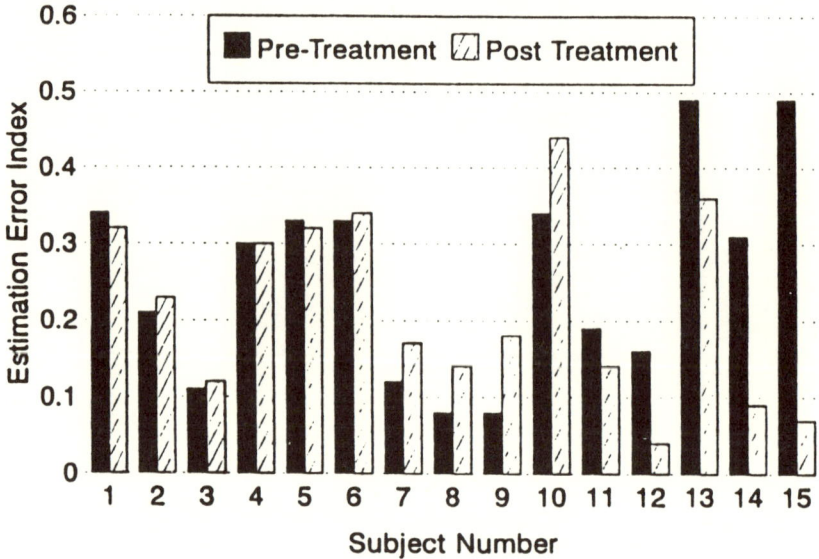

Figure 5. Changes in heartbeat estimation error following treatment (lower values indicate greater accuracy). Reprinted from *Journal of Anxiety Disorders, 8,* Antony, Meadows, Brown, & Barlow, "Cardiac awareness before and after cognitive-behavioral treatment for panic disorder," pp. 341–250. Copyright 1994, with kind permission from Elsevier Science Ltd., The Boulevard, Langford Lane, Kidlington ox5 1GB, UK.

tested groups of patients with either panic disorder or social phobia, as well as normal controls, using the same paradigm in which subjects were asked to count heartbeats. In this experiment, however, the perceptual accuracy of the groups was tested not only at rest but also following a period of strenuous exercise consisting of repeated step-ups. The results are presented in Figure 4. Contrary to the results in Ehlers and Breuer (1992), the results from this experiment suggest that patients with panic disorder were no more accurate in counting their heartbeats than patients with social phobia or non-anxious subjects, although the means were in the expected direction. Nevertheless, subsequent analyses suggested that these mean effects were illusory because differences accounted for only 3% of the variance. All subjects, however, became more accurate as heart rate increased because of exercise. Furthermore, we have recently examined possible changes in cardiac awareness in panic disorder patients following successful cognitive-behavioral treatment (Antony, Meadows, Brown, & Barlow, 1994). Despite significant reduc-

tions in panic attacks and related symptomatology, cardiac awareness did not change on average, although some individual subjects
showed dramatic changes in both directions, reflecting either
greatly increased awareness or greatly decreased awareness (see
Figure 5). In a somewhat related study, Butler and Rapee (1991)
found no relation between perception of heartbeat and total scores
on the Anxiety Sensitivity Index (Reiss, Peterson, Gursky, &
McNally, 1986), which is widely considered to be a measure of anxiety focused on somatic sensations.

The reasons for these discrepant results are not clear, but this
paradigm does not necessarily reflect the self-focused attention and
hypervigilance that may characterize patients with anxiety disorders. It may well be that during the course of the typical day patients
with anxiety disorders *are* more aware of, and hypervigilant for, internal sensations than are people without anxiety disorders. In contrast, the paradigm employed in this study instructs all subjects to
focus on cardiac cues for a limited period of time. Thus these heartbeat estimation studies assess ability to perceive heartbeats when instructed to do so rather than the tendency to focus continually on
cardiac sensations in the natural environment. In any case, this area
needs considerably more work.

RESISTANCE TO DYSFUNCTIONAL MENTALITY

Results from the misattribution studies of sexual arousal (Cranston-
Cuebas et al., 1993; Cranston-Cuebas & Barlow, 1994) may also be interpreted as reflecting a differential vulnerability to the formation of
negative expectancies in a sexual situation. These findings, to be reviewed next, provide a transition to the next major topic to be considered, the role of a sense of controllability in the etiology and process of anxiety. The detraction manipulation may be viewed as
creating a situation in which one might expect subjects to form negative expectancies regarding their sexual performance. Under this
condition, however, functional subjects experienced their greatest
arousal. In contrast, dysfunctional subjects were most aroused under the enhancement condition. Thus, providing them with positive
expectancies from an external source seemed to aid in their arousal.

Our model of sexual functioning (Barlow, 1986) proposes that functional and dysfunctional men enter a sexual situation with different expectancies for their performance. Results from the misattribution experiments and other studies from our laboratory may indicate that sexually functional subjects are resistant to the formation of these negative expectancies. One of the initial studies in our laboratory found that sexually functional subjects overlooked small decrements in their performance and failed to report decreases in their physiological arousal (Abrahamson et al., 1985). This finding, recently replicated (Mitchell, Brown, Barlow, & Marten, 1990), has also been interpreted to suggest that sexually functional men may demonstrate a resistance to "dysfunctional mentality" (Abrahamson et al., 1985) by ignoring evidence that might support negative expectancies of performance. In contrast, because sexually dysfunctional men tend to underreport their physiological arousal (Sakheim et al., 1987), we might conclude that these patients ignore evidence that could support positive performance expectancies.

Findings from another study (Weisberg, Sbrocco, & Barlow, 1994a) also support the possibility that functionals maintain a resistance to the formation of negative expectancies of sexual performance. Fantasy use, or the ability to form vivid, mental representations, has repeatedly been found to be important for the voluntary control of sexual arousal (e.g., Smith & Over, 1987; Stock & Geer, 1982). Because dysfunctionals in our lab report feeling they have less control over their arousal (Mitchell, Marten, Williams, & Barlow, 1990) and also report less use of fantasy in sexual situations (Marten & Barlow, 1991; Weisberg, Sbrocco, & Barlow, 1994b), the relationship between imagery ability, fantasy content, and voluntary arousal was explored (Weisberg et al., 1994a). Sexually functional subjects were asked to engage in either a fantasy in which they would not be able to attain and maintain an erection or a fantasy in which they would not experience any sexual problems. Surprisingly, there were no differences in arousal between fantasy groups. Sexually functional men asked to create a fantasy in which they experienced sexual difficulties evidenced equal penile tumescence and subjective arousal to those asked to engage in a fantasy in which no problems occurred. Examination of the written fantasies of subjects in the "negative" fantasy condition revealed that their fantasies included accounts of sexual problems, as per the instructions, but that these problems were not the focus of the fantasies. In other words, these subjects created arousing fantasies in which problems occurred (such as detumescence), but were not dwelled upon, or they were fantasized as being only temporary.

Overall, it appears that sexually functional men maintain positive expectancies for their performance despite experimental attempts to manipulate this (Cranston-Cuebas et al., 1993; Cranston-Cuebas & Barlow, 1994; Weisberg et al., 1994a) and despite physiological evidence that their performance has decreased (Abrahamson et al., 1985; Mitchell et al., 1990). In contrast, sexually dysfunctional men underreport their erections (Sakheim et al., 1987), maintaining negative expectancies of their performance except when provided with external sources of confidence (Cranston-Cuebas et al., 1993).

Thus these findings from our sexuality research program have altered and extended some of our thinking contributing to the model of anxiety presented in Figure 1. Our focus is now less on attentional allocation within an overall model of attentional capacity and more on the antecedents, components, and consequences and of negative affect itself. As is evident in Figure 1, we suggest that one of the central components of negative affect is the sense of uncontrollability with which one anticipates future events. It is to this topic that we now turn.

A Sense of Control

Preliminary findings regarding a resistance to dysfunctional mentality in normal subjects, as well as the seeming experimental dissection of interoceptive awareness from self-focused attention, reflect back on one of the more fundamental components of anxiety in our model, a sense of lack of control over upcoming events. That is, one could easily interpret the dysfunctional mentality seemingly present in our patient populations as reflecting this profound sense of a lack of control over upcoming situations and responses. In the case of our sexually dysfunctional patients, this sense of uncontrollability and unpredictability is focused on erectile responding. In the case of patients with panic disorder, it is focused on the next unpredictable panic attack and so on. Furthermore, as noted previously, (e.g., Barlow, 1988), it may not be conceptually correct to separate evaluative self-focus or self-preoccupation from the cognitive representations of negative affect (as depicted in Figure 1). It does seem clear, however, that an affectively laden self-preoccupation serves to increase further the intensity of negative affect and the arousal associated with it. Of course, this self-focused attention more likely becomes very much integrated with negative affect over time. That is, unexplained arousal and negative affect may initially trigger a shift to self-focused attention in vulnerable individuals, but eventually self-focused attention becomes an integral part of the core negative affect of anxiety. Thus individuals, caught up with the uncontrollability of upcoming negative events, are trapped in a never-ending cycle of self-evaluative focus or neurotic self-preoccupation. Despite the seeming interrelatedness of the cognitive representations of negative affect, as represented by a sense of uncontrollability and a negative self-evaluative focus, it is still useful to separate self-focused attention in any model of anxiety because this particular component has implications for therapy (Barlow, 1988; Barlow, 1991a).

Returning to the centrality of a sense of control to our model of anxiety, experiments on the construct in the context of producing anxiety in animal laboratories have a long history. Can we produce anxious apprehension in the laboratory? As suggested by Barlow (1988), it appears that we can produce severe anxious apprehension in the laboratory and that we have been doing so for over 50 years. In experiment after experiment, most of them now classic, investigators have produced behavior characterized by extreme agitation, restlessness, distractibility, hypersensitivity, increased autonomic responding, muscle tension, and interference with ongoing performance. The names of the investigators associated with these experiments occupy a prominent place in every textbook of introductory psychology: Pavlov, Masserman, Liddell, and Gantt. The phenomenon they produced was commonly termed experimental neurosis, but it was largely ignored until recently, probably because the subjects were animals rather than people. It took the pioneering and creative efforts of Sue Mineka and her colleagues (e.g., Mineka & Kihlstrom, 1978) to abstract the common themes from the variety of paradigms used to produce experimental neurosis and make a compelling case for the specification of one causal factor running through all of the causal paradigms. They suggested that the cause of anxiety in these animals is that "environmental events of vital importance to the organism become unpredictable, uncontrollable, or both" (p. 257). Since then, a large body of work from Mineka (e.g., 1985a; Barlow, 1988) has underscored the importance of a sense of uncontrollability in the genesis and maintenance of the process of anxiety. In our view, and based largely on the work of Mineka, Gunnar, and Champoux (1986) and others, the sense of uncontrollability that seems to lie at the heart of anxiety may well be a preexisting psychological vulnerability acquired early in the context of experience with mastery or control over one's environment. In other words, early experience associated with mastery or control (coping behaviors) may result in a sense of control over unpredictable life events, even if this control is illusory. Support for this contention is beginning to accumulate in studies targeting the influence of psychosocial variables on development, a topic to which we now turn.

DEVELOPMENTAL ISSUES IN THE FORMATION OF A SENSE OF CONTROL

In discussing how a sense of control might develop, Shear (1991) draws a specific connection between the psychological dimension of control and a child's early experience with parenting when she states, "It is certain that interpersonal relationships influence importantly the development of an individual's sense of control. As already noted, the human infant is almost completely helpless. Its only route to controlling the environment is via its effects on caretakers. In this sense, the infant and small child experience the world much as the yoked control in . . . animal experiments . . . (Mineka et al., 1986). The adults exert control and the child is the passive recipient" (p. 90). When parents are insensitive to their child's expressive, exploratory, and independent behaviors, the child is at risk of developing inhibition and a sense of uncontrollability over his or her world, which may contribute to anxiety. This notion is similar to Bowlby's (1980) attachment-object perspective (see below); however, Shear (1991) states that lack of perceived control need not necessarily be instilled by separation or loss experiences, or by a high frequency of stressful experiences. Rather, a "malfunctioning relationship" involving an intrusive, overprotective, or controlling parenting style could be expected to make a strong contribution to a cognitive vulnerability for anxiety.

Consistent with these notions of parental relationship influences, Mineka (1985a) proposed that the observed sex differences in human fear and anxiety may also be closely related to differential experiences with control as an infant or young child. That is, children who are given more freedom to explore, investigate, and control their environment may be at a lower risk for developing anxiety-related symptoms. Evidence supports the idea that boys are typically given more of these opportunities for independent action, whereas girls are often more closely controlled or protected (LeUnes, Nation, & Turley, 1980). Working in the area of depression, Nolen-Hoeksema (1987) reviewed extensive evidence that the observed sex differences in depression are best accounted for by girls' frequent "opportunities to learn that their responses do not control outcomes" (p. 273). It is well supported that parents respond more consistently to boys' actions, whether positive or negative, and are more likely to ignore girls' behaviors (e.g., Maccoby & Jacklin, 1974).

The findings concerning sex differences in the development of a sense of control are consistent with our present model. In line with Nolen-Hoeksema's (1987) extensive findings, we concluded, "Rather than fundamental biological differences, psychological vulnerabilities associated with an acquired sense of uncontrollability and ineffective coping may be differentially distributed among men and women. That is, women with the same biological vulnerabilities as certain men, may be overrepresented among those with anxiety and depressive disorders because they do not experience the same level of mastery and control over their environment as men do" (Barlow, 1991a, p. 68). Although there are larger implications for the role of sociocultural variables throughout the life span, the implication is equally strong that parenting may play a critical role in the differential formation of these psychological vulnerabilities for emotional disorders. Thus experiments bearing on this hypothesis bear a closer look.

ADDITIONAL DEVELOPMENTAL PERSPECTIVES ON CONTROLLABILITY

Preliminary examinations of cognitive vulnerability for childhood emotional disorders suggest that environmental factors are contributory (e.g., Nolen-Hoeksema, Girgus, & Seligman, 1992); however, the nature of their influence is not well understood (cf. Cole & Turner, 1993). Although some data suggest that environmental stressors interact with a cognitive vulnerability to exacerbate negative affect, other data imply that environmental stressors may actually influence the establishment of these cognitive vulnerabilities at younger ages (Cole & Turner, 1993). Indeed, we have suggested earlier that this cognitive or psychological vulnerability is related to early experiences with uncontrollability that, "when combined with a biological vulnerability and triggered by the stress of negative life-events, leads to clinical anxiety, and sometime later, to possible depression" (Barlow, 1991a, p. 65). Other theorists, as well, have implicated the contribution of early experience to a cognitive vulnerability (e.g., Beck, 1972; Beck & Emery, 1985).

In a review of extensive findings from animal studies, Mineka (1985a) supported the idea that uncontrollability may have a profound influence on the development of anxiety. In a discussion of phenomena that contribute to the increase of fear (which we would term anxiety) to a cs in the absence of cs-us pairing, Mineka (1985a) noted, "There is also increasing evidence that a sense of lack of control or helplessness can clearly lead to increased levels of fear. . . . Furthermore, there is also some evidence that a general history of control over one's environment reduces emotionality" (p. 212). It has been well documented that conditioning involving uncontrollable versus controllable aversive stimuli will result in a greater level of conditioned fear in animals (e.g., Mineka, Cook, & Miller, 1984).

Attending more specifically to the notion of early experience, Mineka et al. (1986) examined the role of mastery and control experiences during rearing of infant monkeys. In this investigation, a "master" group was given a high degree of control over delivery of food, water, and a variety of other reinforcers, and their responses also controlled delivery of identical stimuli to a yoked control group. At seven to nine months, the monkeys were exposed to fear-provoking stimuli, and there were substantial differences between the groups, with the master monkeys showing more approach and exploratory behavior in the face of frightening stimuli. The authors concluded, "It seems that a generalized expectancy of control or a sense of mastery can indeed have profound effects on an animal's reaction to fear or anxiety-provoking situations. This is obviously a way in which personality variables stemming from a person's expe-

rience with control or mastery over his/her environment may influence or interact with the development and maintenance of phobic
fears" (Mineka, 1985a, p. 212).

LOCUS OF CONTROL AND ATTRIBUTIONAL STYLE

In human populations, interest in the dimension of control has a
long history in psychology (e.g., Rotter, 1954). Rotter (1966) developed a self-report instrument to measure perceptions of control,
grading these perceptions along a dimension of internal versus external causality, or "locus of control." Rotter asserted that the degree
to which one is reinforced by an event is mediated by the direction of
one's attribution about the response-stimulus relationship. Under-
standably, this instrument inspired diverse research concerning the
cognitive interpretation of reinforcement. In addition, several attempts were made to construct such an assessment measure for children (e.g., Battle & Rotter, 1963; Bialer, 1961; Crandall, Crandall, &
Katovsky, 1965), but most of these were either difficult to administer
or were psychometrically unsound.

The first reliable and valid measure of locus of control in children, the Nowicki-Strickland Locus of Control Scale (NSLOC, 1973),
was developed by Nowicki and Strickland. In a test of the validity of
the NSLOC, Finch and Nelson (1974) administered the Children's
Manifest Anxiety Scale (Castaneda, McCandless, & Palermo, 1956)
and the NSLOC to a sample of 50 "emotionally disturbed" children.
Scores on the NSLOC were significantly correlated with manifest
anxiety scores, $r = .31$. In other words, a lower sense of control correlated with increased anxiety. More recently, Nunn (1988) evaluated the relationship between the NSLOC and the State-Trait Anxiety
Inventory for Children (STAIC, Trait Version) (Spielberger, 1973). In
a sample of 267 students in grades five through eight, the two measures were also correlated at $r = .31$. Using a clinical population, Mc-
Cauley, Mitchell, Burke, and Moss (1988) examined differences in
various self-report measures of cognition among depressed children
and controls. The groups were 47 children diagnosed with depression, 30 children whose depression had remitted within the past
year, and 31 nondepressed psychiatric controls. Results demonstrated that depressed children showed the most external locus of

control, followed by children in remission, and then by non-depressed controls. Moreover, using a dimensional approach to assess depression, McCauley et al. (1988) found a correlation of .33 between the NSLOC and the Children's Depression Inventory (CDI; Seligman et al., 1984), collapsed across the three groups. The consistency of the degree of association between locus of control scores and measures of negative affectivity is noteworthy, given the diversity of the separate cohorts involved.

Other cognitive dimensions related to control and attribution have emerged subsequent to the efforts of Nowicki and Strickland (1973); however, these findings stem mainly from work in the area of depression. In an exposition of the reformulated learned helplessness theory, Abramson, Seligman, and Teasdale (1978) articulated the construct of attributional style and its possible role in the development of helplessness cognitions, a construct that has since fostered much research attempting to identify possible etiological mechanisms for psychological vulnerability (e.g., Hops, Lewinsohn, Andrews, & Roberts, 1990; Kaslow, Rehm, & Siegel, 1984; Nolen-Hoeksema, Girgus, & Seligman, 1986).

The most rigorous attempts to examine the cognitive vulnerability model have involved prospective methodology. For example, Nolen-Hoeksema et al. (1986) examined attributional style in a sample of 168 schoolchildren in a one-year longitudinal investigation. A composite score from the six scales of the Child Attributional Style Questionnaire (CASQ; Seligman et al., 1984) was used to assess attributional style and was again found to be correlated with concurrent depression as measured by the CDI. More noteworthy, however, the composite CASQ scores were found to be predictive of increases in CDI scores over time. The relationship held in the other direction as well; CDI scores were found to predict change in attributional style over time. Inferences about causal or structural relationships were not possible; however, the study represented some of the stronger support for the longitudinal relationship of attributional style and depression in children.

In a larger prospective investigation, Nolen-Hoeksema et al. (1992) examined the relationship of attributional style, negative life events, and depressive symptoms in children over a five-year period. The investigators hypothesized that attributional style would be predictive of future levels of depression and would interact with negative life events to influence this depression. In addition, they asserted that the relationship of explanatory style to depression might also be moderated by developmental level, stating that children's attributional style may not become fixed or traitlike until after middle childhood.

A sample of 508 children was assessed using a number of measures, including the CDI and the CASQ. Data were collected at nine separate epochs over the five-year period. The results demonstrated the ability of attributional style as well as its interaction with negative life events at Time n to predict change in depression scores at Time $n + 1$. Interestingly, however, these effects emerged during the latter half of the testing sessions only (Times 5, 6, 8, and 9), supporting the hypothesis that a cognitive vulnerability may not be fixed or steady in younger children. In addition, results indicated that the experience of depression itself had an influence on subsequent attributional style, even after depressive symptoms had subsided. This again suggests that early experiences with depression or negative events may contribute to the development of a cognitive vulnerability, which may eventually become relatively enduring over the course of development. The fact that support emerged for a bidirectional longitudinal relationship between depression and attributional style may help to explain the difficulty and limitations of previous cross-sectional and correlational designs.

MODELS OF THE DEVELOPMENT OF COGNITIVE VULNERABILITIES

The findings of Nolen-Hoeksema et al. (1992) are impressive. They not only provide support for longitudinal relationships but also involve multiple replication of the cross-sectional findings. As the authors themselves caution, however, certain methodological issues limit the confidence of any preliminary conclusions about the etiology of cognitive vulnerability. One problem in particular involves the reliability of assessment of attributional style in children. Nolen-Hoeksema et al. (1992) reported internal consistency coefficients ranging from .64 to as low as .42. In addition, others have subsequently questioned the validity of the factor structure of the CASQ, which had never been factor-analyzed until some time after the five-year longitudinal investigation (Cole & Turner, 1993). Moreover, although the correlational methods employed by Nolen-Hoeksema et al. (1992) allowed for the observation of basic patterns of relationships, specific structural relationships of variables over time remain difficult to identify. That is, without the use of linear structural modeling or directed regression, it is difficult to test relationships other than main effects and simple interactions from one epoch to the next.

To that end, Cole and Turner (1993) conducted one of the only examinations of the structural relationship among environmental, cognitive, and clinical variables. They carefully described the lack of specific attention in the literature to the differentiation of moderational and mediational processes implicitly hypothesized to be involved with cognitive or psychological vulnerability. Specifically, a mediational cognitive model is operative when cognitive vulnerability is influenced by an exogenous variable (e.g., stressors) and is simultaneously influential of the outcome variable (e.g., manifest anxiety or depression). A moderational relationship, on the other hand, indicates the statistical interaction of cognitive processes and other variables (e.g., stressors) jointly to influence the outcome variable. The simple structure of this latter model best characterizes the implicit diathesis-stress conceptualizations of most cognitive and cognitive-affective theories (e.g., Alloy, Kelly, Mineka, & Clements, 1990; Barlow, 1991a; Beck & Emery, 1985). (For example, Sanderson, Rapee, and Barlow's [1989] CO_2 challenge study, which examined the cognitive controllability dimension, implicitly demonstrated the moderational effects of a cognitive manipulation of perceived control on the panic-inducing main effects of CO_2 inhalation.)

In an attempt to clarify the structural relationship of cognition, stressors, and depressive symptomatology, Cole and Turner (1993) examined a nonclinical sample of 356 fourth, sixth, and eighth grade students. Using linear structural equation modeling, they comparatively tested models depicting mediational and moderational effects of cognitions on the presumed causal relationship of environmental stressors on depressive symptoms. That is, a model in which cognitive phenomena amplified the effects of stressors on depression (moderation) was compared to a model in which stressors activated cognitive phenomena, which in turn influenced depression (mediation). Despite the consistent theoretical support for a moderational model in adults (e.g., Abramson, Metalsky, & Alloy, 1989), results favored a mediational cognitive model for children in this age range. Specifically, high frequency of negative activities and low frequency of positive activities assessed by the Children's Activity Inventory (CAI; Shelton & Garber, 1987) and low peer ratings of competence were found to engender a depressogenic cognitive style as assessed by items from the CASQ, which then influenced self-report of depression on the Children's Depression Inventory (Kovacs, 1981).

What Cole and Turner highlight as most intriguing is the support for a moderational cognitive model in adults and late adolescents (e.g., Hammen, Adrian, & Hiroto, 1988) and its contrast with evidence for a mediational model in earlier and middle childhood. Consistent with some of the findings of Nolen-Hoeksema et al. (1992), the implications are that cognitive style may not be a steady or traitlike attribute in children. That is, a specific "cognitive program" may not become enduring until late adolescence or adulthood, when it then assumes a moderational role (i.e., exacerbating the effects of life stressors). In younger children, cognitive style may be in a period of fluctuation and formation, a period in which life stressors actually contribute to the development of cognitive vulnerability. The summary of evidence so far supports this compelling proposition; however, empirical work in this area is only in the earliest stages. One of the most notable gaps in the more sophisticated studies is their failure to include a clinical validation of the self-reported symptoms. Cole and Turner (1993) suggest, for example, that future study should be extended to carefully diagnosed clinical populations. Additional assessment strategies are greatly needed that can elucidate the development and subsequent structural influences of a cognitive vulnerability, as well as their relationship to actual clinical disturbance.

Although the examination of attributional style in children with depression has witnessed considerable development, the relationship of attributional style to children with anxiety remains almost entirely unexplored. This is unusual, given the broad empirical support for overlap of childhood anxiety and depression (see King, Gullone, & Tonge, 1991), as well as theoretical support for cognitive vulnerabilities inherent in the development of anxiety (e.g., Barlow, 1991a; Beck & Emery, 1985). In light of this more unitary view, Nolen-

Hoeksema et al. (1992) have suggested, "Our results might be interpreted as showing that some children are prone to negative affectivity (Watson & Clark, 1984), defined as a chronic propensity toward broadly negative affective states such as depression or anxiety, rather than being prone to depression specifically" (p. 419).

Bell-Dolan and Last (1990) conducted one of the first examinations of attributional style in clinically anxious children using the CASQ. Subjects were 36 children with principal diagnoses of a DSM-III-R anxiety disorder, 17 children with attention deficit hyperactivity disorder (ADHD), and 20 never-disordered controls. In this preliminary investigation, composite attributional style scores were significantly correlated with scores from the Revised Children's Manifest Anxiety Scale (RCMAS) ($r = -.43$) and the State-Trait Anxiety Inventory for Children (STAIC) trait version ($r = -.35$). Differences between groups showed some support for more negative attributional style in the two clinical groups over the control group, although with this modest sample size, the magnitude of effect was too small for statistical significance ($p < .10$). In light of the recent progress in the area of depression, these findings demonstrate the importance of continued study of the relationship of explanatory style to anxiety and negative affectivity in general. More important, those data converge on the possible mechanism for development of a sense that events in one's life are uncontrollable, a sense that we propose is the major psychological vulnerability for the development of anxiety and its disorders. We are currently gathering data relevant to these hypotheses in children.

Neurobiological Substrates of Anxiety and Stress: Relation to Uncontrollability

NEUROENDOCRINE RESPONDING

Other chapters in this volume describe in some detail elegant neurobiological models thought to underlie anxiety (e.g., Gray & McNaughton, this volume). But recent reports from an increasingly prominent neuroscientist, Robert M. Sapolsky, highlight the centrality of the effects of a sense of control on neurobiological processes, particularly those processes that are part of the neuroendocrine system (e.g., Sapolsky, 1990, 1992). Indeed, Sapolsky, who studies baboons living freely in a national reserve in Kenya, has isolated the important contribution of a sense of control to the functioning of the neuroendocrine systems and to physical health.

Like many species, baboons arrange themselves in a social hierarchy with dominant members at the top and more submissive members at the bottom. And few experiences in the animal kingdom are more difficult than living at the bottom of a social hierarchy. In baboons, these subordinate animals undergo continual attack from dominant animals and have less access to food, preferred resting places, and sexual partners. Sapolsky (1990) has examined levels of cortisol in these animals as a function of their social rank and discovered that dominant males have lower resting levels of cortisol than subordinate males. When some "emergency" occurred, however, levels of cortisol rose more quickly in the dominant males than in the subordinate males. These findings echo an earlier independent conclusion by Dienstbier (1989) on what constitutes "physiological toughness." The combination of low resting arousal and strong and responsive challenge or stress-induced arousal, according to Dienstbier, is correlated with positive performance in complex tasks, emotional stability, and enhancement of the immune system. Cortisol, of course, is the final step in a cascade of hormone secretion that begins with the limbic system in the brain during periods of stress or anxiety. The hippocampus is very responsive to corticosteroids. When stimulated by these hormones during hypothalamic-pituitary-adrenocortical (HPA) axis activity, the hippocampus helps to turn off the stress response, thus articulating the close link between the limbic system and various parts of the HPA axis. When produced chronically, cortisol can have damaging effects on a variety of physiological systems, ultimately causing damage to the hippocampus and the immune system. This damage to the hippocampus after a period of chronic stress may then lead to chronic secretion of stress hormones and, ultimately, to physical disease and death.

Sapolsky and his colleagues searched out the causes of these differences between dominant and subordinate animals by working backward up the HPA axis. They found that the most likely explanation was excess secretion of corticotrophin-releasing factor (CRF) by the hypothalamus in subordinate animals, combined with a diminished sensitivity of the pituitary gland (which is stimulated by CRF). Therefore, subordinate animals, unlike dominant animals, are continually secreting the hormone cortisol, probably because their lives are so stressful. In addition, they have an HPA system that is less sensitive to the effects of cortisol, making the system less efficient in turning off the stress response, probably related to hippocampal damage.

But Sapolsky's careful observations suggest that it is more than simply being at the top or bottom of a social hierarchy that is crucial in this regard. For example, he observed baboons during years when several males were sitting at the top of the hierarchy with no clear "winner." Although these males dominated the rest of the group, they were continually attacking and stressing each other. Under these conditions they displayed hormonal profiles more like those seen in subordinate males than in dominant males. Thus Sapolsky concludes that the most important factor in regulating stress physiology seems to be a sense of control (Sapolsky, 1992; Sapolsky & Ray, 1989). Those animals who are in control of social situations and are able to cope with any tension that arises can go a long way toward blunting the long-term effects of stress or anxiety. Although Sapolsky characterizes his work as research on stress, and the neuroendocrine responses in the HPA system are typically called "stress hormones," the experience of these baboons with their profound sense of uncontrollability over future threat would certainly fit almost any definition of anxiety, including our own.

AUTONOMIC RESTRICTION

Additional information on neurobiological processes associated with anxiety has come from the important theorizing of Borkovec and Hoehn-Saric and their colleagues, work that bears on the intriguing relationship between disordered cognitive processes found in generalized anxiety disorder (GAD) and somatic arousal. While autonomic hyperactivity has been frequently noted in patients with panic disorder (Holden & Barlow, 1986; Taylor et al., 1986), surprisingly few differences were initially found between patients with GAD and other groups on the basis of physiological measures (Borkovec et al., 1991). For example, individuals with GAD have generally not been distinguished from control subjects on measures such as heart rate, blood pressure, skin conductance, and respiration (Hoehn-Saric & Masec, 1981; Hoehn-Saric & McLeod, 1988). Furthermore, when compared with panic disorder patients, GAD patients typically show lower levels of physiological reactivity as measured, for example, by heart rate (Barlow et al., 1984; Rapee, 1986).

Moreover, this lack of autonomic hyperactivity has also been found in preliminary studies that induced the process of worry experimentally (Borkovec, Robinson, Pruzinsky, & DePree, 1983; Karteroliotis & Gill, 1987). Two notable physiological markers that have been found to correlate with the presence of GAD and worry inductions have been increased muscle tension, as measured by frontalis and gastrocnemius EMG, and electroencephalographic (EEG) beta activity. Several studies have documented that GAD patients show higher muscle tension during periods of rest than normal control subjects, and both manifest increased levels of muscle tension in response to psychological challenges (Fridlund et al., 1986; Hazlett, McLeod, & Hoehn-Saric, 1994; Hoehn-Saric, McLeod, & Zimmerli, 1989). In one of the few studies of brain activity during worry induction, Carter, Johnson, and Borkovec (1986) found that both worriers and nonworriers show a significant increase in EEG beta activity in the frontal lobes during periods of worry. This activity is associated with intense cognitive processing, as opposed to EEG alpha activity, which is related to a calm, relaxed state. Worriers also displayed a greater shift toward left, frontal activation, which is related to verbal-analytic activity associated with worry. Interestingly, these effects were attenuated after relaxation training. At first glance, then, the process of anxious apprehension in GAD patients does not appear to be characterized by autonomic hyperactivity but rather is characterized by CNS activation, chronic muscle tension, and increase in EEG beta activity.

Findings from recent studies, however, suggest more complicated properties associated with autonomic arousal in GAD. Several studies reviewed by Hoehn-Saric and McLeod (1988) suggest that although GAD patients fail to show differences compared with nonanxious controls at rest, GAD patients show a weaker skin conductance response and less variability in skin conductance and heart rate in response to challenge or stress. Moreover, GAD patients appear to take longer to return to baseline than normal subjects. Finally, reductions in variability of electromyographic activity (EMG) have also been found among individuals with GAD, suggesting that low variability may apply to muscle tension as well (Hazlett et al., 1994). These results have led several researchers to postulate that GAD may be characterized by a degree of sympathetic inhibition and a resulting "autonomic inflexibility" (Borkovec, 1994; Hoehn-Saric et al., 1989; Thayer, Friedman, & Borkovec, in press).

Other recent studies have elaborated on the above findings by examining the role of the parasympathetic nervous system (PNS) in autonomic arousal of GAD patients. As Thayer and colleagues (in press) have highlighted, previous studies of autonomic activity in anxiety have generally been assessed via sympathetic nervous system (SNS) indices. This approach neglects the role of the PNS, as well as its relationship within the SNS, factors that may play a particularly important role in heart rate regulation. Lyonfields, Borkovec, and Thayer (1995) compared GAD analog subjects and nonanxious controls during baseline, a period of aversive imagery related to a topic of greatest concern, and a period of worrying about that topic. Throughout the experiment, cardiovascular variability was measured by the Mean Successive Difference of heart rate interbeat interval. This variability assesses the degree of vagal (parasympathetic) control of heart rate activity. In general, low vagal tone is associated with a high and stable heart rate and has been linked with decreased heart rate reactivity (Porges, 1992; Thayer et al., in press).

Results indicated that the GAD analog subjects evidenced very little heart rate variability throughout the experiment and significantly less variability than the control group at baseline. In contrast, the control subjects displayed more variability during baseline but significant reductions in variability from baseline, to aversive imagery, and to worrisome thinking. These findings led the authors to conclude that GAD participants experienced chronically low parasympathetic tone as a result of their perpetual negative thinking, even while at rest. It is noteworthy that all the subjects in the study found worrying to be more anxiety provoking than aversive imagery.

In a related vein, Thayer et al. (in press) examined the autonomic characteristics of generalized anxiety disorder and worry in GAD patients (as opposed to analog subjects) and nonanxious controls during baseline, relaxation, and worry periods. Similar to the above study, cardiovascular responses were measured using parasympathetic indices of heart rate variability. GAD patients showed increased heart rate and less vagally mediated heart rate variability across all conditions. Additionally, relative to baseline and relaxation periods, worry was characterized by decreased cardiac parasympathetic activity (and decreased variability) in both GAD patients and controls. The authors interpreted this finding to suggest that the worry process is directly associated with a lowered parasympathetic control of cardiovascular functioning, which accounts for the autonomic inflexibility seen in GAD. Innovative pilot work in connection with this study suggests that a sample of GAD patients displayed significant increases in heart rate variability and parasympathetic tone following successful intervention with cognitive-behavioral therapy (Friedman, Thayer, Borkovec, & Lyonfields, 1993). Thayer et al. (in press) conclude that GAD may be associated with rigid and unresponsive autonomic nervous system (ANS) activity that is associated with decreased parasympathetic tone but that this situation can be modified with successful treatment.

Autonomic inflexibility found in GAD can be linked to the work of Sapolsky, reviewed above, and Dienstbier (1989), in that the process of anxious apprehension in GAD results in physiological responses that are not optimal for the organism and are opposite to the responses one would observe in an organism that has acquired "physiological toughness" (Dienstbier, 1989). As Thayer and colleagues (in press) highlight, a relationship between anxiety and autonomic inflexibility has been noted by several researchers. In particular, the behaviorally inhibited children studied by Kagan (Kagan, Reznick, & Snidman, 1987; Kagan et al., 1990), typically manifested higher resting heart rates and stability compared with behaviorally uninhibited children. Indeed, inflexibility and loss of variability of various biological systems in response to environmental demands may be indicative of a generic response associated with psychological and physiological dysfunction (Goldberg, 1992; Thayer et al., in press). Borkovec (1994) suggests that the autonomic inflexibility found in GAD patients is related to the fact that the stimuli feared by these patients are not produced by external environmental stressors but are internally generated thoughts about potential future threats. They are, therefore, caught in a perpetual state of scanning for danger (Mathews, 1990) as a function of perceived lack of control over their condition, as are Sapolsky's subordinate baboons, resulting in chronic arousal and reduced reactivity to actual stressors. Thus, is there a possible psychological and neurobiological link between Sapolsky's "stressed" baboons and patients suffering from GAD?

With this brief review of aspects of the process of anxious apprehension, it becomes more possible to examine other aspects of our model of anxiety, including hypothetical distinctions between anxiety and the phenomenon of panic. We begin with a brief examination of panic.

FEAR AND PANIC

If anxiety is, in fact, a coherent emotional structure serving the adaptive purpose of preparation for future challenges or threat, then what is fear? Many emotion theorists, such as Carroll Izard (e.g., Izard, 1992; Izard & Blumberg, 1985; see also Ekman, 1992), suggest that fear is a distinct primitive basic emotion, or perhaps, using Peter Lang's conceptualization, a tightly organized cohesive affective structure stored in memory that is fundamentally a behavioral act. Fear is associated with intense neurobiological and cognitive features. Fear occurs when we are directly and imminently threatened, whether by wild animals, which was so often the case for our distant ancestors living in caves, or more modern-day dangers such as an out-of-control vehicle bearing down on us. The action tendency that is at the heart of this emotion is the well-known fight or flight response. It is, of course, essential that this response be instantaneous because the survival of the organism may depend on it. This is Cannon's (1929) "emergency response" or "alarm reaction." Most theorists would agree that this response is evolutionary favored, ancient, and found far down the phylogenetic scale. Subjectively, the response is characterized by an overwhelming urge to escape, often expressed as "I've got to get out of here." This subjective urge seems to reflect the basic action tendency of fear, which is escape.

What is the clinical manifestation of fear? As noted previously (Barlow, 1988; 1991a), our view is that the summation of developmental and phenomenological evidence to date suggests that the clinical manifestation of the basic emotion of fear is most evident in

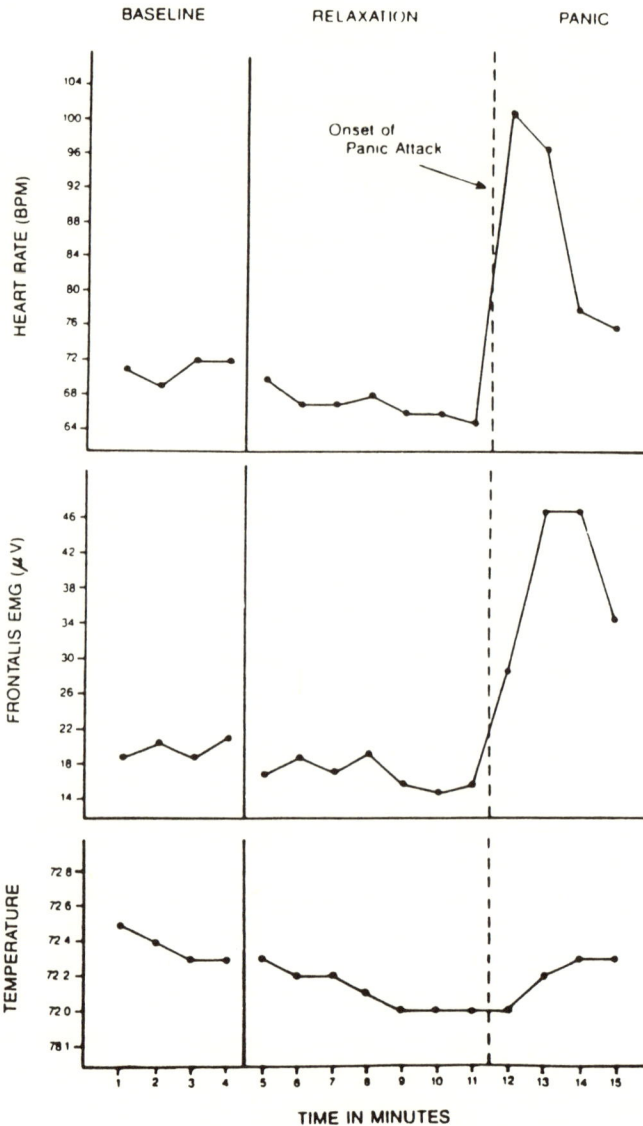

Figure 6. Physiological changes from the start of the recording session through the on-set and peak of the panic attack. From "The Psychophysiology of Relaxation Associ-ated Panic Attacks," by A. S. Cohen, D. H. Barlow, and E. B. Blanchard, 1985, *Journal of Abnormal Psychology, 94,* pp.96–101. Copyright © 1985 by the American Psychologi-cal Association. Reprinted with permission.

the phenomenon of panic attacks. The hair-trigger instantaneous quality of panic (fear) is well illustrated in Figure 6. This figure presents detailed physiological changes preceding and accompanying an "unexpected" panic attack. These data are from one of two patients who serendipitously experienced a panic attack while undergoing a thorough physiological assessment in our laboratory (Cohen, Barlow, & Blanchard, 1985). In this recording, one will notice that the unexpected surge of autonomic arousal, with accompanying subjective manifestations of fear, peaked and then diminished substantially in the space of three minutes.

From a phenomenological point of view, this autonomic surge seems very consistent with the fight/flight response that we call fear. Under these conditions, the emotion of fear mobilizes us physically and cognitively for quick action and sometimes "superhuman" efforts. Although running away or escaping is most often the behavioral manifestation of fear, occasionally directed action to counter the threat is apparent, such as attacking a predator, or single-handedly lifting an automobile so that a child trapped underneath can escape. As we have suggested elsewhere (e.g., Barlow, 1988), sometimes these actions are counterproductive, as in the case of a drowning victim vainly struggling when a rational response would be to lie still and attempt to float. In addition to this autonomic surge, these patients experienced extreme fear and terror, thoughts of dying, and an overwhelming behavioral urge to escape or "get out of here" (which one of our laboratory subjects, in fact, did, with electrodes still attached). Clinically most patients with panic disorder report overwhelming, if irrational, urges to escape during their panic attacks. These urges become a salient part of their experience. For instance, many avoid situations in which this strong emotional urge to act might be blocked (e.g., dentist or beauty salon chairs or formal social gatherings such as churches or movie theaters where sudden escape would attract attention and be embarrassing). An often replicated finding from research on basic emotions is that the intensity of the emotion increases if the action tendency is blocked (e.g., Izard, 1977). The further intensification of the panic attack may contribute to phobic avoidance in patients with anxiety disorders.

Additional data also support the equivalence of fear and panic. For example, most investigators would suppose that the reaction of individuals with specific phobia when confronting their phobic object represents the prototype for a strong fear reaction. But data collected in our clinic and elsewhere show no important differences between the reaction experienced by individuals with specific phobia upon confronting their feared object or situation and the panic attacks experienced by patients with panic disorder who did not report a "cue" for their attack (Barlow, 1988; Barlow et al., 1985; Craske, 1991; Margraf, Taylor, Ehlers, Roth, & Agras, 1987; Street, Craske, & Barlow, 1989). These findings and others are responsible for the essential definitional equivalence of these concepts in DSM-IV (American Psychiatric Association, 1994) in which an unexpected (uncued) panic attack occurring in the context of panic disorder differs from a "situationally based" panic attack occurring in the context of a specific phobia only in the presence of a cue.

But these comparisons between panic attacks and fear responses are made difficult by the considerable variability in commonly accepted definitions of fear and panic (Barlow, Brown, & Craske, 1994). For example, Tomarken and Hollon (1991) and others presume that the strong autonomic surge noticed in Figure 2 might be a necessary component of the definition of fear. But as reviewed elsewhere (Barlow et al., 1994), fear responses in humans, including both subjective reports and escape behavior, seem to occur in the absence of substantial peripheral physiological responding or, for that matter, endocrine responding associated with the HPA axis (e.g., Gorman et al., 1983; Gurguis, Cameron, Ericson, & Curtis, 1988; Kenardy, Fried, Kraemer, & Taylor, 1992; Nesse et al., 1985; Rachman, Levitt, & Lopatka, 1987; Taylor et al., 1986). Recent findings on autonomic restriction and inflexibility may account for this asynchrony in responding, as noted above. Furthermore, marked peripheral physiological surges clearly occur in the absence of reports of panic based on ambulatory monitoring. This well-known discordance among response systems that can occur on occasion does nothing to undermine the phenomenological similarities between fear and panic observed in so many contexts. But this discordance does raise serious problems for any definition of fear or panic, a subject we have struggled with elsewhere (Barlow et al., 1994).

One noted theorist, Donald Klein, presumes that at least some panic attacks differ from fear in that they represent a "suffocation alarm" associated with a centrally based CO_2 sensitivity (Klein, 1993). But neither symptom profiles nor neurobiological functioning (e.g., CO_2 sensitivity, HPA axis responding) suggest that these differences between panic and fear exist. Of course, if the biological substrate of the emotion of fear is in the limbic system, and panic is the basic emotion of fear (Barlow, 1988; 1991a), then one would expect some discontinuities between central and peripheral responding. In fact, this lack of correspondence was demonstrated by none other than Walter Cannon (1929) in his refutation of the specifics of the James-Lange theory of emotion. Nevertheless, a strong autonomic surge is central to any *prototypical* definition of fear or panic (e.g., Barlow et al., 1994; Kenardy, Evans, & Oei, 1988).

Directly examining fear or alarm responses in normals and comparing them to panic attacks would also provide interesting new information. Very few studies have addressed this topic thus far. In one study (Taylor et al., 1986) normal subjects seemed to show differences in subjectively reported response profiles during emergency reactions (e.g., "near miss" car accidents), compared with patients with panic disorder experiencing panic attacks. But Margraf et al. (1987) in a later study demonstrated markedly similar presenting symptoms between normals undergoing a fearful experience resulting in an alarm reaction and patients experiencing panic attacks.

In summary, people experiencing a specific fear response, on the one hand, or a panic attack, on the other, report very similar subjective experiences, including symptomatology; experience similar behavioral tendencies to escape; and seem to experience similar underlying neurobiological processes. But at this time, the evidence is still largely phenomenological and much more work is needed on a more precise functional analysis of fear and panic, particularly at a neurobiological level.

PANIC AND ANXIETY

A stronger network of evidence suggests fundamental differences between panic and anxiety. Both neurobiological and phenomenological evidence suggests that panic attacks are descriptively and functionally unique events when compared with anxiety. Panic attacks present differently from anxious apprehension and are experienced differently by patients (Barlow et al., 1985; Cohen et al., 1985; McNally, 1994; Rapee, 1985; Taylor et al., 1986). It is also worth noting that fear and anxiety, however defined, appear to be psychometrically different constructs (e.g., Tellegen, 1978/1982). For example, fear and anxiety appear to load on largely orthogonal, higher-order factors. Also, in some recent work exploring the dimensions of anxiety and depression in relation to proposing a new diagnosis of mixed anxiety depressive disorder for DSM-IV, Zinbarg et al. (1994) factor analyzed symptomatology in clinically anxious and depressed patients. Among other findings, two separable factors emerged, one characterized by strong autonomic arousal, which seems best described as panic, and the other characterized by the kinds of apprehension and worrying accompanied by arousal and tension that we have described above as "anxious apprehension" (see also Zinbarg & Barlow, in press).

Research demonstrating a strong functional relationship between panic attacks and subsequent anticipatory anxiety has also appeared (e.g., Barlow, 1991b; Rachman and Levitt, 1985; Telch, Lucas, and Nelson, 1989). That is, experiencing a discrete panic attack has differential consequences in individuals, at least one of which is the likelihood of focusing anxiety on potential future panic attacks. Thus, whether a panic attack occurs or not in a specific circumstance, and whether it is expected or not, will influence subsequent anxiety (and avoidance) associated with the phobic situation. In this regard, it is conceptually difficult to consider the alternative of developing anxiety focused on the future experience of anxiety.

EVIDENCE FROM ETHOLOGY: DEFENSIVE REACTIONS, TONIC IMMOBILITY, AND REACTIONS TO RAPE

Additional evidence supporting a functional relationship among these two distinct states comes from the animal ethologists who have demonstrated that animals cycle through a series of antipredator defensive reactions or behavioral action tendencies as a function of distance from the predator. This process begins with the response of "freezing," which seems to reflect a state of behavioral inhibition or anxiety when the animal first notices the potentially threatening predator. As the predator comes ever closer, the next response is a vigorous attempt to escape, reflecting the emotion of fear, which in

Tonic
immobility   Struggle   Flight   Freezing

Near   Far

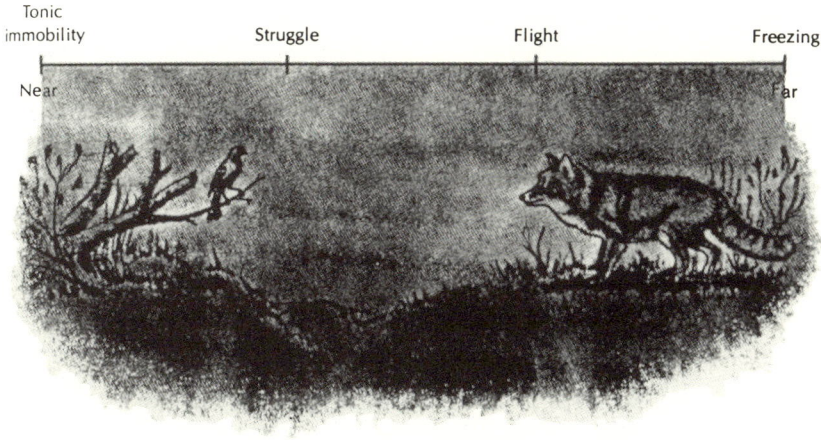

Figure 7. A diagram of Ratner's (1967) defensive distance hypothesis of tonic immobility. From: ELS by Maser and Seligman. Copyright © 1977 by Martin E. P. Seligman and Jack Maser. Used with permission of W. H. Freeman and Company.

turn is followed quickly by fighting and resistance (flight/fight). When contact is actually made, a final defensive reaction characterized by waxy flexibility or "tonic immobility" becomes evident in most species (Gallup, 1974). This response has been referred to colloquially as "playing dead" (Suarez & Gallup, 1981). This dimension of behavior is presented in Figure 7 (see also Gallup & Maser, 1977).

Several studies have demonstrated that discrete responses along this dimension of defensive behaviors will be more robust and vigorous if the animal goes through the whole sequence of behaviors, including the immediately preceding response. For example, the response of tonic immobility will be more robust if the animal has proceeded through freezing, escape, and fighting than if it were placed suddenly in a context prompting tonic immobility (Suarez & Gallup, 1981; Tortora & Borschelt, 1972). This is also consistent with Gray's (1987; 1994) notion that behavioral inhibition in freezing seems to facilitate subsequent vigorous action in animals under threat.

It also seems clear that many animals cycle back through these defensive antipredator reactions (Gallup, Nash, & Ellison, 1971). In other words, animals will come out of a state of tonic immobility fighting, followed by attempts to flee, and so on. The fact that behavioral inhibition or freezing, which seems to reflect anxiety, sets the stage for the vigorous action of escape, parallels research with anxiety-disordered patients, indicating that the best predictor of a

Table 1

Similarities Between Tonic Immobility and Rape-Induced Paralysis

Tonic Immobility	Rape-Induced Paralysis
Profound motor inhibition	Inability to move
Parkinsonian-like tremors	Body shaking
Suppressed vocal behavior	Inability to call out or scream
No loss of consciousness	Recall of details of the attack
Apparent analgesia	Numbness and insensitivity to pain
Reduced core temperature	Sensation of feeling cold
Abrupt onset and termination	Sudden onset and remission of paralysis
Aggressive reactions at termination	Attempts to attack the rapist following recovery

From "Tonic Immobility as a Response to Rape in Humans: A Theoretical Note," by S. D. Suarez and G. G. Gallup Jr., 1979, *Psychological Record, 29*, pp. 315–320. Copyright by the *Psychological Record*.

panic attack (alarm response) in laboratory provocation experiments is a preexisting state of anticipatory anxiety (Barlow, 1988). From an ethological point of view, it would make sense that the emotional state of anxiety lowers the threshold for an alarm response in the event that danger is detected.

We have suggested that freezing, or behavioral inhibition, parallels the experience of anxiety in humans and that the attempt to escape or flee that seems potentiated by freezing or anxiety reflects the basic emotion of fear. But does the response of tonic immobility (sometimes also referred to as freezing) have a parallel in human emotional reactions? As we have pointed out before (e.g., Barlow, 1988), it seems we may have overlooked a tragic but obvious example of this reaction in humans. During brutal rapes, many victims (mostly women) report feeling paralyzed. These women often make comments such as "I felt trembling and cold—I went limp" or "My body felt paralyzed," or "My body went absolutely stiff." Loss of consciousness does not occur during these states, and the victim can almost always report fully on events that occurred during the attack. Burgess and Holmstrom (1976) reported that 22 out of 34 rape victims evidenced physical paralysis at some point during the encounter. Physical parallels between rape-induced paralysis and tonic immobility include reports by rape victims that they feel "freezing cold," which may reflect the characteristic decrease in body temperature that occurs during this defensive reaction, and that they felt numb or insensitive to pain. It is also important that this response does not occur until the rapist actually makes contact with the victim, a condition that is also necessary for the response to occur in animals. Similarities between tonic immobility and rape-induced paralysis as outlined by Suarez and Gallup (1979) are found in Table 1. The observation that tonic immobility may occur in humans suggests that this series of defensive reactions, including anxiety and fear, and the functional relationship among them may have direct implications for anxiety disorders in humans.

HERITABILITY OF DEFENSIVE REACTIONS AND THE ORIGINS OF PANIC

Further circumstantial evidence for the conceptual separation between fear/panic and anxiety is present in genetic studies and studies of the aggregation of emotion-related action tendencies. For example, ancient and seemingly innate defensive reactions, such as becoming tonically immobile when under attack by a predator or fainting at the sight of blood or injections, are highly familial and almost certainly heritable. For example, fully 64% of blood phobics report biological relatives with the same reaction (Öst, 1989). The finding that panic attacks, even in nonclinical panickers, are strongly familial (Norton, Dorward, & Cox, 1986) suggests that experiencing the "defensive" reaction of panic may have a distinct genetic component that differs from heritable qualities associated with the trait of anxiety (Barlow, 1988; Eysenck, 1970). This would be perfectly consistent with evidence that the intensity of the first expression of a coherent fear response (stranger distress) not only occurs at a predictable time in the development of a given species but also seems to have a genetic component.

This hypothetical differential heritability may relate to the onset of the initial panic attack in susceptible individuals, a development that has proven puzzling when considering the etiology of panic disorder. For example, we have suggested that a panic attack, whether or not it ultimately leads to the development of panic disorder, is a normal and appropriate emotional response occurring at an inappropriate time or in an inappropriate situation. In this regard, it is important to emphasize that the response of panic, in our view, does not represent a biological dysfunction per se. In fact, if this response were to occur during a specific threat, such as an impending car accident, it would be seen as adaptive and useful (and would be called the emotion of fear).

It is also clear, as suggested above, that panic attacks seem functionally related to anxiety or stress. That is, an individual genetically vulnerable to be biologically reactive to stressful life events, a reactivity that could potentially develop into anxiety given the right psychological context (e.g., early experiences with uncontrollability), might experience an initial panic attack in at least one of two distinct ways. First, stress-induced biological reactivity could trigger discrete emotions or defensive reactions as a function of differentially inherited thresholds for these action tendencies or perhaps shared neurotransmitter functions. In other words, prolonged stress and its neurochemical consequences, combined with a low threshold for experiencing panic attacks (and/or other stress-related responses such as headaches), might trigger an initial panic attack that would seem "out of the blue." But we have also suggested an alternative explanation (Barlow, 1991a) that would be predicted by Lang's (1985) bioinformational emotion theory. In this model, stressful life events and the resulting activation of various neurobiological systems may present a sufficient number of response and stimulus propositions, such as threatening, negative cognitions, high arousal, and so on, to trigger specific emotional action tendencies stored deep in memory. In this way, a specific action tendency associated with a coherent, tightly organized emotional response may occasionally "fire" out of situational context. The analogy to neuronal discharge is intentional. A possible organization of this sequence is presented in Figure 8.

There is still room within this Langian perspective for a differential heritability of the tendency to experience a panic attack while under stress. Once again, this would be consistent with the notion that a variety of specific stress-related responses such as headaches, hypertension, and irritable bowel syndrome tend to be strongly familial reactions to stress and are probably heritable in some way (Barlow, 1988). In this view, the tendency to experience an initial panic attack would simply be another stress-related response that runs in families. This response may or may not ultimately develop into panic disorder, depending on whether anxiety later develops. Nev-

```
        ┌─────────────────────┐
        │      STRESSOR       │
        └─────────────────────┘
                  │
                  ▼
   ╭──────────────────────────────────────╮
   │  Genetically Determined Biological Reactivity  │
   ╰──────────────────────────────────────╯
                  │
                  ▼
   ┌──────────────────────────────────────┐
   │   Possibly Elaborated Psychologically Into  │
   │   Cognitive-Affective Structure of Anxiety  │
   └──────────────────────────────────────┘
                  │
                  ▼
   ┌──────────────────────────────────────┐
   │  Taps Propositions of Innate Action Tendencies  │
   │      Associated with Discrete Emotion  │
   │                  of                    │
   └──────────────────────────────────────┘
                  │
                  ▼
        ┌─────────────────────┐
        │        FEAR         │
        │       (PANIC)       │
        └─────────────────────┘
```

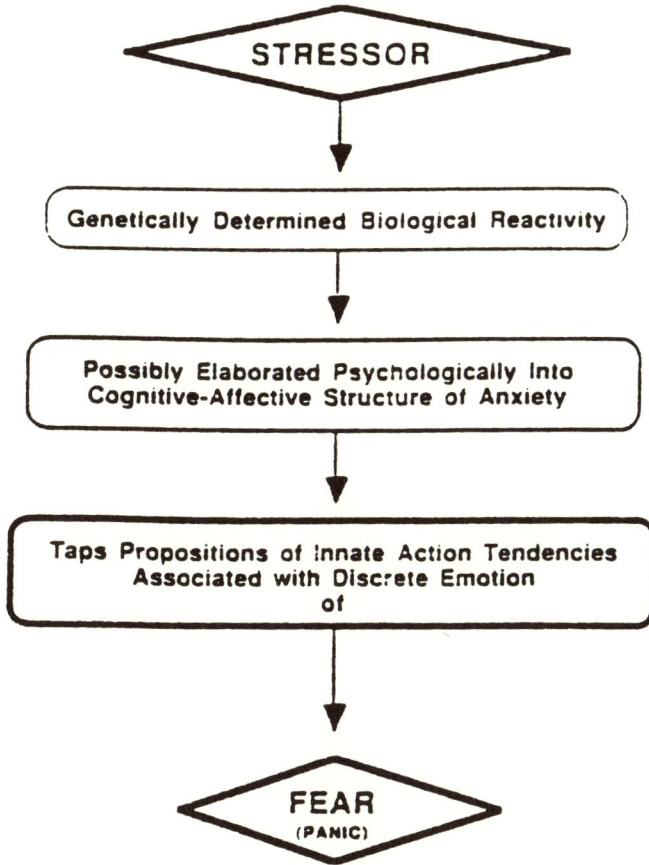

Figure 8. Hypothetical model of the role of genetic vulnerability in producing panic. (From Barlow 1988.)

ertheless, in the difficult area of behavioral genetics, differential heritability of these emotional responses, if it exists, has yet to be confirmed.

THE NEUROBIOLOGY OF FEAR/PANIC

Perhaps the strongest evidence for differences between fear/panic and anxiety comes from the discovery of seemingly different neurobiological substrates for these emotional experiences in the brain (e.g., Gray, 1987, 1995; LeDoux, 1990; Panksepp, 1992). Most prominent among these findings is the work of Jeffrey Gray (1987, 1994, 1995), who has identified the fight/flight system (FFS) as one of three fundamental emotional systems. This system "responds to unconditioned punishment (especially pain) and unconditioned frustrative nonreward by defensive aggression and/or unconditioned escape behavior" (Gray, 1991). Anxiety, on the other hand, emanates from a different system reflecting a high level of activity in the behavioral inhibition system (BIS). For the BIS, Gray has not only elaborated the kinds of inputs operating the system and the mediating brain mechanisms but also the very important information-processing (cognitive) functions that operate as an integral part of this system. As noted above, Gray's pioneering work on BIS has heavily influenced our own view of the nature of anxiety but will not be reviewed here because it is presented elsewhere in this volume.

Curiously, Gray does not call activation of the flight response of the FFS "fear." Rather, he calls the response characterized by overreactivity in the FFS "panic." Gray thinks that the final common pathway for flight or fight behavior lies in the central gray rather than the septo-hippocampal system. "The output from the central gray (as observed in experiments utilizing electrical stimulation in this area of the brain) includes a cluster of major changes in the functioning of the autonomic nervous system that resemble those seen in intact animals engaged in frantic struggle, attack, or flight. In human beings, these autonomic changes are observed during panic attacks" (Gray, 1991).

Most investigators would not agree with Gray's distinction between fear and panic. For example, Ortony and Turner (1990) note, "It strikes us as implausible that the terror-like emotional state associated with a strong urge to flee (the FFS system) should be fundamentally unrelated to the emotion of fear" (p. 320). Nevertheless, these issues may be more semantic than substantive since there is agreement that these two emotional states (fight/flight or panic, on the one hand, and anxiety, on the other) are distinct, irrespective of the labels one puts on them. In summary, most investigators (e.g., Barlow, 1991a, c; Gray, 1991; Mineka , Luten & Pury, 1991; Shear, 1991) would find the phenomenological and physiological evidence on the distinction between panic and anxiety and (presumably) the distinction between fear and anxiety convincing.

THE ROLE OF PANIC AND ANXIETY IN NONANXIETY DISORDERS

Fowles (1993) has made use of these emerging findings on fundamental differences between anxiety and fear in his reanalyses of psychopathy. Reviewing the work of Schalling (1978), Fowles concludes that the theory that psychopaths are deficient in anxiety is severely limited. Rather, the data support the notion that psychopaths are deficient in only one type of anxiety and may even be high in the other type. That is, psychopaths are characterized by less worry and anticipatory concern and are presumably low on BIS-related anxiety compared with nonpsychopaths. Schalling (1978), however, found that psychopaths tend to have more cardiovascular symptoms and panic (described as somatic anxiety) and that this somatic anxiety is positively correlated with impulsivity. Thus, in Gray's terms, a possibly weak BIS, combined with high fight/flight activity, may result in spur-of-the-moment impulsivity that is sometimes characteristic of psychopaths. Fowles also suggests that individuals low on both types of anxiety will show a different type of impulsivity (Whalen, 1989) that could be characterized as "fearlessness."

Fowles also extends the potential utility of this concept to children with attention deficit disorder, who also show spur-of-the-moment impulsivity. Children with aggressive conduct disorder, by contrast, may have more in common with the "fearless" psychopaths described above. In this regard, the high rate of comorbidity between attention deficit disorder and conduct disorder could possibly reflect a common underlying feature of a weak BIS (weak trait anxious apprehension). Greater fight/flight anxiety among some children with attention deficit disorder could account for their impulsivity accompanied by a somewhat lower tendency to aggression (Fowles, 1993).

A MODEL OF CLINICAL ANXIETY DISORDERS

Research reviewed above supporting a clear separation between the states of panic and anxiety leads directly to a model of the development of clinical anxiety disorders that has been articulated in some detail elsewhere (e.g., Barlow, 1988; Craske & Barlow, 1993). The experience of unexpected panic attacks seems to be a common feature in the population at large (Norton, Harrison, Hauch, & Rhodes, 1985; Norton et al., 1986; Salge, Beck, & Logan, 1988; Telch et al., 1989; Wittchen, 1986). But very few of these individuals who experience panic attacks go on to develop a clinical anxiety disorder such as panic disorder. The difference between these "nonclinical" panickers and those who develop panic disorder is striking. Nonclinical panickers show little or no concern over the attacks or the possibility of experiencing another one. Rather, they dismiss the attacks as associated with some passing event or episode such as something they ate or a difficult day at work. They seem to put the experience behind them quickly. Thus the distinguishing characteristic of individuals with panic disorder (or most other anxiety disorders) is the development of anxious apprehension focused on the next potential unexpected panic attack. Thus individuals with panic disorder apprehensively anticipate the next attack, perceive the attacks as uncontrollable, and are extremely vigilant for somatic symptoms that might signal the beginning of the next attack. Criteria defining panic disorder, for example in DSM-IV, specify that unexpected panic attacks must be accompanied by anxiety or concern over future attacks (or a change in behavior reflecting this concern) to meet the criteria for panic disorder (American Psychiatric Association, 1994). Nonclinical panickers also seem to display a kind of illusion of control or a resistance to a dysfunctional mentality that may well reflect the lack of a cognitive vulnerability to develop anxiety concerning what for others would be traumatic events. Thus experiencing what we have called elsewhere (e.g., Barlow, 1988) a false alarm (an unexpected panic attack) would then be followed by the development of anxious apprehension over the next panic attack in order to meet criteria for a disorder. This arrangement is displayed in Figure 9. Notice also in this figure that one might experience a "true alarm," that is, a legitimate traumatic experience, and yet follow the same course on the way to developing a clinical disorder. But the disorder in this case would be posttraumatic stress disorder rather than panic disorder. Evidence has been developed elsewhere that these two disorders probably have much in common (Jones & Barlow, 1990). In a similar vein, other anxiety disorders, such as obsessive-compulsive disorder, social phobia, and specific phobia, may also reflect a combination of the occurrence of alarms or panic attacks and the development of anxious apprehension. For example, social phobia is often

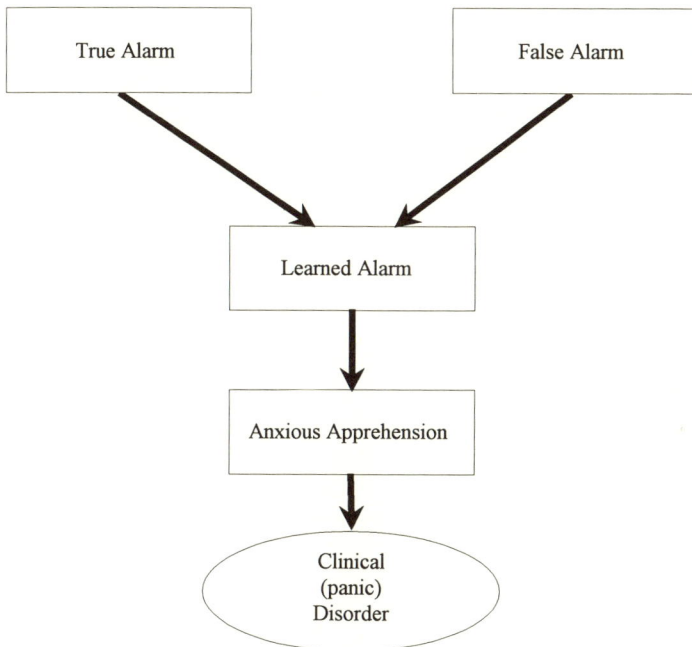

Figure 9. Origins of panic-related disorders.

characterized by false alarms occurring in social evaluative situations following a stressful event. The social phobic individual then focuses anxiety on upcoming social and evaluative situations in which he or she might experience undue anxiety and possibly a panic attack resulting in social failure and ridicule. Anxiety focused on intrusive, unacceptable thoughts that may trigger panic attacks often characterizes OCD. Specific phobia reflects alarms learned to specific cues as well as anxious apprehension in the presence of a specific object or situations.

In any case, these conceptualizations of fear, panic, anxiety, and their functional relationship in the context of clinical anxiety disorders have implications for the structure of other emotional disorders such as stress and mood disorders, as well as for the nature of anger and depression.

Anger and Stress

Throughout the above discussion we have referred to the fight/flight reaction. This is the term that Gray (1987) chooses to describe a single brain system underlying these behavioral action tendencies. Furthermore, on any circumflex of emotion (used by theorists to describe hypothetical relations of one emotional state to another) anger and fear are very closely related.

But it is "flight" which is the hypothetical behavioral action tendency of fear. The "fight" side of the reaction, reflecting as it does resistance to a dangerous threat or attack, is most closely associated with the emotion of anger. The one differentiating characteristic between anger and fear arising out of factor analytic studies is that anger is characterized by a sense of control and mastery (e.g., Lang, 1994b). This may reflect the notion that angry individuals are directing their attention outward toward the source of threat and actively attempting to cope with the situation. Individuals experiencing fear, on the other hand, would not share this sense of actively coping with the threat.

What determines whether one experiences anger or fear? Once again, there is evidence that early experiences with mastery and control over one's environment may have a substantial influence. In one very relevant experiment, Insel, Champoux, Scanlan, and Suomi (1986) reared two groups of rhesus monkeys identically, except for their experiences with nonaversive stimuli in their cages. One group was given free access to toys and food treats. This group served as the control. For a second group, identical toys and food treats were presented only when they were selected by a matched animal in the control group. Thus this Yoked group had the same exposure to the toys and food treats but did not experience control over accessing these items. Later in life, when these groups were exposed to a traumatic social separation, it was the Yoked group that exhibited more anxiety. But the more relevant experimental manipulation occurred next. Insel et al. (1986) administered a benzodiazepine inverse agonist to both groups of monkeys. This drug produces a very severe burst of negative affect. Once again, the Yoked group displayed significantly more anxiety as indicated by social withdrawal and distress vocalizations. But the monkeys that had experienced control over positive aspects of their environment while growing up had a very different response. They evidenced extreme hostility and aggression, often attacking other monkeys that happened to be nearby. Mineka et al. (1986) conducted a similar but even more sophisticated experiment with similarly defined groups without the highly aversive drug manipulation and also found more behavioral signs of anxiety in the Yoked group.

It is tempting to conclude that reactions expressed by the Insel et al. animals reflected either flight or fight and that this varying reaction, at least in this experimental situation, was a function of early experience with mastery and control. Of course, based on the ethological work reviewed above, it seems that all animals will experience either flight reaction or an aggressive or resistive responses under some conditions such as decreasing resistance of the predator. But perhaps the threshold for one reaction or another differs as a function of early experience. In any case, individuals experiencing anger or fear might share the same biological vulnerability to be overresponsive to stress or challenge. Similarly, they might also experience "false alarms" in response to negative life events much as do individuals with panic disorder. But individuals experiencing anger, with their momentary mastery and sense of control, have a different emotional experience than those experiencing fear.

In fact, it seems that there are individuals with clinical disorders, including some entering the treatment system, who experience repeated "anger attacks." In many cases these anger attacks seem to occur in the context of other emotional disorders such as panic disorder or major depressive disorder. One patient treated at our clinic reported experiencing his first "attack" as an inappropriate angry outburst. This event occurred during a business meeting when the individual felt threatened and stressed. The anger he felt was so overwhelming that he found himself temporarily unable to speak in a coherent manner. At that point, he very consciously experienced a lack of control (over his inability to speak or behave appropriately) and found that his anger attack was quickly transformed into a classic panic attack. This preceded the development of social phobia with anxiety and marked vigilance for somatic symptoms that might signal the beginning of the next attack, particularly during business meetings where some participation was expected.

Similar cases of anger attacks appearing in clinics have been reported in other centers (Fava, Anderson, & Rosenbaum, 1990;

Rosenbaum et al., 1993). Thus anger disorder might be analogous to anxiety and mood disorders and might represent yet another emotional disorder. There is also evidence that anger outbursts occur relatively frequently in the population. At least one study (Deffenbacher, 1992) reported that 4% to 7% of college samples experience anger attacks, a frequency similar to the population frequency of nonclinical panics. As with anxiety and mood disorders, the close relationship between stress and anxiety would ensure that individuals may present with considerable overlap between the two. For example, Lee and Cameron (1986) reported that almost 75% of a group of anxiety disordered patients had presented with Type A behavior (based on a questionnaire), which, of course, is characterized by frequent angry outbursts. It is also noteworthy that some investigators have found that it is important to distinguish brief periods of anger or anger attacks from more enduring trait characteristics of anger (Spielberger et al., 1985; Spielberger, Krasner, & Solomon, 1988). Finally, excessive anger is treated in a very similar fashion to anxiety, both psychologically (e.g., Biaggio, 1987; Novaco, 1975) and pharmacologically (Fava et al., 1990; Rosenbaum et al., 1993). Interestingly, in the latter cases, tricyclic antidepressants were often successfully used to treat anger attacks. Thus, experiencing out-of-control attacks of anger to a clinically significant degree may represent another emotional disorder closely paralleling panic disorder. That is, individuals with anger disorder as well as those with panic disorder would share some of the same biological vulnerabilities as well as the experience of false alarms. People experiencing anger attacks exclusively, however, would be relatively unlikely to focus anxiety on the next upcoming attack and, therefore, would seek treatment less often. In describing their patients with anger disorder Fava et al. (1990) noted that the presence of anger attacks was characterized by episodes of anger that were of short duration and grossly out of proportion to precipitating psychosocial stressors. Somatic symptoms associated with the attacks included sudden surges of autonomic arousal, including symptoms such as increased heartbeat, sweating, and flushing, as well as a feeling that the anger was out of control. None of the patients described anxious, panicky, or fearful emotions. The perception that the attack was out of control may well have come after the fact. Nevertheless, it might have ultimately motivated these particular patients to come for help.

Recent research suggests that experiencing repeated anger attacks is dangerous. For example, Ironson and her colleagues (1992) instructed individuals with heart disease to imagine situations or events in their own lives that made them angry, compared to imagining other situations, such as exercise, that also increased heart rate. They found that the emotion of anger actually impaired the pumping efficiency of the heart, putting these individuals at risk for arrhythmias. When the same subjects were asked to imagine getting into situations producing performance anxiety (such as having to give a speech or take a difficult test), these experiences did not have the same effect on their hearts as the emotion of anger, at least in those individuals with preexisting coronary heart disease. This raises the interesting possibility of a differential physiological consequence of experiencing anger versus fear or, perhaps, anxiety. But the finding of impaired pumping efficiency, or lack of it, would have to be first established in individuals without coronary heart disease and then in individuals in the midst of a panic attack to confirm this differential physiological consequence.

Finally, we have suggested that both anxious and stressed individuals may share the same biological vulnerability to be over-responsive to stress or challenge. But individuals presenting with classic "stress disorders" such as hypertension or the loosely defined Type A syndrome display little or no anxiety over the stress they experience. In fact, the process of anxious apprehension never seems to begin because their focus of attention remains external and task oriented. As in the caricature of the hard-driving executive, the coping methods of these individuals seem characterized by hard work, continual attention to achievement, and remarkable confidence in their ability to deal with problems. The exaggerated sense of mastery and control seems to lead to an almost exclusive external focus of attention on the task at hand (Scheier et al., 1983), often at the expense of physical well-being. Evidence suggests that these individuals ignore warning signs of physical malfunctioning associated with stress disorders. As Scheier et al. (1983) point out, this external focus of attention results in a marked decrease in the amount of attention available for internal focus and a subsequent lack of sensitivity to internal bodily events. Suls and Fletcher (1985) confirmed that individuals lower in self-consciousness become ill more often, probably as a result of internal insensitivity. Thus patients with ei-

ther stress or anxiety disorders may differ not only in their perceptions of controllability but also in self-directed versus externally directed focus of attention. These individuals, with the same biological vulnerabilities reflected in a hyperresponsivity to stress, seem to
experience this stress in a very different way with the subsequent
"alarm" response representing flight on the one hand and fight on
the other.

Depression

Much has been written lately about the relation of anxiety to depression (e.g., Barlow, 1991c; Clark & Watson, 1991; Kendall & Watson,
1989). An emerging consensus suggests that both anxiety and depression are variable manifestations of similar (or identical) neurobiological processes (Barlow, 1991a; Gray, 1985) as well as similar
symptom profiles. Groups of patients with either anxiety or depressive disorders are best differentiated by depressive signs and symptoms rather than anxiety signs and symptoms. Specifically, almost
all depressed patients are anxious but not all anxious patients are depressed. This is a robust finding reflected in analyses of self-rating
scales, patterns of comorbidity in clinical studies (Moras, DiNardo,
Brown, & Barlow, 1995; Sanderson, DiNardo, Rapee, & Barlow,
1990), and examination of broad mood factors of negative and positive affect as originally isolated by Auke Tellegen (e.g., 1985). Specific symptoms that seem to discriminate individuals with depression from those with anxiety can be characterized as loss of
pleasurable engagement, or anhedonia, along with cognitive and
motor retardation or "slowing." Broadly speaking, these symptoms
have been characterized as "low positive affect," in Tellegen's terms.
This information, along with the often observed finding that anxiety
tends to precede the occurrence of depression, suggests that at least
certain types of depression seem to grow out of anxiety or are a complication of anxiety occurring in some people under some conditions. Arriving at a similar conclusion, Alloy et al. (1990) referred to
depression emerging out of a state of anxiety as "hopelessness" depression. Thus the origins of depression would be similar if not
identical to the origins of anxiety in that both states would arise out
of common biological vulnerabilities as well as very similar psycho-

logical vulnerabilities emerging from early experiences with (lack of) control. When these biological and psychological vulnerabilities line up correctly, the trigger of a stressful negative life event would lead to clinical anxiety and, possibly some time later, to depression. In this view, then, depression would simply reflect an extreme psychological vulnerability to experiences of unpredictability and uncontrollability based on early experiences with controllability and coping. To put it another way, the determination of whether one becomes anxious and stays that way or also becomes depressed depends on the extent of one's psychological vulnerability, the severity of the current stressor, and coping mechanisms at one's disposal.

But the model suggested above for panic disorder, and possibly anger disorder, also suggest the occurrence of a discrete alarm response (fight/flight) that is elaborated into panic or possibly anger attacks. In the case of panic disorder, there is good evidence that individuals focus apprehensive anxiety onto the possibility of a future panic attack and that it is this state of affairs that accounts for the development of a clinical disorder. In other words, the occurrence of a stress-produced isolated panic attack, with its very short duration, would not lead to a clinical disorder if one did not become anxious about it happening again. Similarly, very few people with angry, hostile outbursts come for treatment of their own accord because they do not usually experience disruptions in their sense of control over their emotional responding. Does something similar happen in depressive disorders? In other words, can one experience a basic and rather acute loss of positive affect with the resulting anhedonia and slowing, much as one might experience the basic emotion of fear or panic? That is, could this reaction occur for no discernible reason (unexpected and uncued) and be experienced by certain individuals as unpredictable or uncontrollable?

Clinically this seems to happen. Earlier John Teasdale (1985) seemed to best capture the essence of this phenomenon when he wrote: "It is not uncommon for depressed patients to misinterpret symptoms of depression as signs of irremediable personal inadequacy: for example, the lack of energy, irritability or loss of interest and affection that characterizes depression are seen as signs of selfishness, weakness, or as evidence that a person is a poor wife or mother. Such interpretations, as well as making the symptoms more aversive, imply that they are going to be very difficult to control"

(p. 160). What this observation reflects is that the basic experience of the symptoms of sudden low positive affect in the form of a major depressive episode is in itself perceived as uncontrollable in these patients. There is also evidence from more normal populations that fear of experiencing episodes of sadness is a distinct factor in factor analytic studies of the Fear Survey Schedule (Taylor & Rachman, 1991, 1992).

This model of depression has two implications. The first is that these major depressive episodes would be time limited and could occur in relative isolation without the emotional complications attendant on perceptions of uncontrollability and hopelessness. In fact, it is very clear that discrete depressive episodes are time limited, with the probability of full remission of an episode approaching 90% even without intervention (Thase, 1990), although the minimum time one must experience the symptoms to qualify for major depressive episode is two weeks based on diagnostic conventions (American Psychiatric Association, 1994). The average length of time of a major depressive episode is six to nine months (Tollefson, 1993). While major depressive episodes are defined by a heterogeneous mix of symptoms, recent research suggests that the somatic or vegetative symptoms, as would be reflected in low positive affect, are most central to these episodes (Buchwald & Rudick-Davis, 1993).

We noted above that panic attacks, representing as we think they do the basic emotion of fear, may serve an adaptive value by promoting the immediate escape from danger (when danger is present). In this case, what would be the purpose of major depressive episodes? Some have speculated (e.g., Beck, 1972) that the shutdown accompanying major depressive episodes would accomplish an important conservation of energies and resources that might be necessary in the event of the loss of important and loved providers. Another possibility is that a depressive episode, if it is appropriate, such as upon the death of a loved one, may marshal social support, empathy, and the establishment of new social networks (Barnett, King, & Howard, 1979; Izard, 1992). Thus this emotional reaction could also be normal and adaptive in its original purpose but inappropriate and untimely in its pathological expression. Therefore, the extension of our model of emotional disorders to mood disorders would posit two fundamentally different kinds of depression: the discrete depressive reaction with its accompanying cognitive

Table 2

Symptom Predictions of the Hopelessness Theory

	Causal Cognition		
Symptoms	Uncertain Helplessness Pure "Aroused" Anxiety Syndrome	Certain Helplessness Mixed "Retarded" Anxiety/Depression Syndrome	Hopelessness Pure Depression Syndrome

Adapted from *Comorbidity of Anxiety and Depressive Disorders: A Helplessness-Hopelessness Perspective*, by L. B. Alloy, K. A. Kelly, S. Mineka, and C. M. Clements, 1990, in J. D. Maser and C. R. Cloninger (Eds.), *Comorbidity of Mood and Anxiety Disorders* (p. 526), Washington DC: American Psychiatric Press.

and motoric shutdown, which we refer to as endogenous depression, and the more chronic neurotic or "hopelessness" type of depression that we, along with Alloy et al. (1990), posit as being an extension of anxious apprehension.

It is also important to consider the usual course of a strong but "normal" major depressive episode in the form of a grief reaction. Although the severe manifestations of most depressive grief reactions resolve within two months, it is not uncommon for some individuals to grieve for a year or longer (Jacobs, Hansen, Berkman, Kasi, & Ostfield, 1989). It is also common for grieving people to experience increases in their grief at significant anniversaries such as births, holidays, and other meaningful occasions, including the one-year anniversary of the death, when symbolic psychosocial representations of the loss become evident. In approximately 20% of bereaved individuals, what we consider a "normal" major depressive reaction will develop into a pathological grief reaction or impacted grief reaction (Jacobs, 1993). This happens when severe incapacitating grief lasts beyond two months, or even one year, and substantial impairment in functioning remains. Interestingly, many of the same psychological and social factors that seem to contribute to the onset of mood disorders in general also predict the development of a "normal" grief response into a formal mood disorder (Jacobs et al., 1989). Thus the major depressive episode most often occurring during the process of grief may be the best representation of a "nonclinical" depressive episode, despite the fact that the suffering can be intense and the impairment in functioning readily evident. The only clear distinction between this reaction and a major depressive disorder, single episode, is the presence of a clear and socially acceptable cue or trigger and the resulting attributions for the episode on the part of the patient.

But the more chronic negative affective states of anxious apprehension and "hopelessness" depression (which may also map closely onto the clinical state of dysthymia) may be more similar than different, as we have suggested above. That is, both may reflect the profound sense of uncontrollability over life events that make one vulnerable to subsequent stressors, particularly when combined with certain biological vulnerabilities. In this view, both panic attacks and discrete major depressive episodes might occur anywhere along the continuum of perceptions of uncontrollability that characterize anxiety and more "chronic" hopelessness depression. For that matter, panic and major depressive episodes may occur outside of the context of these negative affective states. Of course, if one experiences a major depressive episode for any reason, the fact that it may last several weeks or months rather than a few minutes ensures that the episode will be associated with substantially more impairment in functioning and therefore, might need intervention even if it is not part of a recurring pattern against the background of more chronic negative affect. Only when clear precipitants are available, as in the case of the death of a loved one, does society provide the social support and make the necessary allowances, at least for several months, that would obviate the need for more formal intervention.

MANIA (EXCITEMENT DISORDER)

In addition to major depressive episodes, a second fundamental experience contributing to mood disorders is a period of abnormally marked elation, joy, or euphoria referred to as mania. As any clinician knows, this state often seems to resemble a pure emotional experience of elation or excitement. It is also important to note that the average duration of a manic episode, without treatment, is approximately six months, and full remission usually occurs even without the treatment. But recent discoveries provide some interesting parallels with our model of anxiety, stress, and depressive disorders outlined above. It has become apparent over the last decade that a substantial number of patients studied at the peak severity of a

Excitement
(Mania)

STRESS
ANXIETY
DYSTHYMIA

——————— Anger
(Temper Outbursts)

——————Fear
(Panic)

Sadness
(Depression)

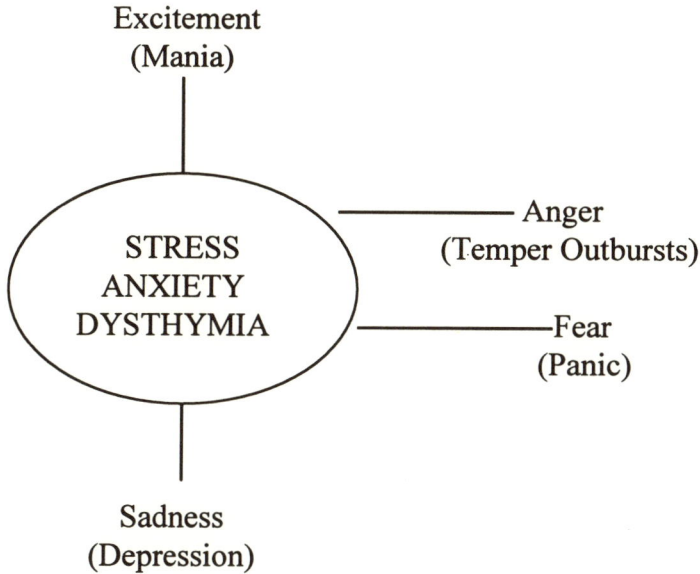

Figure 10. Model of emotional disorders. (From Barlow 1991a.)

manic episode, present with marked degrees of anxiety and negative affect (e.g., Post et al., 1989). In DSM-IV this type of episode is referred to as a dysphoric manic or mixed episode (American Psychiatric Association, 1994; McElroy et al., 1992). Patients with these
episodes are generally more severe than those with manic episodes
without negative affect in that they tend to experience a significantly
greater number of previous hospitalizations and respond less well
to treatment. It also seems clear that manic reactions (excitement),
much like other emotions, can be conditioned to a variety of internal
and external events or stimuli (Post, Rubinow, & Ballenger, 1986).
Clinically, these bipolar patients experiencing mixed episodes report distress over their manic behaviors and feelings, which they experience as out of their control. This would suggest that, much as
with fear, depressive episodes, and anger, a time-limited basic emotion of excitement can emerge frequently and inappropriately in that
it can be perceived as unpredictable and out of one's control, resulting in the emergence of negative affect (anxiety, dysphoria) focused
on the manic episode itself. The phenomenon of mixed mania com-
pletes the better part of a circumflex of emotions associated with

PERSPECTIVES ON ANXIETY, PANIC, AND FEAR

Table 3

Lifetime and Three-Month Prevalence of Cued and Uncued Panic, Anger, Depressive Episodes, and Excitement (N = 317)

	Panic Attack	Anger Outburst	Depressive Episode	Excitement Surge
Liftime				
Cued	191 (60%)	244 (77%)	250 (79%)	298 (94%)
Uncued	43 (14%)	59 (19%)	122 (40%)	137 (44%)
Past three months				
Cued	132 (42%)	204 (64%)	217 (69%)	282 (89%)
Uncued	32 (10%)	55 (17%)	109 (34%)	130 (41%)

NOTE. Percentages are rounded.

emotional disorders. What is common to each of these disorders is a discrete emotion occurring unexpectedly or inappropriately in a manner that is experienced as at least somewhat out of control. This model of emotional disorders is depicted in Figure 10.

Finally, preliminary data now exist directly testing the extension of our model of panic disorder to the emotions of anger, depression/sadness, and excitement in the normal population (Craske, Brown, Meadows, & Barlow, 1995). More than 300 undergraduates were surveyed with a carefully constructed questionnaire to determine the prevalence of both cued and uncued panic attacks, anger outbursts, episodes of sadness, and surges of excitement, as well as the degree of worry or distress over the recurrence of each type of emotional experience. The number and percentage of the sample who answered affirmatively to having experienced either cued or uncued emotions ever and in the past three months are shown in Table 3.

It is noteworthy that 32% of the sample reported no uncued emotional experiences. Overall, significantly more of the sample reported experiencing uncued surges of excitement compared to uncued panic attacks and uncued anger attacks. Ratings of worry about the recurrence of specific emotional episodes and the degree to which they interfered with daily functioning are shown in Table 4. Uncued depressive episodes were more anxiety-provoking than were uncued panic episodes, uncued anger episodes, or uncued surges of excitement. Uncued anger attacks and panic attacks were, in turn, significantly more anxiety-provoking than surges of uncued excitement.

It seems clear based on these data (and pending replication) that

Table 4

Means (and Standard Deviations) for Ratings of Worry about Recurrence and Interference Caused by Cued and Uncued Panic, Anger, Depressive Episodes, and Excitement over the Past Three Months

	Panic Attack	Anger Outburst	Depressive Episode	Excitement Surge
Worry about recurrence (0–8)				
Cued	1.64 (1.6)	1.53 (1.6)	2.65 (2.0)	0.29 (0.9)
Uncued	1.07 (1.1)	1.89 (1.9)	2.90 (2.0)	0.33 (0.9)
Interference with functioning (0–8)				
Cued	1.78 (1.7)	1.92 (1.8)	3.30 (1.9)	1.47 (1.7)
Uncued	1.19 (1.5)	2.33 (1.8)	3.13 (1.9)	1.09 (1.4)

Tables 3 and 4 reprinted from *Journal of Anxiety Disorders*, 9, Craske, Brown, Meadows, & Barlow, "Uncued and cued emotions and associated distress in a college sample," pp. 125–137, Copyright 1995, with kind permisison from Elsevier Science Ltd. The Boulevard, Langford Lane, Kidlington ox5 1GB, UK.

uncued surges of various types of emotion occur in a substantial minority of the population. Although one should expect inflationary reports with this type of study, the proportions are still surprisingly high, with at least 68% of the sample experiencing at least one uncued emotion in the previous three months. The estimate of 10% of the population experiencing uncued panic is consistent with estimates obtained from earlier questionnaire-based studies (e.g., Telch et al., 1989). It is noteworthy, however, that surges of other emotions were evident in much higher proportions, with 34% of the sample reporting depressive episodes. Furthermore, depressive episodes were associated with the most distress. Nevertheless, in this population distress ratings were mild on average, with a very small percentage of the sample "moderately or more so" worried about the recurrence of specific emotions. The percentages meeting this criteria were less than 1% for uncued panic, 4.4% for uncued anger, 14.5% for uncued depression, and almost 0% for uncued excitement.

The convergence of findings from basic and clinical research is only beginning. Findings from cognitive science and emotion theory have become truly applicable to clinical disorders only in the past several years. Additional research integrating findings from basic scientific explorations of affect and cognition should further enhance our knowledge of the nature and treatment of emotional disorders.

Summary and Conclusions

In this chapter we have highlighted three areas in which recent developments in basic science are influencing clinical theorizing concerning the nature of anxiety and its disorders. Each of these areas should be an important focus for future research. The first area concerns findings from cognitive science in general and, more specifically, the allocation of attention within emotional disorders. Whereas previous theorizing suggested that those with emotional disorders displayed excessive self-focus, sometimes characterized as neurotic self-preoccupation, more recent evidence suggests that those with emotional disorders, particularly anxiety disorders, tend to avoid direct observation of their own functioning and evidence a cognitive process that is fundamentally an avoidant technique. As our techniques and methods improve, future research efforts should be better able to ascertain levels of interoceptive awareness and the allocation of attention to personal thoughts and behaviors. It may be, for example, that a negatively affective worry process focusing on self-evaluative concerns combined with a tendency to avoid direct observation of one's functioning (lack of interoceptive awareness or interoceptive focus) may characterize psychopathology associated with emotional disorders and negative affect in general. In this sense, the self-evaluative component of self-focused attention may well be orthogonal to interoceptive awareness or focus.

A second area for future research concerns developmental factors that influence the formation of a sense of control over upcoming situations and responses. A marked lack of control seems to strongly characterize states of anxiety (Barlow, 1988), and the study of the development of a sense of control has strong roots in the basic science of psychology (e.g., Mineka, 1985a). Clinically, this sense of uncontrollability seems manifested in the strong tendency to form negative expectancies or negative predictions of upcoming events that characterizes individuals with emotional disorders. This is in contrast to the strong resistance to dysfunctional mentality that seems present in those without emotional disorders, even in the face of actual experiences of failure. Now a body of work is developing that relates early developmental notions proposed by such theorists as Bowlby (1980) with the development of a psychological vulnerability for emotional disorders, specifically, anxiety and depression. For example, as Nolen-Hoeksema (1987) has suggested, sex differences in emotional disorders may be accounted for by girls' frequent opportunities to learn that their responses do not control outcomes. As we have noted elsewhere, women with the same biological vulnerabilities as certain men may be overrepresented among those with anxiety and depressive disorders because they do not experience the same level of mastery and control over their environment as do men. Unraveling developmental factors that may contribute to emotional disorders, given similar biological dispositions, is a task that lies ahead of us.

Finally, we are just beginning to capitalize on the creative and innovative neurobiological work of Jeffrey Gray (this volume) with recent discoveries on neuroendocrine responding that may characterize part of a biological substrate of emotional disorders. This is a third area for possible research. Specifically, it seems that anxiety is characterized by autonomic restriction and lower levels of physiological reactivity as measured, for example, by heart rate responding. This is consistent with findings from basic neuroscience on the effects of chronic stress on the hypothalamic-pituitary-adrenocortical axis in which the chronic production of cortisol may ultimately damage a variety of physiological systems, including the hippocampus and the immune system. This may, in turn, affect a variety of functions, including memory. Based on the work of Sapolsky (e.g., 1992), it seems that the development of psychological vulnerabilities, specifically an inadequate sense of control over events in one's life, may well interact with neurobiological processes to produce the neuroendocrine functioning that contributes to the chronicity of these conditions. Linking up important and basic psychological science with equally important developments in neuroscience may well provide us with more definitive answers to these questions and facilitate a deeper understanding of the variety of disorders of stress and negative affect.

REFERENCES

Abrahamson, D. J., Barlow, D. H., & Abrahamson, L. S. (1989). Differential effects of performance demand and distraction on sexually functional and dysfunctional males. *Journal of Abnormal Psychology, 98*, 241–247.

Abrahamson, D. J., Barlow, D. H., Beck, J. G., Sakheim, D. K., & Kelly, J. P. (1985). The effects of attentional focus and partner responsiveness on sexual responding: Replication and extension. *Archives of Sexual Behavior,* 14, 361–371.

Abrahamson, D. J., Barlow, D. H., Sakheim, D. K., Beck, J. G., & Athanasiou, R. (1985). Effects of distraction on sexual responding in functional and dysfunctional men. *Behavior Therapy,* 16, 503–515.

Abramson, L. Y., Metalsky, G. I., & Alloy, L. B. (1989). Hopelessness and depression: A theory based subtype of depression. *Psychological Review,* 96, 358–392.

Abramson, L. Y., Seligman, M. E. P., & Teasdale, J. D. (1978). Learned helplessness in humans: Critique and reformulation. *Journal of Abnormal Psychology,* 87, 49–74.

Alloy, L. B., Kelly, K. A., Mineka, S., & Clements, C. M. (1990). Comorbidity of anxiety and depressive disorders: A helplessness-hopelessness perspective. In J. D. Maser & C. R. Cloninger (Eds.), *Comorbidity of mood and anxiety disorders* (pp. 499–543). Washington DC: American Psychiatric Press.

American Psychiatric Association. (1994). *Diagnostic and statistical manual of mental disorders* (4th ed.). Washington DC: Author.

Antony, M. M., Brown, T. A., Craske, M. G., Barlow, D. H., Mitchell, W. B., & Meadows, E. A. (1995). Accuracy of heart beat perception in panic disorder, social phobia, and non-anxious subjects. *Journal of Anxiety Disorders,* 9, 355–371.

Antony, M., Meadows, E., Brown, T. A., & Barlow, D. H. (1994). Cardiac awareness before and after cognitive-behavioral treatment for panic disorder. *Journal of Anxiety Disorders,* 8, 341–350.

Baddeley, A. D. (1986). *Working memory.* Oxford: Clarendon.

Barfield, R., & Sachs, B. (1968). Sexual behavior: Stimulation by painful electric shock to skin in male rats. *Science,* 161, 392–395.

Barlow, D. H. (1986). Causes of sexual dysfunction: The role of anxiety and cognitive interference. *Journal of Consulting and Clinical Psychology,* 54, 140–148.

Barlow, D. H. (1988). *Anxiety and its disorders: The nature and treatment of anxiety disorder.* New York: Guilford.

Barlow, D. H. (1991a). Disorders of emotion. *Psychological Inquiry,* 2(1), 58–71.

Barlow, D. H. (1991b). Disorders of emotions: Clarification, elaboration, and future directions. *Psychological Inquiry,* 2(1), 97–105.

Barlow, D. H. (1991c). The nature of anxiety: Anxiety, depression, and emotional disorders. In R. M. Rapee & D. H. Barlow (Eds.), *Chronic anxiety, generalized anxiety disorder, and mixed anxiety depression* (pp. 1–28). New York: Guilford.

Barlow, D. H., Brown, T. A., & Craske, M. G. (1994). Definitions of panic attacks and panic disorder in the DSM-IV: Implications for research. *Journal of Abnormal Psychology,* 103(3), 553–564.

Barlow, D. H., Cohen, A. S., Waddell, M. T., Vermilyea, B. B., Klosko, J. S., Blanchard, E. B., & DiNardo, P. A. (1984). Panic and generalized anxiety disorders: Nature and treatment. *Behavior Therapy,* 15, 431–449.

Barlow, D. H., Sakheim, D. K., & Beck, J. G. (1983). Anxiety increases sexual arousal. *Journal of Abnormal Psychology, 92,* 49–54.

Barlow, D. H., Vermilyea, J. A., Blanchard, E. B., Vermilyea, B. B., DiNardo, P. A., & Cerny, J. A. (1985). The phenomenon of panic. *Journal of Abnormal Psychology, 94,* 320–328.

Barnett, M. A., King, L. M., & Howard, J. A. (1979). Inducing affect about self or other: Effects on generosity in children. *Developmental Psychology, 15,* 164–167.

Battle, E. S., & Rotter, J. B. (1963). Children's feeling of self-control as related to social class ethnic group. *Journal of Personality, 3,* 482–490.

Beck, A. T. (1972). *Depression: Causes and treatment.* Philadelphia: University of Pennsylvania Press.

Beck, A. T., & Emery, G. (1985). *Anxiety disorders and phobias: A cognitive perspective.* New York: Basic Books.

Beck, D. H., Barlow, D. H., & Sakheim, D. K. (1983). The effect of attentional focus and partner arousal on sexual responding in functional and dysfunctional men. *Behaviour Research and Therapy, 21,* 1–8.

Beck, J. G., Barlow, D. H., Sakheim, D. K., & Abrahamson, D. J. (1984, August). *A cognitive processing account of anxiety and sexual arousal: The role of selective attention, thought content, and affective states.* Paper presented at the annual convention of the American Psychological Association, Toronto, Canada.

Beck, J. G., Barlow, D. H., Sakheim, D. K., & Abrahamson, D. J. (1987). Shock threat and sexual arousal: The role of selective attention, thought content, and affective states. *Psychophysiology, 24,* 165–172.

Bell-Dolan, D., & Last, C. G. (1990, November). *Attributional style of anxious children.* Poster presented at the 24th annual convention of the Association for Advancement of Behavior Therapy, San Francisco.

Biaggio, M. K. (1987). Therapeutic management of anger. *Clinical Psychology Review, 7,* 663–675.

Bialer, I. (1961). Conceptualization of success and failure in mentally retarded and normal children. *Journal of Personality, 29,* 303–320.

Borkovec, T. D. (1994). The nature, functions, and origins of worry. In G. C. L. Davey & F. Tallis (Eds.), *Worrying: Perspectives on theory, assessment, and treatment* (pp. 5–35). Sussex UK: Wiley.

Borkovec, T. D., Robinson, E., Pruzinsky, T., & DePree, J. A. (1983). Preliminary exploration of worry: Some characteristics and processes. *Behaviour Research and Therapy, 21,* 9–16.

Borkovec, T. S., Shadick, R., & Hopkins, M. (1991). The nature of normal and pathological worry. In R. M. Rapee & D. H. Barlow (Eds.), *Chronic anxiety, generalized anxiety disorder, and mixed anxiety depression* (pp. 29–51). New York: Guilford.

Bowlby, J. (1980). *Attachment and loss (Vol. 3): Loss, sadness and depression.* New York: Basic Books.

Brockner, J., & Swap, W. C. (1983). Resolving the relationships between placebos, misattribution, and insomnia: An individual-differences perspective. *Journal of Personality and Social Psychology, 45,* 32–42.

Brown, T. A., Barlow, D. H., & Liebowitz, M. R. (1994). The empirical basis of generalized anxiety disorder. *American Journal of Psychiatry, 151,* 1272–1280.

Brown, T. A., Dowdall, D. J., Côté, G., & Barlow, D. (1994). Worry and obsessions: The distinction between generalized anxiety disorder and obsessive-compulsive disorder. In G. Davey & F. Tallis (Eds.), *Worrying: Perspectives on theory, assessment, and treatment* (pp. 229–246). New York: Wiley.

Brown, T. A., O'Leary, T., & Barlow, D. H. (1993). Generalized anxiety disorder. In D. H. Barlow (Ed.), *Clinical handbook of psychological disorders* (2nd ed., pp. 137–188). New York: Guilford.

Bruce, T. J., & Barlow, D. H. (1990). The nature and role of performance anxiety in sexual dysfunction. In H. Leitenberg (Ed.), *Handbook of social anxiety* (pp. 357–384). New York: Plenum.

Buchwald, A. M., & Rudick-Davis, D. (1993). The symptoms of major depression. *Journal of Abnormal Psychology, 102*(2), 197–205.

Burgess, A. W., & Holmstrom, L. L. (1976). Coping behavior of the rape victim. *American Journal of Psychiatry, 133,* 413–417.

Butler, K. S., & Rapee, R. M. (1991). The influence of anxiety on accuracy of heart rate estimations. *Behaviour Change, 8*(3), 117–123.

Cannon, W. B. (1929). *Bodily changes in pain, hunger, fear and rage.* New York: Appleton-Century-Crofts.

Carter, W. R., Johnson, M. C., & Borkovec, T. D. (1986). Worry: An electrocortical analysis. *Advances in Behaviour Research and Therapy, 8,* 193–204.

Casteneda, A., McCandless, B. R., & Palmermo, D. S. (1956). The children's form of the manifest anxiety scale. *Child Development, 27,* 317–326.

Clark, L. A., & Watson, D. (1991). Tripartite model of anxiety and depression: Psychometric evidence and taxonomic implications. *Journal of Abnormal Psychology, 100,* 316–336.

Cohen, A. S., Barlow, D. H., & Blanchard, E. B. (1985). The psychophysiology of relaxation associated panic attacks. *Journal of Abnormal Psychology, 94,* 96–101.

Cole, D. A., & Turner, J. E. (1993). Models of cognitive mediation and moderation in child depression. *Journal of Abnormal Psychology, 102,* 271–281.

Crandall, V. C., Crandall, V. J., & Katovsky, W. (1965). A children's social desirability questionnaire. *Journal of Consulting Psychology, 29,* 27–36.

Cranston-Cuebas, M. A., & Barlow, D. H. (1990). Cognitive and affective contributions to sexual functioning. In J. Bancroft (Ed.), *Annual review of sex research* (pp. 119–161). Philadelphia: Society for the Scientific Study of Sex.

Cranston-Cuebas, M. A., & Barlow, D. H. (1994). *Attentional focus and the misattribution of male sexual arousal.* Manuscript submitted for publication.

Cranston-Cuebas, M. A., Barlow, D. H., Mitchell, W. B., & Athanasiou, R. (1993). Differential effects of a misattribution manipulation on sexually functional and dysfunctional males. *Journal of Abnormal Psychology, 102,* 525–533.

Craske, M. G. (1991). Phobic fear and panic attacks: The same emotional states triggered by different cues? *Clinical Psychology Review, 11*, 599–620.

Craske, M. G., & Barlow, D. H. (1993). Panic disorder and agoraphobia. In D. H. Barlow (Ed.), *Clinical handbook of psychological disorders* (2nd ed., pp.1–48). New York: Guilford.

Craske, M. G., Brown, T. A., Meadows, E. A., & Barlow, D. H. (1995). Uncued and cued emotions and associated distress in a college sample. *Journal of Anxiety Disorders, 9*(2), 125–137.

Darwin, C. R. (1872). *The expression of emotions in man and animals*. London: John Murray.

Deffenbacher, J. (1992, February). *Cognitive-behavioral approaches to anger reduction*. Paper presented at the meeting of the Banff International Conference on the Behavioral Sciences, Banff, Alberta.

Dienstbier, R. A. (1989). Arousal and physiological toughness: Implications for mental and physical health. *Psychological Review, 96*(1), 84–100.

Dutton, D. G., & Aron, A. P. (1974). Some evidence for heightened sexual attraction under conditions of high anxiety. *Journal of Personality and Social Psychology, 30*, 510–517.

Duval, S., & Wicklund, R. A. (1972). *A theory of objective self-awareness*. New York: Academic.

Ehlers, A., & Breuer, P. (1992). Increased cardiac awareness in panic disorder. *Journal of Abnormal Psychology, 101*(3), 371–382.

Ekman, P. (1992). Are there basic emotions? *Psychological Review, 99*, 550–553.

Eysenck, H. J. (Ed.). (1967). *The biological basis of personality*. Springfield IL: Thomas.

Eysenck, H. J. (1970). *The structure of human personality*. London: Methuen.

Eysenck, H. J. (Ed.). (1981). *A model for personality*. New York: Springer-Verlag.

Fava, M., Anderson, K., & Rosenbaum, J. F. (1990). "Anger attacks": Possible variants of panic and major depressive disorders. *American Journal of Psychiatry, 147*, 867–870.

Fenigstein, A., Scheier, M. F., & Buss, A. H. (1975). Public and private self-consciousness: Assessment and theory. *Journal of Consulting and Clinical Psychology, 43*, 522–527.

Finch, A. J., & Nelson, W. M. (1974). Locus of control and anxiety in emotionally disturbed children. *Psychological Reports, 35*, 469–470.

Fowles, D. C. (1993). A motivational theory of psychopathology. In W. Spaulding (Ed.), *Nebraska Symposium on Motivation: Integrated Views of Motivation, Cognition and Emotion* (Vol. 41). Lincoln: University of Nebraska Press.

Freud, S. (1959). Inhibitions, symptoms and anxiety. In J. Strachey (Ed. and trans.), *The standard edition of the complete psychological works of Sigmund Freud* (Vol. 20). London: Hogarth. (Original work published 1926).

Fridlund, A. J., Hatfield, M. E., Cottam, G. L., & Fowler, J. C. (1986). Anxiety and striate-muscle activation: Evidence from electromyographic pattern analysis. *Journal of Abnormal Psychology, 95*, 228–236.

Friedman, B. H., Thayer, J. F., Borkovec, T. D., & Lyonfields, J. D. (1993, April). *Psychophysiological assessment of generalized anxiety disorder*. Paper presented at the annual meeting of the Midwestern Psychological Association, Chicago.

Gallup, G. G. Jr. (1974). Animal hypnosis: Factual status of a fictional concept. *Psychological Bulletin, 81*, 836–853.

Gallup, G. G. Jr., & Maser, J. D. (1977). Tonic immobility: Evolutionary underpinnings of human catalepsy and catatonia. In J. D. Maser & M. E. P. Seligman (Eds.), *Psychopathology: Experimental models* (pp. 334–357). San Francisco: Freeman.

Gallup, G. G. Jr., Nash, R. F., & Ellison, A. L. Jr. (1971). Tonic immobility as a reaction to predation: Artificial eyes as a fear stimulus for chickens. *Psychonomic Science, 23*, 79–80.

Goldberg, A. L. (1992). Applications of chaos to physiology and medicine. In J. H. Klim & J. Stringer (Eds.), *Applied chaos*. New York: Wiley.

Gorman, J. M., Levy, G. F., Liebowitz, M. R., McGrath, P., Appleby, I. L., Dillon, D. J., Davies, S. O., & Klein, D. F. (1983). Effect of acute beta-adrenergic blockage on lactate-induced panic. *Archives of General Psychiatry, 40*, 1079–1082.

Gray, J. A. (1987). *The psychology of fear and stress* (2nd ed.). Cambridge: Cambridge University Press.

Gray, J. A. (1991). Fear, panic, and anxiety: What's in a name? *Psychological Inquiry, 2*(1), 72–96.

Gray, J. A. (1994). Framework for a taxonomy of psychiatric disorder. In Van Goozen, S. H. M., Van de Poll, N. E., & Sergeant, J. A. (Eds.), *Emotions: Essays on emotion theory* (pp. 29–59). Hillsdale NJ: Erlbaum.

Gray, J. A. (1996). The neuropsychology of anxiety: Reprise. This volume.

Gurguis, N. M., Cameron, O. G., Ericson, N. A., & Curtis, G. C. (1988). The daily distribution of panic attacks. *Comprehensive Psychiatry, 29*, 1–3.

Hammen, C., Adrian, C., & Hiroto, D. (1988). A longitudinal test of the attributional vulnerability model in children at risk for depression. *British Journal of Clinical Psychology, 27*, 37–46.

Hazlett, R. L., McLeod, D. R., & Hoehn-Saric, R. (1994). Muscle tension in generalized anxiety disorder: Elevated muscle tonus or agitated movement? *Psychophysiology, 31*, 189–195.

Hoehn-Saric, R., & Masek, B. J. (1981). Effects of naloxone on normals and chronically anxious patients. *Biological Psychiatry, 16*, 1041–1050.

Hoehn-Saric, R., & McLeod, D. R. (1988). Panic and generalized anxiety disorders. In C. G. Last & M. Hersen (Eds.), *Handbook of anxiety disorders* (pp. 109–126). New York: Pergamon.

Hoehn-Saric, R., McLeod, D. R., & Zimmerli, W. D. (1989). Somatic manifestations in women with generalized anxiety disorder: Psychophysiological responses to psychological stress. *Archives of General Psychiatry, 46*, 1113–1119.

Holden, A. E., & Barlow, D. H. (1986). Heart rate and heart rate variability recorded in vivo agoraphobics and nonphobics. *Behavior Therapy, 17*, 26–42.

Hoon, P., Wincze, J., & Hoon, E. (1977). A test of reciprocal inhibition: Are anxiety and sexual arousal in women mutually inhibitory? *Journal of Abnormal Psychology, 86*, 65–74.

Hops, H., Lewinsohn, P. M., Andrews, J. A., & Roberts, R. E. (1990). Psychosocial correlates of depressive symptomatology among high school students. *Journal of Consulting and Clinical Psychology, 19*, 211–220.

Ingram, R. E. (1990). Self-focused attention in clinical disorders: Review and a conceptual model. *Psychological Bulletin, 107*, 156–176.

Insel, T. R., Champoux, M., Scanlan, J. M., & Suomi, S. J. (1986, May). *Rearing condition and response to anxiogenic drug.* Paper presented at the annual meeting of the American Psychiatric Association, Washington DC.

Ironson, G., Taylor, C. B., Boltwood, M., Bartzokis, T., Dennis, C., Chesney, M., Spitzer, S., & Segall, G. M. (1992). Effects of anger on left ventricular ejection fraction in coronary artery disease. *American Journal of Cardiology, 70*, 281–285.

Izard, C. E. (Ed.). (1977). *Human emotions.* New York: Plenum.

Izard, C. (1992). Basic emotions, relations among emotions, and emotion-cognition relations. *Psychological Review, 99*, 561–565.

Izard, C. E., & Blumberg, M. A. (1985). Emotion theory and the role of emotions in anxiety in children and adults. In A. H. Tuma & J. D. Maser (Eds.), *Anxiety and the anxiety disorders* (pp. 109–129). Hillsdale NJ: Erlbaum.

Jacobs, S. (1993). *Pathologic grief: Maladaptation to loss.* Washington DC: American Psychiatric Press.

Jacobs, S., Hansen, F., Berkman, L., Kasi, S., & Ostfield, A. (1989). Depressions of bereavement. *Comprehensive Psychiatry, 30*(3), 218–224.

Jones, J. C., & Barlow, D. H. (1990). The etiology of posttraumatic stress disorder. *Clinical Psychology Review, 10*, 299–328.

Kagan, J., Reznick, J. S., & Snidman, N. (1987). The physiology and psychology of behavioral inhibition in children. *Child Development, 60*, 1459–1473.

Kagan, J., Reznick, J. S., Snidman, N., Johnson, M. O., Gibbons, J , Gersten, M., Biederman, J., & Rosenbaum, J. F. (1990). Origins of panic disorder. In J. C. Ballenger (Ed.), *Neurobiology of panic disorder* (pp. 71–87). New York: Wiley-Hiss.

Karteroliotis, C., & Gill, D. L. (1987). Temporal changes in psychological and physiological components of state anxiety. *Journal of Sports Psychology, 9*, 261–274.

Kaslow, N. J., Rehm, L. P., & Siegel, A. W. (1984). Social-cognitive and cognitive correlates of depression in children. *Journal of Abnormal Psychology, 12*, 605–620.

Kenardy, J., Evans, L., & Oei, T. P. S. (1988). The importance of cognitions in panic attacks. *Behavior Therapy, 19*, 471–483.

Kenardy, J., Fried, L., Kraemer, H. C., & Taylor, C. B. (1992). Psychological precursors of panic attacks. *British Journal of Psychiatry, 160*, 668–673.

Kendall, P. C., & Watson, D. (Eds.). (1989). *Anxiety and depression: Distinctive and overlapping features.* San Diego: Academic.

King, N. J., Gullone, E., & Tonge, B. J. (1991). Childhood fears and anxiety disorders. *Behaviour Change, 8*, 124–135.

Klein, D. F. (1993). False suffocation alarms, spontaneous panics, and related conditions. *Archives of General Psychiatry, 50*, 306–317.

Kovacs, M. (1980/1981). Rating scales to assess depression in preschool children. *Acta Paedopsychiatry, 46*, 305–315.

Lang, P. J. (1985). The cognitive psychophysiology of emotion: Fear and anxiety. In A. H. Tuma & J. D. Maser (Eds.), *Anxiety and the anxiety disorders* (pp. 131–170). Hillsdale NJ: Erlbaum.

Lang, P. J. (1994a). The varieties of emotional experience: A meditation on James-Lange theory. *Psychological Review, 101*(2), 211–221.

Lang, P. J. (1994b). *The motivational organization of emotion: Affect-reflex connections* (pp. 61–93). Hillsdale NJ: Erlbaum.

LeDoux, J. E. (1990). Information flow from sensation to emotion plasticity in the neural computation of stimulus value. In M. Gabriel & J. Moore (Eds.), *Learning and computational neuroscience: Foundations of adaptive networks* (pp. 3–52). Cambridge: Bradford Books/MIT Press.

Lee, M. A., & Cameron, O. G. (1986). Anxiety disorders, Type A behavior, and cardio-vascular disease. *International Journal of Psychiatry in Medicine, 16*, 123–129.

LeUnes, A. D., Nation, J. R., & Turley, N. M. (1980). Male-female performance in learned helplessness. *Journal of Psychology, 104*, 255–258.

Liddell, H. S. (1949). The role of vigilance in the development of animal neurosis. In P. Hoch & J. Zubin (Eds.), *Anxiety* (pp. 183–197). New York: Grune & Stratton.

Lyonfields, J. D., Borkovec, T. D., & Thayer, J. F. (1995). Vagal tone in generalized anxiety disorder and the effects of aversive imagery and worrisome thinking. *Behavior Therapy, 26*, 457–466.

Maccoby, E. E., & Jacklin, C. N. (1974). *The psychology of sex differences.* Stanford: Stanford University Press.

Margraf, J., Taylor, C. B., Ehlers, A., Roth, W. T., & Agras, W. S. (1987). Panic attacks in the natural environment. *Journal of Nervous and Mental Disease, 175*, 558–566.

Marten, P. A., & Barlow, D. H. (1991, November). *Differences in dimensions of fantasy between sexually functional and dysfunctional males: Preliminary results and treatment implications.* Poster presented at the annual convention of the Association for the Advancement of Behavior Therapy, New York.

Mathews, A. (1990). Why worry? The cognitive function of anxiety. *Behaviour Research and Therapy, 28*, 455–468.

McCauley, E., Mitchell, J. R., Burke, P., & Moss, S. (1988). Cognitive attributes of depression in children and adolescents. *Journal of Consulting and Clinical Psychology, 56*, 903–908.

McElroy, S. L., Keck, P. E., Pope, H. G., Hudson, J. I., Faedda, G. L., & Swann, A. C. (1992). Clinical and research implications of the diagnosis of dysphoric or mixed mania or hypomania. *American Journal of Psychiatry, 149*(12), 1633–1644.

McNally, R. J. (1994). *Panic disorder: A critical analysis.* New York: Guilford.

Miller, L. C., Murphy, R., & Buss, A. H. (1981). Consciousness of body: Private and public. *Journal of Personality and Social Psychology, 41*, 397–401.

Miller, W. R. (1975). Psychological deficit in depression. *Psychological Bulletin, 82*, 238–260.

Mineka, S. (1985a). Animal models of anxiety-based disorders: Their usefulness and limitations. In A. H. Tuma & J. D. Maser (Eds.), *Anxiety and the anxiety disorders* (pp. 199–244). Hillsdale NJ: Erlbaum.

Mineka, S. (1985b). The frightful complexity of the origins of fears. In F. R. Bruch & J. B. Overmier (Eds.), *Affect, conditioning, and cognition: Essays on the determinants of behavior* (pp. 55–73). Hillsdale NJ: Erlbaum.

Mineka, S., Cook, M., & Miller, S. (1984). Fear conditioned with escapable and inescapable shock: The effects of a feedback stimulus. *Journal of Experimental Psychology: Animal Behavior Processes, 10*, 307–323.

Mineka, S., Gunnar, M., & Champoux, M. (1986). Control and early socioemotional development: Infant rhesus monkeys reared in controllable versus uncontrollable environments. *Child Development, 57*, 1241–1256.

Mineka, S., & Kihlstrom, J. (1978). Unpredictable and uncontrollable aversive events. *Journal of Abnormal Psychology, 87*, 256–271.

Mineka, S., Luten, A. G., & Pury, C. L. (1991). Is lack of control over emotions, or over stressful life events, more important in disorders of emotion? *Psychological Inquiry, 2*(1), 83–85.

Mitchell, W. B., Brown, T. A., Barlow, D. H., & Marten, D. H. (1990, November). *The effect of positive and negative affect on sexual responding in functional males.* Paper presented at the annual convention of the Association for the Advancement of Behavior Therapy, San Francisco.

Mitchell, W. B., Marten, P. A., Williams, D. M., & Barlow, D. H. (1990, November). *Control of sexual arousal in sexual dysfunctional males.* Paper presented at the annual convention of the Association for the Advancement of Behavior Therapy, San Francisco.

Moras, K., DiNardo, P. A., Brown, T.A., & Barlow, D. H. (1995). *Comorbidity, fundamental impairment, and depression among the* DSM-III-R *anxiety disorders.* Unpublished manuscript, State University of New York at Albany.

Musson, R. F., & Alloy, L. B. (1988). Depression and self-direction. In L. Alloy (Ed.), *Cognitive processes in depression* (pp. 193–220). New York: Guilford.

Nesse, R. M., Curtis, G. C., Thyer, B. A., McCann, D. S., Huber-Smith, M. J., & Knopf, R. F. (1985). Endocrine and cardiovascular responses during phobic anxiety. *Psychosomatic Medicine, 47*, 320–332.

Nolen-Hoeksema, S. (1987). Sex differences in unipolar depression: Evidence and theory. *Psychological Bulletin, 101*(2), 259–282.

Nolen-Hoeksema, S., Girgus, J. S., & Seligman, M. E. P. (1986). Learned helplessness in children: A longitudinal study of depression, achievement, and attributional style. *Journal of Personality and Social Psychology, 51*, 435–442.

Nolen-Hoeksema, S., Girgus, J. S., & Seligman, M. E. P. (1992). Predictors and consequences of childhood depressive symptoms: A 5-year longitudinal study. *Journal of Abnormal Psychology, 101*(3), 405–422.

Norton, G. R., Dorward, J., & Cox, B. J. (1986). Factors associated with panic attacks in nonclinical subjects. *Behavior Therapy, 17,* 239–252.

Norton, G. R., Harrison, B., Hauch, J., & Rhodes, L. (1985). Characteristics of people with infrequent panic attacks. *Journal of Abnormal Psychology, 94,* 216–221.

Nowicki, S., & Strickland, B. R. (1973). A locus of control scale for children. *Journal of Consulting and Clinical Psychology, 40*(1), 148–154.

Novaco, R. W. (1975). *Anger control: The development and evaluation of an experimental treatment.* Lexington MA: Heath.

Nunn, G. D. (1988). Concurrent validity between the Nowicki-Strickland Locus of Control Scale and the State-Trait Anxiety Inventory for Children. *Educational and Psychological Measurement, 48,* 435–438.

Ortony, A., & Turner, T. J. (1990). What's basic about emotions? *Psychological Review, 97,* 315–331.

Öst, L. G. (1989). *Blood phobia: A specific phobia subtype in DSM-IV.* Paper requested by the Simple Phobia subcommittee of the DSM-IV Anxiety Disorders Work Group.

Palace, E., & Gorzalka, B. (1990). *The enhancing effects of anxiety on arousal in sexually dysfunctional and functional women.* Unpublished manuscript.

Panksepp, J. (1992). A critical role for "affective neuroscience" in resolving what is basic about basic emotions. *Psychological Review, 99,* 554–560.

Porges, S. W. (1992). Autonomic regulation and attention. In B. A. Campbell, H. Hayne, & R. Richardson (Eds.), *Attention and information processing in infants and adults* (pp. 201–223). Hillside NJ: Erlbaum.

Post, R. M., Rubinow, D. R., & Ballenger, J. C. (1986). Conditioning and sensitization in the longitudinal course of affective illness. *British Journal of Psychiatry, 149,* 191–201.

Post, R. M., Rubinow, D. R., Uhde, T. W., Roy-Byrne, P., Linnoila, M., Rosoff, A., & Cowdry, R. (1989). Dysphoric mania: Clinical and biological correlates. *Archives of General Psychiatry, 46,* 353–358.

Rachman, S. J., & Levitt, K. (1985). Panics and their consequences. *Behaviour Research and Therapy, 23,* 585–600.

Rachman, S. J., Levitt, K., & Lopatka, C. (1987). Panic: The links between cognitions and bodily symptoms, I. *Behaviour Research and Therapy, 25,* 411–423.

Ramsey, G. (1943). The sexual development of boys. *American Journal of Psychology, 56,* 217.

Rapee, R. (1985). Distinctions between panic disorder and generalized anxiety disorder: Clinical presentation. *Australian and New Zealand Journal of Psychiatry, 19,* 227–232.

Rapee, R. (1986). Differential response to hyperventilation in panic disorder and generalized anxiety disorder. *Journal of Abnormal Psychology, 95,* 24–28.

Ratner, S. C. (1967). Comparative aspects of hypnosis. In J. E. Gordon (Ed.), *Handbook of clinical and experimental hypnosis* (pp. 550–587). New York: Macmillan.

Reiss, S., Peterson, R. A., Gursky, D. A., & McNally, R. J. (1986). Anxiety sensitivity, anxiety frequency, and the prediction of fearfulness. *Behaviour Research and Therapy, 24,* 1–8.

Riordan, C. (1979). *Interpersonal attraction in aversive situations.* Unpublished doctoral dissertation, State University of New York at Albany.

Roemer, L., & Borkovec, T. D. (1993). Worry: Unwanted cognitive activity that controls unwanted somatic experience. In D. W. Wegner & J. Pennebaker (Eds.), *Handbook of mental control* (pp. 220–238). Englewood Cliffs NJ: Prentice-Hall.

Rosenbaum, J. F., Fava, M., Pava, J. A., McCarthy, M. K., Steingard, R. J., & Bouffides, E. (1993). Anger attacks in unipolar depression, part 2: Neuroendocrine correlates and changes following fluoxetine treatment. *American Journal of Psychiatry, 150*(8), 1164–1168.

Rotter, J. B. (1954). *Social learning and clinical psychology.* Englewood Cliffs NJ: Prentice-Hall.

Rotter, J. B. (1966). Generalized expectancies for internal versus external control of reinforcement. *Psychological Monographs, 80,* No. 609.

Sakheim, D. K., Barlow, D. H., Abrahamson, D. A., & Beck, J. G. (1987). Distinguishing between organogenic and psychogenic erectile dysfunction. *Behaviour Research and Therapy, 23,* 379–390.

Salge, R. A., Beck, J. G., & Logan, A. C. (1988). A community survey of panic. *Journal of Anxiety Disorders, 2,* 157–167.

Sanderson, W. C., DiNardo, P. A., Rapee, R. M., & Barlow, D. H. (1990). Syndrome co-morbidity in patients diagnosed with a DSM-III-Revised anxiety disorder. *Journal of Abnormal Psychology, 99,* 308–312.

Sanderson, W. C., Rapee, R. M., & Barlow, D. H. (1989). The influence of an illusion of control on panic attacks induced via inhalation of 5.5% carbon dioxide-enriched air. *Archives of General Psychiatry, 46,* 157–164.

Sapolsky, R. M. (1990, January). Stress in the wild. *Scientific American,* 116–123.

Sapolsky, R. M. (1992). *Stress, the aging brain, and the mechanisms of neuron death.* Cambridge: MIT Press.

Sapolsky, R., & Ray, J. C. (1989). Styles of dominance and their endocrine correlates among wild, live baboons. *American Journal of Primatology, 18*(1), 1–13.

Sarrel, P. M., & Masters, W. H. (1982). Sexual molestation of men by women. *Archives of Sexual Behavior, 11,* 117–131.

Schalling, D. (1978). Psychopathy-related personality variables and the psychophysiology of socialization. In R. D. Hare & D. Schalling (Eds.), *Psychopathic behavior: Approaches to research* (pp. 85–106). London: Wiley.

Scheier, M. F., Carver, C. S., & Matthews, K. A. (1983). Attentional factors in the perception of bodily states. In J. T. Cacioppo & R. E. Petty (Eds.), *Social psychophysiology: A sourcebook.* New York: Guilford.

Schwarzer, R., & Wicklund, R. A. (1991). *Anxiety and self-focused attention.* Chur: Harwood Academic Publishers.

Seligman, M. E. P., Peterson, C., Kaslow, N. J., Tanenbaum, R. L., Alloy, L. B., & Abramson, L. Y. (1984). Attributional style and depressive symptoms among children. *Journal of Abnormal Psychology, 93,* 235–238.

Shear, M. K. (1991). The concept of uncontrollability. *Psychological Inquiry, 2*(1), 88–93.

Shelton, M. R., & Garber, J. (1987, August). *Development and validation of a children's pleasant and unpleasant events schedule.* Paper presented at the annual convention of the American Psychological Association, New York.

Smith, D. & Over, R. (1987). Male sexual arousal as a function of the content and the vividness of erotic fantasy. *Psychophysiology, 24,* 334–339.

Spielberger, C. D. (1973). *Preliminary test manual for the State-Trait Anxiety Inventory for children.* Palo Alto CA: Consulting Psychological Press.

Spielberger, C. D., Johnson, E. H., Russell, S. F., Crane, R. J., Jacobs, G. A., & Worden, T. J. (1985). The experience and expression of anger: Construction and validation of an anger expression scale. In M. A. Chesney & R. H. Rosenman (Eds.), *Anger and hostility in cardiovascular and behavioral disorders* (pp. 5–30). New York: Hemisphere/McGraw-Hill.

Spielberger, C. D., Krasner, S. S., & Solomon, E. P. (1988). The experience, expression, and control of anger. In M. P. Janisse (Ed.), *Health psychology: Individual differences and stress.* New York: Springer-Verlag.

Stock, W., & Geer, J. (1982). A study of fantasy-based sexual arousal in women. *Archives of Sexual Behavior, 11,* 33–47.

Storms, M. D., & Nisbett, R. E. (1970). Insomnia and the attribution process. *Journal of Personality and Social Psychology, 16,* 319–328.

Street, L. L., Craske, M. G., & Barlow, D. H. (1989). Sensations, cognitions, and the perception of cues associated with expected and unexpected panic attacks. *Behaviour Research and Therapy, 27,* 189–198.

Suarez, S. D., & Gallup, G. G. Jr. (1979). Tonic immobility as a response to rape in humans: A theoretical note. *Psychological Record, 29,* 315–320.

Suarez, S. D., & Gallup, G. G. Jr. (1981). Predatory overtones of open-field testing in chickens. *Animal Learning and Behavior, 9,* 153–163.

Suls, J., & Fletcher, B. (1985). Self-attention, life stress, and illness: A prospective study. *Psychosomatic Medicine, 47,* 469–481.

Taylor, C. B., Sheikh, J., Agras, W. S., Roth, W. T., Margraf, J. Ehlers, A., Maddock, R. J., & Gossard, D. (1986). Self-report of panic attacks: Agreement with heart rate changes. *American Journal of Psychiatry, 143,* 478–482.

Taylor, S., & Rachman, S. J. (1991). Fear of sadness. *Journal of Anxiety Disorders, 5,* 375–381.

Taylor, S., & Rachman, S. J. (1992). Fear and avoidance of aversive affective states: Dimensions and causal relations. *Journal of Anxiety Disorders, 6,* 15–25.

Teasdale, J. D. (1985). Psychological treatments for depression: How do they work? *Behaviour Research and Therapy, 23,* 157–165.

Telch, M. J., Lucas, J. A., & Nelson, P. (1989). Nonclinical panic in college students: An investigation of prevalence and symptomatology. *Journal of Abnormal Psychology, 98*, 300–306.

Tellegen, A. (1982). *Brief manual for the multidimensional personality questionnaire.* Unpublished manuscript, University of Minnesota, Minneapolis. (Original work written 1978.)

Tellegen, A. (1985). Structures of mood and personality and their relevance to assessing anxiety, with an emphasis on self-report. In A. H. Tuma & J. D. Maser (Eds.), *Anxiety and the anxiety disorders* (pp. 681–706). Hillsdale NJ: Erlbaum.

Thase, M. E. (1990). Relapse and recurrence in unipolar major depression: Short-term and long-term approaches. *Journal of Clinical Psychiatry, 51*(6, Suppl.), 51–57.

Thayer, J. F., Friedman, C. H., & Borkovec, T. D. (in press). Autonomic characteristics of generalized anxiety disorder and worry. *Biological Psychiatry.*

Tollefson, G. D. (1993). Major depression. In D. L. Dunner (Ed.), *Current psychiatric therapy.* Philadelphia: W. B. Saunders.

Tomarken, A. J., & Hollon, S. D. (1991). Disorders of emotion: Questions about clarity and integration. *Psychological Inquiry, 2*(1), 94–96.

Tortora, D. F., & Borschelt, P. L. (1972). The effect of escape responses on immobility in bobwhite quail. *Psychonomic Science, 27*, 129–130.

Tyrer, P. J. (1973). Relevance of bodily feelings in emotion. *Lancet,* 915–916.

Tyrer, P. J. (1976). *The role of bodily feelings in anxiety.* London: Oxford University Press.

Watson, D., & Clark, L. A. (1984). Negative affectivity: The disposition to experience negative emotional states. *Psychological Bulletin, 96*, 465–490.

Weisberg, R. B., Sbrocco, T. A., & Barlow, D. H. (1994a, November). *Imagery ability and male sexual arousal.* Paper presented at the annual convention of the Association for Advancement of Behavior Therapy, San Diego.

Weisberg, R. B., Sbrocco, T. A., & Barlow, D. H. (1994b, November). *A comparison of sexual fantasy use between men with situational erectile disorder, generalized erectile disorder, and sexually functional males: Preliminary results.* Paper presented at the annual convention of the Association for Advancement of Behavior Therapy, San Diego.

Weisberg, R. B., Weiner, D. N., Sbrocco, T., Bach, A. K., Brown, T. A., Athanasiou, R., & Barlow, D. H. (1994, November). *Attention allocation and anxiety in sexually functional and dysfunctional males.* Poster presented at the annual convention of the Association for Advancement of Behavior Therapy, San Diego.

Whalen, C. K. (1989). Attention deficit and hyperactivity disorders. In T. H. Ollendick & M. Hersen (Eds.), *Handbook of child psychopathology* (2nd ed., pp. 131–169). New York: Plenum.

Wincze, J., Venditti, E., Barlow, D. H., & Mavissakalian, M. (1980). The effects of a subjective monitoring task on the physiological measure of genital response to erotic stimulation. *Archives of Sexual Behavior, 9*, 533–547.

Wittchen, H. U. (1986). Epidemiology of panic attacks and panic disorders. In I. Hand & H. U. Wittchen (Eds.), *Panic and phobias: Empirical evidence of theoretical models and longterm effects of behavioral treatments* (pp. 18–28). Springer-Verlag.

Yerkes, R. M., & Dodson, J. D. (1908). The relation of strength of stimulus to rapidity of habit-formation. *Journal of Comparative Neurology and Psychology, 18,* 459–482.

Zillmann, D. (1983). Arousal and aggression. In R. G. Geen & E. Donnerstein (Eds.), *Aggression: Theoretical and empirical reviews* (Vol. 1, pp. 75–101). New York: Academic.

Zinbarg, R. E., & Barlow, D. H. (in press). The structure of anxiety and the DSM-III-R anxiety disorders: A hierarchical model. *Journal of Abnormal Psychology.*

Zinbarg, R. E., Barlow, D. H., Liebowitz, M. R., Street, L. L., Broadhead, E., Katon, W., Roy-Byrne, P., Lepine, J. P., Teherani, M., Richards, J., Brantley, P. J., & Kraemer, H. (1994). The DSM-IV field trial for mixed anxiety depression. *American Journal of Psychiatry, 151,* 1153–1162.

Subject Index

Author Index